America Through The Eyes of Its People

Primary Sources in American History

Second Edition

LONGMAN

An Imprint of Addison Wesley Longman, Inc.

New York • Reading, Massachusetts • Menlo Park, California • Harlow, England
Don Mills, Ontario • Sydney • Mexico City • Madrid • Amsterdam

Executive Editor: Bruce Borland
Supplements Editor: Jessica Bayne
Page Design: Judith Anderson
Cover Design: Kay Petronio
Manufacturing and Production: Rohnda Barnes

For permission to use copyrighted material, grateful acknowledgement is made to the copyright holders on pages 357 through 359, which are hereby made part of this copyright page.

America Through The Eyes of Its People, second edition.

ISBN: 0-673-97738-2

98 99 00 01 9 8 7 6 5

Contents

Preface

This reader is a collection of some of the important and representative documents in American history. It is intended to introduce some of the voices form the American past, to impart a sense of how historians write history and to give a hint at some of the complexities of writing the past. The aim of this book, and the series of which it is a part, is to make primary sources readily available to students at low cost.

The objective of this revision has been to broaden the selection of documents to include, in particular, more documents written by women and African Americans and to include more materials describing the social and cultural life of Americans.

Special attention has been paid to making this book more pedagogically useful. Each document is now accompanied by a headnote describing the author of the selection and the circumstances under which the document was written. Chapter introductions place the selections within a broadly drawn historical context. Study questions at the end of each chapter introduction direct the reader to points of special note and suggest comparisons and opportunities for further research.

In the development of this revised volume, invaluable assistance has been received from our thoughtful reviewers: Michael Mayer of the University of Montana, Jo Snider of Southwest Texas State University, and Barbara Oberlander of Santa Fe Community College. Special thanks go to Matthew Shine, our careful and thoughtful copyeditor, Laurie Connole, who assiduously researched the permissions, and Judith Anderson, who designed the book. Comments and suggestions for future editions may be addressed to Jessica Bayne, history supplements editor, Longman Publishers, 10 East 53rd Street, New York, NY 10022.

1

Contact and Colonization

At the end of the fifteenth century, western European monarchs were determined to find new sea routes to the East. Inspired by the Portuguese voyages around Africa, the Spanish sponsored the voyage of Genoan mariner Christopher Columbus, who believed that sailing west would be a quicker and simpler way for Europeans to reach the markets of the East. Columbus's historic trip to the Caribbean was the advent of centuries of western colonization in the Americas. Columbus and subsequent Portuguese, Spanish, French, and English colonists arrived in a region very different from what they expected to find or what they had left at home across the Atlantic. Native Americans already populated much of the Americas, and for many of these peoples, the encounter with Europeans proved devastating. The documents in this chapter reveal some of the motivations and cultural biases of the European explorers and their countrymen.

Spain was the first European country to enjoy the political and economic power an expansive empire in the New World could provide. Undertaken under the banner of, "gold, glory and God," Spanish conquistadors in the sixteenth century conquered many of the richest regions of the New World and exploited natural wealth that would make Spain the greatest power in the world for almost three hundred years.

The first two selections in this chapter describe the reactions of Christopher Columbus and Alvar Núñez Cabeza de Vaca to the Americas and its inhabitants. They provide insight into the changing and varied treatment and perceptions of native peoples by early explorers. The third document, by the sixteenth-century cleric Bartolomé de Las Casas, is a brutal indictment of Spanish colonization which describes the indigenous peoples as "simple" and "delicate" and the conquistadors as "hungry wolves."

The English came late to the game of colonization. Political and economic turmoil in the sixteenth century prevented England from focusing a national effort toward exploration. It was almost a century after John Cabot, sailing under the flag of Henry VII, established the first English claims in the New World before England devoted its energies to colonization. However, unlike in other western European nations, the drive for international expansion came from the private sector. Successful entrepreneurs, like the London merchant Thomas Mun, believed that the private and public sectors could jointly benefit from the wealth of the Americas. Henry VII's Letters Patent granted to John Cabot and excerpts from Thomas Mann's *England's Treasure by Foreign Trade* reveal some of the motivations for English settlement and some of the expectations and demands placed upon foreign trade and the "travelers."

Study Questions

1.   Compare the Cabeza de Vaca and Columbus descriptions of the indigenous peoples they encountered. What do their descriptions reveal about their preconceptions of the New World and about the values of their own cultures?

2.   Discuss the reactions of Columbus and Cabeza de Vaca to the physical environment of the New World. How did it compare to what they left behind in Europe?

3.   Are Las Casas's descriptions of Native Americans more reliable than those of the early explorers? Could he be exploiting the sufferings of Native Americans for his own ends?

4.   How did Native Americans approach the Europeans? How did they communicate?

5.   What were the European expectations of the New World? Is there evidence that the goals of the Spanish and the English were different?

Christopher Columbus, Letter to Luis de Sant' Angel (1493)

In this letter to one of his leading supporters in the Spanish court, Christopher Columbus describes his reaction to the sights of the New World. He is describing the island of Hispaniola, present-day Haiti and the Dominican Republic.*

Sir,

As I know that you will have pleasure of the great victory which out Lord hath given me in my voyage, I write you this, by which you shall know that in [thirty-three] days I passed over the Indies with the fleet which the most illustrious King and Queen, our

---

* From Christopher Columbus' Letter to Luis de Sant' Angel, *Escribano de Racion of the Kingdom of Aragon.* Dated 15 February 1493. Reprinted in Facsimile, Translated and Edited from the Unique Copy of the Original Edition (London: 1891), 22–27.

Lords, gave me: where I found very many islands peopled with inhabitants beyond number. And, of them all, I have taken possession for their Highnesses, with proclamation and the royal standard displayed; and I was not gainsaid. On the first which I found, I put the name Sant Salvador, in commemoration of His High Majesty, who marvelously hath given all this: the Indians call it [Guanhani]. The second I named the Island of Santa María de Concepción, the third Ferrandina, the fourth Fair Island, the fifth La Isla Juana; and so for each one a new name. When I reached Juana, I followed its coast westwardly, and found it so large that I thought it might be the mainland province of Cathay. And as I did not thus find any towns and villages on the seacoast, save small hamlets with the people whereof I could not get speech, because they all fled away forthwith, I went on further in the same direction, thinking I should not miss of great cities or towns. And at the end of many leagues, seeing that there was no change, . . . [I] turned back as far as a port agreed upon; from which I sent two men into the country to learn if there were a king, or any great cities. They traveled for three days, and found interminable small villages and a numberless population, but nought of ruling authority; wherefore they returned.

I understood sufficiently from other Indians . . . that this land, . . . was an island; and so I followed its coast eastwardly for a hundred and seven leagues as far as where it terminated; from which headland I saw another island to the east [eighteen] leagues distant from this, to which I at once gave the name La Spanola. And I proceeded thither, and followed the northern coast, as with La Juana, eastwardly for a hundred and [eighty-eight] great leagues in a direct easterly course, as with La Juana.

The which, and all the others, are more [fertile] to an excessive degree, and this extremely so. In it, there are many havens on the seacoast, incomparable with any others that I know in Christendom, and plenty of rivers so good and great that it is a marvel. The lands thereof are high, and in it are very many ranges of hills, and most lofty mountains incomparably beyond the Island of [Tenerife]; all most beautiful in a thousand shapes, and all accessible, and full of trees of a thousand kinds, so lofty that they seem to reach the sky. And I am assured that they never lose their foliage; as may be imagined, since I saw them as green and as beautiful as they are in Spain during May. . . .

And the nightingale was singing, and other birds of a thousand sorts, in the month of November, round about the way I was going. There are palm trees of six or eight species, wondrous to see for their beautiful variety; but so are the other trees, and fruits, and plants therein. There are wonderful pine groves, and very large plains of verdure, and there is honey, and many kinds of birds, and many various fruits. In the earth there are many mines of metals; and there is a population of incalculable number. Spanola is a marvel; the mountains and hills, and plains, and fields, and land, so beautiful and rich for planting and sowing, for breeding cattle of all sorts, for building of towns and villages.

There could be no believing, without seeing, such harbors as are here, as well as the many and great rivers, and excellent waters, most of which contain gold. In the trees and fruits and plants, there are great differences from those of Juana. In [La Spanola], there are many spiceries, and great mines of gold and other metals.

The people of this island, and of all the others that I have found and seen, or not seen, all go naked, men and women, just as their mothers bring them forth; although some women cover a single place with the leaf of a plant, or a cotton something which they make for that purpose. They have no iron or steel, nor any weapons; nor are they fit thereunto; not be because they be not a well-formed people and of fair stature, but that they are most wondrously timorous. They have no other weapons than the stems of reeds in their seeding state, on the end of which they fix little sharpened stakes. Even these, they dare not use; for many times has it happened that I sent two or three men ashore to some village to parley, and countless numbers of them sallied forth, but as soon as they saw those approach, they fled away in such wise that even a father would not wait for his son. And this was not because any hurt had ever done to any of them:—but such they are, incurably timid. It is true that since they have become more assured, and are losing that terror, they are artless and generous with what they have, to such a degree as no one would believe but him who had seen it. Of anything they have, if it be asked for, they never say no, but do rather invite the person to accept it, and show as much lovingness as though they would give their hearts. And whether it be a thing of value, or one of little worth, they are straightways content with whatsoever trifle of whatsoever kind may be given them in return for it. I forbade that anything so worthless as fragments of broken platters, and pieces of broken glass, and strapbuckles, should be given them; although when they were able to get such things, they seemed to think they had the best jewel in the world. . . .

And they knew no sect, nor idolatry; save that they all believe that power and goodness are in the sky, and they believed very firmly that I, with these ships and crew, came from the sky; and in such opinion, they received me at every place were I landed, after they had lost their terror. And this comes not because they are ignorant; on the contrary, they are men of very subtle wit, who navigate all those seas, and who give a marvellously good account of everything—but because they never saw men wearing clothes nor the like of our ships. And as soon as I arrived in the Indies, in the first island that I found, I took some of them by force to the intent that they should learn [our speech] and give me information of what there was in those parts. And so it was, that very soon they understood [us] and we them, what by speech or what by signs; and those [Indians] have been of much service . . . with loud cries of "Come! come to see the people from heaven!" Then, as soon as their minds were reassured about us, every one came, men as well as women, so that there remained none behind, big or little; and they all brought something to eat and drink, which they gave with wondrous lovingness. . . .

It seems to me that in all those islands, the men are all content with a single wife; and to their chief or king they give as many as twenty. The women, it appears to me, do more work than the men. Nor have I been able to learn whether they held personal property, for it seemed to me that whatever one had, they all took share of, especially of eatable things. Down to the present, I have not found in those islands any monstrous men, as many expected, but on the contrary all the people are very comely; nor are they black like those in Guinea, but have flowing hair; and they are not begotten where there is an excessive violence of the rays of the sun. . . . In those islands, where there are lofty mountains, the cold was very keen there, this winter; but they endured it by being accustomed thereto, and by the help of the meats which they eat with many and inordinately hot spices. . . .

Since thus our Redeemer has given to our most illustrious King and Queen, and to their famous kingdoms, this victory in so high a matter, Christendom should take gladness therein and make great festivals, and give solemn thanks to the Holy Trinity for the great exaltation they shall have by the conversion of so many peoples to our holy faith; and next for the temporal benefit which will bring hither refreshment and profit, not only to Spain, to all Christians. This briefly, in accordance with the facts. Dated, on the caravel, off the Canary Islands, the 15 February of the year 1493.

Alvar Núñez Cabeza de Vaca, "Indians of the Rio Grande" (1528–1536)

In 1528, half of the crew of the Spanish explorer Panfilo de Navarez was stranded in Florida. After sailing in makeshift vessels across the Gulf of Mexico, the crew was shipwrecked and enslaved by coastal peoples. After six years, Cabeza de Vaca, a black slave, Estevancio the Moor (referred to as "the negro" in this excerpt), and two others escaped and made the overland journey from Texas through the Southwest and south to Mexico City. In this selection from his journal, Cabeza de Vaca describes the native peoples and environment of what is now Texas and northern Mexico.*

They are so accustomed to running that, without resting or getting tired, they run from morning till night in pursuit of a deer, and kill a great many, because they follow until the game is worn out, sometimes catching it alive. Their huts are of matting placed over four arches. They carry them on their back and move every two or three days in quest of food; they plant nothing that would be of any use.

They are very merry people, and even when famished do not cease to dance and celebrate their feasts and ceremonials. Their best times are when "tunas" (prickly pears) are ripe, because then they have plenty to eat and spend the time in dancing and eating day and night. As long as these tunas last they squeeze and open them and set them to dry. When dried they are put in baskets like figs and kept to be eaten on the way. The peelings they grind and pulverize.

* From *The Journal of Alvar Nunez Cabeza de Vaca and His Companions from Florida to the Pacific, 1528–1536*, in *His Own Narrative*, ed. A. F. Bandelier (New York: A. S. Barnes & Company, 1905), 91, 94, 108, 143–145, 149–151, 167–168.

All over this country there are a great many deer, fowl and other animals which I have before enumerated. Here also they come up with cows; I have seen them thrice and have eaten their meat. They appear to me of the size of those in Spain. Their horns are small, like those of the Moorish cattle; the hair is very long, like fine wool and like a peajacket; some are brownish and others black, and to my taste they have better and more meat than those from here. Of the small hides the Indians make blankets to cover themselves with, and of the taller ones they make shoes and targets. These cows come from the north, across the country further on, to the coast of Florida, and are found all over the land for over four hundred leagues. On this whole stretch, through the valleys by which they come, people who live there descend to subsist upon their flesh. And a great quantity of hides are met with inland.

We remained with the Avavares Indians for eight months, according to our reckoning of the moons. During that time they came for us from many places and said that verily we were children of the sun. Until then Donates and the negro had not made any cures, but we found ourselves so pressed by the Indians coming from all sides, that all of us had to become medicine men. I was the most daring and reckless of all in undertaking cures. We never treated anyone that did not afterwards say he was well, and they had such confidence in our skill as to believe that none of them would die as long as we were among them. . . .

The women brought many mats, with which they built us houses, one for each of us and those attached to him. After this we would order them to boil all the game, and they did it quickly in ovens built by them for the purpose. We partook of everything a little, giving the rest to the principal man among those who had come with us for distribution among all. Every one then came with the share he had received for us to breathe on it and bless it, without which they left it untouched. Often we had with us three to four thousand persons. And it was very tiresome to have to breathe on and make the sign of the cross over every morsel they ate or drank. For many other things which they wanted to do they would come to ask our permission, so that it is easy to realize how greatly we were bothered. The women brought us tunas, spiders, worms, and whatever else they could find, for they would rather starve than partake of anything that had not first passed through our hands.

While traveling with those, we crossed a big river coming from the north and, traversing about thirty leagues of plains, met a number of people that came from afar to meet us on the trail, who treated us like the foregoing ones.

Thence on there was a change in the manner of reception, insofar as those who would meet us on the trail with gifts were no longer robbed by the Indians of our company, but after we had entered their homes they tendered us all they possessed, and the dwellings also. We turned over everything to the principals for distribution. Invariably those who had been deprived of their belongings would follow us, in order to repair their losses, so that our retinue became very large. They would tell them to be careful and not conceal anything of what they owned, as it could not be done without our knowledge, and then we would cause their death. So much did they frighten them that on the first few days after joining us they would be trembling all the time, and would not dare to speak or lift their eyes to Heaven.

Those guided us for more than fifty leagues through a desert of very rugged mountains, and so arid that there was no game. Consequently we suffered much from lack of food, and finally forded a very big river, with its water reaching to our chest. Thence on many of our people began to show the effects of the hunger and hardships they had undergone in those mountains, which were extremely barren and tiresome to travel.

The next morning all those who were strong enough came along, and at the end of three journeys we halted. Alonso del Castillo and Estevanico, the negro, left with the women as guides, and the woman who was a captive took them to a river that flows between mountains where there was a village in which her father lived, and these were the first adobes we saw that were like unto real houses. Castillo and Estevanico went to these and, after holding parley with the Indians, at the end of three days Castillo returned to where he had left us, bringing with him five or six of the Indians. He told how he had found permanent houses, inhabited, the people of which ate beans and squashes, and that he had also seen maize.

Of all things upon earth that caused us the greatest pleasure, and we gave endless thanks to our Lord for this news. Castillo also said that the negro was coming to meet us on the way, near by, with all the people of the houses. For that reason we started, and after going a league and a half met the negro and the people that came to receive us, who gave us beans and many squashes to eat, gourds to carry water in, robes of cowhide, and other things. As those people and the Indians of our company were enemies, and did not understand each other, we took leave of the latter, leaving them all that had been given to us, while we went on with the former and, six leagues beyond, when night was already approaching, reached their houses, where they received us with great ceremonies. Here we remained one day, and left on the next, taking them with us to other permanent houses, where they subsisted on the same food also, and thence on we found a new custom. . . .

Having seen positive traces of Christians and become satisfied they were very near, we gave many thanks to our Lord for redeeming us from our sad and gloomy condition. Anyone can imagine our delight when he reflects how long we had been in that land, and how many dangers and hardships we had suffered. That night I entreated one of my companions to go after the Christians, who were moving through the part of the country pacified and quieted by us, and who were three days ahead of where we were. They did not like my suggestion, and excused themselves from going, on the ground of being tired and worn out, although any of them might have done it far better than I, being younger and stronger.

Seeing their reluctance, in the morning I took with me the negro and eleven Indians and, following the trail, went in search of the Christians. On that day we made ten leagues, passing three places where they slept. The next morning I came upon four Christians on horseback, who, seeing me in such a strange attire, and in company with Indians, were greatly startled. They stared at me for quite awhile, speechless; so great was their surprise that they could not find words to ask me anything. I spoke first, and told them to lead me to their captain, and we went together to Diego de Alcaraz, their commander.

Bartolomé de Las Casas, "Of the Island of Hispaniola" (1542)

This extract from Las Casas's *Very Brief Account of the Destruction of the Indies* describes the island of Hispaniola (present-day Dominican Republic and Haiti), the island Columbus described in his letter to Luis de Sant' Angel. Las Casas wrote this gory and explosive account in 1542 to be read at a forum on Spanish colonization called by the Holy Roman Emperor Charles V. Widely translated, this account gave rise to a flood of anti-Spanish and anti-Catholic propaganda throughout Europe deriding the Spanish settlement of the Americas.*

God has created all these numberless people to be quite the simplest, without malice or duplicity, most obedient, most faithful to their natural Lords, and to the Christians, whom they serve; the most humble, most patient, most peaceful and calm, without strife nor tumults; not wrangling, nor querulous, as free from uproar, hate and desire of revenge as any in the world. . . .

Among these gentle sheep, gifted by their Maker with the above qualities, the Spaniards entered as soon as soon as they knew them, like wolves, tiger and lions which had been starving for many days, and since forty years they have done nothing else; nor do they afflict, torment, and destroy them with strange and new, and divers kinds of cruelty, never before seen, nor heard of, nor read of. . . . .

The Christians, with their horses and swords and lances, began to slaughter and practice strange cruelty among them. They penetrated into the country and spared neither children nor the aged, nor pregnant women, nor those in child labour, all of whom they ran through the body and lacerated, as though they were assaulting so many lambs herded in their sheepfold.

They made bets as to who would slit a man in two, or cut off his head at one blow: or they opened up his bowels. They tore the babes from their mothers' breast by the feet, and dashed their heads against the rocks. Others they seized by the shoulders and threw into the rivers, laughing and joking, and when they fell into the water they exclaimed: "boil body of so and so!" They spitted the bodies of other babes, together with their mothers and all who were before them, on their swords.

They made a gallows just high enough for the feet to nearly touch the ground, and by thirteens, in honour and reverence of our Redeemer and the twelve Apostles, they put wood underneath and, with fire, they burned the Indians alive.

They wrapped the bodies of others entirely in dry straw, binding them in it and setting fire to it; and so they burned them. They cut off the hands of all they wished to

---

* From Bartolomé de Las Casas, *Very Brief Account of the Destruction of the Indies*, in *Bartolomé de Las Casas*, trans. F. A. McNutt (Cleveland: Arthur H. Clark, 1909), 313–319.

take alive, made them carry them fastened on to them, and said: "Go and carry letters": that is; take the news to those who have fled to the mountains.

They generally killed the lords and nobles in the following way. They made wooden gridirons of stakes, bound them upon them, and made a slow fire beneath; thus the victims gave up the spirit by degrees, emitting cries of despair in their torture. . . .

Henry VII, First Letters Patent Granted to John Cabot and His Sons (1496)

In 1497, inspired by the voyages of Columbus, a young Venetian and his three sons sailed across the Atlantic under the flag of Henry VII. John Cabot did not find a quicker route to Asia, nor any of the profitable markets or cities the English king expected. However, his travels to Newfoundland established England's first claims in the New World. This selection is from Henry VII's royal grant, giving Cabot the right to travel under the English flag and conquer in his name.*

The King, to all whom, etc. Greeting: Be it known and made manifest that we have given and granted as by these presents we give and grant, for us and our heir, to our well-beloved John Cabot, citizen of Venice, and to Lewis, Sebastian and Sancio, sons of the said John, and to the heirs and deputies of them, and of any one of them, full and free authority, faculty and power to sail to all parts, regions and coasts of the eastern, western and northern sea, under our banners, flags and ensigns, five ships or vessels of whatsoever burden and quality they may be and with so many and with such mariners and men as they may wish to take with them in the said ships, at their own proper costs and charges, to find, discover and investigate whatsoever islands, countries, regions or provinces of heathens and infidels, in whatsoever part of the world placed, which before this time were unknown to all Christians. We have also granted to them and to any of them, and to the heirs and deputies of them and any one of them, and have given license to set up our aforesaid banners and ensigns in any town, city, castle, island or mainland whatsoever, newly found by them. And that the before-mentioned John and his sons or their heirs and deputies may conquer, occupy and possess whatsoever such towns, castles, cities and island by them thus discovered that they may be able to conquer, occupy and possess, as our vassals and governors lieutenants and deputies therein, acquiring for us the dominion, title and jurisdiction of the same towns, castles, cities, islands and mainlands so discovered; in such a way nevertheless

---

* From James A. Williamson, *The Cabot Voyages and Bristol Discovery Under Henry VII* (Cambridge, Eng.: Cambridge University Press, 1962), published for the Haklyut Society.

that of all the fruits, profits, emoluments, commodities, gains and revenues accruing from this voyage, the said John and sons and their heirs and deputies shall be bounded and under obligation for every their voyage, as often as they shall arrive at our port of Bristol, at which they are bound and holden only to arrive, all necessary charges and expenses incurred by them having been deducted, to pay us, either in goods or money, the fifth part of the whole capital gained, awe giving and granting to them and to their heirs and deputies, that they should be free and exempt from all payment of customs on all and singular the goods and merchandise that they may bring back with them from those places thus newly discovered.

And further we have given and granted to them and to their heirs and deputies, that all mainlands, islands, towns, cities, castles and other places whatsoever discovered by them, however numerous they may happen to be, may not be frequented or visited by any other subjects of ours whatsoever without the license of the aforesaid John and his sons and of their deputies, on pain of the loss as well of the ships or vessels daring to sail to these places discovered, as of all goods whatsoever. Willing and strictly commanding all singular our subjects as well by land as by sea, that they shall render good assistance to the aforesaid John and his sons and deputies and that they shall give them all their favor and help as well as in fitting out the ships or vessels as in buying stores and provisions with their money and in providing the other things which they must take with them on the said voyage.

Thomas Mun, from England's Treasure by Foreign Trade (1664)

Thomas Mun was a successful London merchant who served as one of the directors of the East India Company. In the late sixteenth and early seventeenth centuries most of the English ventures into the New World were capitalized by joint-stock companies like the East India Company. Mun's treatise, "England's Treasure by Foreign Trade," describes the idea merchant, the theory of mercantilism, and emphasizes the importance of a favorable balance of trade in order to enhance the wealth of a nation.*

The Qualities which are required in a perfect Merchant of Foreign Trade

The Love and service of our Country consisteth not so much in the knowledge of those duties which are to be performed by others, as in the skillful practice of that which is done by our selves; and therefore it is now fit that I say something of the Merchant . . . for the Merchant is worthily called the Steward of the Kingdoms Stock, by way of

* From Thomas Mun, *England's Treasury by Foreign Trade*, in *Early English Tracts on Commerce*, ed. J. R. McCulloch (Cambridge: University Press, 1954), 121–126, 134–141.

Commerce with other Nations; a work of no less Reputation than Trust, which ought to be performed with great skill and conscience, that so the private gain may ever accompany the publique good. . . . I will briefly set down the excellent qualities which are required of a perfect Merchant.

1. He ought to be a good Penman, a good Arithmetician, and a good Accomptant, by that noble order of Debtor and Creditor, which is used only amongst Merchants; also to be expert in the order and form of Charter-parties, Bills of Lading, Invoyces, Contracts, Bills of Exchange, and Policies of Ensurance.

2. He ought to know the Measures, Weights, and Monies of all forraign Countries, especially where we have Trade, & the Monies not onely by their several denominations, but also by their intrinsique values in weight & fineness, compared with the Standard of this Kingdom, without which he cannot well direct his affaires.

3. He ought to know the Customs, Tools, Taxes, Impositions, Conducts and other charges upon all manner of Merchandize exported or imported to and from the said Forraign Countries.

4. He ought to know in what several commodities each Country abounds, and what be the wares which they want, and how and from whence they are furnished with the same.

5. He ought to understand, and to be a diligent observer of the rates of Exchanges by Bills, from one State to another, whereby he may the better direct his affairs, and remit over and receive home his Monies to the most advantage possible.

6. He ought to know what goods are prohibited to be exported or imported in the said forraign Countreys, lest otherwise he should incur great danger and loss in the ordering of his affairs.

7. He ought to know upon what rates and conditions to fraight his Ships, and ensure his adventures from one Countrey to another, and to be well acquainted with the laws, orders and customes of the Ensurance office both here and beyond the Seas, in the many accidents which may happen upon the damage or loss of Ships and goods, or both these.

8. He ought to have knowledge in the goodness and in the prices of all the several materials which are required for the building and repairing of Ships, and the divers workmanships of the same, as also for the Masts, Tackling, Cordage, Ordnance, Victuals, Munition, and Provisions of many kinds; together with the ordinary wages of Commanders, Officers, and Mariners, all which concern the Merchant as he is an Owner of Ships.

9. He ought (by the divers occasions which happen sometimes in the buying and selling of one commodity and sometimes in another) to have indifferent if not perfect knowledge in all manner of Merchandize or wares, which is to be as it were a man of all occupations and trades.

10. He ought by his voyaging on the Seas to become skilful in the Art of Navigation.

11. He ought, as he is a Traveller, and sometimes abiding in forraign Countreys, to attain to the speaking of divers Languages, and to be a diligent observer of the ordinary Revenues and expences of forraign Princes, together with their strength both by Sea and Land, their laws, customes, policies, manners, religions, arts, and the like; to be able to give account thereof in all occasions for the good of his Countrey.

12. Lastly, although there be no necessity that such a Merchant should be a great Scholar; yet it is (at least) required, that in his youth he learn the Latine tongue, which will the better enable him in all the rest of his endeavours.

The Means to Enrich this Kingdom, and to Encrease Our Treasure

The ordinary means therefore to increase our wealth and treasure is by Forraign Trade, wherein wee must ever observe this rule; to sell more to strangers yearly than wee consume of theirs in value. For suppose that when this Kingdom is plentifully served with the Cloth, Lead, Tinn, Iron, Fish and other native commodities, we doe yearly export the overplus to forraign Countreys to the value of twenty two hundred thousand pounds; by which means we are enable beyond the Seas to buy and bring in forraign wares for our use and Consumptions, to the value of twenty hundred thousand pounds.

The Exportation of our Moneys in Trade of Merchandize in a Means to Encrease our Treasure.

If we have such a quantity of wares as doth fully provide us of all things needful from beyond the seas: why should we then doubt that our monys sent out in trade, must not necessarily come back again in treasure; together with the great gains which it may procure in such manner as is before set down? And on the other side, if those Nations which send out their monies do it because they have but few wares of their own, how come they then to have so much Treasure as we ever see in those places which suffer it freely to be exported at all times and by whomsoever? I answer, Even by trading with their Moneys; for by what other means can they get it, having no Mines of Gold or Silver?

2

Dreams and Realities in the Colonies

Within a hundred years of the first settlement in Virginia, England had established thirteen colonies along the North American coastline. These settlements fostered the transplantation of immigrants, whose colonial societies were shaped by their European traditions and the environment of the New World. Many came voluntarily, motivated by hopes and dreams of political, social, and economic opportunities. Others came forcibly: enslaved Africans were brought to the Americas from the countries of western Africa to fill the labor needs of the southern colonies.

This set of documents depicts the development of colonial life during this period, highlighting important events and characteristics that helped to shape an American identity. What should be noted is the contrast between the hopes and dreams of these colonists and the reality of their environment and the emerging frictions in colonial life between newcomers and old settlers, urban and rural areas, the divinely "chosen" and the "consorts of Satan."

These documents, describing life in early Virginia, Massachusetts, and Pennsylvania, describe what happens when dreams clash with reality. Captain John Smith's history of Virginia describes the "starving times" in the colony's early history. The next document, the Laws of Virginia, from 1610 and 1611, reveals how strictly the lives of the early settlers were circumscribed. By 1676, Virginia had developed a distinct lifestyle, a distinct feature of which was the ownership of the best land by a small group of planters. Under the leadership of Governor William Berkeley, these planters dominated the political and economic life of the colony. Later arrivals to the colony were forced to settle further inland in amore hostile and less fertile environment. Realizing the inequity of their situation and believing that they had little support from the colonial government, their frustrations came to a head in an attempt to take control of the colony. The Declaration from Bacon's Rebellion details these settlers' specific grievances and challenges to the authority of colonial rule. It is an important example of the tensions that developed throughout the colonies between the frontier and coastal regions.

Massachusetts was intended to be, in John Winthrop's words, "a city upon a hill." Winthrop envisioned a perfect Christian community that could serve as a model society for the rest of the world. However, the economic success of the colony all but doomed its religious mission: the colony's growth and prosperity made it difficult for citizens to focus on maintaining a closed Christian community, a situation exacerbated by an influx of non-Puritans, which diverted attention from religion to money. The hysteria of the Salem witch trials may be seen as a manifestation of the frustrations of many Puritans as they lost control of their colony.

For William Penn the founding of a colony meant an opportunity to implement his dream for a perfect society in which people lived in perfect harmony. His discourse on the relationship between government and the citizenry, "Model of Government," was written prior to the settlement of Pennsylvania.

Study Questions

1. Many Virginians came to the colony after reading extravagant claims about the opportunities and virtues of life there. How might this have affected their adjustment to life in the colonies?

2. In what ways was life in Virginia different from life in the Massachusetts Bay Colony?

3. Compare Winthrop's and Penn's visions for a perfect society. How did they think the New World would help them form a more perfect society?

4. What grievances did the participants in Bacon's Rebellion have against the governor?

5. Compare the descriptions of gender roles in the Virginia Laws, Anne Bradstreet poetry and Ann Foster's confession.

6. Is there anything in Winthrop's sermon that might foreshadow the witchcraft outbreak in salem or the mind set that produced Ann Foster's confession?

John Smith, "The Starving Time" (1624)

Early colonists endured hard times indeed. Captain John Smith had an extraordinary career as a soldier of fortune, adventurer, and explorer, and within a short time after colonists arrived in Virginia, he became their acknowledged leader. In 1624, he wrote a history of Virginia. This document is from a section called "The Starving Time," which relates the period just after Smith returned to England in 1609. Smith refers to himself in the third person in this account. Note the reference to Pocahontas.[*]

It might well be thought, a Countrie so faire (as Virginia is) and a people so tractable, would long ere this have beene quietly possessed to the satisfaction of the adventurers, & the eternizing of the memory of those that effected it. But because all the world doe see a defailement; this following Treatise shall give satisfaction to all indifferent Readers, how the businesse hath bin carried; where no doubt they will easily understand and answer to their question, how it came to passe there was no better speed and successe in those proceedings. . . .

The day before Captain Smith returned for England with the ships, Captain Davis arrived in a small Pinace, with some sixteene proper men more . . . for the Salvages no sooner understood Smith was gone, but they all revolted, and did spoile and murther all they incountered. Now wee were all constrained to live onely on that Smith had onely for his owne Companie, for the rest had consumed their proportions . . . Sicklemore upon the confidence of Powhatan, with about thirtie others as carelesse as himselfe, were all slaine, onely Jeffrey Shortridge escaped, and Pokahontas the Kings daughter saved a boy called Henry Spilman, that lived many yeeres after, by her meanes, amongst the Patawomekes. . . . Now we all found the losse of Captain Smith, yea his greatest maligners could now curse his losse: as for corne, provision and contribution from the Salvages, we had nothing but mortall wounds, with clubs and arrowes; as for our Hogs, Hens, Goats, Sheepe, Horse, or what lived, our commanders, officers & Salvages daily consumed them, some small proportions sometimes we tasted, till all was devoured; then swords, armes, pieces, or any thing, wee traded with the Salvages, whose cruell fingers were so oft imbrewed in our blouds, that what by their crueltie, our Governours indiscretion, and the losse of our ships, of five hundred within six moneths after Captain Smiths departure, there remained not past sixtie men, women and children, most miserable and poore creatures; and those were preserved for the most part, by roots, herbes, acornes, walnuts, berries, now and then a little fish: they that had startch in these extremities, made no small use of it; yea, even the very

---

[*] From John Smith, *The Generall Historie of Virginia, New England and the Summer Isles*, vol. I (Glasgow: James MacLehoge and Sons, 1907).

skinnes of our horses. Nay, so great was our famine, that a Salvage we slew, and buried, the poorer sort tooke him up againe and eat him, and so did divers one another boyled and stewed with roots and herbs: And one amongst the rest did kill his wife, powdered [salted] her, and had eaten part of her before it was knowne, for which hee was executed, as hee well deserved; now whether shee was better roasted, boyled or carbonado'd [grilled], I know not, but of such a dish as powdered wife I never heard of. This was that time, which still to this day we called the starving time; it were too vile to say, and scarce to be beleeved, what we endured.

The Laws of Virginia (1610–1611)

> Virginia was the first English colony in America, settled in 1607 by representatives of London joint stock companies. Its early years were filled with death and disaster—malaria, starvation, and threat of Indian attack all took a toll on the settlers. The colony's laws strictly controlled the behavior of colonists, emphasizing activities needed to maintain order and to survive. Note the variety of activities deemed capital offenses—and punishable by death.*

Whereas his Majesty, like himself a most zealous prince, has in his own realms a principal care of true religion and reverence to God and has always strictly commanded his generals and governors, with all his forces wheresoever, to let their ways be, like his ends, for the glory of God.

And forasmuch as no good service can be performed, or were well managed, where military discipline is not observed, and military discipline cannot be kept where the rules or chief parts thereof be not certainly set down and generally know, I have, with the advice and counsel of Sir Thomas Gates, Knight, Lieutenant-General, adhered unto the laws divine and orders politic and martial of his lordship, the same exemplified, as addition of such others as I found either the necessity of the present state of the colony to require or the infancy and weakness of the body thereof as yet able to digest, and do now publish them to all persons in the colony, that they may as well take knowledge of the laws themselves as of the penalty and punishment, which, without partiality, shall be inflicted upon the breakers of the same.

1. First, Since we owe our highest and supreme duty, our greatest, and all our allegiance to him from whom all power and authority is derived and flows as from the first and only fountain, and being especial soldiers impressed in this sacred

---

* From "Articles, Lawes, and Orders, Divine, Politique, and Martiall for the Colony of Virginea," in William Strachey, *For the Colony in Virginea Britannia: Lawes, Divine, Morall and Martiall, Etc.* (London: Walter Barre, 1612), 1–7, 19.

cause, we must alone expect our success from him, who is only the blesser of all good attempts, the king of kings, the commander of commanders, and lord of hosts, I do strictly command and charge all captains and officers, of what quality or nature soever, whether commanders in the field or in town or towns, forts or fortresses, to have a care that the Almighty God be duly and daily served and that they call upon their people to hear sermons, as that also they diligently frequent morning and evening prayer themselves by their own exemplar and daily life and duty herein, encouraging others thereunto, and that such who shall often and willfully absent themselves be duly punished according to the martial law in that case provided.

2. That no man speak impiously or maliciously against the holy and blessed Trinity or any of the three persons, that is to say, against God the Father, God the Son, and God the Holy Ghost, or against the known articles of the Christian faith, upon pain of death.

3. That no man blaspheme God's holy name upon pain of death, or use unlawful oaths, taking the name of God in vain, curse, or bane upon pain of severe punishment for the first offense so committed and for the second to have a bodkin thrust through his tongue; and if he continue the blaspheming of God's holy name, for the third time so offending, he shall be brought to a martial court and there receive censure of death of his offense.

4. No man shall use any traitorous words against his Majesty's person or royal authority, upon pain of death.

5. No man shall speak any word or do any act which may tend to the derision or despite of God's holy word, upon pain of death; nor shall any man unworthily demean himself unto any preacher or minister of the same, but generally hold them in all reverent regard and dutiful entreaty; otherwise he the offender shall openly be whipped three times and ask public forgiveness in the assembly of the congregation three several Sabbath days.

6. Every man and woman duly, twice a day upon the first tolling of the bell, shall upon the working days repair unto the church to hear divine service upon pain of losing his or her day's allowance for the first omission, for the second to be whipped, and for the third to be condemned to the galleys for six months. Likewise, no man or woman shall dare to violate or break the Sabbath by any gaming, public or private abroad or at home, but duly sanctify and observe the same, both himself and his family, by preparing themselves at home with private prayer that they may be the better fitted for the public, according to the commandments of God and the orders of our church. As also every man and woman shall repair in the morning to the divine service and sermons preached upon the Sabbath day in the afternoon to divine service and catechizing, upon pain for the first fault to lose their provision and allowance for the whole week following, for the second to lose the said allowance and also to be whipped, and for the third to suffer death.

7. All preachers and ministers within this our colony or colonies shall, in the forts where they are resident, after divine service, duly preach every Sabbath day in the forenoon and catechise in the afternoon and weekly say the divine service twice every day and preach every Wednesday. Likewise, every minister where he is resident, within the same fort or fortress, towns or town, shall choose unto him four of the most religious and better disposed as well to inform of the abuses and neglects of the people in their duties and service of God, as also to the due reparation and keeping of the church handsome and fitted with all reverent observances thereunto belonging. Likewise, every minister shall keep a faithful and true record of church book of all christenings, marriages, and deaths of such our people as shall happen within their fort or fortress, towns or town, at any time, upon the burden of a neglectful conscience and upon pain of losing their entertainment.

8. He that, upon pretended malice, shall murder or take away the life of any man, shall be punished with death.

9. No man shall commit the horrible and detestable sins of sodomy, upon pain of death; and he or she that can be lawfully convict of adultery shall be punished with death. No man shall ravish or force any woman, maid or Indian, or other, upon pain of death; and know that he or she that shall commit fornication, and evident proof made thereof, for their first fault shall be whipped, for their second they shall be whipped, and for their third they shall be whipped three times a week for one month and ask public forgiveness in the assembly of the congregation.

10. No man shall be found guilty of sacrilege, which is a trespass as well committed in violating and abusing any sacred ministry, duty, or office of the church irreverently or prophanely, as by being a church robber to filch, steal, or carry away anything out of the church appertaining thereunto or unto any holy and consecrated place to the divine service of God, which no man shall do upon pain of death. Likewise, he that shall rob the store of any commodities therein of what quality soever, whether provisions of victuals, or of arms, trucking stuff, apparel, linen, or woolen, hose or shoes, hats or caps, instruments or tools of steel, iron, etc., or shall rob from his fellow soldier or neighbor anything that is his, victuals, apparel, household stuff, tool, or what necessary else soever, by water or land, out of boat, house, or knapsack, shall be punished with death. . . .

Every minister or preacher shall, every Sabbath day before catechising, read all these laws and ordinances publicly in the assembly of the congregation upon pain of his entertainment checked for that week.

Bacon's Rebellion: The Declaration (1676)

In 1676, tobacco planters in western Virginia, considered by the authorities in Jamestown to be a backward bunch, requested permission to lead an expedition—a thinly disguised land grab—against the Susquehannock Indians, who had been sporadically attacking settlements nearby. The autocratic royal governor, Sir William Berkeley, who had led Virginia for over thirty years, refused. In response, the frontiersmen, led by Nathaniel Bacon, raised a force of five hundred and marched against not only the Susquehannock but also Governor Berkeley. After burning Jamestown and slaughtering many Indians, Bacon became ill and died in October 1676. Shortly after, British troops arrived and order was restored in the colony. In this declaration, note the broad range of grievances the frontierspeople have and how they appeal in the name of the king in England to justify their actions. *

1. For having, upon specious pretenses of public works, raised great unjust taxes upon the commonalty for the advancement of private favorites and other sinister ends, but no visible effects in any measure adequate; for not having, during this long time of his government, in any measure advanced this hopeful colony either by fortifications, towns, or trade.

2. For having abused and rendered contemptible the magistrates of justice by advancing to places of judicature scandalous and ignorant favorites.

3. For having wronged his Majesty's prerogative and interest by assuming monopoly of the beaver trade and for having in it unjust gain betrayed and sold his Majesty's country and the lives of his loyal subjects to the barbarous heathen.

4. For having protected, favored, and emboldened the Indians against his Majesty's loyal subjects, never contriving, requiring, or appointing any due or proper means of satisfaction for their many invasions, robberies, and murders committed upon us.

5. For having, when the army of English was just upon the track of those Indians, who now in all places burn, spoil, murder and when we might with ease have destroyed them who then were in open hostility, for then having expressly countermanded and sent back our army by passing his word for the peaceable demeanor of the said Indians, who immediately prosecuted their evil intentions,

---

* From "Declaration of Nathaniel Bacon in the Name of the People of Virginia, July 30, 1676," in *Foundations of Colonial America: A Documentary History, Southern Colonies*, ed. Keith Kavenagh (New York: Chelsea House Publishers, 1973), 1783–1784.

committing horrid murders and robberies in all places, being protected by the said engagement and word past of him the said Sir William Berkeley, having ruined and laid desolate a great part of his Majesty's country, and have now drawn themselves into such obscure and remote places and are by their success so emboldened and confirmed by their confederacy so strengthened that the cries of blood are in all places, and the terror and consternation of the people so great, are now become not only difficult but a very formidable enemy who might at first with ease have been destroyed.

6.   And lately, when, upon the loud outcries of blood, the assembly had, with all care, raised and framed an army for the preventing of further mischief and safeguard of this his Majesty's colony.

7.   For having, with only the privacy of some few favorites without acquainting the people, only by the alteration of a figure, forged a commission, by we know not what hand, not only without but even against the consent of the people, for the raising and effecting civil war and destruction, which being happily and without bloodshed prevented; for having the second time attempted the same, thereby calling down our forces from the defense of the frontiers and most weakly exposed places.

8.   For the prevention of civil mischief and ruin amongst ourselves while the barbarous enemy in all places did invade, murder, and spoil us, his Majesty's most faithful subjects.

Of this and the aforesaid articles we accuse Sir William Berkeley as guilty of each and every one of the same, and as one who has traitorously attempted, violated, and injured his Majesty's interest here by a loss of a great part of this his colony and many of his faithful loyal subjects by him betrayed and in a barbarous and shameful manner exposed to the incursions and murder of the heathen. And we do further declare these the ensuing persons in this list to have been his wicked and pernicious councilors, confederates, aiders, and assisters against the commonalty in these our civil commotions.

Sir Henry Chichley	Richard Whitacre
Lt. Col. Christopher Wormeley	Nicholas Spencer
Phillip Ludwell	Joseph Bridger
Robt. Beverley	William Claiburne, Jr.
Ri. Lee	Thomas Hawkins
Thomas Ballard	William Sherwood
William Cole	John Page Clerke
	John Clauffe Clerk

John West, Hubert Farrell, Thomas Reade, Math. Kempe

And we do further demand that the said Sir William Berkeley with all the persons in this list be forthwith delivered up or surrender themselves within four days after the notice hereof, or otherwise we declare as follows.

That in whatsoever place, house, or ship, any of the said persons shall reside, be hid, or protected, we declare the owners, masters, or inhabitants of the said places to be confederates and traitors to the people and the estates of them is also of all the aforesaid persons to be confiscated. And this we, the commons of Virginia, do declare, desiring a firm union amongst ourselves that we may jointly and with one accord defend ourselves against the common enemy. And let not the faults of the guilty be the reproach of the innocent, or the faults or crimes of the oppressors divide and separate us who have suffered by their oppressions.

These are, therefore, in his Majesty's name, to command you forthwith to seize the persons abovementioned as traitors to the King and country and them to bring to Middle Plantation and there to secure them until further order, and, in case of opposition, if you want any further assistance you are forthwith to demand it in the name of the people in all the counties of Virginia.

Nathaniel Bacon
General by Consent of the people.

William Sherwood

John Winthrop, "A Model of Christian Charity" (1630)

John Winthrop, a Cambridge-trained lawyer, was the leader of the group of about a thousand Puritans who settled Massachusetts Bay in 1630. Unlike the Virginians, or perhaps learning from their experience, the Massachusetts settlers arrived with structures of government and social order already established. They founded what became a successful and growing colony. This famous document is a sermon written on board the *Arabella* and delivered to the Puritans on the eve of their settlement of Massachusetts Bay.[*]

God almighty in His most holy and wise providence hath so disposed of the condition of mankind, as in all times some must be rich, some poor, some high and eminent in power and dignity, others mean and in subjection.

---

[*] From *Winthrop Papers: Volume II, 1623–1630* (The Massachusetts Historical Society, 1931).

Reason: First, to hold conformity with the rest of His works, being delighted to show forth the glory of His wisdom in the variety and difference of the creatures and the glory of His power, in ordering all these differences for the preservation and good of the whole.

Reason: Secondly, that He might have the more occasion to manifest the work of His spirit. First, upon the wicked in moderating and restraining them, so that the rich and mighty should not eat up the poor, nor the poor and despised rise up against their superiors and shake off their yoke. Secondly, in the regenerate in exercising His graces in them, as in the great ones, their love, mercy, gentleness, temperance, etc., in the poor and inferior sort, their faith, patience, obedience, etc.

Reason: Thirdly, that every man might have need of other, and from hence they might all be knit more nearly together in the bond of brotherly affection. From hence it appears plainly that no man is made more honorable than another, or more wealthy, etc., out of any particular and singular respect to himself, but for the glory of his creator and the common good of the creature, man.

Thus stands the cause between God and us. We are entered into covenant with Him for this work, we have taken out a commission, the Lord hath given us leave to draw our own articles we have professed to enterprise these actions upon these and these ends, we have hereupon besought Him of favor and blessing. Now if the Lord shall please to hear us, and bring us in peace to the place we desire, then hath He ratified this covenant and sealed our commission, [and] will expect a strict performance of the articles contained in it, but if we shall neglect the observations of these articles which are the ends we have propounded, and dissembling with our God, shall fall to embrace this present world and prosecute our carnal intentions seeking great things for ourselves and our posterity, the Lord will surely break out in wrath against us, be revenged of such a perjured people, and make us know the price of the breach of such a covenant.

Now the only way to avoid this shipwreck and to provide for our posterity is to follow the counsel of Micah, to do justly, to love mercy, to walk humbly with our God. For this end we must be knit together in this work as one man, we must entertain each other in brotherly affection, we must be willing to abridge ourselves of our superfluities for the supply of others' necessities, we must uphold a familiar commerce together in all meekness, gentleness, patience, and liberality, we must delight in each other, make others' conditions our own, rejoice together, mourn together, labor and suffer together, always having before our eyes our commission and community in the work, our community as members of the same body So shall we keep the unity of the spirit in the bond of peace. The Lord will be our God and delight in all our ways, so that we shall see much more of His wisdom, power, goodness, and truth than formerly we have been acquainted with. We shall find that the God of Israel is among us, when ten of us shall be able to resist a thousand of our enemies, when He shall make us a praise and glory, that men shall say of succeeding plantations, the Lord make it like that of New England. For we must consider that we shall be as a city upon a hill, the eyes of all people are upon us. So that if we shall deal falsely with our God in this work we have undertaken and so cause Him to withdraw His present help from us, we shall be made a story and byword throughout the world, we shall open the mouths of enemies to speak evil of the ways of God and all professors for God's sake, we shall shame the faces of many of God's worthy servants, and cause their prayers to be turned into curses upon us till we be consumed out of the good land whither we are going. And to shut up this discourse with that exhortation of Moses, that faithful servant of the Lord in His last farewell to Israel, Deut. 30., Beloved there is now set before us life and good, death and evil, in that we are commanded this day to love the Lord our God, and to love one another, to walk in His ways and to keep His commandments and His ordinance, and His laws, and the articles of our covenant with Him that we may live and be multiplied, and that the Lord our God my bless us in the land whither we go to possess it. But if our hearts shall turn away so that we will not obey, but shall be seduced and worship other Gods, our pleasures, our profits, and serve them, it is propounded unto us this day we shall surely perish out of the good land whither we pass over this vast sea to possess it. Therefore let us choose life, that we, and our seed, may live, and by obeying His voice, and cleaving to Him, for He is our life and our prosperity.

Anne Bradstreet, Before the Birth of One of Her Children (c. 1650)

Ann Bradstreet (1612–1672) is now considered one of the seventeenth century's leading poets. She wrote privately for her family, in part because Puritan culture limited women's freedom to express themselves publicly. During the colonial era, childbirth was frequent (on average, women in New England bore seven children per marriage) and dangerous.[*]

> All things within this fading world have end.
> Adversity doth still our joys attend;
> No ties so strong, no friends so dear and sweet,
> But with death's parting blow are sure to meet.
> The sentence passed is most irrevocable,
> A common thing, yet, oh, inevitable.
> How soon, my dear, death may my steps attend,
> How soon it may be thy lot to lose thy friend,
> We both are ignorant; yet love bids me
> These farewell lines to recommend to thee,
> That when that knot's untied that made us one
> I may seem thine who in effect am none.
> And if I see not half my days that are due,
> What nature would God grant to yours and you.

[*] From Anne Bradstreet, *The Poems of Mrs. Anne Bradstreet* (Boston, 1758).

The many faults that well you know I have
Let be interred in my oblivion's grave;
If any worth or virtue were in me,
Let that live freshly in thy memory,
And when thou feelest no grief, as I no harms,
Yet love thy dead, who long lay in thine arms;
And when thy loss shall be repaid with gains
Look to my little babes, my dear remains,
And if though love thyself, or lovedst me,
These oh protect from stepdam's injury.
And if chance to thine eyes shall bring this verse,
With some sad sighs honor my absent hearse;
And kiss this paper for thy love's dear sake,
Who with salt tears this last farewell did take.

The Examination and Confession of Ann Foster at Salem Village (1692)

In the late winter of 1692, several hysterical girls in Salem Village, Massachusetts, began accusing women in their community of bewitching them. Belief in witchcraft was common in both the new and the old worlds. By the summer, more than 150 people were accused of witchcraft—mostly women, ranging from poor widows to the governor's wife—and nineteen people were hanged. The following is an excerpt from the transcription of the confession of Ann Foster.[*]

After a while Ann ffoster conffesed that the devil apered to her in the shape of a bird at several Times, such a bird as she neuer saw the like before; & that she had had this gift (viz. of striking ye afflicted downe with her eye euer since) & being askt why she thought yt bird was the diuill she answered because he came white & vanished away black & yt the diuill told her yt she should haue this gift & yt she must beliue him & told her she should haue prosperity & she said yt he had apeared to her three times & was always as a bird, and the last time was about half a year since, & sat upon a table had two legs & great eyes & yt it was the second time of his apearance that he promised her prosperity & yt it was Carriers wife about three weeks agoe yt came & perswaded her to hurt these people.

---

[*] Reprinted from *The Colonial Horizon: America in the Sixteenth and Seventeenth Centuries*, 1969, ed. William H. Goetzmann (Reading, MA: Addison Wesley Publishing Company).

16 July 1692. Ann ffoster Examined confessed yt it was Goody Carrier yt made her a witch yt she came to her in person about Six yeares agoe & told her it she would not be a witch ye diuill should tare her in peices & carry her away at which time she promised to Serve the diuill yt she had bewitched a hog of John Loujoys to death & that she had hurt some persons in Salem Villige, yt goody Carier came to her & would have her bewitch two children of Andrew Allins & that she had then two popets made & stuck pins in them to bewitch ye said children by which one of them dyed ye other very sick, that she was at the meeting of the witches at Salem Vilige, yt Goody Carier came & told her of the meeting and would haue her goe, so they got upon Sticks & went said Jorny & being there did see Mr. Buroughs ye minister who spake to them all, & this was about two months agoe that there was then twenty five persons meet together, that she tyed a knot in a Rage & threw it into the fire to hurt Tim. Swan & that she did hurt the rest yt complayned of her by Squesing popets like them & so almost choked them.

18 July 1692. Ann ffoster Examined confessed yt ye deuil in shape of a man apeared to her wth Goody carier about six yeare since when they made her a witch & that she promised to serve the diuill two years, upon which the diuill promised her prosperity and many things but neuer performed it, that she & martha Carier did both ride on a stick or pole when they went to the witch meeting at Salem Village & that the stick broak: as they were caried in the aire aboue the tops of the trees, & they fell but she did hang fast about the neck of Goody Carier & ware presently at the vilage, that she was then much hurt of her Leg, she further saith that she heard some of the witches say there was three hundred & fiue in the whole Country & that they would ruin that place ye Vilige, also said there was present at that meetting two men besides Mr. Burroughs ye minister & one of them had gray haire, she saith yt she formerly frequented the publique metting to worship god. but the diuill had such power ouer her yt she could not profit there & yt was her undoeing: she saith yt about three or foure yeares agoe Martha Carier told her she would bewitch James Hobbs child to death & the child dyed in twenty four hours.

21 July 92. Ann ffoster Examined Owned her former conffesion being read to her and further conffesed that the discourse amongst ye witches at ye meeting at Salem village was that they would afflict there to set up the Diuills Kingdome. This confesion is true as witness my hand.

Ann ffoster Signed & Owned the aboue Examination & Conffesion before me

Salem 10th September 1692.   John Higginson, Just Peace.

William Penn, from "Model of Government" (1681)

William Penn was born to the English gentry but at a young age became a Quaker convert. In 1681, Charles II granted Penn an enormous tract of land north of Maryland and west of the Delaware River. This, Pennsylvania, was the last unsettled segment on America's eastern coast and one of the most fertile. William Penn's Pennsylvania was marked by diversity, prosperity, and fair dealings with the Indians, citizens were also governed liberally—granted freedom of religion, a legislative assembly, and trial by jury. This essay was written prior to William Penn's settlement in Pennsylvania and reveals some of his revolutionary democratic ideas about government.*

For particular frames and models [of government] it will become me to say little. . . . My reasons are: First, that the age is too nice and difficult for it, there being nothing the wits of men are more busy and divided upon. . . .

Secondly, I do not find a model in the world that time, place, and some singular emergencies have not necessarily altered; nor is it easy to frame a civil government that shall serve all places alike.

Thirdly, I know what is said by the several admirers of monarchy, aristocracy, and democracy, which are the rule of one, a few, and many, and are the three common ideas of government when men discourse on that subject. But I choose to solve the controversy with this small distinction, and it belongs to all three: any government is free to the people under it (whatever to be the frame) where the laws rule, and the people are a party to those laws; and more than this is tyranny, oligarchy, and confusion.

---

* From Minutes of the Provincial Council for Pennsylvania . . . (1852), I, 30–31, in Thomas A. Bailey *The American Spirit: U.S. History as Seen by Contemporaries* (Boston: D. C. Heath and Company, 1963), 40-41.

3

Indentured Servants and Slaves

The documents in this chapter contrast voluntary and involuntary servitude in the colonies. In the seventeenth century, indentured servants were considered the best way to meet labor demands in the southern colonies. These young men and women were generally landless Europeans who agreed to work for a set period (usually five to seven years) in return for their transportation to America. The first Africans were brought to the Virginia colony in 1619 but it wasn't until later in the seventeenth century that black African slaves began to replace white indentured servants as field labor. By the 1660s, though, slavery had become institutionalized in Virginia and Maryland, and in the South, slaves had largely replaced indentured servants by the eighteenth century.

The first document in this chapter, selections from the Virginia laws, describes the transition in Virginia from indentured to slave labor and the changing legal system that fostered the institutionalization of slavery. These laws also provide evidence that community standards were strayed from—female servants were impregnated by their masters and love affairs occurred between white women and enslaved men.

These laws support the notion that life was difficult for indentured servants, who were often badly treated by their masters. In *Journey to Pennsylvania in the Year 1750 and Return to Germany in the Year 1754*, Gottlieb Mittelberger narrates the horror of the trans-Atlantic trip and how the end of the journey brought further terror as servants were auctioned off. Richard Frethorne and Elizabeth Sprigs describe their own experiences. Their two letters home, written over one hundred years apart, convey the dreadful loneliness and physical hardships endured by both male and female indentured servants.

But difficult as life was for indentured servants, they lived with the knowledge that their bondage was not permanent and that, eventually, freedom could be achieved. This was not the case for African slaves. *An Account of the African Slave Trade on the Coast of Africa* and *The Interesting Narrative of the Life of Olaudah Equiano* describe the horrors of the "middle passage" and enslavement from two very different points of view—an English surgeon who served on slave ships and an Ibo child who later bought himself out of slavery.

Study Questions

1. Compare the treatment of indentured servants and slaves on the passage to the New World.

2. What effect did indentured servitude and slavery have on families?

3. What does Elizabeth Sprigs's letter reveal about the growing institutionalization of slavery and racism in North America?

4. Contrast Falconbridge's and Equiano's description of the "middle passage."

The Laws of Virginia (1662, 1691, 1705)

These statutes chart the development of regulations on the sexual and reproductive lives of indentured servants and slaves, the growing institutionalization of slavery, and the construction of racism. Note the increasingly harsh penalties and how punishments differed by gender.[*]

[March 1661]

For restraint of the ffilthy sin of ffornication, *Be it enacted* that what man or woman soever shall commit ffornication, he and she soe offending, upon proofe thereof by confession or evidence shall pay each of them five hundred pounds of tobacco fine, *(a)* to the use of the parish or parishes they dwell in, and be bound to their good behavior, and be imprisoned untill they find security to be bound with them, and if they or either of them committing ffornication as aforesaid be servants then the master of such servant soe offending shall pay the said ffive hundred pounds of tobacco as aforesaid to the use of the parish aforesaid, for which the said servant shall serve half a yeare after the time by indenture or custome is expires; and if the master shall refuse to pay the ffine then the servant to be whipped; and if it happen a bastard child to be gotten in such ffornication then the woman if a servant in regard of the losse and trouble her master doth sustaine by her haveing a bastard shall serve two yeares after her time by indenture is expired or pay two thousand pounds of tobacco to her master besides the ffine or punishment for committing the offence and the reputed father to put in security to keep the child and save the parish harmelesse.

---

[*] From the Assembly of Virginia, Act XVI, April 1691, in William Waller Henning, *The Statutes at Large: Being a Collection of All the Laws of Virginia, from the First Session of the Legislature, in the Year 1619*, 13 vols. (New York: 1823), vol. 3: 86–87; and Assembly of Virginia, chap. XLIX, sec. XX, October 1705, in Henning, vol. 3: 453.

[December 1662]

Whereas by act of Assembly every woman servant haveing a bastard is to serve two yeares, and late experience shew that some dissolute masters have gotten their maides with child, and yet claime the benefitt of their service, and on the contrary if a woman gott with child by her master should be freed from that service it might probably induce such loose persons to lay all their bastards to their masters; *it is therefore thought fitt and accordingly enacted, and be it enacted henceforward* that each woman servant gott with child by her master shall after her time by indenture or custome is expired be by the churchwardens of the parish where she lived when she was brought to bed of such bastard, sold for two yeares, and the tobacco to be imployed by the vestry for the use of the parish. . . .

Whereas some doubts have arrisen whether children got by any Englishman upon a negro woman should be slave or ffree, *Be it therefore enacted and declard by this present grand assembly,* that all children bourn in this country shal be held bond of free only according to the condition of the mother, *And* that if any Christian shall comitt ffornication with a negro man or woman, hee or shee soe offending shall pay double the ffines imposed by the former act.

[April 1691]

. . . For prevention of that abominable mixture and spurious issue which hereafter may encrease in this dominion, as well as by negroes, mulattos, and Indians intermarrying with English, or other white women, as by their unlawfull accompanying with one another, *Be it enacted* . . . that . . . whatsoever English or other white man or woman being free, shall intermarry with a negro, mulatto or Indian man or woman bond or free shall within three months after such marriage be banished and removed from this dominion forever. . . .

And be it further enacted . . . That if any English woman being free shall have a bastard child by any negro or mulatto, she pay the sum of fifteen pounds sterling, within one month after such bastard child shall be born, to the Church wardens of the parish . . . and in default of such payment she shall be taken into the possession of the said Church wardens and disposed of for five yeares, and the said fine of fifteen pounds, or whatever the woman shall be disposed of for, shall be paid, one third part to their majesties . . . and one other third part to the use of the parish . . . and the other third part to the informer, and that such bastard child be bound out as a servant by the said Church wardens until he or she shall attain the age of thirty yeares, and in case such English woman that shall have such bastard child be a servant, she shall be sold by the said church wardens (after her time is expired that she ought by law serve her master), for five yeares, and the money she shall be sold for divided as if before appointed, and the child to serve as aforesaid.

[1705]

And be it further enacted, That no minister of the church of England, or other minister, or person whatsoever, within this colony and dominion, shall hereafter wittingly presume to marry a white man with a negro or mulatto woman; or to marry a white woman with a negro or mulatto man, upon paid of forfeiting or paying, for every such marriage the sum of ten thousand pounds of tobacco; one half to our sovereign lady the Queen . . . and the other half to the informer.

Gottlieb Mittelberger, The Passage of Indentured Servants (1750)

Gottlieb Mittelberger was an indentured servant from Germany who worked in Pennsylvania, where he served as a schoolmaster and organist. After only four years, he returned to Germany. The following is a detailed and graphic account of the trans-Atlantic journey and the fate that awaited indentured servants upon arrival in North America.[*]

Both in Rotterdam and in Amsterdam the people are packed densely, like herrings so to say, in the large sea-vessels. One person receives a place of scarcely 2 feet width and 6 feet length in the bedstead, while many a ship carries four to six hundred souls; not to mention the innumerable implements, tools, provisions, water-barrels and other things which likewise occupy such space.

On account of contrary winds it takes the ships sometimes 2, 3, and 4 weeks to make the trip from Holland to . . . England. But when the wind is good, they get there in 8 days or even sooner. Everything is examined there and the custom-duties paid, whence it comes that the ships ride there 8, 10 or 14 days and even longer at anchor, till they have taken in their full cargoes. During that time every one is compelled to spend his last remaining money and to consume his little stock of provisions which had been reserved for the sea; so that most passengers, finding themselves on the ocean where they would be in greater need of them, must greatly suffer from hunger and want. Many suffer want already on the water between Holland and Old England.

When the ships have for the last time weighed their anchors near the city of Kaupp [Cowes] in Old England, the real misery begins with the long voyage. For from there the ships, unless they have good wind, must often sail 8, 9, 10 to 12 weeks before they reach Philadelphia. But even with the best wind the voyage lasts 7 weeks.

---

[*] From Gottlieb Mittelberger, *Journey to Pennsylvania in the Year 1750 and Return to Germany in the Year 1754*, trans. Carl Theo Eben (Philadelphia: John Jos. McVey, n.d.).

But during the voyage there is on board these ships terrible misery, stench, fumes, horror, vomiting, many kinds of sea-sickness, fever, dysentery, headache, heat, constipation, boils, scurvy, cancer, mouth rot, and the like, all of which come from old and sharply salted food and meat, also from very bad and foul water, so that many die miserably.

Add to this want of provisions, hunger, thirst, frost, heat, dampness, anxiety, want, afflictions and lamentations, together with other trouble, as . . . the lice abound so frightfully, especially on sick people, that they can be scraped off the body. The misery reaches the climax when a gale rages for 2 or 3 nights and days, so that every one believes that the ship will go to the bottom with all human beings on board. In such a visitation the people cry and pray most piteously.

Children from 1 to 7 years rarely survive the voyage. I witnessed . . . misery in no less than 32 children in our ship, all of whom were thrown into the sea. The parents grieve all the more since their children find no resting-place in the earth, but are devoured by the monsters of the sea.

That most of the people get sick is not surprising, because, in addition to all other trials and hardships, warm food is served only three times a week, the rations being very poor and very little. Such meals can hardly be eaten, on account of being so unclean. The water which is served out of the ships is often very black, thick and full of worms, so that one cannot drink it without loathing, even with the greatest thirst. Toward the end we were compelled to eat the ship's biscuit which had been spoiled long ago; though in a whole biscuit there was scarcely a piece the size of a dollar that had not been full of red worms and spiders' nests. . . .

At length, when, after a long and tedious voyage, the ships come in sight of land, so that the promontories can be seen, which the people were so eager and anxious to see, all creep from below on deck to see the land from afar, and they weep for joy, and pray and sing, thanking and praising God. The sight of the land makes the people on board the ship, especially the sick and the half dead, alive again, so that their hearts leap within them; they shout and rejoice, and are content to bear their misery in patience, in the hope that they may soon reach the land in safety. But alas!

When the ships have landed at Philadelphia after their long voyage, no one is permitted to leave them except those who pay for their passage or can give good security; the others, who cannot pay, must remain on board the ships till they are purchased, and are released from the ships by their purchasers. The sick always fare the worst, for the healthy are naturally preferred and purchased first; and so the sick and wretched must often remain on board in front of the city for 2 or 3 weeks, and frequently die, whereas many a one, if he could pay his debt and were permitted to leave the ship immediately, might recover and remain alive.

The sale of human beings in the market on board the ship is carried out thus: Every day Englishmen, Dutchmen and High-German people come from the city of Philadelphia and other places, in part from a great distance, say 20, 30, or 40 hours away, and go on board the newly arrived ship that has brought and offers for sale passengers from Europe, and select among the healthy persons such as they deem suitable for their business, and bargain with them how long they will serve for their passage money, which most of them are still in debt for. When they have come to an agreement, it happens that adult persons bind themselves in writing to serve 3, 4, 5 or 6 years for the amount due by them, according to their age and strength. But very young people, from 10 to 15 years, must serve till they are 21 years old.

Many parents must sell and trade away their children like so many head of cattle; for if their children take the debt upon themselves, the parents can leave the ship free and unrestrained; but as the parents often do not know where and to what people their children are going, it often happens that such parents and children, after leaving the ship, do not see each other again for many years, perhaps no more in all their lives. . . .

It often happens that whole families, husband, wife and children, are separated by being sold to different purchasers, especially when they have not paid any part of their passage money.

When a husband or wife has died a sea, when the ship has made more than half of her trip, the survivor must pay or serve not only for himself or herself but also for the deceased.

When both parents have died over half-way at sea, their children, especially when they are young and have nothing to pawn or pay, must stand for their own and their parents' passage, and serve till they are 21 years old. When one has served his or her term, he or she is entitled to a new suit of clothes at parting; and if it has been so stipulated, a man gets in addition a horse, a woman, a cow. When a serf has an opportunity to marry in this country, he or she must pay for each year which he or she would have yet to serve, 5 or 6 pounds.

Richard Frethorne, Letter to His Parents (1623)

This is a letter written by Richard Frethorne, an indentured servant in Virginia, to his parents in England. By 1623, Jamestown was well established. Frethorne lived about ten miles from Jamestown, in Martin's Hundred. Whatever their contract promised, most indentured servants could expect poor food, scant clothing, and overwork. Many did not live out their period of service.*

Loveing and kind father and mother my most humble duty remembered to you hopeing in God of your good health, as I my selfe am at the makeing hereof, this is to let you understand that I your Child am in a most heavie Case by reason of the nature of the Country is such that it Causeth much sicknes [including scurvy and "the bloody flux"] . . . and when wee are sicke there is nothing to comfort us; for since I came out of the ship, I never at anie thing but pease, and loblollie (that is water gruell)[.] as for

---

* Richard Frethorne, "Letter to his Parents, March 20, April 2, 3, 1623," in *The Records of the Virginia Company of London*, vol. IV, ed. Susan M. Kingsbury.

deare or venison I never saw anie since I came into this land there is indeed some foule, but Wee are not allowed to goe, and get yt, but must Worke hard both earelie, and late for a messe of water gruell, and a mouthfull of bread, and beife[.] a mouthfull of bread for a pennie loafe must serve for 4 men which is most pitifull if you did knowe as much as I, when people crie out day, and night, Oh that they were in England without their lymbes and would not care to loose anie lymbe to bee in England againe, yea though they beg from doore to doore. . . . I have nothing at all, no not a shirt to my backe, but two Ragges nor no Clothes, but one poore suite, nor but one paire of shooes, but one paire of stockins, but one Capp, but two bands, my Cloke is stollen by one of my owne fellowes, and to his dying hower would not tell mee what he did with it [although some friends saw the "fellowe" buy butter and beef from a ship, probably purchased with Frethorne's cloak]. . . . but I am not halfe a quarter so strong as I was in England, and all is for want of victualls, for I doe protest unto you, that I have eaten more in a day at home than I have allowed me here for a Weeke. . . .

O that you did see may daylie and hourelie sighes, grones, and teares, and thumpes that I afford mine owne brest, and rue and Curse the time of my birth with holy Job. I thought no head had beene able to hold so much water as hath and doth dailie flow from mine eyes.

Elizabeth Sprigs, Letter to Her Father (1756)

This letter was written by Elizabeth Sprigs, an indentured servant in Maryland, to her father in England. It is clear than conditions for indentured servants had not improved much in the more than 100 years since Richard Freethorne wrote from Virginia to his parents. Note how Sprigs compares her treatment to that of "Negroes."[*]

Maryland, Sept'r 22'd 1756

Honred Father

My being for ever banished from your sight, will I hope pardon the Boldness I now take of troubling you with these, my long silence has been purely owning to my undutifullness to you, and well knowing I had offended in the highest Degree, put a tie to my tongue and pen, for fear I should be extinct from your good Graces and add a further Trouble to you, but too well knowing your care and tenderness for me so long as I retain'd my Duty to you, induced me once again to endeavor if possible, to kindle

---

[*] From Elizabeth Sprigs, "Letter to Mr. John Sprigs in White Cross Street near Cripple Gate, London," September 22, 1756. Reprinted by permission of the Connecticut Chapter of the National Society of Colonial Dames of America.

up that flame again. O Dear Father, believe what I am going to relate the words of truth and sincerity, and Balance my former bad Conduct my sufferings here, and then I am sure you'll pity your Destress Daughter, What we unfortunate English People suffer here is beyond the probability of you in England to Conceive, let it suffice that I one of the unhappy Number, am toiling almost Day and Night, and very often in the Horses drudgery, with only this comfort that you Bitch you do not halfe enough, and then tied up and whipp'd to that Degree that you'd not serve an Animal, scarce any thing but Indian Corn and Salt to eat and that even begrudged nay many Negroes are better used, almost naked no shoes nor stockings to wear, and the comfort after slaving during Masters pleasure, what rest we can get is to rap ourselves up in a Blanket and ly upon the Ground, this is the deplorable Condition your poor Betty endures, and now I beg if you have any Bowels of Compassion left show it by sending me some Relief, Clothing is the principal thing wanting, which if you should condiscend to, may easily send them to me by any of the ships bound to Baltimore Town Patapsco River Maryland, and give me leave to conclude in Duty to you and Uncles and Aunts, and Respect to all Friends

Honored Father

Your undutifull and Disobedient Child
Elizabeth Sprigs

Olaudah Equiano, The Middle Passage (1788)

This is a selection from the autobiography of Olaudah Equiano (or Gustavus Vassa), who was brought to Barbados, Virginia, and, later, England from his home West Africa in the early eighteenth century. He was able to purchase his freedom in England and became an abolitionist. His autobiography was written to describe the inhumanity of slavery as part of his abolitionist activities. These passages describe the middle passage and Equiano's experiences as a slave in Virginia.*

. . . The first object which saluted my eyes when I arrived on the coast was the sea, and a slave ship, which was then riding at anchor, and waiting for its cargo. These filled me with astonishment, which was soon converted into terror when I was carried on board. I was immediately handled and tossed up to see if I were sound by some of the crew;

---

* From *The Interesting Narrative of the Life of Olaudah Equiano, or Gustavus Vassa the African: Written by Himself* (New York, 1791).

and I was now persuaded that I had gotten into a world of bad spirits, and that they were going to kill me. Their complexions too differing so much from ours, their long hair, and the language they spoke, (which was very different from any I had ever heard) united to confirm me in this belief. Indeed such were the horrors of my views and fears at the moment, that, if ten thousand worlds had been my own, I would have freely parted with them all to have exchanged my condition with that of the meanest slave in my own country. When I looked round the ship too and saw a large furnace of copper boiling, and a multitude of black people of every description chained together, every one of their countenances expressing dejection and sorrow, I no longer doubted of my fate; and, quite overpowered with horror and anguish, I fell motionless on the deck and fainted. When I recovered a little I found some black people about me, who I believe were some of those who brought me on board, and had been receiving their pay; they talked to me in order to cheer me, but all in vain. I asked them if we were not to be eaten by those white men with horrible looks, red faces, and loose hair. They told me I was not; and one of the crew brought me a small portion of spirituous liquor in a wine glass; but, being afraid of him, I would not take it out of his hand. One of the blacks therefore took it from him and gave it to me, and I took a little down my palate, which, instead of reviving me, as they thought it would, threw me into the greatest consternation at the strange feeling it produced, having never tasted any such liquor before. Soon after this the blacks who brought me on board went off, and left me abandoned to despair. I now saw myself deprived of all chance or returning to my native country or even the least glimpse of hope of gaining the shore, which I now considered as friendly; and I even wished for my former slavery in preference to my present situation, which was filled with horrors of every kind, still heightened by my ignorance of what I was to undergo. I was not long suffered to indulge my grief; I was soon put down under the decks, and there I received such a salutation in my nostrils as I had never experienced in my life: so that, with the loathsomeness of the stench, and crying together, I became so sick and low that I was not able to eat, nor had I the least desire to taste anything. I now wished for the last friend, death, to relieve me; but soon, to my grief, two of the white men offered me eatables; and, on my refusing to eat, one of them held me fast by the hands, and laid me across I think the windlass, and tied my feet, while the other flogged me severely. I had never experienced anything of this kind before; and although, not being used to the water, I naturally feared that element the first time I saw it, yet nevertheless, could I have got over the nettings, I would have jumped over the side, but I could not; and, besides, the crew used to watch us very closely who were not chained down to the decks, lest we should leap into the water: and I have seen some of these poor African prisoners most severely cut for attempting to do so, and hourly whipped for not eating. This indeed was often the case with myself. In a little time after, amongst the poor chained men, I found some of my own nation, which in a small degree gave ease to my mind. I inquired of these what was to be done with us; they gave me to understand we were to be carried to these white people's country to work for them. I then was a little revived, and thought, if it were no worse than working, my situation was not so desperate: but still I feared I should be put to death, the white people looked and acted, as I thought, in so savage a manner; for I had never seen among any people such instances of brutal cruellty; and this not only shewn towards us blacks, but also to some of the whites themselves. One white man in particular I saw when we were permitted to be on deck, flogged so unmercifully with a large rope near the foremast, that he died in consequence of it; and they tossed him over the side as they would have done a brute. This made me fear these people the more; and I expected nothing less than to be treated in the same manner. I could not help expressing my fears and apprehensions to some of my countrymen: I asked them if these people had no country, but lived in this hollow place (the ship): they told me they did not, but came from a distant one. "Then," said I, "how comes it in all our country we never heard of them?" They told me because they lived so very far off. I then asked where were their women? had they any like themselves? "and why," said I, "do we not see them?" they answered, because they were left behind. . . .

The stench of the hold while we were on the coast was so intolerably loathsome, that it was dangerous to remain there for any time, and some of us had been permitted to stay on the deck for the fresh air; but now that the whole ship's cargo were confined together, it became absolutely pestilential. The closeness of the place, and the heat of the climate, added to the number in the ship, which was so crowded that each had scarcely room to turn himself, almost suffocated us. This produced copious perspirations, so that the air soon became unfit for respiration, from a variety of loathsome smells, and brought on a sickness among the slaves, of which many died, thus falling victims to the improvident avarice, as I may call it, of their purchasers. This wretched situation was again aggravated by the galling of the chains, now become insupportable; and the filth of the necessary tubs, into which the children often fell, and were almost suffocated. The shrieks of the women, and the groans of the dying, rendered the whole a scene of horror almost inconceivable. Happily perhaps for myself I was soon reduced so low here that it was thought necessary to keep me almost always on deck; and from my extreme youth I was not put in fetters. In this situation I expected every hour to share the fate of my companions, some of whom were almost daily brought upon deck at the point of death, which I began to hope would soon put an end to my miseries. Often did I think many of the inhabitants of the deep much more happy than myself. I envied them the freedom they enjoyed, and as often wished I could change my condition for theirs. Every circumstance I met with served only to render my state more painful, and heighten my apprehensions, and my opinion of the cruelty of the whites. One day they had taken a number of fishes; and when they had killed and satisfied themselves with as many as they thought fit, to our astonishment who were on the deck, rather than give any of them to us to eat as we expected, they tossed the remaining fish into the sea again, although we begged and prayed for some as well as we could, but in vain; and some of my countrymen, being pressed by hunger, took an opportunity, when they thought no one saw them, of trying to get a little privately; but they were discovered, and the attempt procured them some very severe floggings. . . .

. . . I and some few more slaves, that were not saleable amongst the rest, from very much fretting, were shipped off in a sloop for North America. . . . While I was in this plantation [in Virginia] the gentleman, to whom I suppose the estate belonged, being unwell, I was one day sent for to his dwelling house to fan him; when I came into the room where he was I was very much affrighted at some things I saw, and the more so as I had seen a black woman slave as I came through the house, who was cooking the dinner, and the poor creature was cruelly loaded with various kinds of iron machines; she had one particularly on her head, which locked her mouth so fast that she could scarcely speak; and could not eat nor drink. I was much astonished and shocked at this contrivance, which I afterwards learned was called the iron muzzle . . .

Alexander Falconbridge, The African Slave Trade (1788)

An Account of the African Slave Trade on the Coast of Africa by Alexander Falconbridge gives a precise description of the inhumanity of the middle passage to the New World. Falconbridge served as a surgeon on slave ships at the end of the eighteenth century. Note his description of the relationships between the white sailors and African women.[*]

As soon as the wretched Africans, purchased at the fairs, fall into the hands of the black traders, they experience an earnest of those dreadful sufferings which they are doomed in future to undergo. And there is not the least room to doubt, but that even before they can reach the fairs, great numbers perish from cruel usage, want of food, travelling through inhospitable deserts, etc. They are brought from the places where they are purchased to Bonny, etc. in canoes; at the bottom of which they lie, having their hands tied with a kind of willow twigs, and a strict watch is kept over them. Their usage in other respects, during the time of passage, which generally lasts several days, is equally cruel. Their allowance of food is so scanty, that it is barely sufficient to support nature. They are, besides, much exposed to the violent rains which frequently fall here, being covered only with mats that afford but a slight defense; and as there is usually water at the bottom of the canoes, from their leaking, they are scarcely every dry.

Nor do these unhappying beings, after they become the property of the Europeans (from whom as a more civilized people, more humanity might naturally be expected), find their situation in the least amended. Their treatment is no less rigorous. The men Negroes, on being brought aboard the ship, are immediately fastened together, two and two, by handcuffs on their wrists, and irons riveted on their legs. They are then sent down between the decks, and placed in an apartment partitioned off for that purpose. The women likewise are placed in a separate room, on the same deck, but without being ironed. And an adjoining room, on the same deck is besides appointed for the boys. Thus are they placed in different apartments.

[*] From Alexander Falconbridge, An Account of the Slave Trade on the Coast of Africa (London: 1788).

But at the same time, they are frequently stowed so close, as to admit of no other posture than lying on their sides. Neither will the height between decks, unless directly under the grating, permit them the indulgence of an erect posture; especially where there are platforms, which is generally the case. These platforms are a kind of shelf, about eight or nine feet in breadth, extending from the side of the ship towards the centre. They are placed nearly midway between the decks, at the distance of two or three feet from each deck. Upon these the Negroes are stowed in the same manner as they are on the deck underneath.

. . . About eight o'clock in the morning the Negroes are generally brought upon deck. Their irons being examined, a long chain, which is locked to a ring-bolt, fixed in the deck, is run through the rings of the shackles of the men, and then locked to another ring-bolt, fixed also in the deck. By this means fifty or sixty, and sometimes more, are fastened to one chain, in order to prevent them from rising, or endeavoring to escape. If the weather proves favorable, they are permitted to remain in that situation till four or five in the afternoon, when they are disengaged from the chain, and sent down.

. . . Upon the Negroes refusing to take sustenance, I have seen coals of fire, glowing hot, put on a shovel, and placed so near their lips, as to scorch and burn them. And this has been accompanied with threats, of forcing them to swallow the coals, if they any longer persisted in refusing to eat. These means have generally had the desired effect. I have also been credibly informed that a certain captain in the slave trade poured melted lead on such of the Negroes as obstinately refused their food.

Exercise being deemed necessary for the preservation of their health, they are sometimes obligated to dance, when the weather will permit their coming on deck. If they go about it reluctantly, or do not move with agility, they are flogged; a person standing by them all the time with at cat-o'-nine-tails in his hand for that purpose. Their music, upon these occasions, consists of a drum, sometimes with only one head; and when that is worn out, they do not scruple to make use of the bottom of one of the tubs before described. The poor wretches are frequently compelled to sing also; but when they do so, their songs are generally, as may naturally be expected, melancholy lamentations of their exile from their native country.

. . . On board some ships, the common sailors are allowed to have intercourse with such of the black women whose consent they can procure. And some of them have been known to take the inconstancy of their paramours so much to heart, as to leap overboard and drown themselves. The officers are permitted to indulge their passions among them at pleasure, and sometimes are guilty of such brutal excesses as disgrace human nature.

The hardships and inconveniences suffered by the Negroes during the passage are scarcely to be enumerated or conceived. They are far more violently affected by the seasickness than the Europeans. It frequently terminates in death, especially among the women. But the exclusion of the fresh air is among the most intolerable. For the purpose of admitting this needful refreshment, most of the ships in the slave trade are provided, between the decks, with five or six air-ports on each side of the ship, of about six inches in length, and four in breadth; in addition to which, some few ships, but not one in twenty, have what they denominate wind-sails. But whenever the sea is rough and the rain heavy, it becomes necessary to shut these, and every other conveyance by which the air is admitted. The fresh air being thus excluded, the Negroes' rooms very soon grow intolerably hot. The confined air, rendered noxious by the effluvia exhaled from their bodies, and by being repeatedly breathed, soon produces fevers and fluxes, which generally carries off great numbers of them.

. . . One morning, upon examining the place allotted for the sick Negroes, I perceived that one of them, who was so emaciated as scarcely to be able to walk, was missing, and was convinced that he must have gone overboard in the night, probably to put a more expeditious period to his sufferings. And, to conclude on this subject, I could not help being sensibly affected, on a former voyage, at observing with what apparent eagerness a black woman seized some dirt from off an African yam, and put it into her mouth, seeming to rejoice at the opportunity of possessing some of her native earth.

From these instances I think it may have been clearly deduced that the unhappy Africans are not bereft of the finer feelings, but have a strong attachment to their native country, together with a just sense of the value of liberty. And the situation of the miserable beings above described, more forcibly urges the necessity of abolishing a trade which is the source of such evils, than the most eloquent harangue, or persuasive arguments could do.

4

Uniquely American

The interaction of European people and culture with the wilderness of the Americas produced a new culture and a new people, which we identify as American. The transformation was not always easy. In this chapter, William Byrd, a member of the Virginia gentry, reveals his desperate attempt to become an English gentleman in his diary while Michel-Guillaume-Jean de Crèvecoeur, a French immigrant who settled in New York State, embraced his lot as a new "American." Taken together, Byrd and Crèvecoeur illustrate how individuals grappled with leaving their Old World cultures behind and accepting the new cultures and customs of the New World.

The religious revivals of the early eighteenth century also served to shaped American society. The Great Awakening not only rekindled religious enthusiasm in the colonies, it served as a common and unifying experience for Americans. Three documents in this section describe the religious revivalism that swept the East. Benjamin Franklin describes the preaching of the famous English evangelist George Whitefield. American Jonathan Edwards' famous sermon "Sinners in the Hands of an Angry God" is an example of this fantastic jeremiad genre. His "Some Thoughts Concerning the Present Revival of Religion in New England" discusses the special destiny of the New World.

Study Questions

1. Why was it so difficult for Byrd to accept being an American gentleman? Did his embrace of things English make him less "American"?

2. How does Crèvecoeur's description of an American apply to Byrd?

3. In what ways does Franklin's account betray a certain provincialism? What has made him aware of conditions in Georgia? How does he regard the settlers of Georgia?

4. Franklin was impressed with the immediate impact of Whitefield's sermon. Would Edwards's sermon have the same kind of impact? What were the key ingredients Edwards used to sway his audience?

5. What does Edwards's "Some Thoughts Concerning the Present Religious Revival in New England" reveal about a growing sense of a common American identity? Could this piece support the argument that the Great Awakening contained an element of social subversion?

6. Compare Edwards's and Crèvecoeur's descriptions of the new American character.

7. Discuss Edwards's sense of America's special destiny. Compare this with that of John Winthrop.

William Byrd II, Diary (1709)

William Byrd II of Westover, Virginia was a prime example of a "new American." Byrd was a member of the American gentry, but spent his life in a desperate attempt to live up to his own conception of an English gentleman. He compulsively ordered his life in an attempt to reflect the lifestyle of the English gentry he had only read about. For all his efforts, however, Byrd never really lived the life of English gentry. For one thing, his perception of the life of an English gentleman was a bit off the mark—he was self-taught, relying on his reading of instruction manuals. He had to fashion himself a gentleman literally by the book. Naturally, this produced a somewhat skewed image of what it meant to be a British gentleman. Moreover, the realities of life in the colonies were far different from those in England, guaranteeing Byrd's quest to be quixotic at best. In fact, unknown to himself, he represented something entirely new—an American gentleman.*

7. I rose at 5 o'clock and read a chapter in Hebrew and some Greek in Josephus. I said my prayers and ate milk for breakfast. I danced my dance, and settled my accounts. I read some Latin. It was extremely hot. I ate stewed mutton for dinner. In the afternoon it began to rain and blow very violently so that it blew down my fence. It likewise thundered. In all the time I have been in Virginia I never heard it blow harder. I read

---

* From William Byrd, *The Secret Diary of William Byrd of Westover*, 1709–1712, eds. Louis B. Wright and Marion Tinling (Richmond, VA: Dietz Press, 1941).

Latin again and Greek in Homer. In the evening we took a walk in the garden. I said my prayers and had good health, good humor, and good thoughts, thanks be to God Almighty.

8. I rose at 5 o'clock and read a chapter in Hebrew and some Greek in Josephus. I said my prayers and ate milk for breakfast. I danced my dance. I read some Latin. Tom returned from Williamsburg and brought me a letter from Mr. Bland which told me the wine came out very well. I ate nothing but pudding for dinner. In the afternoon I read some more Latin and Greek in Homer. Then I took a walk about the plantation. I said my prayers and had good health, good thoughts, and good humor, thanks be to God Almighty.

9. I rose at 5 o'clock and read two chapters in Hebrew and some Greek in Josephus. I said my prayers and ate milk and apples for breakfast with Captain Wilcox who called here this morning. I danced my dance. I wrote a letter to England and read some Latin. I ate roast chicken for dinner. In the afternoon I saluted my wife and took a nap. I read more Latin and Greek in Homer. Then I took a walk about the plantation. I neglected to say my prayers. I had good health, good thoughts, and good humor, thanks be to God Almighty.

Michel-Guillaume-Jean de Crèvecoeur, from *Letters from an American Farmer* (1782)

Michel-Guillaume-Jean de Crèvecoeur (1735–1813) was born in Caen, Normandy. In 1755, he migrated to French Canada, where he served with the French in the French and Indian War against the British. While serving under Montcalm in the defense of Quebec, Crèvecoeur was wounded and hospitalized. He made his way to New York, where he worked as an Indian trader and surveyor. Eventually, he married and began a new life as a farmer in Orange County, New York, where he lived as "an American farmer" from 1769 to 1780. His American is a mixture of European cultures, changed by contact with the wilderness.*

He [an "enlightened Englishman" on first seeing America] is arrived on a new continent; a modern society offers itself to his contemplation, different from what he had hitherto seen. It is not composed, as in Europe, of great lords who possess every thing, and of a herd of people who have nothing. Here are no aristocratical families, no

---

* From Michel-Guilluame-Jean de Crèvecoeur, *Letters from an American Farmer* (New York, 1782).

courts, no kings, no bishops, no ecclesiastical dominion, no invisible power giving to a few a very visible one; no great manufacturers employing thousands, no great refinements of luxury. The rich and poor are not so far removed from each other as they are in Europe. . . .

The next wish of this traveller will be to know whence came all these people? They are a mixture of English, Scotch, Irish, French, Dutch, Germans, and Swedes. From this promiscuous breed, that race now called Americans have arisen. . . .

What then is the American, this new man? He is either an European, or the descendant of an European, hence that strange mixture of blood, which you will find in no other country. I could point out to you a family whose grandfather was an Englishman, whose wife was Dutch, whose son married a French woman, and whose present four sons have now four wives of different nations. He is an American, who leaving behind him all his ancient prejudices and manners, receives new ones from the new mode of life he has embraced, the new government he obeys, and the new rank he holds. . . . The Americans were once scattered all over Europe; here they are incorporated into one of the finest systems of population which has ever appeared, and which will hereafter become distinct by the power of the different climates they inhabit. . . .

But to return to our back settlers. I must tell you, that there is something in the proximity of the woods, which is very singular. It is with men as it is with the plants and animals that grow and live in the forests; they are entirely different from those that live in the plains. . . . By living in or near the woods, their actions are regulated by the wildness of the neighbourhood. . . .

Benjamin Franklin, from *The Autobiography of Benjamin Franklin* (1771)

Benjamin Franklin wrote and rewrote his autobiography in the years between 1771 and his death in 1790. In it, he recalled the impact of hearing George Whitefield preach in 1739. As Franklin was recalling an incident that took place many years earlier, this excerpt may be colored by the time that passed.*

In 1739 arriv'd among us from England the Rev. Mr. Whitefield, who had made himself remarkable there as an itinerant preacher. . . . The Multitudes of all Sects and Denominations that attended his Sermons were enormous, and it was matter of Speculation to me who was one of the Number, to observe the extraordinary Influence

---

* From Benjamin Franklin., *The Autobiography of Benjamin Franklin* (New York: Penguin, 1986).

of his Oratory on his Hearers, and how much they admir'd & respected him, notwithstanding his common Abuse of them, by assuring them they were naturally half Beasts and half Devils. It was wonderful to see the Change soon made in the Manners of our Inhabitants; from being thoughtless or indifferent about Religion, it seem'd as if all the World were growing Religious; so that one could not walk thro' the Town in an Evening without Hearing Psalms sung in different Families of every Street. . . . Mr. Whitefield, in leaving us, went preaching all the Way thro' the Colonies to Georgia. The Settlement of that Province had lately been begun; but instead of being made with hardy industrious Husbandmen accustomed to Labor, the only People fit for such an Enterprise, it was with Families of broken Shopkeepers and other insolvent Debtors, many of indolent & idle habits, taken out of the Gaols, who being set down in the Woods, unqualified for clearing Land, & unable to endure the Hardships of a new Settlement, perished in Numbers, leaving many helpless Children unprovided for. The Sight of their miserable Situation inspired the benevolent Heart of Mr. Whitefield with the idea of building an Orphan House there. . . . Returning northward he preached up this Charity, & made large Collections; for his Eloquence had a wonderful Power over the Hearts and Purses of his Hearers, of which I myself was an Instance. I did not disapprove of the Design, but as Georgia was then destitute of Materials & Workmen, and it was propos'd to send them from Philadelphia at a great Expense, I thought it would have been better to have built the House here & Brought the Children to it. This I advis'd, but he was resolute in his first Project, and rejected my Counsel, and I thereupon refus'd to contribute. I happened soon after on one of his Sermons, in the Course of which I perceived he intended to finish with a Collection, & I silently resolved he should get nothing from me. I had in my Pocket a Handful of Copper Money, three or four silver Dollars, and five Pistoles in gold. As he proceeded I began to soften, and concluded to give the Coppers. Another Stroke of his Oratory made me asham'd of that, and determin'd me to give the Silver & he finished so admirably, that I empty'd my Pocket wholly into the Collector's Dish, Gold and all. At this Sermon there was also one of our Club, who being of my Sentiments respecting the Building in Georgia, and suspecting a Collection might be intended, had by Precaution emptied his Pockets before he came from home; towards the Conclusion of the Discourse, however, he felt a strong Desire to give, and apply'd to a Neighbor who stood near him to borrow some Money for the Purpose.

Jonathan Edwards, from "Sinners in the Hands of an Angry God" (1741)

Jonathan Edwards was the greatest American-born revivalist preacher. "Sinners in the Hands of an Angry God," delivered first at Northampton, Massachusetts, in 1741, was his most famous sermon. No record was kept of the sermon's impact the first time Edwards delivered it, but Reverend Stephen Williams of Longmeadow noted in his diary that when Edwards preached later in Enfield, Connecticut, "the shrieks and cries were piercing and amazing." The emotionalism of the sermon and its description of the moment of tension as man dangles over the fire produced the sermon's impact. In Edwards's sermon, God finally tires of protecting unworthy man from the flames; revealing its most disturbing part: its message of the insecurity of temporary protection by an all-powerful and infinitely angry God.[*]

. . . This that you have heard is the case of every one of you that are out of Christ. That world of misery, that lake of burning brimstone, is extended abroad under you. There is the dreadful pit of the glowing flames of the wrath of God; there is hell's wide gaping mouth open; and you have nothing to stand upon, nor any thing to take hold of; there is nothing between you and hell but the air; 'tis only the power and mere pleasure of God that holds you up.

You probably are not sensible of this; you find you are kept out of hell, but don't see the hand of God in it, but look at other things, as the good state of your bodily constitution, your care of your own life, and the means you use for your own preservation. But indeed these things are nothing; if God should withdraw his hand, they would avail no more to keep you from falling, than the thin air to hold up a person that is suspended in it.

Your wickedness makes you as it were heavy as lead, and to tend downwards with great weight and pressure towards hell; and, if God should let you go, you would immediately sink, and swiftly descend and plunge into the bottomless gulf; and your healthy constitution, and your own care and prudence, and best contrivance, and all your righteousness, would have no more influence to uphold you and keep you out of hell, than a spider's web would have to stop a falling rock. . . .

The God that holds you over the pit of hell, much as one holds a spider or some loathsome insect over the fire, abhors you, and is dreadfully provoked. His wrath towards you burns like fire; he looks upon you as worthy of nothing else but to be cast into the fire. He is of purer eyes than to bear you in his sight; you are ten thousand

---

[*] From Johnathan Edwards, "Sinners in the Hands of an Angry God (1741)," in *The Great Awakening*, eds. Alan Heimert and Perry Miller (Indianpolis: Bobbs-Merrill, 1969).

times as abominable in his eyes as the most hateful, venomous serpent is in ours. You have offended him infinitely more than ever a stubborn rebel did his prince, and yet 'tis nothing but his hand that holds you from falling into the fire every moment. . . .

O sinner! Consider the fearful danger you are in! 'Tis a great furnace of wrath, a wide and bottomless pit, full of fire and of wrath that you are held over in the hand of that God whose wrath is provoked and incensed as much against you as against many of the damned in hell. You hang by a slender thread, with the flames of Divine wrath flashing about it, and ready every moment to singe it and burn it asunder. . . .

It would be dreadful to suffer this fierceness and wrath of Almighty God one moment; but you must suffer it to all eternity. There will be no end to this exquisite, horrible, misery. . . .

How dreadful is the state of those that are daily and hourly in danger of this great wrath and infinite misery! But this is the dismal case of every soul in this congregation that has not been born again, however moral and strict, sober and religious, they may otherwise be. Oh! that you would consider it, whether you be young or old!

Jonathan Edwards, from "Some Thoughts Concerning the Present Revival of Religion in New England" (1742)

This is one of Jonathan Edwards's written works (in contrast to "Sinners in the Hands of an Angry God," a sermon meant to be delivered orally). Note the ways in which this piece, written in 1742, both reflects a sense of an American identity and acknowledges divisions in American society.*

God has made as it were two worlds here below, the old and the new (according to the names they are now called by), two great habitable continents, far separated one from the other; the latter is but newly discovered, . . . it has been, until of late, wholly the possession of Satan, the church of God having never been in it, as it has been in the other continent, from the beginning of the world. This new world is probably now discovered, that the new and most glorious state of God's church on earth might commence there; that God might in it begin a new world in a spiritual respect, when he creates the new heavens and new earth. . . .

The old continent has been the source and original of mankind, in several respects. The first parents of mankind dwelt there; and there dwelt Noah and his sons; and there the second Adam was born, and was crucified and rose again; and it is probable that, in some measure to balance these things, the most glorious renovation of the world shall

---

* From Johnathan Edwards, "Some Thoughts Concerning the Present Revival of Religion in New England (1742)," in *The Great Awakening*, eds. Alan Heimert and Perry Miller (Indianapolis: Bobbs-Merrill, 1969).

originate from the new continent, and the church of God in that respect be from hence. And so it is probable that that will come to pass in spirituals, that has in temporals, with respect to America; that whereas till of late, the world was supplied with its silver and gold and earthly treasures from the old continent, now it is supplied chiefly from the new, so the course of things in spiritual respects will be in like manner turned.

And it is worthy to be noted that America was discovered about the time of the reformation, or but little before: which reformation was the first thing that God did towards the glorious renovation of the world, after it had sunk into the depths of darkness and ruin, under the great antichristian apostasy. So that as soon as this new world is (as it were) created, and stands forth in view, God presently goes about doing some great thing to make way for the introduction of the church's latter day glory, that is to have its first seat in, and is to take its rise from that new world. . . .

I observed before, that when God is about to do some great work for his church, his manner is to begin at the lower end; so when he is about to renew the whole habitable earth, it is probable that he will begin in this utmost, meanest, youngest and weakest part of it, where the church of God has been planted last of all; and so the first shall be last, and the last first. . . .

5

What Price Freedom?

It is difficult to discern the exact moment in which the path of the American colonies and the British government diverged. Perhaps it was inevitable, given the changes within the colonies as they developed an American identity. Prior to 1756, the British imperial government made a number of attempts to assert greater control over the economic and political arrangements it had with the colonies. However, turmoil within its own political system made it almost difficult to achieve these objectives. It was only after the French and Indian War that a new, coherent imperial policy calling for tighter restrictions over the colonies developed.

Within ten years, differences between England and its colonies blossomed into an ideological and political dispute that drove them apart. This set of documents centers on the major political debates of the period, following the path of the American colonists as they considered independence and what the promise of a new nation held for Americans.

Americans were divided about their relationship with Britain, and some of the most vociferous among them were radicalized by the taxes and duties imposed on the colonies in the 1760s. Benjamin Franklin was a colonial agent in England at the time and his 1766 testimony to Parliament represents the views of many in America who opposed the Stamp Act. John Dickinson, also a Philadelphian, typified many Americans; he was loyal to Great Britain but nonetheless opposed the imposition of taxes on the colonists by Parliament. Some Americans, however, still believed that the British government had the right to tax them, as demonstrated by the 1774 letter from colonial loyalists to North Carolina Governor Josiah Martin. Expressing a contrary sentiment, Patrick Henry's famous speech, "Give Me Liberty or Give Me Death," is from the meeting of the Virginia Convention in 1775. It is probably the best-known statement of the opinion that the colonists had no choice other than to break with Britain.

This chapter ends with documents exposing the limits of revolutionary freedom and liberal promises. Abigail Adams's plea that her husband, John Adams, "Remember the Ladies" went unheard, and Benjamin Banneker's letter to Thomas Jefferson reminds us and the then secretary of state that the Declaration of Independence, promising that "all men are created equal," did not apply to slaves.

Study Questions

1. Compare the similarities and differences in the arguments of Franklin and Dickinson concerning the passage of internal colonial taxes by Parliament.

2. According to Franklin, what actions were the colonists willing to take to show their disapproval of the passage of the Stamp Act?

3. What did Dickinson fear would happen if the Townshend Duties were collected?

4. Compare Patrick Henry and the North Carolina Loyalists on the role of the English government.

5. Why was Patrick Henry's rhetoric so popular?

6. How do Abigail Adams and Benjamin Bannaeker use the rhetoric of the American Revolution to support their claims for equality?

Benjamin Franklin, Testimony Against the Stamp Act (1766)

In 1765 Parliament passed the first internal tax on the colonists, known as the Stamp Act. Benjamin Franklin was a colonial agent in London at the time and, as colonial opposition to the act grew, found himself representing these views to the British government. In his testimony from Parliament he describes the role of taxes in Pennsylvania and the economic relationship between the colonies and the mother country.[*]

Q. What is your name, and place of abode?

A. Franklin, of Philadelphia.

Q. Do the Americans pay any considerable taxes among themselves?

A. Certainly many, and very heavy taxes.

Q. What are the present taxes in Pennsylvania, laid by the laws of the colony?

---

[*] From *The Parliamentary History of England* (London: 1813), XVI, 138–159.

A. There are taxes on all estates, real and personal; a poll tax; a tax on all offices, professions, trades, and businesses, according to their profits; an excise on all wine, rum, and other spirit; and a duty of ten pounds per head on all Negroes imported, with some other duties.

Q. For what purposes are those taxes laid?

A. For the support of the civil and military establishments of the country, and to discharge the heavy debt contracted in the last [Seven Years'] war. . . .

Q. Are not all the people very able to pay those taxes?

A. No. The frontier counties, all along the continent, have been frequently ravaged by the enemy and greatly impoverished, are able to pay very little tax. . . .

Q. Are not the colonies, from their circumstances, very able to pay the stamp duty?

A. In my opinion there is not gold and silver enough in the colonies to pay the stamp duty for one year.

Q. Don't you know that the money arising from the stamps was all to be laid out in America?

A. I know it is appropriated by the act to the American service; but it will be spent in the conquered colonies, where the soldiers are, not in the colonies that pay it. . . .

Q. Do you think it right that America should be protected by this country and pay no part of the expense?

A. That is not the case. The colonies raised, clothed, and paid, during the last war, near 25,000 men, and spent many millions.

Q. Where you not reimbursed by Parliament?

A. We were only reimbursed what, in your opinion, we had advanced beyond our proportion, or beyond what might reasonably be expected from us; and it was a very small part of what we spent. Pennsylvania, in particular, disbursed about 500,000 pounds, and the reimbursements, in the whole, did not exceed 60,000 pounds. . . .

Q. Do you think the people of America would submit to pay the stamp duty, if it was moderated?

A. No, never, unless compelled by force of arms. . . .

Q. What was the temper of America towards Great Britain before the year 1763?

A. The best in the world. They submitted willingly to the government of the Crown, and paid, in all their courts, obedience to acts of Parliament. . . .

Q. What is your opinion of a future tax, imposed on the same principle with that of the Stamp Act? How would the Americans receive it?

A. Just as they do this. They would not pay it.

Q. Have not you heard of the resolutions of this House, and of the House of Lords, asserting the right of Parliament relating to America, including a power to tax the people there?

A. Yes, I have heard of such resolutions.

Q. What will be the opinion of the Americans on those resolutions?

A. They will think them unconstitutional and unjust.

Q. Was it an opinion in America before 1763 that the Parliament had no right to lay taxes and duties there?

A. I never heard any objection to the right of laying duties to regulate commerce; but a right to lay internal taxes was never supposed to be in Parliament, as we are not represented there. . . .

Q. Did the Americans ever dispute the controlling power of Parliament to regulate the commerce?

A. No.

Q. Can anything less than a military force carry the Stamp Act into execution?

A. I do not see how a military force can be applied to that purpose.

Q. Why may it not?

A. Suppose a military force sent into America; they will find nobody in arms; what are they then to do? They cannot force a man to take stamps who chooses to do without them. They will not find a rebellion; they may indeed make one.

Q. If the act is not repealed, what do you think will be the consequences?

A. A total loss of the respect and affection the people of America bear to this country, and of all the commerce that depends on that respect and affection.

Q. How can the commerce be affected?

A. You will find that, if the act is not repealed, they will take very little of your manufactures in a short time.

Q. Is it in their power to do without them?

A. I think they may very well do without them.

Q. Is it their interest not to take them?

A. The goods they take from Britain are either necessaries, mere conveniences, or superfluities. The first, as cloth, etc., with a little industry they can make at home; the second they can do without till they are able to provide them among themselves; and the last, which are mere articles of fashion, purchased and consumed because the fashion in a respected country; but will now be detested and rejected. The people have already struck off, by general agreement, the use of all goods fashionable in mourning. . . .

Q. If the Stamp Act should be repealed, would it induce the assemblies of America to acknowledge the right of Parliament to tax them, and would they erase their resolutions [against the Stamp Act]?

A. No, never.

Q. Is there no means of obliging them to erase those resolutions?

A. None that I know of; they will never do it, unless compelled by force of arms.

Q. Is there a power on earth that can force them to erase them?

A. No power, how great soever, can force men to change their opinions. . . .

Q. What used to be the pride of the Americans?

A. To indulge in the fashions and manufactures of Great Britain.

Q. What is now their pride?

A. To wear their old clothes over again, till they can make new ones.

John Dickinson, from *Letters from a Farmer in Pennsylvania* (1768)

John Dickinson's *Letters from a Pennsylvania Farmer*, were written in protest to the passage of the Townshend Duties in 1767. Dickinson was not really a farmer; he was one of the wealthiest lawyers in Philadelphia and considered himself a loyal subject of the British crown. Nonetheless, he believed that Parliament had no right to tax the colonies. The following is an excerpt from his defense of the legal rights of free-born Englishmen.[*]

There is [a] late act of Parliament, which seems to me to be . . . destructive to the liberty of these colonies, . . . that is the act for granting duties on paper, glass, etc. It appears to me to be unconstitutional.

The Parliament unquestionably possesses a legal authority to regulate the trade of Great Britain and all its colonies. Such an authority is essential to the relation between a mother country and its colonies and necessary for the common good of all. He who

[*] From John Dickinson, *Letters from a Farmer in Pennsylvania to the Inhabitants of the British Colonies* (Boston: John Mein, 1768), 5–35.

considers these provinces as states distinct from the British Empire has very slender notions of justice or of their interests. We are but parts of a whole; and therefore there must exist a power somewhere to preside, and preserve the connection in due order. This power is lodged in the Parliament, and we are as much dependent on Great Britain as a perfectly free people can be on another.

I have looked over every statute relating to these colonies, from their first settlement to this time; and I find every one of them founded on this principle till the Stamp Act administration. All before are calculated to preserve or promote a mutually beneficial intercourse between the several constituent parts of the Empire. And though many of them imposed duties on trade, yet those duties were always imposed with design to restrain the commerce of one part that was injurious to another, and thus to promote the general welfare. . . . Never did the British Parliament, till the period abovementioned, think of imposing duties in American for the purpose of raising a revenue. . . . This I call an innovation, and a most dangerous innovation.

That we may be legally bound to pay any general duties on these commodities, relative to the regulation of trade, is granted. But we being obliged by her laws to take them from Great Britain, any special duties imposed on their exportation to us only, with intention to raise a revenue from us only, are as much taxes upon us as those imposed by the Stamp Act. . . . It is nothing but the edition of a former book with a new title page, . . . and will be attended with the very same consequences to American liberty.

Sorry I am to learn that there are some few persons, [who] shake their heads with solemn motion, and pretend to wonder what can be the meaning of these letters. . . . I will now tell the gentlemen. . . . The meaning of them is to convince the people of these colonies that they are at this moment exposed to the most imminent dangers, and persuade them immediately, vigorously, and unanimously to exert themselves, in the most firm, but most peaceable manner for obtaining relief. The cause of liberty is a cause of too much dignity to be sullied by turbulence and tumult. It ought to be maintained in a manner suitable to her nature. . . . I hope, my dear countrymen, that you will in every colony be upon your guard against those who may at any time endeavour to stir you up, under pretences of patriotism, to any measures disrespectful to our sovereign and our mother country. Hot, rash, disorderly proceedings injure the reputation of a people as to wisdom, valour and virtue, without procuring them the least benefit. . . .

Every government, at some time or other, falls into wrong measures. They may proceed from mistake or passion. But every such measure does not dissolve the obligation between the governors and the governed. The mistake may be corrected, the passion may pass over. It is the duty of the governed to endeavour to rectify the mistake and appease the passion. They have not at first any other right than to represent their grievances and to pray for redress. . . .

Address of the Inhabitants of Anson County to Governor Martin (1774)

Many Americans remained loyal to England before, during, and after the Revolutionary War. Loyalists were particularly strong where British government was stable (like around New York City) and where colonists relied on the British for protection (like on the Carolina frontiers). This is a letter sent by colonial Loyalists from Anson County, North Carolina, to their governor, pledging their loyalty and asking, in part, for protection.*

To His Excellency, Josiah Martin Esquire, Captain General, Governor, &c,

Most Excellent Governor:

Permit us, in behalf of ourselves, and many others of His Majesty's most dutiful and loyal subjects within the County of Anson, to take the earliest opportunity of addressing your Excellency, and expressing our abomination of the many outrageous attempts now forming on this side of the Atlantick, against the peace and tranquillity His Majesty's Dominions in North America, and to witness to your Excellency, by this our Protest, a disapprobation and abhorence of the many lawless combinations and unwarrantable practices actually carrying on by a gross tribe of infatuated anti-Monarchists in the several Colonies in these Dominions; the baneful consequence of whose audacious contrivance can, *in fine*, only tend to extirpate the fundamental principles of all Government, and illegally to shake off their obedience to, and dependence upon, the imperial Crown and Parliament of Great Britain; the infection of whose pernicious example being already extended to this particular County, of which we now bear the fullest testimony.

It is with the deepest concern (though with infinite indignation) that we see in all public places and papers disagreeable votes, speeches and resolutions, said to be entered into by our sister Colonies, in the highest contempt and derogation of the superintending power of the legislative authority of Great Britain. And we further, with sorrow, behold their wanton endeavors to vilify and arraign the honour and integrity of His Majesty's most honourable Ministry and Council, tending to sow the seed of discord and sedition, in open violation of their duty and allegiance. . . .

. . . We are truly invigorated with the warmest zeal and attachment in favour of the British Parliament, Constitution and Laws, which our forefathers gloriously struggled to establish, and which are now become the noblest birthright and inheritance of all Britannia's Sons. . . .

---

* From *The Colonial Records of North Carolina, Volume IX, 1771 to 1775*, ed. William I. Saunders (Raleigh: North Carolina Printers, 1890), 1161-1164.

We are truly sensible that those invaluable blessings which we have hitherto enjoyed under His Majesty's auspicious Government, can only be secured to us by the stability of his Throne, supported and defended by the British Parliament, the only grand bulwark and guardian of our civil and religious liberties.

Duty and affection oblige us further to express our grateful acknowledgements for the inestimate blessings flowing from such a Constitution. And we do assure your Excellency that we are determined, by the assistance of Almighty God, in our respective stations, steadfastly to continue His Majesty's loyal Subjects, and to contribute all in our power for the preservation of the publick peace; so, that, by our unanimous example, we hope to discourage the desperate endeavours of a deluded multitude, and to see a misled people turn again from their atrocious offences to a proper exercise of their obedience and duty.

And we do furthermore assure your Excellency, that we shall endeavor to cultivate such sentiments in all those under our care, and to warm their breasts with a true zeal for His Majesty, and affection for his illustrious family. And may the Almighty God be pleased to direct his Councils, his Parliament, and all those in authority under him, that their endeavors may be for the advancement of piety, and the safety, honour and welfare of our Sovereign and his Kingdoms, that the malice of his enemies may be assuaged, and their evil designs confounded and defeated; so that all the world may be convinced that his sacred person, his Royal family, his Parliament, and our Country, are the special objects of Divine dispensation and Providence.

[Signed by two hundred twenty-seven of the inhabitants of Anson County.]

Patrick Henry, "Give Me Liberty or Give Me Death" (1775)

There are few Americans who are not familiar with Patrick Henry's cry "give me liberty or give me death." This fiery speech is popular not only as a document of the revolutionary struggle but as one of the great speeches of all time. Patrick Henry served in the French and Indian Wars and first attracted attention as the leader of the objections to the Stamp Act in the Virginia House of Burgesses. In this speech, he argues that the colonists have no other choice after exhausting all the avenues for reconciliation with Britain.*

Mr. President:

It is natural to man to indulge in the illusions of hope. We are apt to shut our eyes against a painful truth, and listen to the song of the siren till she transforms us into beasts. Is this the part of wise men, engaged in a great and arduous struggle for liberty?

---

* From Patrick Henry, "Speech in the Virginia Convention, March 23, 1775," In *Library of the World's Best Literature, Ancient and Modern*, vol. XII, ed. Charles D. Warner (New York: R. S. Peale and J. A. Hill, 1897), 7242–7244.

Are we disposed to be of the number of those who having eyes see not, and having ears hear not, the things which so nearly concern their temporal salvation? For my part, whatever anguish of spirit it may cost, I am willing to know the whole truth; to know the worst and to provide for it.

I have but one lamp by which my feet are guided; and that is the lamp of experience. I know of no way of judging of the future but by the past. And judging by the past, I wish to know what there has been in the conduct of the British ministry for the last ten years, to justify those hopes with which gentlemen have been pleased to solace themselves and the house? Is it that insidious smile with which our petition has been lately received? Trust it not, sir: It will prove a snare to your feet. Suffer not yourselves to be betrayed with a kiss. Ask yourselves how this gracious reception of our petition comports with those warlike preparations which cover our waters and darken our land. Are fleets and armies necessary to a work of love and reconciliation? Have we shown ourselves so unwilling to be reconciled that force must be called in to win back our love? Let us not deceive ourselves, sir. These are the implements of war and subjugation—the last arguments to which kings resort. I ask gentlemen, sir, what means this martial array, if its purpose be not to force us to submission? Can gentlemen assign any other possible motive for it? Has Britain any enemy in this quarter of the world, to call for all this accumulation of navies and armies? No, sir, she has none. They are meant for us; they can be meant for no other. They are sent over to bind and rivet upon us those chains which the British ministry have been so long forging. And what have we to oppose them? Shall we try argument? Sir, we have been trying that for the last ten years. Have we anything new to offer upon the subject? Nothing. We have held the subject up in every light of which it is capable; but it has been all in vain. Shall we resort to entreaty and humble supplication? What terms shall we find which have not been already exhausted? Let us not, I beseech you, sir, deceive ourselves longer.

Sir, we have done everything that could be done to avert the storm which is now coming on. We have petitioned, we have remonstrated, we have supplicated, we have prostrated ourselves before the throne, and have implored its interposition to arrest the tyrannical hands of the ministry and Parliament. Our petitions have been slighted; our remonstrances have produced additional violence and insult; our supplications have been disregarded; and we have been spurned with contempt from the foot of the throne. In vain, after these things, may we indulge the fond hope of peace and reconciliation. There is no longer any room for hope. If we wish to be free, if we mean to preserve inviolate those inestimable privileges for which we have been so long contending, if we mean not basely to abandon the noble struggle in which we have been so long engaged, and which we have pledged ourselves never to abandon until the glorious object of our contest shall be obtained—we must fight! I repeat, sir, we must fight! An appeal to arms and to the God of Hosts is all that is left us!

They tell us, sir, that we are weak—unable to cope with so formidable an adversary. But when shall we be stronger? Will it be the next week, or the next year? Will it be when we are totally disarmed, and when a British guard shall be stationed in every house? Shall we gather strength by irresolution and inaction? Shall we acquire the means of effectual resistance by lying supinely on our backs, and hugging the delusive phantom of hope until our enemies shall have bound us hand and foot? Sir, we are not weak, if we make a proper use of those means which the God of nature hath placed in our power. Three millions of people, armed in the holy cause of liberty, and in such a country as that which we possess, are invincible by any force which our enemy can send against us. Besides, sir, we shall not fight our battles alone. There is a just God who presides over the destinies of nations; and who will raise up friends to fight our battles for us. The battle, sir, is not to the strong alone; it is to the vigilant, the active, the brave. Besides, sir, we have no election. If we were base enough to desire it, it is not too late to retire from the contest. There is no retreat but in submission and slavery! Our chains are forged; their clanking may be heard on the plains of Boston! The war is inevitable—and let it come! I repeat it, sir, let it come!

It is in vain, sir, to extenuate the matter. Gentlemen may cry, Peace, peace; but there is no peace. The war is actually begun. The next gale that sweeps from the north will bring to our ears the clash of resounding arms. Our brethren are already in the field. Why stand we here idle? What is it that gentlemen wish? What would they have? If life so dear, or peace sweet, as to be purchased at the price of chains and slavery? Forbid it Almighty God—I know not what course others may take; but as for me, give me liberty or give me death!

Abigail Adams and John Adams Letters; Abigail Adams Letter to Mercy Otis Warren (1776)

These letters are written between Abigail Adams and her husband John, the future president, then a member of the Continental Congress in Pennsylvania. Many women were active in the Revolutionary War—from supporting the war effort by raising money to billeting soldiers—and Abigail Adams's letter is an example of how involvement in the Revolution raised questions about what freedom for all would mean. Abigail Adams's letter to her husband is followed by one to their friend, the historian, poet, and playwright, Mercy Otis Warren.[*]

[Abigail Adams to John Adams, March 31, 1776]

I long to hear that you have declared an independancy [sic]—and by the way in the new Code of Laws which I suppose it will be necessary for you to make I would desire you would Remember the Ladies, and be more generous and favourable to them than

---

[*] From *The Adams Family Correspondence*, eds. L. H. Butterfield et al. (Cambridge: Belknap Press of Harvard University Press, 1963), vol. I, 29–31.

your ancestors. Do not put such unlimited power into the hands of the Husbands. Remember all men would be tyrants if they could. If perticuliar care and attention is not paid to the Ladies we are determined to foment a Rebelion, and will not hold ourselves bound by any Laws in which we have no voice, or Representation.

That your Sex are Naturally Tyrannical is a Truth so thoroughly established as to admit of no dispute, but such of you as wish to be happy willingly give up the harsh title of Master for the more tender and endearing one of Friend. Why then, not put it out of the power of the vicious and the Lawless to use us with cruelty and indignity with impunity. Men of Sense in all Ages abhor those customs which treat us only as the vassals of your Sex. Regard us then as Beings placed by providence under your protection and in immitation of the Supreem Being make use of that power only for our happiness.

[John Adams to Abigail Adams, April 14, 1776]

As to Declarations of Independency, be patient. Read our Privateering Laws, and our Commercial Laws. What signifies a Word.

As to your extraordinary Code of Laws, I cannot but laugh. We have been told that our Struggle has loosened the bands of Government every where. That Children and Apprentices were disobedient—that schools and Colledges were grown turbulent —that Indians slighted their Guardians and Negroes grew insolent to their Masters. But your Letter was the first Intimation that another Tribe more numerous and powerfull than all the rest were grown discontented.—This is rather too coarse a Compliment but you are so saucy, I wont blot it out.

Depend upon it, We know better than to repeal our Masculine systems. Altho they are in full Force, you know they are little more than Theory. We dare not exert our Power in its full Latitude. We are obliged to go fair, and softly, and in Practice you know We are the subjects. We have only the Name of Masters, and rather than give up this, which would compleatly subject Us to the Despotism of the Peticoat, I hope General Washington, and all our brave Heroes would fight. . . .

[Abigail Adams to Mercy Otis Warren]

Braintree April 27 1776

He is very saucy to me in return for a List of Female Grievances which I transmitted to him. I think I will get you to join me in a petition to Congress. I thought it was very probable our wise Statesmen would erect a New Government and form a new code of Laws. I ventured to speak a word on behalf of our Sex, who are rather hardly dealte with by the Laws of England which gives such unlimited power to the Husband to use his wife Ill.

I requested that our Legislators would consider our case and as all Men of Delicacy and Sentiment are adverse to Exercising the power they possess, yet as there is a natural propensity in Human Nature to domination, I thought the most generous plan was to put it out of the power of the Arbitrary and tyranick to injure us with impunity by Establishing some Laws in favour upon just and Liberal principals.

I believe I even threatened fomenting a Rebellion in case we were not considered and assured him we would not hold ourselves bound by any Laws in which we had neither a voice nor representation.

In return he tells me he cannot but Laugh at my extraordinary Code of Laws. That he had heard their Struggle had loosened the bands of Government, that children and apprentices were disobedient, that Schools and Colleges had grown turbulent, that Indians slighted their Guardians, and Negroes grew insolent to their Masters. But my Letter was the first intimation that another Tribe more numerous and powerful than all the rest were grown discontented. This is rather too coarse a complement, he adds, but that I am so saucy he wont blot it out.

So I have helped the Sex abundantly, but I will tell him I have only been making trial of the Disinterestedness of his Virtue, and when weigh'd in the balance have found it wanting.

It would be bad policy to grant us greater power say they since under all the disadvantages we Labour we have the ascendency over their Hearts.

And charm by accepting, by submitting sway.

[Abigail Adams to John Adams, May 7, 1776]

I can not say that I think you very generous to the Ladies, for whilst you are proclaiming peace and good will to men, Emancipating all Nations, you insist upon retaining an absolute power over Wives. But you must remember that Arbitrary power is like most other things which are very hard, very liable to be broken—and notwithstanding all your wise Laws and Maxims we have it in our power not only to free our selves but to subdue our Masters, and without violence throw both your natural and legal authority at our feet—

> "Charm by accepting, by submitting sway
> Yet have our Humour most when we obey."

Benjamin Banneker, Letter to Thomas Jefferson (1791)

Benjamin Banneker was a free black mathematician and surveyor living in Maryland who helped lay out Washington, D.C. He also published an astronomical almanac which was sold throughout the Middle Atlantic states. This is an excerpt from his letter to the then secretary of state Thomas Jefferson, inspired by Banneker's reading of Jefferson's *Notes on the State of Virginia.* [*]

Sir, I am fully sensible of the greatness of that freedom which I take with you on the present occasion; a liberty which Seemed to me Scarcely allowable, when I reflected on that distibguished, and dignifying station in which you Stand; and the almost general prejudice and prepossession which is so previlent in the world against those of my complexion. . . .

Sir I freely and Chearfully acknoweldge, that I am of the African race, and, in that colour which is natural to them of the deepest dye:[†] and it is under a Sense of the most profound gratitude to the Supreme Ruler of the universe, that I do now confess to you, that I am not under that State of tyrannical thralldom, and inhuman capivity, to which too many of my bretheren are doomed; but that I have abundantly tasted of the fruition of those bessings which proceed from that free and unequalled liberty with which you are favoured and which I hope you will willingly allow you have received from the immediate Hand of that Being from whom proceedeth every good and perfect gift.

Sir, Suffer me to recall to your mind that time in which the Arms and tyranny of the British Crown were exerted with powerful effort, in order to reduce you to a State of Servitude; look back I entreat you on the variety of dangers to which you were exposed, reflect on that time in which every human aid appeared unavailable, and in which even hope and fortitude wore the greatful Sense of your miraculous and providential preservation; You cannot but acknowledge, that the present freedom and tranquility which you enjoy you have mercifully received, and that it is the peculiar blessing of Heaven.

This, Sir, was a time in whch you clearly saw into the injustice of a State of Slavery, and in which you have Just apprehension of the horrors of its condition, it was now Sir, that you abhorrence thereof was so excited, that you publickly held forth this true and invaluable doctrine, which is worthy to be recorded and remembered in all Succeeding ages. "We hold these truths to be Self evident, that all men are created equal, and that they are endowed by their creator with certain inalienable rights, that amongst them are life, liberty, and the persuit of happiness." . . .

Sir, I suppose that your knowledge of the situation of my brethern is too extensive to need a recital here; neither shall I presume to prescribe methods by which they may be relieved, otherwise than by recommending to you, and all others, to wean yourselves from those narrow prejudices which you have imbibed with respect to them, and as Job proposed to his friends, "Put your Souls in their Souls' stead," thus shall your hearts be enlarged with kindness and benevolence towards them, and thus shall you need neither the direction of myself or others in what manner to proceed herein.

---

[*] From Silvio A. Bedini, *The Life of Benjamin Banneker* (New York: Landmark Enterprises, 1984), 152–159.
[†] My Father was Brought here a Slave from Africa.

And now, Sir, altho my Sympathy and affection for my brethern hath caused my enlargement thus far, I ardently hope that your candour and generosity will plead with you in my behalf, when I make known to you, that it was not originally my design; but that having taken up my pen in order to direct to you as a present, a copy of an Almanack which I have calculated for the Succeeding year, I was unexpectedly and unavoidably led thereto. . . .

6

Forming the Young Republic

As the American Revolution drew to a close, the new nation took its first shaky steps toward unity. Many Americans hoped that the sacrifices of war meant a better future for them and the nation. Unfortunately, many met frustration and disappointment as the country learned the difficulties of self-government. They would spend the decade searching to create national and local governments that could provide stability and unity and protect their liberties. Many Americans, particularly women and most especially African Americans, found less liberty after the Revolution than they anticipated.

It became evident during the American Revolution that the central government was in a financial dilemma. Determined to maintain a level of solvency, it had withheld the pay of the soldiers and officers in the early 1780s. In 1783, future president George Washington, appealed to the army for their loyalty—revealing how precarious the unity and existence of the new nation was.

The first national government, under the Articles of Confederation, was unable to deal with the economic problems of the postwar period. A lack of a national currency, runaway inflation, interstate tariffs, and little foreign trade combined to drive the nation into a depression by the mid-1780s. With a restricted marketplace and mounting debts, many American farmers were driven to economic ruin. In western Massachusetts, believing they had no other recourse, a group of farmers led by Daniel Shays marched on the state government offices in Worcester and Springfield to force it to address their problems. Two letters, written by two state militia generals, reveal why generals sent by the state government in Boston took action against the farmers and why they felt they had no alternative.

In 1787 there was little doubt that the national government was no longer able to govern as it was then configured. Delegates from 12 states met in Philadelphia in May to revise the Articles of Confederation. The Virginia, or Randolph, Plan, written by James Madison and excerpted here, laid the basis for the new national government formulated by the Constitution.

The newly written Constitution made a powerful argument for a republican government rooted in a strong central government. Ratification was not easy, given the vivid memories of life under the rule of the British government. What have become known as the Federalist papers sought to win Americans over. In 85 pamphlets and newspaper articles, "Publius" (Alexander Hamilton, John Jay, and James Madison) argued the strengths of this new government. James Madison's Federalist Paper #10 is one of the most well-known of these documents and provides one of the clearest analyses of American federalism.

The Revolution set in motion changes unanticipated by its architects. Its rhetoric inspired women and free blacks to aspire to equal treatment and education. The years after the Revolution witnessed a great expansion of educational opportunity, based on the belief that a republic required a well-educated citizenry to function properly. Women's education received a boost from this idea. The ideal republican woman was a patriot, a virtuous wife, and the mother and teacher of good citizens of the republic. Nevertheless, women's education lagged far behind that of men. Blacks enjoyed even less opportunity. Molly Wallace's valedictory oration from the Young Ladies Academy in Philadelphia and the petition of Massachusetts blacks for inclusion in the state's system of public education are examples of how eager diverse Americans were to be well-educated members of the republic.

Study Questions

1. What did Washington mean when he told the officers, "give the world another subject of wonder . . . an army victorious over its enemies—victorious over itself."

2. What fears did Washington express regarding the threatened actions of the army?

3. Can a comparison be made between the actions of the officers at Newburgh and the group led by Daniel Shays?

4. Given the tone of the letters by Shepherd and Lincoln, what were their feelings concerning the rebellion?

5. What are the similarities and differences between the Virginia Plan of government and the present federal government? Why would Virginia have taken the leadership in presenting a new structure of government?

6. According to James Madison, how would the new constitution balance the "cabals of a few" with the "confusion of the multitude"?

7. What connections can be drawn between the ideology of the Revolution, the arguments for women's education and the African-American petition for access to public schools?

George Washington, The Newburgh Address (1783)

A number of officers met in Newburgh, New York, in 1783 to discuss ways to address their grievances after the central government had withheld their pay for many months. As they debated a course of action, Washington appeared and spoke to them. In his address, he acknowledges the hardships under which they won the war and appeals to them to find "greater strength not to succumb" to their anger. This speech forestalled further actions by the officers.[*]

To the Officers of the Army

Gentlemen—A fellow soldier, whose interest and affections bind him strongly to you, whose past sufferings have been as great, and whose future fortune may be as desperate as yours—would beg leave to address you.

Age has its claims, and rank is not without its pretensions to advise: but, though unsupported by both, he flatters himself, that the plain language of sincerity and experience will neither be unheard nor unregarded.

Like many of you, he loved private life, and left it with regret. He left it, determined to retire from the field, with the necessity that called him to it, and not till then—not till the enemies of his country, the slaves of power, and the hirelings of injustice, were compelled to abandon their schemes, and acknowledge America as terrible in arms as she had been humble in remonstrance. With this object in view, he has long shared in your toils and mingled in your dangers. He has felt the cold hand of poverty without a murmur, and has seen the insolence of wealth without a sigh. But, too much under the direction of his wishes, and sometimes weak enough to mistake desire for opinion, he has till lately—very lately—believed in the justice of his country. He hoped that, as the clouds of adversity scattered, and as the sunshine of peace and better fortune broke in upon us, the coldness and severity of government would relax, and that, more than justice, that gratitude would blaze forth upon those hands, which had upheld her, in the darkest stages of her passage, from impending servitude to acknowledged independence. But faith has its limits as well as temper, and there are points beyond which neither can be stretched, without sinking into cowardice or plunging into credulity.—This, my friends, I conceive to be your situation.—Hurried to the very verge of both, another step would ruin you forever.—To be tame and unprovoked when injuries press hard upon you, is more than weakness; but to look up for kinder usage, without one manly effort of your own, would fix your character, and shew the world how richly you deserve those chains you broke. To guard against

[*] From *Journals of the Continental Congress*, 34 vols., eds. W. C. Ford, et al., (Washington D.C., 1904–1937), XXIV, 295–297.

this evil, let us take a review of the ground upon which we now stand, and from thence carry our thoughts forward for a moment, into the unexplored field of expedient.

After a pursuit of seven long years, the object for which we set out is at length brought within our reach. Yes, my friends, that suffering courage of yours was active once—it has conducted the United States of America through a doubtful and a bloody war. It has placed her in the chair of independency, and peace returns again to bless— whom? A country willing to redress your wrongs, cherish your worth and reward your services, a country courting your return to private life, with tears of gratitude and smiles of admiration, longing to divide with you that independency which your gallantry has given, and those riches which your wounds have preserved? Is this the case? Or is it rather a country that tramples upon your rights, disdains your cries and insults your distresses? Have you not, more than once, suggested your wishes, and made known your wants to Congress? Wants and wishes which gratitude and policy should have anticipated, rather than evaded. And have you not lately, in the meek language of entreating memorials, begged from their justice, what you would no longer expect from their favour? How have you been answered? Let the letter which you are called to consider to-morrow make reply.

If this, then, be your treatment, while the swords you wear are necessary for the defence of America, what have you to expect from peace, when your voice shall sink, and your strength dissipate by division? When those very swords, the instruments and companions of your glory, shall be taken from your sides, and no remaining mark of military distinction left but your wants, infirmities and scars? Can you then consent to be the only sufferers by this revolution, and retiring from he field, grow old in poverty, wretchedness and contempt? Can you consent to wade through the vile mire of dependency, and owe the miserable remnant of that life to charity, which has hitherto been spent in honor? If you can—GO—and carry with you the jest of tories and scorn of whigs—the ridicule, and what is worse, the pity of the world. Go, starve, and be forgotten! But, if your spirit should revolt at this; if you have sense enough to discover, and spirit enough to oppose tyranny under whatever garb it may assume; whether it be the plain coat of republicanism, or the splendid robe of royalty; if you have yet learned to discriminate between a people and a cause, between men and principles—awake; attend to your situation and redress yourselves. If the present moment be lost, every future effort is in vain; and your threats then, will be as empty as your entreaties now.

I would advise you, therefore, to come to some final opinion upon what you can bear, and what you will suffer. If your determination be in any proportion to your wrongs, carry your appeal from the justice to the fears of government. Change the milk-and-water style of your last memorial; assume a bolder tone—decent, but lively, spirited and determined, and suspect the man who would advise to more moderation and longer forbearance. Let two or three men, who can feel as well as write, be appointed to draw up your last remonstrance; for, I would no longer give it the sueing, soft, unsuccessful epithet of memorial. Let it be represented in language that will neither dishonor you by its rudeness, nor betray you by its fears, what has been promised by Congress, and what has been performed, how long and how patiently you have suffered, how little you have asked, and how much of that little has been denied. Tell them that, though you were the first, and would wish to be the last to encounter danger: though despair itself can never drive you into dishonor, it may drive you from the field: that the wound often irritated, and never healed, may at length become incurable; and that the slightest mark of indignity from Congress now, must operate like the grave, and part you forever: that in any political event, the army has its alternative. If peace, that nothing shall separate them from your arms but death: if war, that courting the auspices, and inviting the direction of your illustrious leader, you will retire to some unsettled country, smile in your turn, and "mock when their fear cometh on." But let it represent also, that should they comply with the request of your late memorial, it would make you more happy and them more respectable. That while war should continue, you would follow their standard into the field, and when it came to an end, you would withdraw into the shade of private life, and give the world another subject of wonder and applause; an army victorious over its enemies—victorious over itself.

Shays's Rebellion: Letters of Generals William Shepard and Benjamin Lincoln to Governor James Bowdoin of Massachusetts (1787)

In the summer of 1786, Massachusetts farmers began to stop foreclosures by breaking up court sessions. The Massachusetts Assembly had denied their petition for tax relief, and, under the leadership of (unpaid) war veteran Daniel Shays, the farmers took the law into their own hands. After Shays and his armed supporters marched on Worcester and threatened to shut down the Supreme Court at Springfield, Governor James Bowdoin sent out 4,400 soldiers to stop Shays and his 1,200 men. The rebellious farmers were driven back and Shays later escaped into Vermont. The following are letters from Governor Bowdoin's militia generals, reporting on the scene as they prepared to fight the insurrection.[*]

[General Shepard to Governor Bowdoin]
Springfield
January 26, 1787

The unhappy time is come in which we have been obliged to shed blood. Shays, who was at the head of about twelve hundred men, marched yesterday afternoon about four o'clock, towards the public buildings in battle array. He marched his men in an open

---

[*] Reprinted from The Massachusetts Archives, 190, 317–320.

column by platoons. I sent several times by one of my aides, and two other gentlemen, Captains Buffington and Woodbridge, to him to know what he was after, or what he wanted. His reply was, he wanted barracks, and barracks he would have and stores. The answer returned was he must purchase them dear, if he had them.

He still proceeded on his march until he approached within two hundred and fifty yards of the arsenal. He then made a halt. I immediately sent Major Lyman, one of my aides, and Capt. Buffington to inform him not to march his troops any nearer the arsenal on his peril, as I was stationed here by order of your Excellency and the Secretary at War, for the defence of the public property; in case he did I should surely fire on him and his men. A Mr. Wheeler, who appeared to be one of Shays' aides, met Mr. Lyman, after he had delivered my orders in the most peremptory manner, and made answer, that was all he wanted. Mr. Lyman returned with his answer.

Shays immediately put his troops in motion, and marched on rapidly near one hundred yards. I then ordered Major Stephens, who commanded the artillery, to fire upon them. He accordingly did. The two first shots he endeavored to overshoot them, in hopes they would have taken warning without firing among them, but it had no effect on them. Major Stephens then directed his shot through the center of his column. The fourth or fifth shot put their whole column into the utmost confusion. Shays made an attempt to display the column, but in vain. We had one howitz which was loaded with grapeshot, which when fired, gave them great uneasiness.

Had I been disposed to destroy them, I might have charged upon their rear and flanks with my infantry and the two field pieces, and could have killed the greater part of his whole army within twenty-five minutes. There was not a single musket fired on either side. I found three men dead on the spot, and one wounded, who is since dead. One of our artillery men by inattention was badly wounded. Three muskets were taken up with the dead, which were all deeply loaded.

I have received no reinforcement yet, and expect to be attacked this day by their whole force combined.

[General Lincoln to Governor Bowdoin]
Head Quarters, Springfield
January 28th, 1787

We arrived here yesterday about noon with one regiment from Suffolk, one from Essex, one from Middlesex, and one from Worcester, with three companies of artillery, a corps of horse, and a volunteer corps under the command of Colonel Baldwin; the other company of artillery with the other regiment from Middlesex and another from Worcester which were as a cover to our stores arrived about eight o'clock in the evening. On my arrival, I found that Shays had taken a post at a little village six miles north of this, with the whole force under his immediate command, and that Day had taken post in West Springfield, and that he had fixed a guard at the ferry house on the west side of the river, and that he had a guard at the bridge over Agawam river. By this disposition all communication from the north and west in the usual paths was cut off.

From a consideration of this insult on Government, that by an early move we should instantly convince the insurgents of its ability and determination speedily to disperse them; that we wanted the houses occupied by these men to cover our own troops; that General Patterson was on his march to join us, which to obstruct was an object with them; that a successful movement would give spirits to the troops; that it would be so was reduced to as great a certainty, as can be had in operations of this kind; from these considerations, Sir, with many others, I was induced to order the troops under arms at three o'clock in the afternoon, although the most of them had been so from one in the morning.

We moved about half after three, and crossed the river upon the ice, with the four regiments; four pieces of artillery; the light horse, and the troops of this division, under General Shepard moved up the river on the ice, with an intention to fall in between Shays who was on the east side of the river, and Day on the west, and to prevent a junction as well as to cut off Day's retreat. We supposed that we should hereby encircle him with a force so superior that he would not dare to fire upon us which would effectually prevent bloodshed, as our troops were enjoined in the most positive manner not to fire without orders. The moment we showed ourselves upon the river the guard at the ferry house turned out and left the pass open to us. They made a little show of force for a minute or two near the meeting house, and then retired in the utmost confusion and disorder. Our horse met them at the west end of the village, but the insurgents found means by crossing the fields and taking to the woods to escape them; some were taken who are aggravatedly guilty, but not the most so.

The next news we had of them, was by an express from Northampton, that part of them arrived in the south end of their town about eleven o'clock. Shays also in a very precipitate manner left his post a[t] Chickabee, and some time in the night passed through South Hadley, on his way to Amherst.

As soon as our men are refreshed this morning, we shall move northward, leaving General Shepard here as a cover to the magazines; perhaps we may overtake Shays and his party, we shall do it, unless they disperse. If they disperse, I shall cover the troops in some convenient place, and carry on our operations in a very different way.

The Virginia, or Randolph, Plan (1787)

The Virginia Plan, written by James Madison, was inspired by Madison's readings of European writers on natural law and republican government. Presented by the Virginia Governor Edmund Randolph, it provided the basis for the new constitution. It was supported by many large states and provided for a stronger national government than that established under the Articles of Confederation.*

1. Resolved that the Articles of Confederation ought to be so corrected and enlarged as to accomplish the objects proposed by their institution; namely "common defence, security of liberty and general welfare."

2. Resolved therefore that the rights of suffrage in the National Legislature ought to be proportioned to the Quotas of contribution, or to the number of free inhabitants, as the one or the other rule may seem best in different cases.

3. Resolved that the National Legislature ought to consist of two branches.

4. Resolved that the members of the first branch of the National Legislature ought to be elected by the people of the several States. . . . to receive liberal stipends by which they may be compensated for the devotion of their time to public service, to be ineligible to any office established by a particular State, or under the authority of the United States, except those peculiarly belonging to the functions of the first branch, during the term of service, and for the space of after its expiration; to be incapable of reelection for the space of after the expiration of their term of service, and to be subject to recall.

5. Resolved that the members of the second branch of the National Legislature ought to be elected by those of the first, out of a proper number of persons nominated by the individual Legislatures, to be of the age of years at least; to hold their offices for a term sufficient to ensure their independency; to receive liberal stipends, by which they may be compensated for the devotion of their time to public service; and to be ineligible to any office established by a particular State, or under the authority of the United States, except those peculiarly belonging to the functions of the second branch, during the term of service, and for the space of after the expiration thereof.

6. Resolved that each branch ought to possess the right of originating Acts; that the National Legislature ought to be impowered to enjoy the Legislative Rights vested in Congress by the Confederation and moreover to legislate in all cases to which the separate States are incompetent, or in which the harmony of the United States may be interrupted by the exercise of individual Legislation; to negative all laws passed by the several States, contravening in the opinion of the national Legislature the articles of Union; and to call forth the force of the Union against any member of the Union failing in its duty under the articles thereof.

7. Resolved that a National Executive be instituted; [to be chosen by the National Legislature for the terms of years; to be chosen by the National Legislature for the

---

* Reprinted from Richard B. Morris, *Basic Documents on the Confederation and Constitution–Anvil Series* (Malabar, FL: Krieger Publishing Co., 1985).

terms of years;] to receive punctually, at stated times, a fixed compensation for the services rendered, in which no increase or diminution shall be made so as to affect the Magistracy, existing at the time of the increase of diminution, and to be ineligible a second time; and that besides a general authority to execute the National laws, it ought to enjoy the Executive rights vested in Congress by the Confederation.

8.   Resolved that the Executive and a convenient number of the national Judiciary, ought to compose a Council of revision with authority to examine every act of the National Legislature before it shall operate, and every act of a particular Legislature before a Negative thereon shall be final; and that the dissent of the said Council shall amount to a rejection, unless the Act of the National Legislature be passed again, or what of a particular Legislature be again negatived by the members of each branch.

9.   Resolved that National Judiciary be established to consist of one or more supreme tribunals, and of inferior tribunals to be chosen by the National Legislature, to hold their offices during good behaviour; and to receive punctually at stated times fixed compensation for their services, in which no increase or diminution shall be made so as to affect the persons actually in office at the time of such increase or diminution. That the jurisdiction of the inferior tribunals shall be to hear and determine in the dernier resort, all piracies and felonies on the high seas, captures from an enemy; cases in which foreigners or citizens of other States applying to such jurisdictions may be interested, or which respect the collection of the National revenue; impeachments of any National officers, and questions which may involve the national peace and harmony.

10.   Resolved that provision ought to be made for the admission of States Lawfully arising within the limits of the United States, whether from a voluntary junction of Government and Territory or otherwise, with the consent of a number of voices in the National legislature less than the whole.

11.   Resolved that a Republican Government and the territory of each State, except in the instance of a voluntary junction of Government and territory, ought to be guaranteed by the United States to each State.

12.   Resolved that provision ought to be made for the continuance of Congress and their authorities and privileges, until a given day after the reform of the articles of Union shall be adopted, and for the completion of all their engagements.

13.   Resolved that provision ought to be made for the amendment of the Articles of Union whensoever it shall seem necessary, and that the assent of the National Legislature ought not to be required thereto.

14.   Resolved that the Legislative Executive and Judiciary powers within the several States ought to be bound by oath to support the articles of Union.

15. Resolved that the amendments which shall be offered to the Confederation, by the Convention ought at a proper time, or times, after the approbation of Congress to be submitted to an assembly or assemblies of Representatives, recommended by the several Legislatures to be expressly chosen by the people, to consider and decide thereon.

Publius (James Madison), Federalist Paper #10 (1788)

The Federalist Papers, of which this is one of the best known, were published in support of ratification of the Constitution by James Madison, Alexander Hamilton, and John Jay under the pseudonym Publius. This document rebuts the anti-federalists' argument that a republic would soon crumble under the pressure of factional divisions. Madison outlined how a republican government could balance the needs of the minority and majority while preserving liberty and diversity.*

. . . [I]t may be concluded that a pure democracy, by which I mean a society, consisting of a small number of citizens, who assemble and administer the government in person, can admit of no cure for the mischiefs of faction. A common passion or interest will, in almost every case, be felt by a majority of the whole; a communication and concert results from the form of government itself; and there is nothing to check the inducements to sacrifice the weaker party, or an obnoxious individual. Hence it is, that such democracies have ever been spectacles of turbulence and contention; have ever been found incompatible with personal security, or the rights of property; and have in general been short in their lives, as they have been violent in their deaths. Theoretic politicians, who have patronized this species of government, have erroneously supposed, that by reducing mankind to a perfect equality in their political rights, they would, at the same time, be perfectly equalized, and assimilated in their possessions, their opinions, and their passions.

A republic, by which I mean a government in which the scheme of representation takes place, opens a different prospect, and promises the cure for which we are seeking. Let us examine the points in which it varies from pure democracy, and we shall comprehend both the nature of the cure, and the efficacy which it must derive from the union.

---

* From James Madison, The Federalist, Number 10, November 22, 1787, in *The Papers of James Madison, Volume 10*, May 27, 1783–March 3, 1788, eds. et al., Robert Rutland (Chicago: University of Chicago Press, 1977), 267–270.

The two great points of difference between a democracy and a republic, are first, the delegation of the government, in the latter, to a small number of citizens elected by the rest; secondly, the greater number of citizens, and greater sphere of country, over which the latter may be extended.

The effect of the first difference is, on the one hand, to refine and enlarge the public views, by passing them through the medium of a chosen body of citizens, whose wisdom may best discern the true interest of their country, and whose patriotism and love of justice, will be least likely to sacrifice it to temporary or partial considerations. Under such a regulation, it may well happen that the public voice pronounced by the representatives of the people, will be more consonant to the public good, than if pronounced by the people themselves convened for the purpose. On the other hand, the effect may be inverted. Men of factious tempers, of local prejudices, or of sinister designs, may by intrigue, by corruption, or by other means, first obtain the suffrages, and then betray the interests of the people. The question resulting is, whether small or extensive republics are most favourable to the election of proper guardians of the public wealth; and it is clearly decided in favour of the latter by two obvious considerations.

In the first place it is to be remarked, that however small the republic may be, the representatives must be raised to a certain number, in order to guard against the cabals of a few; and that however large it may be, they must be limited to a certain number, in order to guard against the confusion of a multitude. Hence the number of representatives in the two cases not being in proportion to that of the constituents, and being proportionally greatest in the small republic, it follows, that if the proportion of fit characters be not less in the large than in the small republic, the former will present a greater opinion, and consequently a greater probability of a fit choice.

In the next place, as each representative will be chosen by a greater number of citizens in the large than in the small republic, it will be more difficult for unworthy candidates to practise with success the vicious arts, by which elections are too often carried; and the suffrages of the people being more free, will be more likely to centre on men who possess the most attractive merit, and the most diffusive and established characters.

It must be confessed, that in this, as in most other cases, there is a mean, on both sides of which inconveniences will be found to lie. By enlarging too much the number of electors, you render the representative too little acquainted with all their local circumstances and lesser interests; as by reducing it too much, you render him unduly attached to these, and too little fit to comprehend and pursue great and national objects. The federal constitution forms a happy combination in this respect; the great and aggregate interests being referred to the national, the local and particular to the state legislatures.

The other point of difference is, the greater number of citizens and extent of territory which may be brought within the compass of republican, than of democratic government; and it is this circumstance principally which renders factious combinations less to be dreaded in the former, than in the latter. The smaller the society the fewer probably will be the distinct parties and interests composing it; the fewer the distinct parties and interests, the more frequently will a majority be found of the same party; and the smaller the number of individuals composing a majority, and the smaller the compass within which they are placed, the more easily will they concert and execute their plans of oppression. Extend the sphere, and you take in a greater variety of parties and interests; you make it less probable that a majority of the whole will have a common motive to invade the rights of other citizens; or if such a common motive exists, it will be more difficult for all who feel it to discover their own strength, and to act in unison with each other. Besides other impediments, it may be remarked, that where there is a consciousness of unjust dishonourable purposes, communication is always checked by distrust, in proportion to the number whose concurrence is necessary.

Hence it clearly appears, that the same advantage, which a republic has over a democracy, in controlling the effects of faction, is enjoyed by a large over a small republic—is enjoyed by the union over the states composing it. Does this advantage consist in the substitution of representatives, whose enlightened views and virtuous sentiments render them superior to local prejudices and to schemes of injustice? It will not be denied, that the representation of the union will be most likely to possess these requisite endowments. Does it consist in the greater security afforded by a greater variety of parties, against the event of any one party being able to outnumber or oppress the rest? In an equal degree does the encreased variety of parties, comprised within the union, encrease this security. Does it, *in fine*, consist in the greater obstacles opposed to the concert and accomplishment of the secret wishes of an unjust and interested majority? Here, again, the extent of the union gives it the most palpable advantage.

The influence of factious leaders may kindle a flame within their particular states, but will be unable to spread a general conflagration through the other states: A religious sect, may degenerate into a political faction in a part of the confederacy; but the variety of sects dispersed over the entire face of it, must secure the national councils against any danger from that source: A range of paper money, for an abolition of debts, for an equal division of property, or for any other improper or wicked project, will be less apt to pervade the whole body of the union, than a particular member of it; in the sample proportion as such a malady is more likely to taint a particular county or district, than an entire sate.

In the extent an proper structure of the union, therefore, we behold a republican remedy for the diseases most incident to republican government. And according to the degree of pleasure and pride, we feel in being republicans, ought to be our zeal in cherishing the spirit, and supporting the character of federalists.

Publius.

Molly Wallace, Valedictory Oration (1792)

Molly Wallace delivered this valedictory oration to the Young Ladies' Academy in Philadelphia, which offered girls a curriculum similar to that offered in schools for boys. Men founded and taught in the school and, although the education was similar to that available to boys, the young ladies were expected to apply their education within the home.*

The silent and solemn attention of a respectable audience, has often, at the beginning of discourses intimidated, even veterans, in the art of public elocution. What then must my situation be, when my sex, my youth and inexperience all conspire to make me tremble at the talk which I have undertaken? . . . With some, however, it has been made a question, whether we ought ever to appear in so public a manner. Our natural timidity, the domestic situation to which by nature and custom we seem destined, are, urged as arguments against what I have now undertaken:—Many sarcastical observations have been handed out against female oratory: But to what do they amount? Do they not plainly inform us, that, because we are females, we ought therefore to be deprived of what is perhaps the most effectual means of acquiring a just, natural and graceful delivery? No one will pretend to deny, that we should be taught to read in the best manner. And if to read, why not to speak? . . . But yet it might be asked, what, has a female character to do with declamation? That she should harangue at the head of an Army, in the Senate, or before a popular Assembly, is not pretended, neither is it requested that she ought to be an adept in the stormy and contentious eloquence of the bar, or in the abstract and subtle reasoning of the Senate; —we look not for a female Pitt, Cicero, or Demosthenes.

There are more humble and milder scenes than those which I have mentioned, in which a woman may display her elocution. There are numerous topics, on which she may discourse without impropriety, in the discussion of which, she may instruct and please others, and in which she may exercise and improve her own understanding. After all, we do not expect women should become perfect orators. Why then should they be taught to speak in public? This question may possibly be answered by asking several others.

Why is a boy diligently and carefully taught the Latin, the Greek, or the Hebrew language, in which he will seldom have occasion, either to write or to converse? Why is he taught to demonstrate the propositions of Euclid, when during his whole life, he will not perhaps make use of one of them? Are we taught to dance merely for the sake of becoming dancers? No, certainly. These things are commonly studied, more on account of the habits, which the learning of them establishes, than on account of any

* From Molly Wallace, *The Rise and Progress of the Young Ladies' Academy of Philadelphia* (Philadelphia: Stewart and Cochran, 1794), 212–213.

important advantages which the mere knowledge of them can afford. So a young lady, from the exercise of speaking before a properly selected audience, may acquire some valuable habits, which, otherwise she can obtain from no examples, and that no precept can give. But, this exercise can with propriety be performed only before a select audience: a promiscuous and indiscriminate one, for obvious reasons, would be absolutely unsuitable, and should always be carefully avoided. . . .

Petition for Access to Education (1787)

After the Revolution, African Americans arrived in northern cities (like Boston, Philadelphia, and New York) in greater numbers, developing new community institutions which sometimes were granted equal treatment as those of whites. This is a petition to the Massachusetts legislature protesting the exclusion of blacks from public education; one of the movement's organizers was Prince Hall, the founder of the Negro Masonic Order.[*]

To the Honorable the Senate and House of Representatives of the Commonwealth of Massachusetts Bay, in General Court assembled.

The petition of a great number of blacks, freemen of this Commonwealth, humbly sheweth, that your petitioners are held in common with other freemen of this town and Commonwealth and have never been backward in paying our proportionate part of the burdens under which they have, or may labor under; and as we are willing to pay our equal part of these burdens, we are of the humble opinion that we have the right to enjoy the privileges of free men. But that we do not will appear in many instances, and we beg leave to mention one out of many, and that is of the education of our children which now receive no benefit from the free schools in the town of Boston, which we think is a great grievance, as by woeful experience we now feel the want of a common education. We, therefore, must fear for our rising offspring to see them in ignorance in a land of gospel light when there is provision made for them as well as others and yet can't enjoy them, and for no other reason can be given than they are black. . . .

We therefore pray your Honors that you would in your wisdom make some provision . . . for the education of our dear children. And in duty bound shall ever pray.

---

[*] From "Petition for Equal Education," 1787, in *A Documentary History of the Negro People in the United States*, ed. Herbert Aptheker (Secaucus, NJ: Carol Publishing Group, 1951). Copyright © 1951 by Carol Publishing Group. A Citadel Press Book.

7

Settling the Government

The writers of the Constitution provided a framework for a government for the new nation. It would be left to the first four presidential administrations, of Washington, Adams, Jefferson, and Madison, to prove that it was a workable compact. Their task was a difficult one, as policies, programs, and procedures had to be developed for the nation and divisions quickly appeared within the leadership over which policies and programs would be the most effective for the nation and how to implement them. These differences led to the rise of political parties, something that the framers of the Constitution had hoped to avoid. But despite these obstacles, by the end of the War of 1812, the country had settled into its institutional structures and learned that politics could be a natural part of the political process, while at the same time it almost doubled in size, withstood a war with a major European power, and re-established independence from Europe.

This chapter begins with George Washington's melancholy farewell address, an argument for national unity by a man who personified the nation. Washington was disheartened by the disputes between Republicans and Federalists, believed in strong economic development, and argued for an America independent in foreign affairs.

After serving one term as John Adams's vice president, Thomas Jefferson, a Democratic-Republican, became the third president of the United States in 1801. When Jefferson took office, the Republicans detested the judiciary. Not a single Republican judge had been appointed to the federal judiciary in the 1790s, and Republican newspaper editors were regularly hauled before federal courts under the Sedition Act. As soon as it met, the Republican Congress repealed the Federal Judiciary Act of 1801, which had created new courts, packed by John Adams with Federalists. One of Adam's appointees, William Marbury, petitioned the Supreme Court for a writ of mandamus, or order, to restore his commission as a justice of the peace for Washington, D.C.

John Marshall, the chief justice of the Supreme Court, ruled in *Marbury v. Madison* that the Supreme Court's right of mandamus was unconstitutional and incorrectly based on a clause in the Judiciary Act of 1789. He thereby established the Court's right to review and reverse federal state court decisions that conflicted with federal law or the Constitution, or the principle of judicial review.

Judicial review was not explicitly mentioned in the Constitution, although Alexander Hamilton asserted it in Federalist Paper #78, and future cases codified and strengthened it. Perhaps the best known of these was *Martin v. Hunter's Lessee,* in which the Court powerfully reasserted the supremacy of federal law as interpreted by the Supreme Court of the United States. In later Court decisions, including *Fletcher v. Peck*, the Marshall Court overturned state actions that came into conflict with the Constitution.

One of the important Marshall Court decisions that encouraged economic growth and supported a strong national government was *McCulloch v. Maryland,* which established the legality of the Bank of the United States and the power of the Congress to act within the "letter and spirit of the Constitution."

At the same time as it fleshed out the scope and limits of its governing and judicial institutions, the nation also experienced significant territorial growth under Jefferson. The Louisiana Purchase is considered one of the greatest accomplishments of the Jefferson administration. With one act, Jefferson doubled the size of the nation and laid the foundation for one of the largest territorial expansions undertaken by any country in history. He asked his private secretary, Meriwether Lewis, to lead an expedition to explore and map the newly purchased land. Led by Lewis and his partner, William Clark, the party trekked for over two years, reaching the Pacific in 1805. Included in this chapter is a series of selections from the journals they kept during their journey.

Following the War of 1812, seen by many as a second war of independence, the United States began to establish an identity separate from Europe, entering into a period of patriotism as Europe itself settled into a period of peace. The Monroe Doctrine was issued in response to the new independence of many Latin American states and the prospect of Russian and European interference in North and South American affairs and it manifests this new American nationalism. The policy stated that the political system of the Americas differed fundamentally from that of Europe, that any extension of European influence in the region would be considered a threat to the "peace and safety" of the United States, that the Western Hemisphere was closed to further colonization, and that the United states would not interfere with existing European colonies or European internal affairs. The Monroe Doctrine was later seen by many as the enunciation of the end of America's colonization by Europe.

Study Questions

1. What did Washington mean in his statement, "the jealousy of a free people ought to be constantly awake"?

2. When Washington wrote, "foreign influences is one of the most baneful foes of republican government," was he concerned about a particular country?

3. Was it realistic in 1796 to expect the nation to "steer clear of permanent alliances"?

4. How did the Lewis and Clark expedition relate to Native Americans? How do they describe the Native American reactions to their expedition?

George Washington, Farewell Address (1796)

George Washington delivered his farewell address in September 1796, stating that he would not accept a third term as president. He was 64 years old and disheartened: the patriot, war hero, president, and national symbol had been unable to stay above the fray of political argument. In his address, he argues for a nation united rather than divided by parties, economic policies, and foreign affairs.*

Observe good faith and justice toward all nations. Cultivate peace and harmony with all. Religion and morality enjoin this conduct. And can it be that good policy does not equally enjoin it? It will be worthy of a free, enlightened, and, at no distant period, a great nation to give to mankind the magnanimous and too novel example of a people always guided by an exalted justice and benevolence. . . .

In the execution of such a plan nothing is more essential than that permanent, inveterate antipathies against particular nations and passionate attachments for others should be excluded, and that, in place of them just and amicable feelings toward all should be cultivated. The nation which indulges toward another an habitual hatred or an habitual fondness is in some degree a slave. It is a slave to its animosity or to its affection either of which is sufficient to lead it astray from its duty and its interest. . . .

The nation prompted by ill will and resentment sometimes impels to war the government, contrary to the best calculations of policy. The government sometimes participates in the national propensity, and adopts through passion what reason would reject. . . .

So, likewise, a passionate attachment of one nation for another produces a variety of evils. Sympathy for the favorite nation, facilitating the illusion of an imaginary common interest in cases where no real common interest exists, and infusing into one the enmities of the other, betrays the former into a participation in the quarrels and wars of the latter without adequate inducement or justification. . . .

As avenues to foreign influence in innumerable ways, such attachments are particularly alarming to the truly enlightened and independent patriot. How many opportunities do they afford to tamper with domestic factions to practice the arts of seduction, to mislead public opinion, to influence or awe the public councils! Such an attachment of a small or weak toward a great and powerful nation dooms the former to be the satellite of the latter.

Against the insidious wiles of foreign influence (I conjure you to believe me, fellow citizens) the jealousy of a free people ought to be constantly awake, since

---

* From *Messages and Papers of the Presidents*, ed. J. D. Richardson, National Archives and Records Administration, (1986) 1, 221–223.

history and experience prove that foreign influence is one of the most baneful foes of republican government. . . .

The great rule of conduct for us in regard to foreign nations is, in extending our commercial relation, to have with them as little political connection as possible. So far as we have already formed engagements, let them be fulfilled with perfect good faith. Here let us stop.

Europe has a set of primary interests which to us have no, or a very remote, relation. Hence she must be engaged in frequent controversies, the causes of which are essentially foreign to our concerns. Hence, therefore, it must be unwise in us to implicate ourselves by artificial ties in the ordinary vicissitudes of her politics, or the ordinary combinations and collisions of her friendships or enmities.

Our detached and distant situation invites and enables us to pursue a different course. If we remain one people, under an efficient government, the period is not far off when we may defy material injury from external annoyance; when we may take such an attitude as will cause the neutrality we may at any time resolve upon to be scrupulously respected; when belligerent nations, under the impossibility of making acquisitions upon us, will not lightly hazard the giving us provocation; when we may choose peace or war, as our interest, guided by justice, shall counsel.

Why forego the advantages of so peculiar a situation? Why quit our own to stand upon foreign ground? Why, by interweaving our destiny with that of any part of Europe, entangle our peace and prosperity in the toils of European ambition, rivalship, interest, humor, or caprice?

It is our true policy to steer clear of permanent alliances with any portion of the foreign world, so far, I mean, as we are now at liberty to do it. For let me not be understood as capable of patronizing infidelity to existing engagements. I hold the maxim of less applicable to public than to private affairs that honesty is always the best policy. I repeat, therefore, let those engagements be observed in their genuine sense. But in my opinion it is unnecessary and would be unwise to extend them.

Taking care always to keep ourselves by suitable establishments on a respectable defensive posture, we may safely trust to temporary alliances for extraordinary emergencies.

Harmony, liberal intercourse with all nations, are recommended by policy, humanity, and interest. But even our commercial policy should hold an equal an impartial hand, neither seeking nor granting exclusive favors or preference; . . . constantly keeping in view that it is folly in one nation to look for disinterested favors from another; that it must pay with a portion of its independence for whatever it may accept under that character; that by such acceptance it may place itself in the condition of having given equivalents for nominal favors, and yet of being reproached with ingratitude for not giving more. There can be no greater error than to expect or calculate upon real favors from nation to nation. It is an illusion which experience must cure, which a just pride ought to discard.

Marbury v. Madison (1803)

In *Marbury v. Madison*, John Marshall, the Federalist chief justice, deflected much of the Republican hostility directed at the Supreme Court and laid the foundation for the Court's eventual independence from purely political interests. Just as important, he established the principle of judicial review and the supremacy of the national government over the states. Among the tactics Marshall used was the device of having one justice's opinion (in this case, and often elsewhere, his own) speak for the whole Court. By making his claim cautiously and tentatively, Marshall deflected possible opposition while establishing an important precedent.

[Chief Justice Marshall delivered the opinion of the Court.]

In the order in which the Court has viewed this subject, the following questions have been considered and decided: 1st. Has the applicant a right to the commission he demands? 2d. If he has a right, and that right has been violated, do the laws of this country afford him a remedy? 3d. If they do afford him a remedy, is it a mandamus issuing from this court? . . .

It is . . . the opinion of the Court: 1st. That by signing the commission of Mr. Marbury, the President of the United States appointed him a justice of the peace for the county of Washington, in the District of Columbia; and that the seal of the United States, affixed thereto by the secretary of state, is conclusive testimony of the verity of the signature, and of the completion of the appointment; and that the appointment conferred on him a legal right to the office for the space of five years. 2d. That, having this legal title to the office, he has a consequent right to the commission; a refusal to deliver which is a plain violation of that right, for which the laws of his country afford him a remedy. 3d. It remains to be inquired whether he is entitled to the remedy for which he applies? . . .

This . . . is a plain case for a mandamus, either to deliver the commission, or a copy of it from the record; and it only remains to be inquired, whether it can issue from this court?

The act to establish the judicial courts of the United States authorizes the Supreme Court, "to issue writs of mandamus, in cases warranted by the principles and usages of law, to any courts appointed or persons holding office, under the authority of the United States." The secretary of state, being a person holding an office under the authority of the United States, is precisely within the letter of this description; and if this court is not authorized to issue a writ of mandamus to such an officer, it must be because the law is unconstitutional . . .

The Constitution vests the whole judicial power of the United States in one Supreme Court, and such inferior courts as Congress shall, from time to time, ordain and establish....

In the distribution of this power, it is declared that "the Supreme Court shall have original jurisdiction in all cases affecting ambassadors, other public ministers and consuls, and those in which a state shall be a party. In all other cases, the Supreme Court shall have appellate jurisdiction." . . .

If it had been intended to leave it in the discretion of the legislature to apportion the judicial power between the supreme and inferior courts according to the will of that body, it would certainly have been useless to have proceeded further than to have defined the judicial power, and the tribunals in which it should be vested. The subsequent part of the section is mere surplusage, is entirely without meaning, . . .

It cannot be presumed that any clause in the Constitution is intended to be without effect . . .

To enable this court, then, to issue a mandamus, it must be shown to be an exercise of appellate jurisdiction . . .

The authority, therefore, given to the Supreme Court, by the Act establishing the judicial courts of the United States, to issue writs of mandamus to public officers, appears not to be warranted by the Constitution . . .

Martin v. Hunter's Lessee (1816)

This case is the best-known in which the Supreme Court established its right to review and reverse state decisions. This case concerned a Loyalist, Lord Fairfax, who fled to England during the Revolution. Fairfax owned substantial land in Virginia which he passed on to his nephew, Denny Fairfax, a British subject. Virginia passed an act in 1782 voiding this grant based on the contention that, under Virginia law, aliens could not inherit property. In addition, various confiscation measures enacted, but never implemented, during the war had transferred Lord Fairfax's property to the state. David Hunter obtained a grant of a portion of the Fairfax land from Virginia and brought an act of ejectment against the Fairfax interests. In ensuing challenges, the Supreme Court of Virginia decided for Hunter, but the United States Supreme Court reversed the Virginia court in 1813. In response, Virginia's judges claimed that, although bound by the Constitution and federal laws, they were not bound by the Supreme Court's interpretation of those laws. They therefore refused to obey the United States Supreme Court's order requiring them to enter judgment for the Fairfax interests. This brought the case back to the Supreme Court. Justice Joseph Storey's opinion powerfully asserted the supremacy of federal law as interpreted by the Supreme Court of the United States.

Justice Storey delivered the opinion of the Court.

. . . But it is plain that the framers of the constitution did contemplate that cases within the judicial cognizance of the United States not only might but would arise in the state courts, in the exercise of their ordinary jurisdiction. With this view the sixth article declares, that "this constitution, and the laws of the United States which shall be made in pursuance thereof, and all treaties made, or which shall be made, under the authority of the United States, shall be the supreme law of the land, and the judges in every State shall be bound thereby, any thing in the constitution, or laws of any State to the contrary notwithstanding." It is obvious that this obligation is imperative upon the state judges in their official, and not merely in their private, capacities. From the very nature of their judicial duties they would be called upon to pronounce the law applicable to the case in judgment. They were not to decide merely according to the laws or constitution of the State, but according to the constitution, laws, and treaties of the United States, "the supreme law of the land.". . .

It must, therefore, be conceded that the Constitution not only contemplated, but meant to provide for cases within the scope of the judicial power of the United States, which might yet depend before state tribunals. It was foreseen that in the exercise of their ordinary jurisdiction, state courts would incidentally take cognizance of cases arising under the Constitution, the laws, and treaties of the United States. Yet to all these cases the judicial power, by the very terms of the Constitution, is to extend. It cannot extend by original jurisdiction if that was already rightfully and exclusively attached in the state courts, which (as has been already shown) may occur; it must therefore extend by appellate jurisdiction, or not at all. It would seem to follow that the appellate powers of the United States must, in such cases, extend to state tribunals; and if in such cases, there is no reason why it should not equally attach upon all others within the purview of the Constitution. . . .

On the whole, the Court are of opinion, that the appellate power of the United States does extend to cases pending in the state courts. . . .

McCulloch v. Maryland (1819)

In this landmark decision, the Marshall Court struck down a Maryland law that applied a $15,000 tax on "foreign banks" to the Second Bank of the United States. The Court declared the tax unconstitutional because it interfered with the Bank, which had been legally chartered by Congress. In *McCulloch*, the implied powers of Congress were strengthened and the legality of the Bank was established.*

That the power of taxation is one of vital importance; that it is retained by the states; that it is not abridged by the grant of a similar power to the government of the Union; that it is to be concurrently exercised by the two governments—are truths which have never been denied. But such is the paramount character of the Constitution that its capacity to withdraw any subject from the action of even this power is admitted. The states are expressly forbidden to lay any duties on imports or exports, except what may be absolutely necessary for executing their inspection laws. . . . The same paramount character would seem to restrain . . . a state from such other exercise of this power as is in its nature incompatible with, and repugnant to, the constitutional laws of the Union. A law absolutely repugnant to another, as entirely repeals that other as if express terms of repeal were used.

On this ground the counsel for the Bank place its claim to be exempted from the power of a state to tax its operations. There is no express provision for the case, but the claim has been sustained on a principle which so entirely pervades the Constitution, is so intermixed with the materials which compose it, so interwoven with its web, so blended with its texture, as to be incapable of being separated from it without rending it into shreds.

This great principle is that the Constitution, and laws made in pursuance thereof, are supreme; that they control the constitutions and laws of the respective states, and cannot be controlled by them. From this, which may be almost termed an axiom, other propositions are deduced as corollaries. . . . These are: 1. That a power to create implies a power to preserve. 2. That a power to destroy, if wielded by a different hand, is hostile to, and incompatible with, these powers to create an preserve. 3. That where this repugnancy exists, that authority which is supreme must control, not yield to that over which it is supreme. . . .

That the power to tax involves the power to destroy; that the power to destroy may defeat and render useless the power to create; that there is a plain repugnance in conferring on one government a power to control the constitutional measures of another . . . are propositions not to be denied. . . .

If we apply the principle for which the state of Maryland contends, to the Constitution generally, we shall find it capable of changing totally the character of that instrument. We shall find it capable of arresting all the measures of the government, and of prostrating it at the foot of the states. The American people have declared their Constitution, and the laws made in pursuance thereof, to be supreme; and this principle would transfer the supremacy, in fact, to the states.

If the states may tax one instrument employed by the government in the execution of its powers, they may tax any and every other instrument. They may tax the mail; they may tax the mint; they may tax patent rights; they may tax the papers of the

---

* From 4 Wheaton 316, (432–433, 436, 437).

custom-house; they may tax judicial process; they may tax all the means employed by the government, to an excess which would defeat all the ends of government. This was not intended by the American people. They did not design to make their government dependent on the states. . . .

The question is, in truth, a question of supremacy. And if the right of the states to tax the means employed by the general government be conceded, the declaration that the Constitution, and the laws made in pursuance thereof, shall be the supreme law of the land, is empty and unmeaning declamation.

Meriwether Lewis, Journal (1805)

Meriwether Lewis, Jefferson's personal secretary, and Lewis's friend William Clark had both served in the West in the army. In 1803 they were sent on a mission by President Jefferson to gather scientific information, explore the Louisiana Purchase territory, establish formal relationships with the Native American groups, and evaluate the fur trade. Lewis and Clark, with a party of almost fifty experienced men, left from St. Louis and traveled to the Pacific along the Missouri, Yellowstone, and Columbia Rivers with the help of a Shoshone guide, Sacajawea, and her French-Canadian husband, Toussaint Charbonneau. Their journals expanded interest in and disseminated information about the West.*

Saturday August 17th 1805

we made them [the Indians] sensible of their dependance on the will of our government for every species of merchandize as well for their defence & comfort; and apprized them of the strength of our government and its friendly dispositions toward them. we also gave them as a reason why we wished to pe[ne]trate the country as far as the ocean to the west of them was to examine and find out a more direct way to bring merchandize to them. that as no trade could by carryed on with them before our return to our homes that it was mutually advantageous to them as well as to ourselves that they should render us such aids as they had in their power to furnish in order to haisten our voyage and of course our return home. that such were their horses to transport our baggage without which we could not subsist, and that a pilot to conduct us through the mountains was also necessary if we could not decend the river by water. but that we did not ask either their horses or their services without giving a satisfactory

* From *The Journals of Lewis and Clark*, ed., Barnard De Voto (Boston: Houghton Mifflin, 1981), 202–206, 207–211, 213–214. Copyright © 1953 by Barnard De Voto. Copyright © renewed 1981 by Avis Devoto. Reprinted by permission of Houghton Mifflin Company.

compensation in return. that at present we wished them to collect as many horses as were necessary to transport our baggage to their village on the Columbia where we would then trade with them at our leasure for such horses as they could spare us.

the chief thanked us for friendship towards himself and nation & declared his wish to serve us in every rispect. that he was sorry to find that it must yet be some time before they could be furnished with firearms but said they could live as they had done heretofore until we brought them as we had promised. he said they had not horses enough with them at present to remove our baggage to their village over the mountain, but that he would return tomorrow and encourage his people to come over with their horses and that he would bring his own and assist us. this was complying with all we wished at present.

Sunday August 18th 1805

this morning while Capt. Clark was busily engaged in preparing for his rout, I exposed some articles to barter with the Indians for horses as I wished a few at this moment to releive the men who were going with Capt. Clark from the labour of carrying their baggage, and also one to keep here in order to pack the meat to camp which the hunters might kill. i soon obtained three very good horses for which I gave an uniform coat, a pair of legings, a few handkerchiefs, three knives and some other small article the whole of which did not cost more than about 20$ in the U'States. the Indians seemed quite as well pleased with their bargin as I was. the men also purchased one for an old checked shirt a pair of old legings and a knife. two of those I purchased Capt. C. took on him. At 10 a.m. Capt. Clark departed with his detachment and all the Indians except 2 men and 2 women who remained with us.

Tuesday August 20, 1805

i now prevailed on the Chief to instruct me with rispect to the geography of his country. This he undertook very cheerfully, by delineating the rivers on the ground. but I soon found that his information fell far short of my expectation or wishes. He drew the river on which we now are [the Lemhi] to which he placed two branches just above us, which he shewed me from the openings on the mountains were in view; he next made it discharge itself into a large river which flowed from the S.W. about ten miles below us [the Salmon], then continued this joint stream in the same direction of this valley or N.W. for one days march and then enclined to the West for 2 more days march. here we placed a number of heaps of sand on each side which he informed me represented the vast mountains of rock eternally covered with snow through which the river passed. that the perpendicular and even juting rocks so closely hemmed in the river that there was no possibil[it]y of passing along the shore; that the bed of the river was obstructed by sharp pointed rocks and the rapidity of the stream such that the whole surface of the river was beat into perfect foam as far as the eye could reach. that the mountains were also inaccessible to man or horse. he said that this being the state of the country in that direction that himself nor none of his nation had ever been further down the river than these mountains.

in this manner I spend the day smoking with them and acquiring what information I could with respect to their country. they informed me that they could pass the Spaniards by the way of the yellowstone river in 10 days. I can discover that these people are by no means friendly to the Spaniards. their complaint is, that the Spaniards will not let them have fire arms and ammunition, that they put them off by telling them that if they suffer them to have guns they will kill each other, thus leaving them defenceless and an easy prey to their bloodthirsty neighbours to the East of them who being in possession of fire arms hunt them up and murder them without rispect to sex or age and plunder them of their horses on all occasions. they told me that to avoid their enemies who were eternally harrassing them that they were obliged to remain in the interior of these mountains at least two thirds of the year where the[y] suffered as we then saw great hardships for the want of food sometimes living for weeks without meat and only a little fish roots and berries. but this added Cameahwait, with his ferce eyes and lank jaws grown meager for the want of food, would not be the case if we had guns, we could then live in the country of buffaloe and eat as our enimies do and not be compelled to hide ourselves in these mountains and live on roots and berries as the bear do. whitemen would come to them with an abundance of guns and every other article necessary to their defence and comfort, and that they would be enabled to supply themselves with these articles on reasonable terms in exchange for the skins of the beaver Otter and Ermin so abundant in their country. they expressed great pleasure at this information and said they had been long anxious to see the whitemen that traded guns; and that we might rest assured of their friendship and that they would do whatever we wished them.

The Monroe Doctrine and a Reaction (1823)

This policy statement was introduced in a message to Congress delivered by President James Monroe in December 1823. When European policymakers heard it, they thought it "arrogant" and "blustering." The Monroe Doctrine nevertheless became important as a declaration of principles later in the nineteenth century, as the economic and military power of the United States caught up with Monroe's vision. The reaction to the doctrine, an editorial in the Baltimore *Chronicle*, is typical of some of the patriotic acclaim the statement received.[*]

---

[*] From *Messages and Papers of the Presidents*, ed. J. D. Richardson, National Archives and Records Administration, (1896), II, 209, 218–219.

In the discussion to which this interest [Russia's on the northwest coast] has given rise, the occasion has been judged proper for asserting, as a principle in which the rights and interests of the United States are involved, that the American continents, by the free and independent condition which they have assumed and maintain, are henceforth not to be considered as subjects for the future colonization by any European powers. . . .

The political system of the Allied Powers [Holy Alliance] is essentially different . . . from that of America. This difference proceeds from that which exists in their prospective [monarchical] governments; and to the defence of our own . . . this whole nation is devoted. We owe it, therefore, to candor and to the amicable relations existing between the United States and those powers to declare that we should consider any attempt on their part to extend their system to any portion of this hemisphere as dangerous to our peace and safety.

With the existing colonies or dependencies of any European power, we have not interfered and shall not interfere. But with the governments [of Spanish America] who have declared their independence and maintained it, and whose independence we have, on great consideration and on just principles, acknowledged, we could not view any interposition for the purpose of oppressing them, or controlling in any other light than as the manifestation of an unfriendly disposition toward the United States. . . .

Our policy in regard to Europe, which was adopted at an early stage of the wars which have so long agitated that quarter of the globe, nevertheless remains the same, which is, not to interfere in the internal concerns of any of its powers; to consider the government *de facto* as the legitimate government for us; to cultivate friendly relations with it, and to preserve those relations by a frank, firm, and manly policy, meeting in all instances the just claims of every power, submitting to injuries from none.

But in regard to those [American] continents, circumstances are eminently and conspicuously different. It is impossible that the Allied Powers should extend their political system to a portion of either continent without endangering our peace and happiness. Nor can anyone believe that our southern brethren, if left to themselves, would adopt it of their own accord. It is equally impossible, therefore, that we should behold such interposition in any form with indifference.

[Baltimore *Chronicle*, Editorial]

We can tell . . . further that this high-toned, independent, and dignified message will not be read by the crowned heads of Europe without a revolting stare of astonishment. The conquerors of Bonaparte, with their laurels still green and blooming on their brows, and their disciplined animal machines, called armies, at their backs, could not have anticipated that their united force would so soon be defied by a young republic, whose existence, as yet, cannot be measured with the ordinary life of man.

This message itself constitutes an era in American history, worthy of commemoration. . . . We are confident that, on this occasion, we speak the great body of American sentiment, such as exulting millions are ready to re-echo. . . . We are very far from being confident that, if Congress occupy the high and elevated ground taken in the Message, it may not, under the smiles of Divine Providence, be the means of breaking up the Holy Alliance.

Of this we are positively sure: that all timidity, wavering imbecility, an backwardness on our part will confirm these detested tyrants in their confederacy; paralyze the exertions of freedom in every country; accelerate the fall of those young sister republics whom we have recently recognized; and, perhaps, eventually destroy our own at the feet of absolute monarchy.

8

Jacksonian Expansion and Egalitarianism

The election of Andrew Jackson to the presidency in 1828 marked a revolution in American politics. Jackson's era saw a return to the two-party system, now markedly changed since the era of the Federalists and Republicans as a result of the enfranchisement of poorer male white voters, territorial expansion into the West, and the resultant rise of political power there. And while altering the political landscape, expansion also exposed some of the limitations of democracy, as Native Americans were removed from the East and whites moved farther west, bringing slavery with them.

By 1829 it had become clear that America's expansion westward would require a national policy. Since most of the expansion was confined to east of the Mississippi, Americans believed transplanting Native Americas west of the river would solve the problem they presented. In his annual address to Congress included here, Jackson, who had gained fame as a professional Indian fighter, supported the Indian Removal Act and pursued a policy of removing Indians from the path of white settlement.

The Cherokee had attempted to hold their lands by adjusting to white ways. However, in spite of several treaties that had seemed to establish the legitimacy of their government, in 1829 Georgia refused to recognize the Cherokee and passed a law declaring all Cherokee laws void and Cherokee lands part of Georgia. In *Worcester v. Georgia*, the Marshall Supreme Court ruled that the Georgia law was "repugnant to the Constitution" and did not apply to the Cherokee.

President Jackson, taking a state's rights position, backed Georgia and defied the Supreme Court. He insisted that no independent nation could exist within the United States. Between 1837 and 1839 the army drove about 15,000 Cherokee to leave Georgia for lands in Oklahoma; about 4,000 died on the way.

Andrew Jackson came into the White House intending to "reform" and "purify" the government. He ushered in a new political culture, one that appeared more egalitarian and democratic, filled with political conventions, rallies, and parades, all engineered to increase voter participation. One of the most well-known and symbolic figures from this time period is Davy Crockett—a Tennessee frontiersman and two-time member of Congress—whose backwoods dress, back-country language, and political independence endeared him to his contemporaries. His advice to politicians reprinted here is a somewhat ironic commentary on the new Jacksonian politics.

Davy Crockett's fame was guaranteed when he died at the Alamo, the Texas garrison attacked by forces of the Mexican general Santa Ana in 1836 during Texas's war for independence from Mexico. During the Jacksonian period, white southerners (and their slaves) were moving onto Mexican territory in what is now Texas. The selection included here, by José María Sánchez, provides a vivid picture of the mixture of cultures in eastern Texas during in the late 1820s. In the next decade, Texas declared its independence, and in 1845 it was annexed by the United States to become the twenty-eighth state.

While Jackson personified the frontiers, many Americans were moving away from rural areas into rapidly industrializing cities and towns like Lowell, Massachusetts, and Cincinnati, Ohio. Lowell, founded in 1823 by a group of Boston entrepreneurs led by Francis Cabot Lowell, was considered the birthplace of the American factory system and the prototype for the soon-widespread employment of young rural women in the production of textiles.

Textile corporations built boardinghouses around their mills to accommodate the recent migrants and established paternalistic regulations governing these women. Regulations required that women workers be in their boardinghouses by ten o'clock each evening and that operators of the boardinghouses report violations to the mill's management. At least in the early years, the women were required to attend church. Such controls were designed to "protect" the workers and to assure Yankee parents that their daughters might leave home to work in the mills without injury to their persons or their reputations. In the mid-1830s, the women earned about $3.25 for a seventy-three-hour week; room and board in a company boardinghouse cost about $1.25 per week. These earnings compared favorably with incomes from other areas open to women, like teaching, domestic service, or sewing. The *Harbinger* report on textile mills and the letters of Mary Paul, a worker, provide contrasting pictures of the textile factories of Lowell.

Like the expansion of white settlers westward, the industrialization of the north was not entirely without conflict. The Lowell women struck in 1834 and several times during the 1840s. An earlier strike occurred in 1825 in Boston among skilled hand-workers, master and journeyman carpenters. Over six hundred journeymen participated in the strike, demanding, among other things, a ten-hour workday. The strike failed after business leaders indicated that they would not hire any master carpenters (who employed the junior carpenters) acceding the journeymen's demands.

Study Questions

1. Why did Andrew Jackson appeal to "humanity and national honor" while advocating removal of southeastern Indians?

2. What kind of life did the Cherokee expect to find in the western territory?

3. Could different peoples live together? Why did Jackson and María Sánchez seem to indicate that peoples would be better separate?

4. "Egalitarian democracy" included only white males. In what way does Davy Crockett's advice to politicians reflect this?

5. Why were women attracted to the factory system? Why were they willing to work under the conditions it imposed?

6. Why might early industrialists prefer to hire unmarried women?

7. How did factory work compare to the ideology of the day that considered women to be best suited to domestic pursuits? How might the *Harbinger* report reflect assumptions about female work capabilities?

8. What treatment did the journeymen and master carpenters expect? What precedents did both the journeymen and master carpenters refer to in order to support their point of view?

9. Could the Boston carpenters' strike be described as a democratic event? Why?

10. How did expansion and industrialization effect political culture? Did they work to encourage democratization? For whom?

Andrew Jackson, First Annual Message to Congress (1829)

In the early nineteenth century, the lands occupied by southeastern and northwestern Native American groups, including the Cherokee, Chickasaw, Choctaw, Seminole, Fox, and Creek, were closed in upon by an expanding frontier of white settlement. In this address, President Jackson, a former frontiersman and Indian fighter, cloaked his argument for the relocation of Native Americans in the language of concern and honor. Indian removal helped bring about economic expansion for the new republic, but at tremendous cost to both the Native Americans who fought displacement and who moved west.*

The condition and ulterior destiny of the Indian tribes within the limits of some of our states have become objects of much interest and importance. It has long been the policy of government to introduce among them the arts of civilization, in the hope of

* From *Messages and Papers of the Presidents*, ed. J. D. Richardson, National Archives and Records Administration, (1896), II, 456–459 (Dec. 8, 1829).

gradually reclaiming them from a wandering life. This policy has, however, been coupled with another wholly incompatible with its success. Professing a desire to civilize and settle them, we have at the same time lost no opportunity to purchase their lands and thrust them farther into the wilderness. By this means they have not only been kept in a wandering state, but been led to look upon us as unjust and indifferent to their fate. . . .

Our conduct toward these people is deeply interesting to our national character. Their present condition, contrasted with what they once were, makes a most powerful appeal to our sympathies. Our ancestors found them the uncontrolled possessors of these vast regions. By persuasion and force they have been made to retire from river to river and from mountain to mountain, until some of the tribes have become extinct and others have left but remnants to preserve for awhile their once terrible names. Surrounded by the whites with their arts of civilization, which, by destroying the resources of the savage, doom him to weakness and decay, the fate of the Mohegan, the Narragansett, and the Delaware is fast overtaking the Choctaw, the Cherokee, and the Creek. That this fate surely awaits them if they remain within the limits of the states does not admit of a doubt. Humanity and national honor demand that every effort should be made to avert so great a calamity. . . .

As a means of effecting this end, I suggest for our consideration the propriety of setting apart an ample district west of the Mississippi, and without [outside] the limits of any state or territory now formed, to be guaranteed to the Indian tribes as long as they shall occupy it, each tribe having a distinct control over the portion designated for its use. There they may be secured in the enjoyment of governments of their own choice, subject to no other control from the United States than such as may be necessary to preserve peace on the frontier and between the several tribes. There the benevolent may endeavor to teach them the arts of civilization, and, by promoting union and harmony among them, to raise up an interesting commonwealth, destined to perpetuate the race and to attest the humanity and justice of this government.

This emigration should be voluntary, for it would be as cruel as unjust to compel the aborigines to abandon the graves of their fathers and seek a home in a distant land. But they should be distinctly informed that if they remain within the limits of the states they must be subject to their laws.

"Memorial of the Cherokee Nation" (1830)

The Washington administration had established a policy designed to "civilize" the Indians, and the Cherokee, more than any other Native American group, had done so—by codifying their own legal system, printing their own newspapers, and even owning slaves. However, no amount of assimilation helped the Cherokee when the state of Georgia demanded their land. During the "trail of tears," when the Cherokee were forced to march to Oklahoma, more than 4,000 Cherokee died. The "Memorial of the Cherokee Nation" appeared in *Nile's Weekly Register* in 1830.*

We are aware that some persons suppose it will be for our advantage to remove beyond the Mississippi. We think otherwise. Our people universally think otherwise. Thinking that it would be fatal to their interests, they have almost to a man sent their memorial to Congress, deprecating the necessity of a removal. . . . It is incredible that Georgia should ever have enacted the oppressive laws to which reference is here made, unless she had supposed that something extremely terrific in its character was necessary in order to make the Cherokees willing to remove. We are not willing to remove; and if we could be brought to this extremity, it would be not by argument, nor because our judgment was satisfied, not because our condition will be improved; but only because we cannot endure to be deprived of our national and individual rights and subjected to a process of intolerable oppression.

We wish to remain on the land of our fathers. We have a perfect and original right to remain without interruption or molestation. The treaties with us, and laws of the United States made in pursuance of treaties, guaranty our residence and our privileges, and secure us against intruders. Our only request is, that these treaties may be fulfilled, and these laws executed.

But if we are compelled to leave our country, we see nothing but ruin before us. The country west of the Arkansas territory is unknown to us. From what we can learn of it, we have no prepossessions in its favor. All the inviting parts of it, as we believe, are preoccupied by various Indian nations, to which it has been assigned. They would regard us as intruders. . . . The far greater part of that region is, beyond all controversy, badly supplied with wood and water; and no Indian tribe can live as agriculturists without these articles. All our neighbors . . . would speak a language totally different from ours, and practice different customs. The original possessors of that region are now wandering savages lurking for prey in the neighborhood. . . . Were the country to which we are urged much better than it is represented to be, . . . still it is not the land of our birth, nor of our affections. It contains neither the scenes of our childhood, nor the graves of our fathers.

. . . We have been called a poor, ignorant, and degraded people. We certainly are not rich; nor have we ever boasted of our knowledge, or our moral or intellectual elevation. But there is not a man within our limits so ignorant as not to know that he has a right to live on the land of his fathers, in the possession of his immemorial privileges, and that this right has been acknowledged by the United States; nor is there a man so degraded as not to feel a keen sense of injury, on being deprived of his right and driven into exile. . . .

---

* Reprinted from "Memorial of the Cherokee Nation," in *Nile's Weekly Register*, 1830.

Davy Crockett, Advice to Politicians (1833)

Like Andrew Jackson, Davy Crockett was from the frontier state of Tennessee. He had even fought under Jackson in the Creek War in 1813 and 1814. He was a former congressman as well as a famous frontiersman, and his advice to politicians reflects the new political culture of the Jacksonian era.*

"Attend all public meetings," says I, "and get some friend to move that you take the chair. If you fail in this attempt, make a push to be appointed secretary. The proceeding of course will be published, and your name is introduced to the public. But should you fail in both undertakings, get two or three acquaintances, over a bottle of whisky, to pass some resolutions, no matter on what subject. Publish them, even if you pay the printer. It will answer the purpose of breaking the ice, which is the main point in these matters.

"Intrigue until you are elected an officer of the militia. This is the second step toward promotion, and can be accomplished with ease, as I know an instance of an election being advertised, and no one attending, the innkeeper at whose house it was to be held, having a military turn, elected himself colonel of his regiment." Says I, "You may not accomplish your ends with as little difficulty, but do not be discouraged—Rome wasn't built in a day.

"If your ambition or circumstances compel you to serve your country and earn three dollars a day, by becoming a member of the legislature, you must first publicly avow that the constitution of the state is a shackle upon free and liberal legislation, and is, therefore, of as little use in the present enlightened age as an old almanac of the year in which the instrument was framed. There is policy in this measure, for by making the constitution a mere dead letter, your headlong proceedings will be attributed to a bold and unshackled mind; whereas, it might otherwise be thought they arose from sheer mulish ignorance. 'The Government' has set the example in his [Jackson's] attack upon the Constitution of the United States, and who should fear to follow where 'the Government' leads?

"When the day of election approaches, visit your constituents far and wide. Treat liberally, and drink freely, in order to rise in their estimation, though you fall in your own. True, you may be called a drunken dog by some of the clean-shirt and silk-stocking gentry, but the real roughnecks will style you a jovial fellow. Their votes are certain, and frequently count double.

---

* From *David Crockett, Exploits and Adventures in Texas* (1836), 56–59.

"Do all you can to appear to advantage in the eyes of the women. That's easily done. You have but to kiss and slabber [slobber over] their children, wipe their noses, and pat them on the head. This cannot fail to please their mothers, and you may rely on your business being done in that quarter.

"Promise all that is asked," said I, "and more if you can think of anything. Offer to build a bridge or a church, to divide a county, create a batch of new offices, make a turnpike, or anything they like. Promises cost nothing; therefore, deny nobody who has a vote or sufficient influence to obtain one.

"Get up on all occasions, and sometimes on no occasion at all, and make long-winded speeches, though composed of nothing else than wind. Talk of your devotion to your country, your modesty and disinterestedness, or on any such fanciful subject. Rail against taxes of all kinds, officeholders, and bad harvest weather; and wind up with a flourish abut the heroes who fought and bled for our liberties in the times that tried men's souls. To be sure, you run the risk of being considered a bladder of wind, or an empty barrel. But never mind that; you will find enough of the same fraternity to keep you in countenance.

"If any charity be going forward, be at the top of it, provided it is to be advertised publicly. If not, it isn't worth your while. None but a fool would place his candle under a bushel on such an occasion.

"These few directions." said I, "if properly attended to, will do your business. And when once elected—why, a fig for the dirty children, the promises, the bridges, the churches, the taxes, the offices, and the subscriptions. For it is absolutely necessary to forget all these before you can become a thoroughgoing politician, and a patriot of the first water."

José María Sánchez, *A Trip to Texas* (1828)

José María Sánchez was sent by the Mexican government to survey and report on conditions in southeastern Texas, where increasing numbers of southern white Americans had settled. The Mexican government had encouraged immigration into their relatively unpopulated borderlands, provided that the settlers convert to Roman Catholicism and become Mexican citizens. Few did either, however. José María Sánchez's report reveals the increasing tensions in the area.*

* From José María Sánchez "A Trip to Texas" (1828), trans. Carlos E. Castaneda in *Southwestern Historical Quarterly*, Vol. 29, No. 4, April 1926, 270–273. Reprinted with permission of the Texas State Historicial Association.

The Americans from the north have taken possession of practically all the eastern portion of Texas, in most cases without the permission of the authorities. They immigrate constantly, finding no one to prevent them, and take possession of the site that best suits them without asking leave or going through any formality other than that of building their homes. Thus the majority of inhabitants in the Department are North Americans, the Mexican population being reduced to only Bejar, Nacadoches, and La Bahía del Espíritu Santo, wretched settlements that between them do not number three thousand inhabitants, and the new village of Guadeloupe Victoria that has scarcely more than seventy settlers. The government of the state, with its seat at Saltillo, that should watch over the preservation of its most precious and interesting department, taking measures to prevent its being stolen by foreign hands, is the only that knows the least not only about actual conditions, but even about its territory. . . .

The Mexicans that live here are very humble people and perhaps their intentions are good, but because of their education and environment they are ignorant not only of the customs of our great cities, but even of the occurrences of our Revolution, exception a few persons who have heard about them. Accustomed to the continued trade with the North Americans, they have adopted their customs and habits and one may say truly that they are not Mexicans except by birth, for they even speak Spanish with marked incorrectness. . . .

This village [San Felipe de Austin] has been settled by Mr. Stephen Austin, a native of the United States of the North. It consists, at present, of forty or fifty wooden houses on the western bank of the large river known as Rio de los Brazos de Dios, but the houses are not arranged symmetrically so as to form streets, but on the contrary, lie in an irregular and desultory manner. Its population is nearly two hundred persons, of which only ten are Mexicans, for the balance are all Americans from the North with an occasional European. Two wretched little stores supply the inhabitants of the colony: one sells only whiskey, rum, sugar, and coffee; the other, rice, flour, lard, and cheap cloth. It may seem that these items are too few for the needs of the inhabitants, but they are not because the American from the North, at least the greater part of those I have seen, eat only salted meat, bread made by themselves out of corn meal, coffee and home-made cheese. To these the greater part of those who live in the village add strong liquor, for they are in general, in my opinion, lazy people of vicious character. Some of them cultivate their small farms by planting corn; but this task they usually entrust to their negro slaves, whom they treat with considerable harshness. Beyond the village in an immense stretch of land formed by rolling hills are scattered the families brought by Stephen Austin, which today number more than two thousand persons. The diplomatic policy of this impresario, evident in all his actions, has, as one may say, lulled the authorities into a sense of security, while he works diligently for his own ends. In my judgment, the spark that will start the conflagration that will deprive us of Texas, will start from this colony. All because the government does not take vigorous measures to prevent it. Perhaps it does not realize the value of what it is about to lose.

The Harbinger, Female Workers of Lowell (1836)

The following is a selection from a magazine report investigating the textile mills of New England. Textile mills formed the backbone of the rapidly industrializing north while other industrial operations expanding during the period included paper mills (primarily in Philadelphia), iron and metalworking, refineries, and shoemaking (again, like textiles, primarily in New England). In 1836 Lowell had 17,000 inhabitants, and women composed nearly 70 percent of the laboring population. In addition to providing relatively cheap and dependable labor, it was hoped that the young unmarried women would keep the factories clean, Christian, and productive.*

We have lately visited the cities of Lowell [Mass.] and Manchester [N.H.] and have had an opportunity of examining the factory system more closely than before. We had distrusted the accounts which we had heard from persons engaged in the labor reform now beginning to agitate New England. We could scarcely credit the statements made in relation to the exhausting nature of the labor in the mills, and to the manner in which the young women—the operatives—lived in their boardinghouses, six sleeping in a room, poorly ventilated.

We went through many of the mills, talked particularly to a large number of the operatives, and ate at their boardinghouses, on purpose to ascertain by personal inspection the facts of the case. We assure our readers that very little information is possessed, and no correct judgments formed, by the public at large, of our factory system, which is the first germ of the industrial or commercial feudalism that is to spread over our land. . . .

In Lowell live between seven and eight thousand young women, who are generally daughters of farmers of the different states of New England. Some of them are members of families that were rich in the generation before. . . .

The operatives work thirteen hours a day in the summer time, and from daylight to dark in the winter. At half past four in the morning the factory bell rings, and at five the girls must be in the mills. A clerk, placed as a watch, observes those who are a few minutes behind the time, and effectual means are taken to stimulate to punctuality. This is the morning commencement of the industrial discipline (should we not rather say industrial tyranny?) which is established in these associations of this moral and Christian community.

At seven the girls are allowed thirty minutes for breakfast, and at noon thirty minutes more for dinner, except during the first quarter of the year, when the time is extended to forty-five minutes. But within this time they must hurry to their boardinghouses and return to the factory, and that through the hot sun or the rain or the

*From *The Harbinger*, Nov. 14, 1836.

cold. A meal eaten under such circumstances must be quite unfavorable to digestion and health, as any medical man will inform us. After seven o'clock in the evening the factory bell sounds the close of the day's work.

Thus thirteen hours per day of close attention and monotonous labor are extracted from the young women in these manufactories. . . . So fatigued—we should say, exhausted and worn out, but we wish to speak of the system in the simplest language—are numbers of girls that they go to bed soon after their evening meal, and endeavor by a comparatively long sleep to resuscitate their weakened frames for the toil of the coming day.

When capital has got thirteen hours of labor daily out of a being, it can get nothing more. It would be a poor speculation in an industrial point of view to own the operative; for the trouble and expense of providing for times of sickness and old age would more than counterbalance the difference between the price of wages and the expenses of board and clothing. The far greater number of fortunes accumulated by the North in comparison with the South shows that hireling labor is more profitable for capital than slave labor.

Now let us examine the nature of the labor itself, and the conditions under which it is performed. Enter with us into the large rooms, when the looms are at work. The largest that we saw is in the Amoskeag Mills at Manchester. . . . The din and clatter of these five hundred looms, under full operation, struck us on first entering as something frightful and infernal, for it seemed such an atrocious violation of one of the faculties of the human soul, the sense of hearing. After a while we became somewhat used to it, and by speaking quite close to the ear of an operative and quite loud, we could hold a conversation and make the inquiries we wished.

The girls attended upon an average three looms; many attended four, but this requires a very active person, and the most unremitting care. However, a great many do it. Attention to two is as much as should be demanded of an operative. This gives us some idea of the application required during the thirteen hours of daily labor. The atmosphere of such a room cannot of course be pure; on the contrary, it is charged with cotton filaments and dust, which, we are told, are very injurious to the lungs.

On entering the room, although the day was warm, we remarked that the windows were down. We asked the reason, and a young woman answered very naively, and without seeming to be in the least aware that this privation of fresh air was anything else than perfectly natural, that "when the wind blew, the threads did not work well." After we had been in the room for fifteen or twenty minutes, we found ourselves, as did the persons who accompanied us, in quite a perspiration, produced by a certain moisture which we observed in the air, as well as by the heat. . . .

The young women sleep upon an average six in a room, three beds to a room. There is no privacy, no retirement, here. It is almost impossible to read or write alone, as the parlor is full and so many sleep in the same chamber. A young woman remarked to us that if she had a letter to write, she did it on the head of a bandbox, sitting on a trunk, as there was no space for a table.

So live and toil the young women of our country in the boardinghouses and manufactories which the rich an influential of our land have built for them.

Mary Paul, Letters Home (1845, 1846)

The following documents are letters from Mary Paul, an operative at the Lowell mills, to her father in Claremont, New Hampshire. Mary was fifteen years old, and typical of many of the young women who worked in Lowell and similar mill towns. Mill work offered women like Mary the possibility of independence—Mary herself worked away from home for twelve years before her marriage. And, like Mary Paul, most women did not make a permanent commitment to factory work. Because of this and other factors, rural women proved only to be a temporary fix to the needs of industrialization, and by the 1840s and 1850s they were replaced by immigrant, largely Irish, labor.[*]

Saturday Sept. 13th 1845

Dear Father

. . . I want you to consent to let me go to Lowell if you can. I think it would be much better for me than to stay about here. I could earn more to begin with than I can any where about here. I am in need of clothes which I cannot get if I stay about here and for that reason I want to go to Lowell or some other place. We all think if I could go with some steady girl that I might do well. I want you to think of it and make up your mind. . . .

Mary

Woodstock Nov 8 1845

Dear Father

As you wanted me to let you know when I am going to start for Lowell, I improve this opportunity to write you. Next Thursday the 13th of this month is the day set or the Thursday afternoon. I should like to have you come down. If you come bring Henry if you can for I should like to see him before I go. . . .

Mary

---

[*] From "The Letters of Mary Paul, 1845–1849," in *Vermont History* 48, ed. Thomas Dublin, (Montpelier, VT: Vermont Historical Society, 1980). Reprinted with permission of Vermont Historical Society.

Lowell Nov 20th 1845

Dear Father

. . . Went to a boarding house and staid until Monday night. On Saturday after I got here Luthera Griffith went round with me to find a place but we were unsuccessful. On Monday we started again and were more successful. We found a place in a spinning room and the next morning I went to work. I like very well have 50 cts first payment increasing every payment as I get along in work have a first rate overseer and a very good boarding place. . . . It cost me $3.25 to come. Stage fare was $3.00 and lodging at Windsor, 25 cts. Had to pay only 25 cts for board for 9 days after I got here before I went into the mill. Had 2.50 left with which I got a bonnet and some other small articles. . . .

excuse bad writing and mistakes

This from your own daughter

Mary

Lowell Dec 21st 1845

Dear Father

. . . I am well which is one comfort. My life and health are spared while others are cut off. Last Thursday one girl fell down and broke her neck which caused instant death. She was going in or coming out of the mill and slipped down it being very icy. The same day a man was killed by the cars. Another had nearly all of his ribs broken. Another was nearly killed by falling down and having a bale of cotton fall on him. Last Tuesday we were paid. In all I had six dollars and sixty cents paid $4.68 for board. With the rest I got me a pair of rubbers and a pair of 50.cts shoes. Next payment I am to have a dollar a week beside my board. . . . Perhaps you would like something about our regulations about going in and coming out of the mill. At 5 o'clock in the morning the bell rings for the folks to get up and get breakfast. At half past six it rings for the girls to get up and at seven they are called into the mill. At half past 12 we have dinner are called back again at one and stay till half past seven. I get along very well with my work. . . .

This from

Mary S Paul

Lowell April 12th 1846

Dear Father

. . . The overseer tells me that he never had a girl get along better than I do and that he will do the best he can by me. I stand it well, though they tell me that I am growing very poor. I was paid nine shillings a week last payment and am to have more this one though we have been out considerable for backwater which will take off a good deal.* The Agent promises to pay us nearly as much as we should have made but I do not think that he will. . . . I have a very good boarding place have enough to eat and that which is good enough. The girls are all kind and obliging. The girls that I room with are all from Vermont and good girls too. . . .

Resolutions of the Boston Carpenters' Strike (1845)

The Boston Carpenters' strike was one of the earliest in which the ten-hour day was a principal issue. Work hours (in addition to pay) were a prominent issue in later factory strikes in Lowell and elsewhere in New England. The journeymen in the Boston strike also expected a "family wage." Unlike the girls at Lowell, men needed to support families on their salaries. The master carpenters, however, suggest that the strike may not be the work of native Bostonians but some "foreign growth"—perhaps some of the newly arrived Irish and German immigrants.†

Resolutions of Journeymen Carpenters

Notice to house carpenters and housewrights in the country. An advertisement having appeared in the papers of this city, giving information that there is at this time a great demand for workmen in this branch of mechanical business in this city, it is considered a duty to state for the benefit of our brethren of the trade that we are not aware of any considerable demand for labor in this business, as there is, at this time, a very considerable number of journeymen carpenters who are out of employ, and the probable inducement which led to the communication refereed to arises from a disposition manifested on the part of the builders in this city to make their own terms

---

* Mary quoted her wages in English currency, but she was almost certainly paid in American money. Nine shillings would be equal to $1.50. Mary was referring to her wages exclusive of room and board charges. "Backwater" was caused by heavy run-off from rains and melting snow. The high water levels caused water to back up and block the waterwheel.

† From *A Documentary History of American Industrial Society*, John R. Commons et al, eds. (Cleveland: Arthur H. Clark Company, 1910), VI, 76–77, 79–81.

as to the price of labor and the number of hours labor which shall hereafter constitute a day's work. It being a well-known fact that the most unreasonable requirements have been hitherto extracted with regard to the terms of labor of journeymen mechanics in this city; and it is further well known that in the cities of New York, Philadelphia, Baltimore, and most of the other cities of much more liberal and equitable course of policy has been adopted by the master-builders, on this subject, giving to their journeymen that fair and liberal support to which they are unquestionably entitled. It is an undoubted fact that, on the present system, it is impossible for a journeyman housewright and house carpenter to maintain a family at the present time with the wages which are now usually given to the journeymen house carpenters in this city.

Resolutions of Master Carpenters

Resolved, That we learn with surprise and regret that a large number of those who are employed as journeymen in this city have entered into a combination for the purpose of altering the time of commencing and terminating their daily labor from that which has been customary from time immemorial, thereby lessening the amount of labor each day in a very considerable degree.

Resolved, That we consider such a combination as unworthy of that useful and industrious class of the community who are engaged in it; that it is fraught with numerous and pernicious evils, not only as respect their employers but the public at large, and especially themselves; for all journeymen of good character and of skill may expect very soon to become masters and, like us, the employers of others; and by the measure which they are now inclined to adopt they will entail upon themselves the inconvenience to which they seem desirous that we should not be exposed?

Resolved, That we consider the measure proposed, as calculated to exert a very unhappy influence on our apprentices—by seducing them from that course of industry and economy of time to which we are anxious to inure them. That it will expose the journeymen themselves to many temptations and improvident practices from which they are happily secure; while they attend to that wise and salutary maxim of mechanics, "Mind your business." That we consider idleness as the most deadly bane to usefulness and honorable living; and knowing (such is human nature that, where there is no necessity, there is no exertion, we fear and dread the consequences of such a measure upon the morals and well-being of society).

Resolved, That we cannot believe this project to have originated with many of the faithful and industrious sons of New England but are compelled to consider it an evil of foreign growth, and one which, we hope and trust, will not take root in the favored soil of Massachusetts. And especially that our city, the early rising and industry of whose inhabitants are universally proverbial, may not be infested with the unnatural production.

Resolved, That if such a measure were ever to be proper and necessary, the time has not yet arrived when it is so; if it would ever be just, it cannot be at a time like the present, when builders have generally made their engagements and contracts for the season, having predicated their estimates and prices upon the original state of things in reference to journeymen. And we appeal therefore to the good sense, the honesty, and justice of all who are engaged in this combination, and ask them to review their doings, contemplate their consequences, and then act as becomes men of sober sense and of prudence.

Resolved, finally, That we will make no alteration in the manner of employing journeymen as respects the time of commencing and leaving work and that we will employ no man who persists in adhering to the project of which we complain.

9

The Ferment of Reform

American society in the antebellum period experienced many rapid cultural, economic, and social changes. One of the responses to these changes was a "reform" movement that permeated all parts of society. Rooted in the ideals of the Second Great Awakening, many American reformers believed in and strove for the perfectibility of man. While some groups focused on individual reform, others looked toward reforming specific American institutions. Most of the reform groups were located in the North, where the Industrial Revolution had begun to affect all aspects of its society and change was occurring at a far more accelerated rate than in the South. Ironically, while many of these groups wanted to perfect life in America, they would only end up exacerbating the growing tensions and strains between the North and the South.

The wave of religious revivals that ran through New England and the frontier from the turn of the century through the 1830s was reenergized in upstate New York and the Midwest under the influence of a new generation of revivalists like Charles Finney, a former lawyer, who was one of the most compelling speakers of his day. In the 1820s and 1830s, Finney believed anyone could be converted and "saved" through the magical effects of the "powerful excitement" brought on by a revival. The selection included here is Finney's description of revivalism and his defense of revivals to those who would suggest the church pursue its mission in more discreet ways.

As the northern economy industrialized, many began to question industrialization's effect on the people of the region. Like the revivalists, they believed in human perfectibility and did not see industrialization as the path to that ideal. Some withdrew from a world they thought flawed and created their own "utopian" communities. George Ripley, a Boston Unitarian minister organized Brook Farm in Massachusetts in 1841, believing that self-realization could be found through communal sharing in a pastoral setting. Among the literary figures who came to the farm was Nathaniel Hawthorne, a writer who celebrated the transcendence of the human heart in the face of social intolerance. Hawthorne's letter from Brook Farm to his wife describes his experiences there.

One of the most effective reforms of this period concerned the changes in northern schools. As industrialization took hold, it became painfully clear that the educational system was inadequate. Traditional classical education had no relevance in preparing a workforce necessary for an industrial economic system. Recognizing this, Massachusetts, under the leadership of Horace Mann, created the blueprint for the modern American school system. Appointed the first state superintendent of schools in 1837, Mann introduced programs that led to the institution of universal public education (for white children) across the country. In his *Report of the Massachusetts Board of Education*, Mann explained why public education was integral to the economic success of the United States.

No reform movement, however, had a more dramatic effect on antebellum America than abolitionism. This movement had a long history that began with the Quakers during the colonial period. After 1830, its activity would be centered in the North. While earlier antislavery groups, like the American Colonization Society, had sought amicable solutions for planters and slaves—"gradual abolition," colonization, or humanization of the institution—the new reformers stridently sought immediate abolition of slavery.

One of the catalysts for this change was William Lloyd Garrison, the founder of the New England Anti-Slavery Society and the publisher of *The Liberator*, the leading abolitionist journal. Beginning with the first articles published in the *The Liberator*, Garrison's challenged northern—as well as southern—society to consider its relationship to slavery.

African Americans were active in the abolitionist movement—many were prominent speakers on the mainstream abolitionist circuit and organized their own, separate, abolitionist societies as well, in part because some northern abolitionist groups discriminated against them. The most prominent African-American abolitionist leader was Frederick Douglass, a former slave from Maryland. In general, white abolitionist leaders (including the radical Garrison) preferred to have black leaders like Douglass describe the horrors of slavery and appeal to sentiments rather than offer political analysis. Partly because of this, Douglass eventually broke from Garrison and began endorsing more radical analysis of slavery and speaking out about political events. This excerpt from Douglass's Independence Day speech in 1851 showcases his rhetorical powers.

Not all activists in the antebellum period were abolitionists and reformers. Some white southerners, in particular, dedicated themselves to the defense and justification of slavery. Slavery's defenders referred to its biblical antecedents and "scientific" justification and argued that it was the destiny of slaves (read: blacks) to be taken care of by benevolent masters (read: whites). Among these defenders was George Fitzhugh, who believed that the "Negro is but grown child and must be governed as a child." In the selection included here, Fitzhugh compares the treatment of slaves with that of "wage slaves"—northern factory workers, "slaves" to capital—who worked under more difficult circumstances than those of southern slaves.

Women, including Angelina and Sarah Grimke, Lucretia Mott, and Elizabeth Cady Stanton, were actively involved in the antislavery movement and through it developed a growing awareness of their own disenfranchisement. Within the abolitionist community, there were considerable misgivings about the equality of women and women's rights. At the World Anti-Slavery Congress in 1840, Elizabeth

Cady Stanton and Lucretia Mott were not permitted to speak—because they were women. In response, they called a convention at Seneca Falls, New York, in 1848, to advocate the rights of women. The Declaration of Sentiments, reprinted here, resulted from that convention and articulates the women's desire for equality.

Study Questions

1. What similar assumptions about human nature and society do the reformers and revivalists in this chapter share?

2. In what ways is Finney's revivalist strategy—encouraging "excitement"— reflected in the strategies of other reformers like Garrison and Douglass?

3. Are there hints of Hawthorne's later criticisms of utopian communitarianism in his letter from Brook Farm? Why might he believe that he had "gained strength wonderfully" from his farming experience?

4. What were Horace Mann's expectations of the common school? What were his expectations of American society?

5. How did Garrison's and Douglass's rhetoric differ? Were there differences between the audiences they addressed? the audiences' expectations of the speakers?

6. Itemize Fitzhugh's many justifications for slavery. Why does he argue that prejudice is stronger against African Americans in the North than in the South. Would Garrison and/or Douglass agree with him on this point?

7. In what way did the Declaration of Sentiments deny or uphold the view of women's moral superiority?

Charles Finney, "Religious Revival" (1835)

Some Christians, including Catholics and upper-class individuals, believed revivalism—with its group conversions, camp meetings, and abundance of religious fervor that sometimes included speaking in tongues, screaming, and dancing—to be an embarrassment or a perversion. Finney, perhaps the most successful revivalist of his day, believed in the possibility of group conversion through the hypnotic work of an effective minister, and thought the revival movement absolutely essential to the future of Christianity.[*]

---

[*] From Charles G. Finney, *What a Revival of Religion is* (1835).

It is altogether improbable that religion will ever make progress among *heathen* nations except through the influence of revivals. The attempt is now making to do it by education, and other cautious and gradual improvements. But so long as the laws of mind remain what they are, it cannot be done in this way. There must be excitement sufficient to wake up the dormant moral powers, and roll back the tide of degradation and sin. And precisely so far as our own land approximately to heathenism, it is impossible for God or man to promote religion is such a state of things but by powerful excitements.—This is evident from the fact that this has always been the way in which God has done it. God does not create these excitements, and choose this method to promote religion for nothing, or without reason. Where mankind are so reluctant to obey God, they will not obey until they are excited. For instance, how many there are who know that they ought to be religious, but they are afraid if they become pious they will be laughed at by their companions. Many are wedded to idols, others are procrastinating repentance, until they are settled in life, or until they have secured some favorite worldly interest. Such persons never will give up their false shame, or relinquish their ambitious schemes, till they are so excited that they cannot contain themselves any longer. . . .

It is presupposed that the church is sunk down in a backslidden state, and a revival consists in the return of the church from her backsliding, and in the conversion of sinners.

1. A revival always includes conviction of sin on the part of the church. Backslidden professors cannot wake up and begin right away in the service of God, without deep searching of heart. The fountains of sin need to be broken up. In a true revival, Christians are always brought under such convictions; they see their sins in such a light, that often they find it impossible to maintain a hope of their acceptance with God. It does not always go to that extent; but there are always, in a genuine revival, deep convictions of sin, and often cases of abandoning all hope.

2. Backslidden Christians will be brought to repentance. A revival is nothing else than a new beginning of obedience to God. Just as the case of a converted sinner, the first step is a deep repentance, a breaking down of heart, a getting down into the dust before God, with deep humility, and forsaking of sin.

3. Christians will have their fair renewed. While they are in their backslidden state they are blind to the state of sinners. Their hearts are as hard as marble. The truths of the Bible only appear like a dream. They admit it to be all true; their conscience and their judgment assent to it; but their faith does not see it standing out in bold relief, in all the burning realities of eternity. But when they enter into a revival, they no longer see men as trees walking, but they see things in that strong light which will renew the love of God in their hearts. This will lead them to labor zealously to bring others to him. They will feel grieved that others do not love God, when they love him so much. And they will set themselves feelingly to persuade their neighbors to give him their heart. So their love to men will be renewed. They will be filled with a tender and burning love for souls. They will have a longing desire for the salvation of the whole world. They will be in agony for individuals whom they want to have saves; their friends, relations, enemies. They will not only be urging them to give their hearts to

God, but they will carry them to God in the arms of faith, and with strong crying and tears beseech God to have mercy on them, and save their souls from endless burning.

4. A revival breaks the power of the world and sin over Christians. It bring them to such vantage ground that they get a fresh I pulse towards heaven. They have a new foretaste of heaven, and new desires after union to God; and the charm of the world is broken, and the power of sin overcome.

5. When the churches are thus awakened and reformed, the reformation and salvation of sinners will follow, going through the same stages of conviction, repentance, and reformation. Their hearts will be broken down and changed. Very often the most abandoned profligates are among the subjects. Harlots, and drunkards, infidels, and all sorts of abandoned characters, are awakened and converted. The worst part of human society are softened, and reclaimed, and made to appear as lovely specimens of the beauty of holiness. . . .

You see the error of those who are beginning to think that religion can be better promoted in the world without revivals, and who are disposed to give up all efforts to produce religious excitements. Because there are evils arising in some instances out of great excitements on the subject of religion, they are of opinion that it is best to dispense with them altogether. This cannot, and must not be. True, there is danger of abuses. In cases of great *religious* as well as all other excitements, more for less incidental evils may be expected of course. . . . So in revivals of religion, it is found by experience, that in the present state of the world, religion cannot be promoted to any considerable extent without them.

Nathaniel Hawthorne, A Letter from Brook Farm (1841)

Brook Farm was a utopian community dedicated to merging "intellectual and manual labor" founded in Massachusetts by George Ripley and Bronson Alcott, friends of Ralph Waldo Emerson. Hawthorne lived on Brook Farm in 1841 and his later book *The Blithedale Romance* (1852) was harshly critical of unflinching and naïve optimism of the community. This letter to his wife, however, provides a detailed and sympathetic account of the daily life of the community.*

As the weather precludes all possibility of ploughing, hoeing, sowing and other such operations, I bethink me that you may have no objection to hear something of my whereabout and whatabout. You are to know then, that I took up my abode here on the

* Reprinted from *Voices from America's Past*, eds. Richard B. Morris and James Woodress (New York: E. P. Dutton & Co., 1961, 1962, 1963), 2:46–47.

12th ultimo, in the midst of a snowstorm, which kept us all idle for a day or two. At the first glimpse of fair weather, Mr. Ripley summoned us into the cowyard and introduced me to an instrument with four prongs, commonly called a dung-fork. With this tool, I have already assisted to load twenty or thirty carts of manure, and shall take part in loading nearly three hundred more. Besides, I have planted potatoes and peas, cut straw and hay for the cattle, and done various other mighty works. This very morning, I milked three cows; and I milk two or three every night and morning. The weather has been so unfavorable, that we have worked comparatively little in the fields; but, nevertheless, I have gained strength wonderfully—grown quite a giant, in fact—and can do a day's work without the slightest inconvenience. In short, I am transformed into a complete farmer.

This is one of the most beautiful places I ever saw in my life, and as secluded as if it were a hundred miles from any city or village. There are woods, in which we can ramble all day, without meeting anybody, or scarcely seeing a house. Our house stands apart from the main road; so that we are not troubled even with passengers looking at us. Once in a while, we have a transcendental visitor, such as Mr. [Bronson] Alcott; but, generally, we pass whole days without seeing a single face, save those of the brethren. At this present time, our effective force consists of Mr. Ripley, Mr. Farley (a farmer from the far west), Rev. Warren Burton (author of various celebrated works), three young men and boys, who are under Mr. Ripley's care, and William Allen, his hired man, who has the chief direction of our agricultural labors. In the female part of the establishment there is Mrs. Ripley and two women folks. The whole fraternity eat together; and such a delectable way of life has never been seen on earth, since the days of the early Christians. We get up at half-past four, breakfast at half-past six, dine at half-past twelve, and go to bed at nine.

The thin frock, which you made for me, is considered a most splendid article; and I should not wonder if it were to become the summer uniform of the community. I have a thick frock, likewise; but it is rather deficient in grace, though extremely warm and comfortable. I wear a tremendous pair of cow-hide boots, with soles two inches thick. Of course, when I come to see you, I shall wear my farmer's dress.

We shall be very much occupied during most of this month, ploughing and planting; so that I doubt whether you will see me for two or three weeks. You have the portrait by this time, I suppose; so you can very well dispense with the original. When you write to me (which I beg you will do soon) direct your letter to West Roxbury, as there are two post offices in the town. I would write more; but William Allen is going to the village, and must have this letter; so good-bye.

Nath Hawthorne
Ploughman

Horace Mann, from *Report of the Massachusetts Board of Education* (1848)

Horace Mann was a typical reformer who was atypically successful in institutionalizing his idealism. Under his direction, the state of Massachusetts standardized the operation of schools designed to produce the employees of the future—literate but also obedient, industrious, and punctual. Mann believed the "common school" would support and further the basic ideals of the Republic.*

Without undervaluing any other human agency, it may be safely affirmed that the common school, improved and energized as it can easily be, may become the most effective and benignant of all the forces of civilization. Two reasons sustain this position. In the first place, there is an universality in its operation, which can be affirmed of no other institution whatever. If administered in the spirit of justice and conciliation, all the rising generation may be brought within the circle of its reformatory and elevating influences. And, in the second place, the materials upon which it operates are so pliant and ductile as to be susceptible of assuming a greater variety of forms than any other earthly work of the Creator. . . .

According to the European theory, men are divided into classes—some to toil and earn, others to seize and enjoy. According to the Massachusetts theory, all are to have an equal chance for earning, and equal security in the enjoyment of what they earn. A republican form of government, without intelligence in the people, must be, on a vast scale, what a mad-house without superintendent or keepers would be on a small one. . . . However elevated the moral character of a constituency may be, however, well-informed in matters of general science or history, yet they must, if citizens of a republic, understand something of the true nature and functions of the government under which they live. . . .

The establishment of a republican government, without well-appointed and efficient means for the universal education of the people, is the most rash and foolhardy experiment ever tried by man. . . . It may be an easy thing to make a republic, but it a very laborious thing to make republicans; and woe to the republic that rests upon no better foundations than ignorance, selfishness, and passion! . . .

Such, then, . . . is the Massachusetts system of common schools. Reverently it recognizes and affirms the sovereign rights of the Creator, sedulously and sacredly it guards the religious rights of the creature. . . . In a social and political sense, it is a free school system. It knows no distinction of rich and poor, of bond and free, or between those, who, in the imperfect light of this world, are seeking, through different avenues, to reach the gate of heaven. Without money and without price, it throws open its doors,

* From Twelfth Annual Report, 1848, *Annual Reports on Education* (Boston: Horace B. Fuller, 1868), 650–754.

and spreads the table of its bounty, for all the children of the State. Like the sun, it shines not only upon the good, but upon the evil, that they may become good; and, like the rain, its blessings descend not only upon the just, but upon the unjust, that their injustice may depart from them, and be know no more.

William Lloyd Garrison, from *The Liberator* (1831)

William Lloyd Garrison was a radical abolitionist from Massachusetts who advocated immediate abolition of slavery. Garrison outraged his contemporaries, was attacked and harassed by mobs, and alienated moderate abolitionists—who advocated "gradual" emancipation. *The Liberator* was Garrison's newspaper and this excerpt is from its first issue, declaring its editorial stand bravely and unequivocally.*

During my recent tour for the purpose of exciting the minds of the people by a series of discourses on the subject of slavery, every place that I visited gave fresh evidence of the fact that a great revolution in public sentiment was to be effected in the free states—and particularly in New England—than at the South. I find contempt more bitter, opposition more active, detraction more relentless, prejudice more stubborn, and apathy more frozen, than among slaveowners themselves. Of course, there were individual exceptions to the contrary.

This state of things afflicted but did not dishearten me. I determined, at every hazard, to lift up the standard of emancipation in the eyes of the nation, within sight of Bunker Hill and in the birthplace of liberty. That standard is now unfurled; and long may it float, unhurt by the spoliations of time or the missiles of a desperate foe—yea, till every chain be broken, and every bondman set free! Let Southern oppressors tremble—let all the enemies of the persecuted blacks tremble. . . .

Assenting to the "self-evident truth" maintained in the American Declaration of Independence "that all men are created equal, and endowed by their Creator with certain inalienable rights—among which are life, liberty, and the pursuit of happiness," I shall strenuously contend for the immediate enfranchisement of our slave population. . . . In Park Street Church, on the Fourth of July, 1829, in an address on slavery, I unreflectingly assented to the popular but pernicious doctrine of gradual abolition. I seize this opportunity to make a full and unequivocal recantation, and thus publicly to ask pardon of my God, of my country, and of my brethren the poor slaves, for having uttered a sentiment so full of timidity, injustice, and absurdity. . . .

---

* *The Liberator* (Boston), Jan. 1, 1831.

I am aware that many object to the severity of my language; but is there not cause for severity? I will be as harsh as truth, and as uncompromising as justice. On this subject I do not wish to think, or speak, or write, with moderation. No! No! Tell a man whose house is on fire to give a moderate alarm; tell him to moderately rescue his wife from the hands of the ravisher; tell the mother to gradually extricate her babe from the fire into which it has fallen—but urge me not to use moderation in a cause like the present. I am in earnest—will not equivocate—I will not excuse—I will not retreat in a single inch—and I will be heard. The apathy of the people is enough to make every statue leap from its pedestal, and to hasten the resurrection of the dead.

It is pretended that I am retarding the cause of emancipation by the coarseness of my invective and the precipitancy of my measures. The charge is not true. On this question my influence—humble as it is—is felt at this moment to a considerable extent, and shall be felt in coming years—not perniciously, but beneficially—not as a curse, but as a blessing. And posterity will bear testimony that I was right.

Frederick Douglass, Independence Day Speech (1852)

Fred Douglass spent his young years as a slave in Maryland where he was (illegally) taught to read and write. As a young man, he escaped to New York City and later Massachusetts. In his twenties, he became an abolitionist speaker of renown and was the leading black abolitionist of his time. This speech was given in Rochester, New York on Independence Day 1852.*

Fellow citizens above your national, tumultuous joy, I hear the mournful wail of millions! whose chains, heave and grievous yesterday, are, today, rendered more intolerable by the jubilee shouts that reach them. If I do forget, it I do not faithfully remember those bleeding children of sorrow this day, "may my right hand forger her cunning, and may ny tongue cleave to the roof of my mouth"! To forget them, to pass lightly over their wrongs, and to chime in with the popular theme would be treason most scandalous and shocking, and would make me a reproach before God and the world. My subject, them, fellow citizens, is *American Slavery*. I shall see this day and its popular characteristics from the slav;s point of view. Standing there identified with the American bondman, making his wrongs mine. I do not hesitate to declare with all my soul that the character and conduct of this nation never looked blacker to me than on this Fourth of July! Whether we turn to the declarations of the past or to the professions of the present, the conduct of the nation seems equally hideous and

* Reprinted from *The American Reader: Words That Moved a Nation*, ed. Diane Ravitch (New York: HarperCollins, 1991), 155–156.

revolting. America is false to the past, false to the present, and solemnly binds herself to be false to the future. Standing with God and the crushed and bleeding slave on this occasion, I will,in the name of humanity which is outraged, in the name of liberty which is fettered, in the name of the Constitution and the Bible which are disregarded and trampled upon, All the emphasis I can command, everything that serves to perpetuate slavery the great sin and shame of America! "I will not equivocate, I will not excuse"; I will use the severest of language I can command; and yet not one word shall escape that any man, whose judgment is not blinded by prejudice, or who is not at heart a slaveholder, shall not confess to be right and just.

But I fancy I hear someone of my audience say, "It is just in this circumstance that your and your brother abolitionists fail to make a favorable impression on the public mind. Would you argue more and denounce less, would you persuade more and rebuke less, your cause would be much more likely to succeed." But, I submit, where all is plain, there is nothing to be argued. What point in the antislavery creed would you have me argue? On what branch of the subject do the people of this country need light? Must I undertake to prove that the slave is a man? That point is conceded already. Nobody doubts it. The slaveholders themselves acknowledge it the enactment of laws for their government. They acknowledge it when they punish disobedience on the part of the slave. There are seventy-two crimes in the state of Virginia which, if committed by a black man (no matter how ignorant he be), subject him to the punishment of death, while only two of the same crimes will subject a white man to the like punishment. What is this but the acknowledgment that the slave is a moral, intellectual, and responsible being? The manhood of the slave is conceded. It is admitted in the fact that the Southern statute books are covered with enactments forbidding, under severe fines and penalties, the teaching of the slave to read or to write. When you can point to any such laws in reference to the beasts of the field, then I may consent to argue the manhood of the slave. When the dogs in your streets, when the fowls of the air, when the cattle on your hills, when the fish of the sea and the reptiles that crawl shall be unable to distinguish the slave from a brute, then will I argue with you that the slave is a man!

For the present, it is enough to affirm the equal manhood of the Negro race. It is not astonishing that, while we are plowing, planting, and reaping, using all kinds of mechanical tools erecting houses, constructing bridges, building ships, working in metals of brass, iron, copper and silver, and gold; that, while we are reading, writing, and ciphering, acting as clerks, merchants and secretaries, having among us lawyers, doctors, ministers, poets, authors, editors, orators, and teachers; that, while we are engaged in all manner of enterprises common to other men, digging gold in California, capturing the whale in the Pacific, feeding sheep and cattle on the hillside, living, moving, acting, thinking, planning, living in families as husbands, wives, and children, and, above all, confessing and worshipping the Christian's God, and looking hopefully for life and immortality beyond the grave, we are called upon to prove that we are men!

Would you have me argue that man is entitled to liberty? That he is the rightful owner of his own body? You have already declared it. Must I argue the wrongfulness of slavery? Is that a question for republicans? Is it to be settled by the rules of logic and argumentation, as a matter beset with great difficulty, involving a doubtful application of the principle of justice, hart to be understood? How should I look today, in the presence of Americans, dividing and subdividing a discourse, to show that men have a natural right to freedom? speaking of it relatively and positively, negatively and affirmatively? To do so would be to make myself ridiculous and to offer an insult to your understanding. There is not a man beneath the canopy of heaven that does not know that slaver is wrong for him.

What, am I to argue that is wrong to make men brutes, to rob them of their liberty, to work them without wages, to keep them ignorant of their relations to their fellow men, to beat them with sticks, to flay their flesh with the last, to load their limbs with irons, to hunt them with dogs, to sell them at auction, to sunder their families, to knock out their teeth, to burn their flesh, to starve them into obedience and submission to their masters? Must I argue that a system them marked with blood, and stained with pollution, is wrong? No! I will not. I have better employment for my time and strength than such arguments would imply.

What, then remains to be argued? Is it that slavery is not divine; that God did not establish it; that our doctors of divinity are mistaken? There is blasphemy in the thought. That which is inhuman cannot be divine? Who can reason on such a proposition? They that can may; I cannot. The time for such argument is past.

At a time like this, scorching iron, not convincing argument, is needed. O! had I the ability, and could I reach the nation's ear, I would today pour out a fiery stream of biting ridicule, blasting reproach, withering sarcasm, and stern rebuke. For it is not light that is needed, but fire; it is not the gentle shower, but thunder. We need the storm, the whirlwind, and the earthquake. The feeling of the nation must be quickened, the conscience of the nation must be startled; the hypocrisy of the nation must be exposed; and its crimes against God and man must be proclaimed and denounced.

What, to the American slave is your Fourth of July? I answer: a day that reveals to him, more than all other days in the year, the gross injustice and cruelty to which he s the constant victim. To him, your celebration is a sham; your boasted liberty an unholy license; your national greatness, swelling vanity; your sound of rejoicing are empty and heartless; your denunciation of tyrants, brass-fronted impudence; your shouts of liberty and equality, hollow mockery; your prayers and hymns, your sermons and thanksgivings with all your religious parade and solemnity, are, to Him, mere bombast, fraud, deception, impiety, and hypocrisy a thin veil to cover up crimes which would disgrace a nation of savages. There is not a nation of savages. There is not a nation on earth guilty of practices more shocking and bloody than are the people of the United States at this very hour.

Go where you may, search where you will, roam through all the monarchies and despotisms of the Old World, travel through South America, search out every abuse, and when you have found the last, lay your facts by the side of the everyday practices of this nation, and you will say with that, for revolting barbarity and shameless hypocrisy, America reigns without a rival.

George Fitzhugh, "The Blessings of Slavery" (1857)

This selection, from Fitzhugh's *Cannibals All! or Slaves Without Masters*, is a justification and defense of slavery. In other portions of his radical book, Fitzhugh argued that (as his title implies) work relations made cannibals of everyone and that, ideally, liberty was meant only for the few—that "some were born with saddles on their backs, and others booted and spurred to ride them—and the riding does them good." In justifying slavery in principle rather than as only a natural state for nonwhites, Fitzhugh ran counter to the general ideology of the antebellum period, a time of increasing democratization, expansion, and participation. In doing so, he became fodder for those northerners who were terrified of a "slave power" conspiracy emanating from the South.[*]

The negro slaves of the South are the happiest, and in some sense, the freest people in the world. The children and the aged and infirm work not at all, and yet have all the comforts and necessaries of life provided for them. They enjoy liberty, because they are oppressed neither by care or labor. The women do little hard work, and are protected from the despotism of their husbands by their masters. The negro men and stout boys work, on the average, in good weather, no more than nine hours a day. The balance of their time is spent in perfect abandon. Besides, they have their Sabbaths and holidays. White men, with som muh of license and abandon, would die of ennui; but negroes luxuriate in corporeal and mental repose. With their faces upturned to the sun, they can sleep at any hour; and quiet sleep is the gretest of human enjoyments. "Blessed be the man who invented sleep." 'Tis happiness in itself—and results from contentment in the present, and confident assurance of the future. We do not know whether free laborers ever sleep. They are fools to do so; for, whilst they sleep, the wily and watchful capitalist is devising means to ensnare and exploit them. The free laborer must work or starve. He is more of a slave than the negro, because he works longer and harder for less allowance than the slave, and has no holiday, because the cares of life with him begin when its labors end. He has no liberty and not a single right. . . .

Until the lands of America are appropriated by a few, population becomes dense, competition among laborers active, employment uncertain, and wages low, the personal liberty of all the whites will continue to be a blessing. We have vast unsettled territories; population may cease to increase slowly, as in most countries, and many centuries may elapse before the question will be practically suggested, whether slavery to capital be preferable to slavery to human masters. But the negro has neither energy

---

[*] From George Fitzhugh, *Cannibals All! or Slaves Without Masters* (Richmond, Va.: A. Morris, 1857), 294–299.

nor enterprise, and, even in our sparser populations, finds with his improvident habits, that his liberty is a curse to himself, and a greater curse to the society around him. These considerations, and others equally obvious, have induced the South to attempt to defend negro slavery as an exceptional institution, admitting, nay asserting, that slavery, in the general or in the abstract, is morally wrong, and against common right. With singular inconsistency, after making this admission, which admits away the authority of the Bible, of profane history, and of the almost universal practice of mankind—they turn around and attempt to bolster up the cause of negro slavery by these very exploded authorities. If we mean not to repudiate all divine, and almost all human authority in favor of slavery, we must vindicate that institution in the abstract.

To insist that a status of society, which has been almost universal, and which is expressly and continually justified by Holy Writ, is its natural, normal, and necessary status, under the ordinary circumstances, is on its face a plausible and probable proposition. To insist on less, is to yield our cause, and to give up our religion; for if white slavery be morally wrong, be a violation of natural rights, the Bible cannot be true. Human and divine authority do seem in the general to concur, in establishing the expediency of having masters and slaves of different races. In very many nations of antiquity, and in some of modern times, the law has permitted the native citizens to become slaves to each other. But few take advantage of such laws; and the infrequency of the practice establishes the general truth that master and slave should be of different national descent. In some respects the wider the difference the better, as the slave will feel less mortified by his position. In other respects, it may be that too wide a difference hardens the hearts and brutalizes the feeling of both master and slave. The civilized man hates the savage, and the savage returns the hatred with interest. Hence West India slavery of newly caught negroes is not a very humane, affectionate, or civilizing institution. Virginia negroes have become moral and intelligent. They love their master and his family, and the attachment is reciprocated. Still, we like the idle, but intelligent house-servants, better than the hard-used, but stupid outhands; and we like the mulatto better than the negro; yet the negro is generally more affectionate, contented, and faithful.

The world at large looks on negro slavery as much the worst form of slavery; because it is only acquainted with West India slavery. But our Southern slavery has become a benign and protective institution, and our negroes are confessedly better off than any free laboring population in the world. How can we contend that white slavery is wrong, whilst all the great body of free laborers are starving; and slaves, white or black, throughout the world, are enjoying comfort? . . .

The aversion to negroes, the antipathy of race, is much greater at the North than at the South; and it is very probable that this antipathy to the person of the negro, is confounded with or generates hatred of the institution with which he is usually connected. Hatred to slavery is very generally little more than hatred of negroes.

There is one strong argument in favor of negro slavery over all other slavery; that he, being unfitted for the mechanic arts, for trade, and all skillful pursuits, leaves those pursuits to be carried on by the whites; and does not bring all industry into disrepute, as in Greece and Rome, where the slaves were not only the artists and mechanics, but also the merchants.

Whilst, as a general and abstract question, negro slavery has no other claims over other forms of slavery, except that from inferiority, or rather peculiarity, of race, almost all negroes require masters, whilst only the children, the women, and the very weak, poor, and ignorant, &c., among the whites, need some protective and governing relation of this kind; yet as a subject of temporary, but worldwide importance, negro slavery has become the most necessary of all human institutions.

The African slave trade to America commenced three centuries and a half since. By the time of the American Revolution, the supply of slaves had exceeded the demand for slave labor, and the slaveholders, to get rid of a burden, and to prevent the increase of a nuisance, became violent opponents of the slave trade, and many of them abolitionists. New England, Bristol, and Liverpool, who reaped the profits of the trade, without suffering from the nuisance, stood out for a long time against its abolition. Finally, laws and treaties were made, and fleets fitted out to abolish it; and after a while, the slaves of most of South America, of the West Indies, and of Mexico were liberated. In the meantime, cotton, rice, sugar, coffee, tobacco, and other products of slave labor, came into universal use as necessaries of life. The population of Western Europe, sustained and stimulated by those products, was trebled, and that of the North increased tenfold. The products of slave labor became scarce and dear, and famines frequent. Now, it is obvious, that to emancipate all the negroes would be to starve Western Europe and our North. Not to extend and increase negro slavery, *pari passu*, with the extension and multiplication of free society, will produce much suffering. If all South America, Mexico, the West Indies, and our Union south of Mason and Dixon's line, of the Ohio and Missouri, were slaveholding, slave products would be abundant and cheap in free society; and their market for their merchandise, manufactures, commerce, &c., illimitable. Free white laborers might live in comfort and luxury on light work, but for the exacting and greedy landlords, bosses, and other capitalists.

We must confess, that overstock the world as you will with comforts and with luxuries, we do not see how to make capital relax its monopoly—how to do aught but tantalize the hireling. Capital, irresponsible capital, begets, and ever will beget, the *immedicabile vulnus* of so-called Free Society. It invades every recess of domestic life, infects its food, its clothing, its drink, its very atmosphere, and pursues the hireling, from the hovel to the poor-house, the prison and the grave. Do what he will, go where he will, capital pursues and persecutes him. "*Haeret lateri lethalis arundo!*"

Capital supports and protects the domestic slave; taxes, oppresses, and persecutes the free laborer.

Elizabeth Cady Stanton, Declaration of Sentiments (1848)

Elizabeth Cady Stanton (1815–1902) along with Lucretia Mott, played a major role in drafting the declaration that was presented at the Seneca Falls convention in 1848. The document paralleled the Declaration of Independence and listed the grievances of women, ending with the controversial request for women's rights.*

When, in the course of human events, it becomes necessary for one portion of the family of man to assume among the people of the earth a position different from that which they have hitherto occupied, but one to which the laws of nature and of nature's God entitle them, a decent respect to the opinions of mankind requires that they should declare the causes that impel them to such a course.

We hold these truths to be self-evident: that all men and women are created equal; that they are endowed by their Creator with certain inalienable rights; that among these are life, liberty, and the pursuit of happiness; that to secure these rights governments are instituted, deriving their just powers from the consent of the governed. Whenever any form of government becomes destructive of these ends, it is the right of those who suffer from it to refuse allegiance to it, and to insist upon the institution of a new government, laying its foundation on such principles, and organizing its powers in such form, as to them shall seem most likely to effect their safety and happiness. Prudence, indeed, will dictate that governments long established should not be changed for light and transient causes; and accordingly all experience has shown that mankind are more disposed to suffer, while evils are sufferable, than to right themselves by abolishing the forms to which they are accustomed. But when a long train of abuses and usurpations, pursuing invariably the same object, evinces a design to reduce them under absolute despotism, it is their duty to throw off such government, and to provide new guards for their future security. Such has been the patient sufferance of the women under this government, and such is now the necessity which constrains them to demand the equal station to which they are entitled.

The history of mankind is a history of repeated injuries and usurpations on the part of man toward woman, having in direct object the establishment of an absolute tyranny over her. To prove this, let facts be submitted to a candid word.

He has never permitted her to exercise her inalienable right to the elective franchise.

He has compelled her to submit to laws, in the formation of which she had no voice.

He has withheld from her rights which are given to the most ignorant and degraded men—both natives and foreigners.

Having deprived her of this first right of a citizen, the elective franchise, thereby leaving her without representation in the halls of legislation, he has oppressed her on all sides.

He has made her, if married, in the eye of the law, civilly dead.

He has taken from her all right in property, even to the wages she earns.

---

* From Elizabeth Cady Stanton, Susan B. Anthony, and Matilda J. Gage, eds., "Declaration of Sentiments," in *History of Woman Suffrage* (Rochester, N.Y.: Charles Mann, 1881), I: 67–94.

He has made her, morally, an irresponsible being, as she can commit many crimes with impunity, provided they be done in the presence of her husband. In the covenant of marriage, she is compelled to promise obedience to her husband, he becoming, to all intents and purposes, her master, the law giving him power to deprive her of her liberty, and to administer chastisement.

He has so framed the laws of divorce, as to what shall be the proper causes, and in case of separation, to whom the guardianship of the children shall be given, as to be wholly regardless of the happiness of women—the law, in all cases, going upon a false supposition of the supremacy of man, and giving all power into his hands.

After depriving her of all rights as a married woman, if single, and the owner of property, he has taxed her to support a government which recognizes her only when her property can be made profitable to it.

He has monopolized nearly all the profitable employments, and from those she is permitted to follow, she receives but a scanty remuneration. He closes against her all the avenues to wealth and distinction which he considers most honorable to himself. As a teacher of theology, medicine, or law, she is not known.

He has denied her the facilities for obtaining a thorough education, all colleges being closed against her.

He allows her in Church, as well as in State, but a subordinate position, claiming Apostolic authority for her exclusion from the ministry, and, with some exceptions, from any public participation in the affairs of the Church.

He has created a false public sentiment by giving to the world a different code of morals for men and women, by which the moral delinquencies which exclude women from society are not only tolerated, but deemed of little account in man.

He has usurped the prerogative of Jehovah himself, claiming it as his right to assign for her a sphere of action, when that belongs to her conscience and to her God.

He has endeavored, in every way he could, to destroy her confidence in her own powers, to lessen her self-respect, and to make her willing to lead a dependent and abject life.

Now, in the view of this entire disfranchisement of one-half of the people of this country, their social and religious degradation, in view of the unjust laws above mentioned, and because women do feel themselves aggrieved, oppressed, and fraudulently deprived of their most sacred rights, we insist that they have immediate admission to all the rights and privileges which belong to them as citizens of the United States.

In entering upon the great work before us, we anticipate no small amount of misconception, misrepresentation, and ridicule; but we shall use every instrumentality within our power to effect our object. We shall employ agents, circulate tracts, petition the State and National legislatures, and endeavor to enlist the pulpit and the press on our behalf. We hope this Convention will be followed by a series of Conventions embracing every part of the country.

10

Living in and Rebelling Against Antebellum America

By 1850 America was on the verge of becoming a modern society. The North and the West were undergoing revolutions in their economies. These changes would draw them closer together as they began to reap the benefits of technological advances that would revolutionize every segment of their societies. The South did not industrialize and instead maintained its traditional agriculturally based economy, and found itself increasingly isolated from the rest of country.

Northern society leaped toward modernization as its economy shifted to large-scale factory production of commodities. This economic transformation affected all aspects of its society. In the generation or so before the Civil War, middle-class men and women faced new expectations, obligations, and roles. A woman was expected to stay home and to take care of the house, her children, and her husband, while men were expected to provide for their families. These expectations are revealed in some of the letters reprinted here: Two of the letters are from a larger correspondence, in which Joshua Wilson, a Presbyterian minister from Cincinnati, Ohio, and his wife, Sarah, counsel their son, George, on becoming an adult. The two letters included here, signed by Joshua and his daughter, George's sister Sally, deal with courtship. The last letter is from a planter in eastern North Carolina to his daughter who was considering marriage. Against her father's advice, Mary Matilda Norcom married her suitor; her parents disowned her.

While Northern society changed, the South held onto its agrarian slave-labor system. The next set of documents in this selection concerns the daily lives, everyday violence, and occasional extraordinary resistance of slaves. Slavery was more than an economic system; it was a social arrangement based on violence. The documents in this section—excerpts from the North Carolina Supreme Court case concerning murder of a slave, *State v. Boon*; a selection from the confessions of Nat Turner following his famous slave revolt in 1831; and the narratives of two escaped slaves, Mrs. James Steward and Mrs. Nancy Howard—reveal the (often legally sanctioned) violence that undergirded the slave system and the attempts of African Americans to preserve their families, their religious faith, and their dignity in its face.

The legal institution of slavery codified the rights of masters over their slaves and provided protection for slaves (as their master's property) against excessively abusive masters and from strangers. Slaves could not raise a hand against a white, even in self-defense; slaves could not testify against whites in court. The law did not recognize slave marriages. A cursory examination of the cases concerning the criminal law of slavery reveals the conflicting interests at work. The excerpt here from *State v. Boon* reveals the court's profound ambivalence about slave's legal rights and the court's responsibility to protect slaves.

The Nat Turner revolt was perhaps the most famous and most violent slave uprising of the antebellum period. It was also the slave revolt that galvanized white fears and antipathy toward their slaves—manumission became increasingly difficult and interest in ending slavery faded soon afterwards. Nat Turner, the leader of the revolt, was a religious, educated slave who believed himself to be on a religious mission. In August 1831, before the revolt was crushed, Turner and his compatriots murdered fifty-five white men, women and children, including the family of his master, Joseph Travis. Turner was caught and executed. Before he was killed he dictated a confession, excerpted here, to his white lawyer.

Most slaves did not revolt like Nat Turner or other organizers like Denmark Vesey and Gabriel Prosser. A few slaves, however, did try to escape from slavery to the North or to escaped-slave communities in Florida. The narratives of Mrs. James Steward and Mrs. Nancy Howard reveal not only the sufferings and indignities suffered by slave women, but also their attempts to maintain dignity and family ties.

Study Questions

1. From the role played by fathers in the Wilson and Norcom letters and from the expectations about a husband and father's role described in the letters, describe the position of husband and father in the antebellum period.

2. In the antebellum period, most land holdings were too small and too many children survived into adulthood for most families to be able to endow children with substantial patrimonies and dowries. Might this situation limit the authority of the parent?

3. Analyze the grounds for the North Carolina Supreme Court's overturning of Boon's conviction. What conflicting property interests might have influenced the justices' decision? If the state took Boon's life, how would the owner of the slave recover damages?

4. How different was Nat Turner from most slaves of this period? Why did he think himself qualified to lead a rebellion?

5. How do the daily lives and gender roles described in the narratives of escaped slaves compare to those described in the Wilson and Norcom letters? Examine, in particular, Mrs. James Steward's courtship.

Joshua and Sally Wilson Letters to George Wilson (1823)

These letters, from George Wilson's father, Joshua, and his sister Sally, offer advice on courtship and illuminate the expectations placed on young men during this period—to act as breadwinners and be the heads of their families, while young women were expected to stay in their "separate sphere"—the home—and take care of domestic affairs. In earlier periods, the work of an entire family contributed to a family's economic survival, but in an industrializing society men worked outside the home, for money, and women's home-work became less economically significant.*

November 23, 1823

We presume you are already informed that your letter of the 28th was duly received. The delicate and important subject suggested for our consideration form a sufficient reason for some delay that we might not give advice in a matter of such moment without meditation, prayer, and serious conference. It would be very unreasonable for us to attempt to restrain the lawful and laudable desires of our children, all we ought to do is to endeavor to direct and regulate their innocent wishes and curb and conquer those which are vicious. Nor are we ignorant of the great advantages which frequently result from virtuous love and honorable wedlock. But there is a time for all things, and such are the fixed laws of nature that things are only beautiful and useful when they occupy their own time and place. Premature love and marriage are often blighted by the frosts of adversity and satiety leaving hasty lovers to droop in the meridian of life and drag out a miserable existence under the withering influence of disappointment and disgust. . . . We do not say you have been hasty but we wish you to reflect seriously upon this question. Is not the whole affair premature? We know from experience and observation that schemes which appear reasonable and desirable at the age of twenty wear a very different aspect at twenty five. We think it probable that greater maturity, more experience in business and a larger acquaintance with the world might change your views and feelings. Besides we are not sure that you have sufficiently considered the weighty responsibility. We feel no disposition to place any insuperable barrier in your way. Our advice is that you give the subject that consideration which its importance demands, that you unite with us in praying for divine direction, that every thing be done deliberately, decently, orderly, honorably, and devoutly.

[Joshua Wilson]

---

* From Donald M. Scott and Bernard Wishy, *Americas Families, A Documentary History* (Chicago: Dorsey Press, 1988).

December 9, 1823

Your letter of Nov 18 has been duly received. On its contents we have meditated with deep solicitude. . . . You seem confident that your decision is not premature nor hasty. Here we feel compelled to demur and beg you to weigh the matter again. You express a hope that before great length of time we shall have an opportunity of receiving Miss B much to our satisfaction. Dear George, it will not be any satisfaction to us to see you place a lady in a more precarious condition than you found her and this we are sure would be the case if marriage with this young lady should take place shortly. We must remind you of a pledge given in your former letter and insist upon its obligation, that you marry no woman without the prospect of supporting her in a suitable manner. Think of the circumstances in which she has been educated, of the circle of society in which she has been accustomed to move, of her delicate constitution and refined sensibility and then imagine to yourself her disappointment upon entering into a poor dependent family occupying an indifferent tenement without the means of affording a comfortable lodging or decently accommodating her friends. She has been accustomed to see you in the agreeable aspect of the scholar and a gentleman and she has seen your father also in flattering circumstances. . . . We do not say things to discourage you but to show you the necessity of prudence in your plans, diligence in your studies and such application to business as will afford a reasonable prospect of success before you become the head of a family.

[Sally Wilson]

Ja Norcom, Letter to Mary Matilda Norcom (1846)

> This letter from Mary Matilda Norcom's father urges her to settle on a man who could "support a family." As mentioned in the introduction to this chapter, Mary did not. Along with an increase in the responsibility placed on a man, who had to provide for his family in the antebellum period by working outside of the home, there was a new emphasis in the nineteenth century on the "affectionate" family—a husband and wife who married for love.*

Edenton, N. C., 19 August 1846

My dear Daughter,

. . . You must remember, my daughter, what I have said to you, *on a certain subject*. I would not *acknowledge* myself to be *engaged*, affianced, to any man not in a condition

---

* From Donald M. Scott and Bernard Wishy, *Americas Families, A Documentary History* (Chicago: Dorsey Press, 1988).

to give me a comfortable & respectable support—to place me beyond the chance of want or poverty. I, my dear, could *never never* ratify such an engagement were you to make it. Everything, therefore, in relation to this matter must be *conditional*. It cannot be positive, for, however meritorious a man may be, & how high he might be in my opinion or esteem, I could not sanction his connexion with a daughter of mine, in the "Holy Estate" with the prospect of poverty & wretchedness before her.

Treat the man who honors you with his partiality & preference with candor, politeness—nay, with kindness, *but let him not hope*, if he is inconsiderate enough to wish it, to draw you into a situation in which you would be less comfortable than you are in your father's dwelling, or less comfortable than you could be among your friends, in your present condition. W—is a meritorious and respectable young man, an honour to his family, & worthy of general esteem; and had I a fortune, my daughter, to give you, or the means of making you independent, I see nothing in his character to object to. But his inability to support a family, *as long as it lasts*, is an insurmountable objection, & of the probability of its removal no correct opinion can *now* be formed. Time alone can instruct us on the subject. Pray be prudent, my daughter, and do nothing in your absence from us, that *you would not do in the presence of* your father,

Ja Norcom

State v. Boon (1801)

Early North Carolina statutes treated the murder of a slave differently than other murders. According to laws in 1741 and 1774, people who murdered slaves were required to compensate their owners (unless they killed in the supression of an insurrection) and they risked jail time if they failed to do so. In 1791 an act of the legislature noted that the "distinction of criminality between the murder of a white person and of one who is equally a human creature, but merely of a different complexion, is disgraceful to humanity and degrading in the highest degree to the laws and principles of a free, Christian and enlightened country." The law then provided that the murderer would suffer the same punishment as he would if he "killed a free man," but provided exceptions for slaves killed in insurrections and slaves "dying under moderate correction." This is an excerpt from the North Carolina Supreme Court decision in the first case brought under the new law, concerning a man, Boon, indicted, convicted, and sentenced to death for killing a slave that belonged to another man.

HALL, J.   The prisoner has been found guilty of the offence charged in the indictment [Boon was indicted and convicted under the third section of the act of 1791 for killing a slave belonging to another]; whether any, or what punishment, can be inflicted upon him in consequence thereof, is not to be decided. . . .

We must consider the words of the enacting clause, without regard to the preamble. . . . If any person hereafter shall be guilty of killing a slave &c. such offender shall be adjudged guilty of murder &c. and shall suffer the same punishment, as if he had killed a free man. In case the person had killed a free man what punishment would the law have inflicted upon him? Before this question can be solved another must be asked; because upon that, the solution of the first depends. What sort of a killing was it? or what circumstances of aggravation or mitigation attended it? . . . That to which the Legislature referred us for the purpose of ascertaining the punishment, proper to be inflicted is, in itself, so doubtful and uncertain that I think no punishment whatever can be inflicted; without using a discretion and indulging a latitude, which in criminal cases, ought never to be allowed a Judge.

. . . Much latitude of construction ought not to be permitted to operate against life; if it operate at all, it should be in favor of it. Punishments ought to be plainly defined and easy to be understood; they ought not to depend upon construction or arbitrary discretion. . . .

But it has been also contended, on behalf of the state, that the offense with which the prisoner is charged, is a felony at common law, and that having been found guilty by the jury, he ought to be punished, independently of any Act of Assembly on the subject. . . .

Slaves in this country possess no such rights; their condition is . . . abject; . . . they are not parties to our constitution; it was not made for them.

. . . it is doubtful whether the offense with which he is charged is a felony at common law or not. It is doubtful whether he ought to be punished or not, that, certainly, is a sufficient reason for discharging him . . . I cannot hesitate to say, that he ought to be discharged.

JOHNSTON, J.   The murder of a slave, appears to me, a crime of the most atrocious and barbarous nature; much more so than killing a person who is free, and on an equal footing. It is an evidence of a most depraved and cruel disposition, to murder one, so much in your power, that he is incapable of making resistance, even in his own defence . . . and had there been nothing in our acts of Assembly, I should not hesitate on this occasion to have pronounced sentence of death on the prisoner.

. . . From the context, and taking every part of the section [of the act of 1791] under consideration, there remains no doubt in my mind respecting the intention of the Legislature; but the judges in this country . . . have laid down, and invariably adhered to, very strict rules in the construction of penal statutes in favor of life . . .

. . . judgment in this case should be arrested.

TAYLOR, JR.   . . . But when the court is called upon, under an act of Assembly, to pronounce the highest punishment known to the law, they must be satisfied that the language used is clear and explicit to the object intended . . . I think no judgment can be pronounced.

Nat Turner, Confession (1831)

This is a selection from Nat Turner's confessions, collected by his white lawyer after he had been apprehended for leading a revolt that culminated in the murder of fifty-five whites and the death of at least that many African Americans from white retaliation. The revolt, intended, in Turner's words, to "carry terror and devastation," was spurred by his divine vision. This selection describes the origins of Turner's sense of his own uniqueness and his divine revelation.*

... To a mind like mine, restless, inquisitive and observant of every thing that was passing, it is easy to suppose that religion was the subject to which it would be directed, and although this subject principally occupied my thoughts—there was nothing that I saw or heard of to which my attention was not directed—The manner in which I learned to read and write, not only had great influence on my own mind, as I acquired it with the most perfect ease, so much so, that I have no recollection whatever of learning the alphabet—but to the astonishment of the family, one day, when a book was shewn to me to keep me from crying, I began spelling the names of different objects—this was a source of wonder to all in the neighborhood, particularly the blacks—and this learning was constantly improved at all opportunities—when I got large enough to go to work, while employed, I was reflecting on many things that would present themselves to my imagination, and whenever an opportunity occurred of looking at a book, when the school children were getting their lessons, I would find many things that the fertility of my own imagination had depicted to me before. . . .

[A]ll my time, not devoted to my master's service, was spent either in prayer, or in making experiments in casting different things in moulds made of earth, in attempting to make paper, gun-powder, and many other experiments, that although I could not perfect, yet convinced me of its practicability if I had the means.

I was not addicted to stealing in my youth, nor have ever been—Yet such was the confidence of the negroes in the neighborhood, even at this early period of my life, in my superior judgment, that they would often carry me with them when they were going on any roguery, to plan for them. Growing up among them, with this confidence in my superior judgment, and when this, in their opinions, was perfected by Divine inspiration, from the circumstances already alluded to in my infancy, and which belief was ever afterwards zealously inculcated by the austerity of my life and manners, which became the subject of remark by white and black.

---

* From Thomas R. Gray, *The Confessions of Nat Turner, The Leader of the Late Insurrection in Southamton Virginia* (Baltimore, 1831).

—Having soon discovered to be great, I must appear so, and therefore studiously avoided mixing in society, and wrapped myself in mystery, devoting my time to fasting and prayer—by this time, having arrived to man's estate, and hearing the scriptures commented on at meetings, I was struck with that particular passage which says: "Seek ye the kingdom of Heaven and all things shall be added unto you." I reflected much on this passage, and prayed daily for light on this subject—As I was praying one day at my plough, the spirit spoke to me, saying "Seek ye the kingdom of Heaven and all things shall be added unto you."

Question—what do you mean by the Spirit? Ans.—The Spirit that spoke to the prophets in former days—and I was greatly astonished, and for two years prayed continually, whenever my duty would permit—and then again I had the same revelation, which fully confirmed me in the impression that I was ordained for some great purpose in the hands of the Almighty.

Several years rolled round, in which many events occurred to strengthen me in this my belief. At this time I reverted in my mind to the remarks made of me in my childhood, and the things that had been shewn me—and as it had been said of me in my childhood by those by whom I had been taught to pray, both white and black, and in whom I had the greatest confidence, that I had too much sense to be raised, and if I was, I would never be of any use to any one as a slave. Now finding I had arrived to man's estate, and was a slave, and these revelations being made known to me, I began to direct my attention to this great object, to fulfill the purpose for which, by this time, I felt assured I was intended.

Knowing the influence I had obtained over the minds of my fellow servants (not by the means of conjuring and such like tricks—for to them I always spoke of such things with contempt) but by the communion of the Spirit whose revelations I often communicated to them, and they believed and said my wisdom came from God. I now began to prepare them for my purpose, by telling them something was about to happen that would terminate in fulfilling the great promise that had been made to me— . . . .

Benjamin Drew, Narratives of Escaped Slaves (1855)

These two stories of fugitive slaves who escaped from Maryland to freedom in Canada were recorded by Benjamin Drew, an abolitionist. Most runaway slaves were young men, who, like these young women, had suffered physical abuse. Relatively few women were able to make the dangerous journey to freedom because of the difficulty of fleeing with children. These women's stories document some of the sadistic physical abuse many slaves—men and women alike—suffered at the hands of their masters: whippings, brandings, and confinement, for instance. They also provide evidence of the attempt by women to maintain family ties, relationships, and commitments.*

[Mrs. James Steward]

The slaves want to get away bad enough. They are not contented with their situation.

I am from the eastern shore of Maryland. I never belonged but to one master; he was very bad indeed. I was never sent to school, nor allowed to go to church. They were afraid we would have more sense than they. I have a father there, three sisters, and a brother. My father is quite an old man, and he is used very badly. Many a time he has been kept at work a whole long summer day without sufficient food. A sister of mine has been punished by his taking away her clothes and locking them up, because she used to run when master whipped her. He kept her at work with only what she could pick up to tie on her for decency. He took away her child which had just begun to walk, and gave it to another woman—but she went and got it afterward. He had a large farm eight miles from home. Four servants were kept at the house. My master could not manage to whip my sister when she was strong. He waited until she was confined, and the second week after her confinement he said, "Now I can handle you, now you are weak." She ran from him, however, and had to go through water, and was sick in consequence.

I was beaten at one time over the head by my master, until the blood ran from my mouth and nose: then he tied me up in the garret, with my hands over my head—then he brought me down and put me in a little cupboard, where I had to sit cramped up, part of the evening, all night, and until between four and five o'clock, next day, without any food. The cupboard was near a fire, and I thought I should suffocate.

My brother was whipped on one occasion until his back was as raw as a piece of beef, and before it got well, master whipped him again. His back was an awful sight.

We were all afraid of master: when I saw him coming, my heart would jump up into my mouth, as if I had seen a serpent.

I have been wanting to come away for eight years back. I waited for Jim Seward to get ready. Jim had promised to take me away and marry me. Our master would allow no marriages on the farm. When Jim had got ready, he let me know—he brought to me two suits of clothes—men's clothes—which he had bought on purpose for me. I put on both suits to keep me warm. We eluded pursuit and reached Canada in safety.

[Mrs. Nancy Howard]

I was born in Anne Arundel County, Maryland—was brought up in Baltimore. After my escape, I lived in Lynn, Mass., seven years, but I left there through fear of being carried back, owing to the fugitive slave law. I have lived in St. Catherines [Ontario, Canada] less than a year.

---

* From *A Northside View of Slavery: The Refuge, or The Narratives of Fugitive Slaves in Canada, Related by Themselves*, ed. Benjamin Drew (Boston: John P. Jowett, 1856), 41–43, 50–51, 138, 140–141, 224–227.

The way I got away was—my mistress was sick, and went into the country for her health. I went to stay with her cousin. After a month, my mistress was sent back to the city to her cousin's, and I waited on her. My daughter had been off three years. A friend said to me—"Now is your chance to get off." At last I concluded to go—the friend supplying me with money. I was asked no questions on the way north.

My idea of slavery is, that it is one of the blackest, the wickedest things everywhere in the world. When you tell them the truth, they whip you to make you lie. I have taken more lashes for this, than for any other thing, because I would not lie.

One day I set the table, and forgot to put on the carving-fork—the knife was there. I went to the table to put it on a plate. My master said,—"Where is the fork?" I told him "I forgot it." He says,—"You d——d black b——, I'll forget you!"—at the same time hitting me on the head with the carving knife. The blood spurted out—you can see. (Here the woman removed her turban and showed a circular cicatrices denuded of hair, about an inch in diameter, on the top of her head.) My mistress took me into the kitchen and put on camphor, but she could not stop the bleeding. A doctor was sent for. He came but asked no questions. I was frequently punished with raw hides—was hit with tongs and poker and anything. I used when I went out, to look up at the sky, and say, "Blessed Lord, oh, do take me out of this!" It seemed to me I could not bear another lick. I can't forget it. I sometimes dream that I am pursued, and when I wake, I am scared almost to death.

11

Manifest Destiny and Its Consequences

Westward expansion was an integral part of the development of the United States. From the first settlers, Americans assumed it was their destiny to move across the continent. By the 1830s this ideology strongly influenced the policies and actions of the national government. During the next twenty years, through peace and war and by peaceful and aggressive means, the government helped fill settlers in the continent.

"Manifest Destiny" helped to make the United States a powerful industrial world power in the late nineteenth and twentieth centuries. However, in the antebellum period, it was a driving force in the sectional tensions between the North and the South. Each new territorial acquisition brought debate over whether or not such areas should be free or slave territory. Some Americans sought a compromise through popular sovereignty, which would allow the residents of a territory to determine their status.

This chapter examines manifest destiny and its effect on the American nation. It begins with the author of the term, John L. O'Sullivan. In "The Great Nation of Futurity," O'Sullivan proposed to the American public that they were "a nation . . . destined to be the great nation of futurity" and glorified America as a nation connected to the future.

Westward expansion also led to an inevitable conflict with Mexico. Texas had declared its independence in 1836, and in 1845, in a move defended as an expansion of American civilization (or manifest destiny), Texas was annexed by the United States.

After losing Texas, Mexico had little interest in selling California and the New Mexico territory to President James Polk. In 1846, border dispute in Texas provided the opportunity for the United States to send the military to the region and war broke out. Though it appeared to be a popular undertaking, many Americans were skeptical of the country's motives and feared the consequences of the Mexican-American War. Abraham Lincoln, then a Whig Congressman, introduced a resolution demanding to know the exact spot at which American troops had been fired on. Many from the North were afraid of the expansion of slavery into the new territories. Thomas Corwin, a Whig Senator from Ohio, argued before Congress that the Mexican-American War would heighten the tensions between pro- and anti- slavery groups in the United States and feared that the external war would lead to a civil war.

Further north American settlers had been streaming into the Oregon Territory in the early 1840s, while it was still jointly occupied by the United States and Great Britain. In the treaty of 1846, the United States gained sole possession of the lands south of the forty-eighth parallel—opening the way for more settlement of the territory. Settlers in search of their fortune or a new life moved with their families to Oregon and California on tortuous overland routes. The journal of Elizabeth Greer, excerpted here, reveals the difficulties of making the journey.

Settlers in virtually all cases were moving into lands that had been occupied by Native American groups, including the Sioux Indians of the Great Plains, and the Blackfoot, Nez Percé and Crow Indians of the Plateau. Chief Seattle was the leader of six Native American tribes in the Oregon Territory. In 1854 he was told that the United States government wanted to buy his lands and establish reservations for his people. As his oration describes, he accepted the offer, fearing what a bloody war would do to his people.

Study Questions

1.   According to John L. O'Sullivan, what characteristics of the American nation determine its future? How is the United States different from other nations? How could his rhetoric drive expansionism?

2.   Compare John O'Sullivan's discussion of America's special destiny with the ideas of John Winthrop in chapter two.

3.   What does Corwin fear will be the consequence of a war with Mexico? Discuss his critique of manifest destiny.

4.   What do Greer's writings suggest about the sexual division of labor or the mutability of gender roles on the trail?

5.   In Chief Seattle's terms, what were the major differences between Native American and white societies?

John L. O'Sullivan, "The Great Nation of Futurity" (1845)

In this selection from "The Great Nation of Futurity," John O'Sullivan glorified America and proclaimed its destiny to spread its civilization. In his magazine, *The United States Magazine and Democratic Review*, O'Sullivan reminded Americans that "America is destined for better deeds" and spread the expansionist doctrine.*

---

* From *The United States Magazine and Democratic Review*, VI (November, 1839), 2–3, 6.

The American people having derived their origin from many other nations, and the Declaration of National Independence being entirely based on the great principle of human equality, these facts demonstrate at once our disconnected position as regards any other nation; that we have, in reality, but little connection with the past history of any of them and still less with all antiquity, its glories, or its crimes. On the contrary, our national birth was the beginning of a new history, the formation and progress of an untried political system, which separates us from the past and connects us with the future only; and so far as regards the entire development of the natural rights of man, in moral, political, and national life, we may confidently assume that our country is destined to be the great nation of futurity.

It is so destined, because the principle upon which a nation is organized fixes its destiny, and that of equality is perfect, is universal. It presides in all the operations of the physical world, and it is also the conscious law of the soul—the self-evident dictate of morality, which accurately defines the duty of man to man, and consequently man's rights as man. Besides, the truthful annals of any nation furnish abundant evidence that its happiness, its greatness, its duration, were always proportionate to the democratic equality in its system of government.

How many nations have had their decline and fall because the equal rights of the minority were trampled on by the despotism of the majority; or the interests of the many sacrificed to the aristocracy of the few; or the rights and interests of all given up to the monarchy of one? These three kinds of government have figured so frequently and so largely in the ages that have passed away that their history, through all time to come, can only furnish a resemblance. Like causes produce like effects, and the true philosopher of history will easily discern the principle of equality, or of privilege, working out its inevitable result. The first is regenerative, because it is natural and right; and the latter is destructive to society, because it is unnatural and wrong.

What friend of human liberty, civilization, and refinement can cast his view over the past history of the monarchies and aristocracies of antiquity, and not deplore that they ever existed? What philanthropist can contemplate the oppressions, the cruelties, and injustice inflicted by them on the masses of mankind and not turn with moral horror from the retrospect?

America is destined for better deeds. It is our unparalleled glory that we have no reminiscences of battlefields, but in defense of humanity, of the oppressed of all nations, of the rights of conscience, the rights of personal enfranchisement. Our annals describe no scenes of horrid carnage, where men were led on by hundreds of thousands to slay one another, dupes and victims to emperors, kings, nobles, demons in the human form called heroes. We have had patriots to defend our homes, our liberties, but no aspirants to crowns or thrones; nor have the American people ever suffered themselves to be led on by wicked ambition to depopulate the land, to spread desolation far and wide, that a human being might be placed on a seat of supremacy.

We have no interest in the scenes of antiquity, only as lessons of avoidance of nearly all their examples. The expansive future is our arena and for our history. We are entering on its untrodden space with the truths of God in our minds, beneficent objects in our hearts, and with a clear conscience unsullied by the past. We are the nation of human progress, and who will, what can, set limits to our onward march? Providence is with us, and no earthly power can. We point to the everlasting truth on the first page of our national declaration, and we proclaim to the millions of other lands that "the gates of hell"—the powers of aristocracy and monarchy—"shall not prevail against it."

The far-reaching, the boundless future, will be the era of American greatness. In its magnificent domain of space and time, the nation of many nations is destined to manifest to mankind the excellence of divine principles; to establish on earth the noblest temple ever dedicated to the worship of the Most High, the Sacred, and the True. Its floor shall be a hemisphere, roof the firmament of the star-studded heavens, and its congregation of Union of many Republics, comprising hundreds of happy millions, calling owning no man master, but governed by God's natural and moral law of equality, the law of brotherhood—of "peace and good will amongst men."

Yes, we are the nation of progress, of individual freedom, of universal enfranchisement. Equality of rights is the cynosure of our union of states, the grand exemplar of the correlative equality of individuals; and, while truth sheds its effulgence, we cannot retrograde without dissolving the one and subverting the other. We must onward to the fulfillment of our mission—to the entire development of the principle of our organization—freedom of conscience, freedom of person, freedom of trade and business pursuits, universality of freedom and equality. This is our high destiny, and in nature's eternal, inevitable decree of cause and effect we must accomplish it. All this will be our future history, to establish on earth the moral dignity and salvation of man—the immutable truth and beneficence of God. For this blessed mission to the nations of the world, which are shut out from the lifegiving light of truth, has America been chosen; and her high example shall smite unto death the tyranny of kings, hierarchs, and oligarchs and carry the glad tidings of peace and good will where myriads now endure in existence scarcely more enviable than that of beasts of the field. Who, then, can doubt that our country is destined to be the great nation of futurity?

Thomas Corwin, Against the Mexican War (1847)

The Mexican-American war began in early 1846 and ended abruptly—after Americans had marched all the way to Mexico City—less than a year later. The question of who would win the war was never really seriously debated. What was in debate was the character of the American expansion and the question of slavery. Corwin, a Whig senator from Ohio, questioned expansionism and feared that the South would carry slavery wherever it went.[*]

---

[*] From *The American Reader: Words That Moved a Nation*, ed. Diane Ravitch (New York: HarperCollins, 1991), 77–79.

What is the territory, Mr. President, which you propose to wrest from Mexico? It is consecrated to the heart of the Mexican by many a well-fought battle with his old Castilian master. His Bunker Hills, and Saratogas, and Yorktowns are there! The Mexican can say, "There I bled for liberty! and shall I surrender that consecrated home of my affections to the Anglo-Saxon invaders? What do they want with it? They have Texas already. They have possessed themselves of the territory between the Nueces and the Rio Grande. What else do they want? To what shall I point my children as memorials of that independence which I bequeath to them, when those battlefields shall have passed from my possession?"

Sir, had one come and demanded Bunker Hill of the people of Massachusetts, had England's lion ever showed himself there, is there a man over thirteen and under ninety who would not have been ready to meet him? Is there a river on this continent that would not have run red with blood? Is there a field but would have been piled high with the unburied bones of slaughtered Americans before these consecrated battlefields of liberty should have been wrested from us? But this same American goes into a sister republic, and says to poor, weak Mexico, "Give up your territory, you are unworthy to possess it; I have got one half already, and all I ask of you is to give up the other!" . . . .

Sir, look at this pretense of want of room. With twenty millions of people, you have about one thousand millions of acres of land, inviting settlement by every conceivable argument, bringing them down to a quarter of a dollar an acre, and allowing every man to squat where the pleases. . . .

There is one topic connected with this subject which I tremble when I approach, and yet I cannot forbear to notice it. It meets you in every step you take; it threatens you which way soever you go in the prosecution of this war. I allude to the question of slavery. Opposition to its further extension, it must be obvious to everyone, is a deeply rooted determination with men of all parties in what we call the nonslaveholding states. New York, Pennsylvania, and Ohio, three of the most powerful, have already sent their legislative instructions here. So it will be, I doubt not, in all the rest. It is vain now to speculate about the reasons for this. Gentlemen of the South may call it prejudice, passion, hypocrisy, fanaticism. I shall not dispute with them now on that point. You and I cannot alter or change this opinion, if we would. These people only say we will not, cannot consent that you shall carry slavery where it does not already exist. They do not seek to disturb you in that institution as it exists in your states. Enjoy it if you will and as you will. This is their language; this their determination. How is it in the South? Can it be expected that they should expend in common their blood and their treasure in the acquisition of immense territory, and then willingly forgo the right to carry thither their slaves, and inhabit the conquered country if they please to do so? Sir, I know the feelings and opinions of the South too well to calculate on this. Nay, I believe they would even contend to any extremity for the mere right, had they no wish to exert it. I believe (and I confess I tremble when the conviction presses upon me) that there is equal obstinacy on both sides of this fearful question.

If, then, we persist in war, which, if it terminates in anything short of a mere wanton waste of blood as well as money, must end (as this bill proposes) in the acquisition of territory, to which at once this controversy must attach—this bill would seem to be nothing less than a bill to produce internal commotion. Should we prosecute this war another moment, or expend one dollar in the purchase or conquest of a single acre of Mexican land, the North and the South are brought into collision on a point where neither will yield. Who can foresee or foretell the result! Who so bold or reckless as to look such a conflict in the face unmoved! I do not envy the heart of him who can realize the possibility of such a conflict without emotions too painful to be endured. Why, then, shall we, the representatives of the sovereign states of the Union—the chosen guardians of this confederated Republic, why should we precipitate this fearful struggle, by continuing a war the result of which must be to force us at once upon a civil conflict? Sir, rightly considered, this is treason, treason to the Union, treason to the dearest interests, the loftiest aspirations, the most cherished hopes of our constituents. It is a crime to risk the possibility of such a contest. It is a crime of such infernal hue that every other in the catalogue of iniquity, when compared with it, whitens into virtue. . . . Let us abandon all idea of acquiring further territory and by consequence cease at once to prosecute this war. Let us call home our armies, and bring them at once within our own acknowledged limits. Show Mexico that you are sincere when you say you desire nothing by conquest. She has learned that she cannot encounter you in war, and if she had not, she is too weak to disturb you here. Tender her peace, and, my life on it, she will then accept it. But whether she shall or not, you will have peace without her consent. It is your invasion that has made war; your retreat will restore peace. Let us then close forever the approaches of internal feud, and so return to the ancient concord and the old ways of national prosperity and permanent glory. Let us here, in this temple consecrated to the Union, perform a solemn lustration; let us wash Mexican blood from our hands, and on these altars, and in the presence of that image of the Father of his Country that looks down upon us, swear to preserve honorable peace with all the world and eternal brotherhood with each other.

Elizabeth Dixon Smith Greer, Journal (1847–1850)

Like many during the 1840s and 1850s, Elizabeth Dixon Smith Greer, her husband, and her small children made the journey along the Oregon Trail from Indiana. The migrants' motivations were often complex, but all hoped to improve their lives. Oregon settlers like the Greers were promised 640 acres in the territory. In this selection from her journal, kept for friends back home, Elizabeth Greer documents the difficulties of the overland journey.*

---

* From *The Thirty-fifth Transactions of the Oregon Pioneer Association* (1907), 153, 171–78.

Dear Friends—By your request I have endeavored to keep a record of our journey from "the States" to Oregon, though it is poorly done, owing to my having a young babe and besides a large family to do for; and, worst of all, my education is very limited.

April 21, 1847—Commenced our journey from La Porte, Indiana, to Oregon; made fourteen miles. . . .

November 18—My husband is sick. It rains and snows. We start this morning around the falls with our wagons. We have 5 miles to go. I carry my babe and lead, or rather carry, another through snow, mud and water, almost to my knees. It is the worst road that a team could possibly travel. I went ahead with my children, and I was afraid to look behind me for fear of seeing the wagons turn over into the mud and water with everything in them. My children gave out with cold and fatigue and could not travel, and the boys had to unhitch the oxen and bring them and carry the children on to camp. I was so cold and numb that I could not tell by the feeling that I had any feet at all. We started this morning at sunrise and did not get to camp until after dark, and there was not one dry thread on one of us—not even my babe. I had carried my babe and I was so fatigued that I could scarcely speak or step. When I got here I found my husband lying in Welch's wagon, very sick. He had brought Mrs. Polk down the day before and was taken sick here. We had to stay up all night, for our wagons are left halfway back. I have not told half we suffered. I am not adequate to the task. Here were some hundreds camped, waiting for boats to come and take them down the Columbia to Vancouver or Portland or Oregon City.

November 19—My husband is sick and can have but little care. Rain all day.

November 20—Rain all day. It is almost an impossibility to cook, and quite so to keep warm or dry. I froze or chilled my feet so that I cannot wear a shoe, so I have to go around in the cold water barefooted.

November 21—Rain all day. The whole care of everything falls upon my shoulders. I cannot write any more at present.

November 30—Raining. This morning I ran about trying to get a house to get into with my sick husband. At last I found a small, leaky concern, with two families already in it. Mrs. Polk had got down before us. She and another widow was in this house. My family and Welch's went in with them, and you could have stirred us with a stick. Welch and my oldest boy was driving the cattle around. My children and I carried up a bed. The distance was nearly a quarter of a mile. Made it down on the floor in the mud. I got some men to carry my husband up through the rain and lay him on it, and he never was out of that shed until he was carried out in his coffin. Here lay five of us bedfast at one time . . . and we had no money, and what few things we had left that would bring money, I had to sell. I had to give 10 cents a pound for fresh pork, 75 cents per bushel for potatoes, 4 cents a pound for fish. There are so many of us sick that I cannot write any more at present. I have not time to write much, but I thought it would be interesting to know what kind of weather we have in the winter.

1848—January 14—Rain this morning. Warm weather. We suppose it has rained half of the time that I have neglected writing.

January 15—My husband is still alive, but very sick. There is no medicine here except at Fort Vancouver, and the people there will not sell one bit—not even a bottle of wine.

February 1—Rain all day. This day my dear husband, my last remaining friend, died.

February 2—Today we buried my earthly companion. Now I know what none but widows know; that is, how comfortless is a widow's life, especially when left in a strange land, without money or friends, and the care of seven children. Cloudy. . . .

Chief Seattle, Oration (1854)

Native Americans were devastated by the effects of American expansion: 70,000 Indians died in California alone between 1849 and 1859; the Paiute were shot for sport by trappers. Between 1853 and 1857, the United States forced the secession of 147 million acres of Native American land. This land included those of Chief Seattle, who chose to capitulate to the government rather than risk conflict with an army that had been singularly effective in crushing other Indian groups.[*]

. . . Yonder sky that has wept tears of compassion upon my people for centuries untold, and which to us appears changeless and eternal, may change. Today is fair. Tomorrow it may be overcast with clouds. My words are like the stars that never change. Whatever Seattle says the great chief at Washington can rely upon with as much certainty as he can upon the return of the sun or the seasons. The White Chief says that Big Chief at Washington sends us greetings of friendship and goodwill. This is kind of him for we know he has little need of our friendship in return. His people are many. They are like the grass that covers vast prairies. My people are few. They resemble the scattering trees of a storm-swept plain. The great, and—I presume—good White Chief sends us word that he wishes to buy our lands but is willing to allow us enough to live comfortably. This indeed appears just, even generous, for the Red Man no longer has rights that he need respect, and the offer may be wise also, as we are no longer in need of an extensive country.

---

[*] Reprinted from *The American Reader: Words That Moved a Nation*, ed. Diane Ravitch (New York: HarperCollins, 1991), 92–94.

There was a time when our people covered the land as the waves of a wind-ruffled sea cover its shell-paved floor, but that time long since passed away with the greatness of tribes that are now but a mournful memory. I will not dwell on nor mourn over, our untimely decay, nor reproach my paleface brothers with hastening it as we too may have been somewhat to blame.

Youth is impulsive. When our young men grow angry at some real or imaginary wrong, and disfigure their faces with black paint, it denotes that their hearts are black, and that they are often cruel and relentless, and our old men and old women are unable to restrain them. Thus has ever been. Thus it was when the White Men first began to push our forefathers further westward. But let us hope that the hostilities between us may never return. We would have everything to lose and nothing to gain. Revenge by young men is considered gain, even at the cost of their own lives, but old men who stay at home in times of war, and mothers who have sons to lose, know better.

Our good father at Washington—for I presume he is now our father as well as yours . . . sends us word that if we do as he desires he will protect us. His brave warriors will be to us a bristling wall of strength, and his wonderful ships of war will fill our harbors so that our ancient enemies far to the northward—the Hydas and Tsimpsians,—will cease to frighten our women, children, and old men. Then in reality will he be our father and we his children. But can that ever be? Your God is not our God! Your God loves your people and hates mine. He folds his strong protecting arms lovingly about the paleface and leads him by the hand as a father leads his infant son— but He has forsaken His red children—if they really are his. Our God, the Great Spirit, seems also to have forsaken us. Your God makes your people wax strong every day. Soon they will fill all the land. Our people are ebbing away like a rapidly receding tide that will never return. The White Man's God cannot love our people or He would protect them. They seem to be orphans who can look nowhere for help. How then can we be brothers? How can your God become our God and renew our prosperity and awaken in us dreams of returning greatness? If we have a common heavenly father He must be partial—for He came to His paleface children. We never saw Him. He gave you laws but had no word for His red children whose teeming multitudes once filled this vast continent as stars fill the firmament. No; we are two distinct races with separate origins and separate destinies. There is little in common between us.

To us the ashes of our ancestors are sacred and their resting place is hallowed ground. You wander far from the graves of your ancestors and seemingly without regret. Your religion was written upon tables of stone by the iron finger of your God so that you could not forget. The Red Man could never comprehend nor remember it. Our religion is the traditions of our ancestors—the dreams of our old men, given them in solemn hours of night by the Great Spirit; and the visions of our sachems, and is written in the hearts of our people.

Your dead cease to love you and the land of their nativity as soon as they pass the portals of the tomb and wander away beyond the stars. They are soon forgotten and never return. Our dead never forget the beautiful world that gave them being. They still love its verdant valleys, its murmuring rivers, its magnificent mountains, sequestered vales and verdant lined lakes and bays, and even yearn in tender, fond affection over the lonely heartened living, and often return from the Happy Hunting Ground to visit, guide, console and comfort them.

Day and night cannot dwell together. The Red Man has ever fled the approach of the White Man, as the morning mist flees before the morning sun.

However, your proposition seems fair and I think that my people will accept it and will retire to the reservation you offer them. Then we will dwell apart in peace. . . .

It matters little where we pass the remnant of our days. They will not be many. The Indians' night promises to be dark. Not a single star of hope hovers above his horizon. Sad-voiced winds moan in the distance. Grim fate seems to be on the Red Man's trail, and wherever he goes he will hear the approaching footsteps of his fell destroyer and prepare stolidly to meet his doom, as does the wounded doe that hears the approaching footsteps of the hunter.

. . . But why would I mourn at the untimely fate of my people? Tribe follows tribe, and nation follows nation, like the waves of the sea. It is the order of nature, and regret is useless. Your time of decay may be distant, but it will surely come, for even the White Man whose God walked and talked with him as friend with friend, cannot be exempt from the common destiny. We may be brothers after all. We will see.

We will ponder your proposition and when we decide we will let you know. But should we accept it, I here and now make this condition that we will not be denied the privilege without molestation of visiting at any time the tombs of our ancestors, friends, and children. . . .

And when the last Red Man shall have perished, and the memory of my tribe shall have become a myth among the White Men, these shores will swarm with the invisible dead of my tribe, and when your children's children think themselves alone in the field, the store, the ship, upon the highway, or in the silence of the pathless woods, they will not be alone. In all the earth there is no place dedicated to solitude. At night when the streets of your cities and villages are silent and you think them deserted, they will throng with the returning hosts that once filled them and still love this beautiful land. The White Man will never be alone.

Let him be just and deal kindly with my people, for the dead are not powerless. Dead, did I say? There is no death, only a change of worlds.

12

Road to War

The 1850s was a decade of crisis, as the last hopes for peace between the North and South were shattered. The Compromise of 1850 quickly proved to be a failure, and as the years progressed, the political system became deadlocked and was unable to deal with the growing sectional divisions. Each day seemed to bring another occasion for northerners and southerners to become hardened in their stands. This chapter describes some of the events that inflamed sectional differences.

It begins with John C. Calhoun's fiery defense of the southern cause in opposition to the Compromise of 1850, engineered by Henry Clay, which allowed that California be brought into the Union as a free state, the admission of New Mexico and Utah as slave states, abolition of the slave trade in Washington, D.C., and stricter enforcement of the Fugitive Slave Law in the North. While it is filled with rhetoric and arguments in favor of secession, Calhoun described his speech as a plan to save the Union.

The northern side was as unwavering in its cause as Calhoun was in his. The Fugitive Slave Act, part of the Compromise of 1850, angered and impassioned many northerners, including Harriet Beecher Stowe. It inspired Stowe to write her bestselling novel, *Uncle Tom's Cabin*, which sold over 300,000 copies in the first year after its publication in 1852. So influential was it that during the Civil War Abraham Lincoln introduced Stowe as "the little lady who started the Civil War." The selection from *Uncle Tom's Cabin* excerpted here showcases the sensationalist and heartrending aspects of the novel, which brought the ethics of slavery into question for a wide audience.

While debate raged, until 1857 the United States Supreme Court had not been directly involved in the sectional conflict. However, a case on appeal from the circuit court afforded the Supreme Court the opportunity to finally render a decision on the constitutionality of the Missouri Compromise. Dred Scott and his wife Harriet sued the state of Missouri for their freedom. They argued that because they had been taken into territories where slavery was prohibited, they should be freed.

The Supreme Court's decision in *Dred Scott v. Sanford* was one of the most controversial events in a decade full of political controversy. Historians have long debated why Chief Justice Roger B. Taney, a staunch Jacksonian and a southern

Democrat, would abandon his hesitancy to impose judicial solutions on political problems. Taney's appointment in 1836 roughly coincided with the emergence of slavery as a national issue. At that time, the law, as it related to the status of slaves and free blacks, consisted of the Constitution, a few isolated Supreme Court cases, and a few, similarly isolated, acts of Congress and the executive branch. The Constitution clearly recognized slavery. The three-fifths compromise and the provision prohibiting the outlawing of the African slave trade until 1808 both implicitly recognized the institution of slavery. Moreover, the Constitution specifically provided that persons who owed service or labor in one state and escaped should, upon recapture, be returned to the person to whom such service was due.

The Supreme Court, led by Chief Justice Taney, who wrote one of nine opinions, argued that blacks—whether free or slave—were not citizens and thus could not sue in federal court. In addition, the Court declared that, because Congress did not have the power to ban slavery, the Missouri Compromise was unconstitutional. Dred Scott and his wife remained slaves.

The Dred Scott decision did not resolve the slavery issue and, in fact, further fueled the sectional fires already alight. Stephen Douglas, the Democratic senator from Illinois, had been active in passing the Compromise of 1850 and the Kansas-Nebraska Act and was in the national limelight throughout most of this period. His support of popular sovereignty made him seem a moderate in a time of political extremism. Many believed that Douglas could win the presidential election of 1860. In 1858 Douglas sought reelection to the Senate. His Republican opponent was Abraham Lincoln.

"A House Divided" was Lincoln's speech accepting the Republican nomination for that senate race. Up to that point, Lincoln had been a member of the House of Representatives and a lawyer in Springfield, Illinois. Although Douglas won reelection, the campaign brought Lincoln national attention. "A House Divided" was used later, during Lincoln's run for president, by southern politicians uneasy about the future and alarmed at the prospect of a Lincoln presidency

Study Questions

1. One observer noted that "Calhoun thought his plan would save the Union, but his speech was an argument for secession." In what ways does his speech bear this out?

2. Given the demographic and economic developments of the mid-nineteenth century, how reasonable were Calhoun's fears of northern domination?

3. How did *Uncle Tom's Cabin* foster northern abolitionist beliefs?

4. How are racial stereotypes embedded in Stowe's characterization of southern plantation life?

5. In his opinion, Taney stated that the "only issue" before the Court was whether African Americans could be citizens. In his decision, he argued that they could not, and went on to declare the Missouri Compromise unconstitutional. Why might Taney have gone on to address the issue of the constitutionality of the Missouri Compromise?

6. Why might southern politicians have seized on Lincoln's "A House Divided" speech to prove their own positions?

John C. Calhoun, Proposal to Preserve the Union (1850)

The debate over the Compromise of 1850 was one of the most extraordinary moments in the history of the Senate. Powerful orators eloquently defended their causes. The triumvirate of Henry Clay, John C. Calhoun, and Daniel Webster, who had dominated legislative politics for a generation, gave their last great performances. Younger politicians, such as Stephen Douglas, who would shape the politics of the next decade, grasped for leadership. The nation tottered on the brink of disunion, but both sides stared into the chasm and pulled back. This is Calhoun's impassioned defense of the southern cause. Only four weeks from death and too ill to read it for himself, Calhoun sat and listened while Senator James Mason of Virginia read it for him.

I have, Senators, believed from the first that the agitation of the subject of slavery would, if not prevented by some timely and effective measure, end in disunion. . . . The agitation has been permitted to proceed, with almost no attempt to resist it, until it has reached a period when it can no longer be disguised or denied that the Union is in danger. You have thus had forced upon you the greatest and the gravest question that can ever come under your consideration: How can the Union be preserved?

. . . The first question, then, presented for consideration, in the investigation I propose to make, in order to obtain such knowledge, is: What is it that has endangered the Union?

To this question there can be but one answer: That the immediate cause is the almost universal discontent which pervades all the States composing the southern section of the Union. . . .

It is a great mistake to suppose, as is by some, that it originated with demagogues. . . . No; some cause, far deeper and more powerful than the one supposed must exist to account for discontent so wide and deep. The question, then, recurs: What is the cause of this discontent? It will be found in the belief of the people of the southern States, as prevalent as the discontent itself, that they cannot remain, as things now are, consistently with honor and safety, in the Union. The next question to be considered is: What has caused this belief?

One of the causes is, undoubtedly, to be traced to the long-continued agitation of the slave question on the part of the North, and the many aggressions which they have made on the rights of the South during the time. . . .

There is another, lying back of it, with which this is intimately connected, that may be regarded as the great and primary cause. That is to be found in the fact that the equilibrium between the two sections in the Government, as it stood when the Constitution was ratified and the Government put in action has been destroyed. At that time there was nearly a perfect equilibrium between the two, which afforded ample means to each to protect itself against the aggression of the other; but, as it now stands, one section has the exclusive power of controlling the Government, which leaves the other without any adequate means of protecting itself against its encroachment and oppression. . . .

[The] great increase of Senators, added to the great increase of the House of Representatives and the electoral college on the part of the North, which must take place under the next decade, will effectually and irretrievably destroy the equilibrium which existed when the Government commenced. . . .

What was once a constitutional federal republic is now converted, in reality, into one as absolute as that of the Autocrat of Russia, and as despotic in its tendency as any absolute Government that ever existed.

As, then, the North has the absolute control over the Government, it is manifest that on all questions between it and the South, where there is a diversity of interests, the interests of the latter will be sacrificed to the former, however oppressive the effects may be. . . . But if there was no question of vital importance to the South, in reference to which there was a diversity of views between the two sections, this state of things might be endured without the hazard of destruction to the South. But such is not the fact. . . .

I refer to the relation between the two races in the southern section, which constitutes a vital portion of her social organization. Every portion of the North entertains views and feelings more or less hostile to it. . . .

If the agitation goes on, the same force, acting with increased intensity, as has been shown, will finally snap every cord, when nothing will be left to bind the States together except force. . . .

How can the Union be saved? To this I answer, there is but one way by which it can be, and that is by adopting such measures as will satisfy the States belonging to the southern section that they can remain in the Union consistently with their honor and their safety.

Harriet Beecher Stowe, from *Uncle Tom's Cabin* (1852)

This selection from *Uncle Tom's Cabin* describes a violent exchange between the slave master Simon Legree (a transplanted Connecticut native) and the patient slave Uncle Tom. Southerners criticized Stowe, who had very little (if any) experience of plantation life, for an atypical, distorted perception of slavery. Most northern readers were taken in by Stowe's tale and its somewhat sensationalized and sentimental portrayal of slavery.[*]

"And now," said Legree, "come here, you Tom. You see, I told ye I didn't buy ye jest for the common work. I mean to promote ye, and make a driver of ye; and tonight ye may jest as well begin to get ye hand in. Now, ye jest take this yer gal and flog her; ye've seen enough on't [of it] to know how." "I beg Mas'r' pardon," said Tom; "hopes Mas'r won't set me at that. It's what I an't used to—never did—and can't do, no way possible."

"Ye'll larn a pretty smart chance of things ye never did know, before I've done with ye!" said Legree, taking up a cowhide and striking Tom a heavy blow across the cheek, and following up the infliction by a shower of blows.

"There!" he said, as he stopped to rest; "now, will ye tell me ye can't do it?"

"Yes, Mas'r," said Tom, putting up his hand, to wipe the blood that trickled down his face. "I'm willin' to work, night and day, and work while there's life and breath in me. But this yer thing I can't feel it right to do; and, Mas'r, I never shall do it—never!"

Tom had a remarkably smooth, soft voice, and a habitually respectful manner that had given Legree an idea that he would be cowardly and easily subdued. When he spoke these last words, a thrill of amazement went through everyone. The poor woman clasped her hands and said, "O Lord!" and everyone involuntarily looked at each other and drew in their breath, as if to prepare for the storm that was about to burst.

Legree looked stupefied and confounded; but at last burst forth: "What! Ye blasted black beast! Tell me ye don't think it right to do what I tell ye! What have any of you cussed cattle to do with thinking what's right? I'll put a stop to it! Why, what do ye think ye are? May be ye think ye're a gentleman, master Tom, to be a telling your master what's right, and what an't! So you pretend it's wrong to flog the gal!"

"I think so, Mas'r," said Tom; "the poor crittur's sick and feeble; 'twould be downright cruel, and it's what I never will do, nor begin to. Mas'r, if you mean to kill me, kill me; but, as to my raising my hand again any one here, I never shall—I'll die first!"

Tom spoke in a mild voice, but with a decision that could not be mistaken. Legree shook with anger; his greenish eyes glared fiercely, and his very whiskers seemed to curl with passion. But, like some ferocious beast, that plays with its victim before he

[*] From Harriet B. Stowe, *Uncle Tom's Cabin* (Cleveland, 1852) .

devours it, he kept back his strong impulse to proceed to immediate violence, and broke out into bitterly raillery.

"Well, here's a pious dog, at last, let down among us sinners—a saint, a gentleman, and no less, to talk to us sinners about our sins! Powerful holy crittur, he must be! Here, you rascal, you make believe to be so pious—didn't you never hear, out of yer Bible, 'Servants, obey yer masters'? An't I yer master? Didn't I pay down twelve hundred dollars, cash, for all there is inside yer old cussed black shell? An't yer mine, now, body and soul?" he said, giving Tom a violent kick with his heavy boot; "tell me!"

In the very depth of physical suffering, bowed by brutal oppression, this question shot a gleam of joy an triumph through Tom's soul. He suddenly stretched himself up, and, looking earnestly to heaven, while the tears and blood that flowed down his face mingled, he exclaimed, " No! no! no! my soul an't yours, Mas'r! You haven't bought it—ye can't buy it! It's been bought and paid for by One that is able to keep it. No matter, no matter, you can't harm me!"

"I can't!" said Legree, with a sneer; "we'll see-we'll see! Here Sambo, Quimbo, give this dog such a breakin' in as he won't get over this month!"

The two gigantic Negroes that now laid hold of Tom, with fiendish exultation in their faces, might have formed no unapt personification of powers of darkness. The poor woman screamed with apprehension, and all rose, as by a general impulse, while they dragged him unresisting from the place.

Dred Scott v. Sanford (1857)

Dred and Harriet Scott first sued for their freedom in 1846, after their master, a doctor, had brought them from Missouri to Minnesota and Wisconsin. They waited more than ten years before the Supreme Court decision, which ultimately denied them their freedom, was handed down. This excerpt is from Chief Justice Roger Taney's decision.

The Question is simply this: Can a negro, whose ancestors were imported into this country, and sold as slaves, become a member of the political community formed and brought into existence by the Constitution of the United States, and as such become entitled to all the rights, and privileges, and immunities, guarantied [sic] by that instrument to the citizen? One of which rights is the privilege of suing in a court of the United States in the cases specified in the constitution.

... The only matter in issue before the Court, therefore, is, whether the descendants of such slaves, when they shall be emancipated, or who are born of parents who had become free before their birth, are citizens of a State, in the sense which the word citizen is used in the Constitution. . . .

The words "people of the United States" and "citizens" are synonymous terms. . . . They both describe the political body who, according to our republican institutions, form the sovereignty, and who hold the power and conduct the government through their representatives. . . . The question before us is, whether the class of persons described in the plea in abatement compose a portion of this people, and are constituent members of this sovereignty? We think they are not, under the word "citizens" in the Constitution, and can therefore claim none of the rights and privileges which that instrument provides for and secures to citizens of the United States. On the contrary, they were at that time considered as a subordinate and inferior class of beings, who had been subjugated by the dominant race, and whether emancipated or not, yet remained subject to their authority, and had no rights or privileges but such as those who held the power and the government might choose to grant them. . . .

In discussing the question, we must not confound the rights of citizenship which a State may confer within its own limits, and the rights of citizenship as a member of the Union. It does not by any means follow, because he has all the rights and privileges of a citizen of a State, that he must be a citizen of the United States. . . .

In the opinion of the court, the legislation and histories of the times, and the language used in the Declaration of Independence, show, that neither the class of persons who had been imported as slaves, nor their descendants, whether they had become free or not, were then acknowledged as a part of the people, nor intended to be included in the general words used in that memorable instrument. . . .

They had for more than a century before been regarded as beings of an inferior order, and altogether unfit to associate with the white race, either in social or political relations, and so far inferior, that they had no rights which the white man was bound to respect; and that the negro might justly and lawfully be reduced to slavery for his benefit. . . .

... there are two clauses in the constitution which point directly and specifically to the negro race as a separate class of persons, and show clearly that they were not regarded as a portion of the people or citizens of the government then formed.

... upon full and careful consideration of the subject, the court is of opinion, that, upon the facts stated. . . , Dred Scott was not a citizen of Missouri within the meaning of the constitution of the United States and not entitled as such to sue in its courts. . . .

Abraham Lincoln, "A House Divided" (1858)

This speech, one of the Lincoln's first as he came into the national spotlight, showcases his simple, clear style and persuasive rhetoric. Lincoln opposed the Dred Scott decision and believed that the South exerted an undue influence on national policy making. Far from a radical abolitionist, however, Lincoln believed blacks were inferior to whites and opposed allowing blacks to vote, marry whites, or to become citizens.[*]

If we could first know where we are, and whither we are tending, we could better judge what to do and how to do it. We are now far into the fifth year since a policy was initiated with the avowed object, and confident promise, of putting an end to slavery agitation. Under the operation of that policy, that agitation has not only not ceased but has constantly augmented. In my opinion, it will not cease until a crisis shall have been reached and passed. "A house divided against itself cannot stand." I believe this government cannot endure permanently half-slave and half-free. I do not expect the Union to be dissolved—I do not expect the house to fall—but I do expect it will cease to be divided. It will become all one thing or all the other. Either the opponents of slavery will arrest the further spread of it and place it where the public mind shall rest in the belief that it is in the course of ultimate extinction or its advocates will push it forward, till it shall become alike lawful in all the states, old as well as new—North as well as South.

---

[*] From *Political Debates between Hon. Abraham Lincoln and Hon. Stephen A. Douglas* . . . (Columbus, Ohio, 1860). Published as a campaign document by the Ohio Republican State Central Committee.

13

The World Turned Upside Down

The Civil War began with an outpouring of support in both the North and the South—thousands of young men rushed to volunteer to fight for the Union or for an independent Confederacy. Troops went off to battle expecting a brief engagement. However, the war was brutal and by the end of the fighting in 1865, over 600,000 men had been killed. In many ways, the Civil War transformed American society. Slavery was ended, the South was physically damaged and forced to adapt its distinctive economic system, and technological advancements and industries became more important in both North and South.

Slavery was not part of the rhetoric of the early part of the war. Most Northerners believed the war was being fought to preserve the Union and most southerners believed they were fighting for self-determination—not over the question of the spread of slavery or the emancipation of slaves. In fact, Lincoln argued that "If I could save the Union without freeing any slave, I would do it; and if I could save it by freeing all the slaves, I would do it." But in 1863, Lincoln did issue the Emancipation Proclamation freeing the slaves. Although the proclamation had little practical effect, it had great symbolic resonance, elevating the war to save the Union into a war to end slavery.

From the beginning of the war, blacks attempted to participate in the war effort, although they were initially rebuffed by the Union side. But war's end, over 186,000 African Americans had served in the Union forces. They received lower pay, had poorer supplies and equipment, and were led by white officers. The first two documents in this chapter describe the difficulties encountered by African Americans in the Union army during the war. In a 1863 letter to President Lincoln, an African American soldier, James Gooding, protests the lower pay received by black soldiers. In her reminiscences of the Civil War, Susie King Taylor, a slave who escaped to the Union army and followed her husband in the Thirty-third Colored Regiment, recalls that the men in her regiment refused their pay altogether until the government gave them their full pay.

There were many women, like Susie King Taylor, who served the army on the field and many more who took on increased responsibilities on the home front. Clara

Barton, nicknamed the "Angel of the Battlefield," was one of thousands of women who served as a field nurse during the Civil War. Until the Civil War, nursing was considered "unladylike" and an improper occupation for a well-bred woman, and Barton encountered tremendous resistance to her work in the war. In this selection, she describes her difficulties caring for thousands of suffering men dying on a battlefield in Virginia.

On the home front in the South as well as the North, women suffered great privations in addition to personal grief. A number of southern women kept diaries, and these offer powerful and personal insights into life in the Confederacy during the war. The selection here from the diary of Lucy Breckinridge of Virginia describes some of the personal losses she suffered.

Gettysburg is probably the most famous and arguably the most important battle of the Civil War. In the first three days of July 1863, Union troops, commanded by General George G. Mead, turned back a Confederate advance into Pennsylvania. It was the first time the Confederate General Robert E. Lee was clearly beaten on the battlefield and that marked a crucial military turning point. After the carnage, the South would never again mount an offensive into northern territory. In the following November, Lincoln came to Gettysburg to dedicate a memorial cemetery. The last document is Lincoln's famous Gettysburg Address.

Study Questions

1. What was James Gooding's rationale for asking for increased wages from President Lincoln?

2. Compare Susie King Taylor's and James Gooding's rhetoric.

3. Why might Clara Barton's nursing activity have been considered improper or unladylike?

4. Compare Clara Barton's reaction to the general carnage of the battlefield with Lucy Breckinridge's reaction to the death of her brother.

5. Why is the Gettysburg Address one of the great symbols of the Civil War and American history? To whom did Lincoln extend new "freedom?"

James Henry Gooding, Letter to President Lincoln (1863)

In this eloquent letter, written after the Emancipation proclamation, James Henry Gooding wrote to his president, complaining about his ill-treatment and that he had not been paid in over a month. No answer from President Lincoln is recorded. [*]

Morris Island, S.C.

September 28, 1863

Your Excellency, Abraham Lincoln:

Your Excellency will pardon the presumption of an humble individual like myself, in addressing you, but the earnest solicitation of my comrades in arms besides the genuine interest felt by myself in the matter is my excuse, for placing before the Executive head of the Nation our Common Grievance.

On the 6th of the last Month, the Paymaster of the Department informed us, that if we would decide to receive the sum of $10 (ten dollars) per month, he would come and pay us that sum, but that, on the sitting of Congress, the Regt. [regiment] would, in his opinion, be allowed the other 3 (three). He did not give us any guarantee that this would be, as he hoped; certainly he had no authority for making any such guarantee, and we cannot suppose him acting in any way interested.

Now the main question is, are we Soldiers, or are we Laborers? We are fully armed, and equipped, have done all the various duties pertaining to a Soldier's life, have conducted ourselves to the complete satisfaction of General Officers, who were, if anything, prejudiced against us, but who now accord us all the encouragement and honors due us; have shared the perils an labor of reducing the first strong-hold that flaunted a Traitor Flag; and more, Mr. President, to-day the Anglo-Saxon Mother, Wife, or Sister are not alone in tears for departed Sons, Husbands, and Brothers. The patient, trusting descendant of Afric's Clime have dyed the ground with blood, in defence of the Union, and Democracy. Men, too, your Excellency, who know in a measure the cruelties of the iron heel of oppression, which in years gone by, the very power their blood is now being spilled to maintain, ever ground them in the dust.

But when the war trumpet sounded o'er the land, when men knew not the Friend from the Traitor, the black man laid his life at the altar of the Nation,—and he was refused. When the arms of the Union were beaten, in the first year of the war, and the Executive called for more food for its ravenous maw, again the black man begged the privilege of aiding his country in her need, to be again refused.

And now he is in the War, and how has he conducted himself? Let their dusky forms rise up, out of the mires of James Island, and give the answer. Let the rich mould

[*] Reprinted from *A Documentary History of the Negro People in the U.S.* ed. Herbert Aptheker (New York: Citadel Press, 1951), 482–484.

around Wagner's parapet be upturned, and there will be found an eloquent answer. Obedient and patient and solid as a wall are they. All we lack is a paler hue and a better acquaintance with the alphabet.

Now your Excellency, we have done a Soldier's duty. Why can't we have a Soldier's pay? You caution the Rebel chieftain, that the United States knows no distinction in her soldiers. She insists on having all her soldiers of whatever creed or color, to be treated according to the usages of War. Now if the United States exacts uniformity of treatment of her soldiers from the insurgents, would it not be well and consistent to set the example herself by paying all her soldiers alike?

We of this Regt. were not enlisted under any "contraband" act. But we do not wish to be understood as rating our service of more value to the Government than the service of the ex-slave. Their service is undoubtedly worth much to the Nation, but Congress made express provision touching their case, as slaves freed by military necessity, and assuming the Government to be their temporary Guardian. Not so with us. Freemen by birth and consequently having the advantage of thinking and acting for ourselves so far as the Laws would allow us, we do not consider ourselves fit subjects for the Contraband act.

We appeal to you, Sir, as the Executive of the Nation, to have us justly dealt with. The Regt. do pray that they be assured their service will be fairly appreciated by paying them as American Soldiers, not as menial hirelings. Black men, you may well know, are poor; three dollars per month, for a year, will supply their needy wives and little ones with fuel. If you, as Chief Magistrate of the Nation, will assure us of our whole pay, we are content. Our Patriotism, our enthusiasm will have a new impetus, to exert our energy more and more to aid our Country. Not that our hearts ever flagged in devotion, spite the evident apathy displayed in our behalf, but we feel as though our country spurned us, now we are sworn to serve her. Please give this a moment's attention.

Susie King Taylor, Reminiscences of an Army Laundress (1902)

Susie King Taylor traveled with the Thirty-third U.S. Colored Regiment in which her husband served. She and her husband were two of five thousand slaves who escaped to the Union army. This excerpt describes some of the daily life of a soldier and a soldier's wife and the special indignities suffered by African-American fighting men.*

---

* From Susie King Taylor, *Reminiscences of My Life in Camp with the 33rd United States Colored Troops* (Boston: 1902), 15–16, 26–28, 32–35.

I was enrolled as company laundress, but I did very little of it, because I was always busy doing other things through camp, and was employed all the time doing something for the officers and comrades. . . .

The first colored troops did not receive any pay for eighteen months, and the men had to depend wholly on what they received from the commissary, established by Gen. Saxton. A great many of these men had large families, and as they had no money to give them, their wives were obliged to support themselves and children by washing for the officers of the gunboats and the soldiers, and making cakes and pies, which they sold to the boys in camp. Finally, in 1863, the government decided to give them half pay, but the men would not accept this. They wanted "full pay or nothing." They preferred rather to give their services to the state, which they did until 1864, when the government granted them full pay with all the back pay due. . .

I learned to handle a musket very well while in the regiment and could shoot straight and often hit the target. I assisted in cleaning the guns and used to fire them off, to see if the cartridges were dry, before cleaning and re-loading, each day. I thought this was great fun. I was also able to take a gun all apart and put it together again. . . .

We had fresh beef once in a while, and we would have soup, and the vegetables they put in the soup were dried and pressed; they looked like hops. Salt beef was our standby. Sometimes the men would have what we called slap-jacks. This was flour made into bread and spread thin on the bottom of the mess-pan to cook; each man had one of them with a pint of tea for his supper, or a pint of tea and five or six hardtack. I often got my own meals and would fix some dishes for the noncommissioned officers also.

About the first of June, 1864, the regiment was ordered to Folly Island, staying there until the latter part of the month, when it was ordered to Morris Island. We landed on Morris Island between June and July, 1864. This island was a narrow strip of sandy soil, nothing growing on it but a few bushes and shrubs. The camp was one mile from the boat landing, called Pawnell Landing, and the landing one mile from Fort Wagner. . . .

About four o'clock, July 2, the charge was made. The firing could be plainly heard in camp. I hastened down to the landing and remained there until eight o'clock that morning. When the wounded arrived, or rather began to arrive, the first one brought in was Samuel Anderson of our company. He was badly wounded. Then others of our boys, some with their legs off, arm gone, foot off, and wounds of all kinds imaginable. They had to wade through creeks and marshes, as they were discovered by the enemy and shelled very badly. A number of the men were lost, some got fastened in the mud and had to cut off the legs of their pants, to free themselves. The 103rd New York suffered the most, as their men were very badly wounded.

My work now began. I gave my assistance to try to alleviate their sufferings. I asked the doctor at the hospital what I could get for them to eat. They wanted soup, but that I could not get; but I had a few cans of condensed milk and some turtle eggs, so I thought I would try to make some custard. I had doubts as to my success, for cooking with turtle eggs was something new to me, but the adage has it, "Nothing ventured, nothing done," so I made a venture and the result was a very delicious custard. This I carried to the men, who enjoyed it very much. My services were given at all times for the comfort of these men. I was on hand to assist whenever needed.

Clara Barton, Medical Life at the Battlefield (1862)

Clara Barton was one of many women who worked in support of the war effort by nursing troops, raising funds, and making clothes and bandages. This selection from her memoirs describes her initial ambivalence about going to work in the war effort and the nightmarish conditions she found on the battlefield.*

I was strong and thought I might go to the rescue of the men who fell. . . . What could I do but go with them, or work for them and my country? The patriot blood of my father was warm in my veins. The country which he had fought for, I might at least work for. . . .

But I struggled long and hard with my sense of propriety—with the appalling fact that I was only a woman whispering in one ear, and thundering in the other the groans of suffering men dying like dogs—unfed and unsheltered, for the life of every institution which had protected and educated me!

I said that I struggled with my sense of propriety and I say it with humiliation and shame. I am ashamed that I thought of such a thing.

When our armies fought on Cedar Mountain, I broke the shackles and went to the field. . . .

Five days and nights with three hours sleep—a narrow escape from capture—and some days of getting the wounded into hospitals at Washington, brought Saturday, August 30. And if you chance to feel, that the positions I occupied were rough and unseemly for a *woman*—I can only reply that they were rough and unseemly for *men*. But under all, lay the life of the nation. I had inherited the rich blessing of health and strength of constitution—such as are seldom given to woman—and I felt that some return was due from me and that I ought to be there. . . .

. . . . Our coaches were not elegant or commodious; they had no seats, no platforms, no steps, a slide door on the side the only entrance, and this higher than my head. For my man attaining my elevated position, I must beg of you to draw on your imaginations and spare me the labor of reproducing the boxes, boards, and rails, which in those days, seemed to help me up and down the world. We did not criticize the unsightly helpers and were thankful that the stiff springs did not quite jostle us out. This need not be limited to this particular trip or train, but will for all that I have known in Army life. This is the kind of conveyance which your tons of generous gifts

* From Perry H. Epler, *Life of Clara Barton* (Macmillan, 1915), 31–32, 35–43, 45, 59, 96–98.

have reached the field with the freights. These trains through day and night, sunshine and heat and cold, have thundered over heights, across plains, the ravines, and over hastily built army bridges 90 feet across the stream beneath.

At 10 o'clock Sunday (August 31) our train drew up at Fairfax Station. The ground, for acres, was a thinly wooded slope—and among the trees on the leaves and grass, were laid the wounded who pouring in by scores of wagon loads, as picked up on the field the flag of truce. All day they came and the whole hillside was red. Bales of hay were broken open and scattered over the ground littering of cattle, and the sore, famishing men were laid upon it.

And when the night shut in, in the mist and darkness about us, we knew that standing apart from the world of anxious hearts, throbbing over the whole country, we were a little band of almost empty handed workers literally by ourselves in the wild woods of Virginia, with 3,000 suffering men crowded upon the few acres within our reach.

After gathering up every available implement or convenience for our work, our domestic inventory stood 2 water buckets, 5 tin cups, 1 camp kettle, 1 stew pan, 2 lanterns, 4 bread knives, 3 plates, and a 2-quart tin dish, and 3,000 guest to serve.

You will perceive by this, that I had not yet learned to equip myself, for I was no Pallas, ready armed, but grew into my work by hard thinking and sad experience. It may serve to relieve your apprehension for the future of my labors if I assure you that I was never caught so again.

But the most fearful scene was reserved for the night. I have said that the ground was littered with dry hay and that we had only two lanterns, but there were plenty of candles. The wounded were laid so close that it was impossible to move about in the dark. The slightest misstep brought a torrent of groans from some poor mangled fellow in your path.

Consequently here were seen persons of all grades from the careful man of God who walked with a prayer upon his lips to the careless driver hunting for his lost whip,—each wandering about among this hay with an open flaming candle in his hands.

The slightest accident, the mere dropping of a light could have enveloped in flames this whole mass of helpless men.

How we watched and pleaded and cautioned as we worked and wept that night! How we put socks and slippers upon their cold feet, wrapped your blankets and quilts about them, and when we no longer these to give, how we covered them in the hay and left them to their rest! . . .

The slight, naked chest of a fair-haired lad caught my eye, dropping down beside him, I bent low to draw the remnant of his blouse about him, when with a quick cry he threw his left arm across my neck and, burying his face in the folds of my dress, wept like a child at his mother's knee. I took his head in my hands and held it until great burst of grief passed away. "And do you know me?" he asked at length, "I am Charley Hamilton, we used to carry your satchel home from school!" My faithful pupil, poor Charley. That mangled right hand would never carry a satchel again.

About three o'clock in the morning I observed a surgeon with a little flickering candle in hand approaching me with cautious step up in the wood. "Lady," he said as he drew near, "will you go with me? Out on the hills is a poor distressed lad, mortally wounded, and dying. His piteous cries for his sister have touched all our hearts none of us can relieve him but rather seem to distress him by presence."

By this time I was following him back over the bloody track, with great beseeching eyes of anguish on every side looking up into our faces, saying so plainly, "Don't step on us."

Lucy Breckinridge, Diary (1862)

Only eighteen when the war began, Lucy Gilmer Breckinridge, a member of an old-line Virginia family, began keeping a diary in the summer of 1862. Before the war ended, five of her brothers had joined the Confederate army. Given its location south and west of the fighting in the Valley Campaign, the family home, Grove Hill, was spared the devastation of battle. Still, the war was part of daily life. Women at Grove Hill sewed clothing, made bandages, cared for the sick and wounded, read, prayed, and worried about their loved ones.*

Sunday, August 12th, 1862

It rained so steadily today that we could not go to church. I sat all the morning in the library with George talking about "reds" and marriages. He said very earnestly, "Well, Luce, take my advice and do not get married until the war is over. There are many reasons why you should not; for instance, you might be a widow in a short time." Then, after thinking a few minutes, it seemed to strike him that it would not be such a bad thing to be a pretty young widow. He has an idea that I am engaged, and seems to take a great deal more interest in me; treats me with marked respect and unwonted tenderness. He is a funny boy and a very sweet one. I never loved him so much before, because all my special love was given to John [Lucy's brother]. He and I were so nearly the same age, and never were separated in any way until the last two or three years. I loved him better than anyone on earth. Though we were playmates from our babyhood, I do not ever remember having been angry with John. I was more intimate with him and stayed with him more than I did with Eliza [Lucy's sister]. We never formed a plan for the future in which we were not connected. Everything seems changed to me since he died. He was the noblest and best of us all, and all his life had

---

* From *Lucy Breckinridge of Grove Hill*, ed. Mary Robertson (Kent, Ohio: Kent State University Press, 1979).

been the favorite with his brothers and sisters. "God takes our dearest even so; the reason why we cannot know; helpless he leaves us crushed with woe."

Eliza and Emma went over to the graveyard and put up a white cross with John's name on it and the date of the Battle of Seven Pines with the inscription, "He hath entered into peace," and put garlands of ivy on it. It is only a temporary mark for the grave. All of his brothers and sisters wish to raise a monument to his memory, the first of our band who has been taken from us. What a sad summer this has been.

Abraham Lincoln, Gettysburg Address (1863)

In this memorial speech, Lincoln, with characteristic rhetorical power, connected the sufferings of individual soldiers with the larger purposes of the Civil War—to preserve the Union and to preserve freedom for all. Although Lincoln spoke of "all men being equal" it is not quite clear how "equal" he found African Americans to be.[*]

Four score and seven years ago our fathers brought forth on this continent a new nation, conceived in liberty, and dedicated to the proposition that all men are created equal.

Now we are engaged in a great civil war, testing whether that nation, or any nation so conceived and so dedicated, can long endure. We are met on a great battlefield of that war. We have come to dedicate a portion of that field as a final resting-place for those who here gave their lives that nation might live. It is altogether fitting and proper that we should do this.

But, in a larger sense, we cannot dedicate—we cannot consecrate—we cannot hallow—this ground. The brave men, living and dead, who struggled here, have consecrated it far above our poor power to add or detract. The world will little note nor long remember what we say here, but it can never forget what they did here. It is for us, the living, rather, to be dedicated here to the unfinished work which they who fought here have thus far so nobly advanced. It is rather for us to be here dedicated to the great task remaining before us—that from these honored dead we take increased devotion to that cause for which they gave the last full measure of devotion; that we here highly resolve that these dead shall not have died in vain; that this nation, under God, shall have a new birth of freedom; and that government of the people, by the people, for the people, shall not perish from the earth.

---

[*] From *Abraham Lincoln, Complete Works* . . . , eds. John G. Nicolay and John Hay (New York, 1905), IX, 209–210.

14

To Heal the Nation's Wounds

At the end of the Civil War, the nation remained in crisis. The most pressing question facing it was how to reconstruct the Union—what to do with the newly emancipated slaves and in what capacity and under what conditions to readmit the states of the Confederacy to the Union. While these issues were debated nationally, the South quickly attempted to find solutions for the economic and social disruptions that had occurred as a result of the war.

As an agrarian economy, the South had depended on land and slave labor for its wealth. The war had destroyed much of the land and had eliminated the institution of slavery. In the first years after the war ended, the white power structure devised new political and economic arrangements to revive the economy. The Black Codes were instituted by southern legislatures immediately following the war as a means of reestablishing white dominance and assuaging white fear. The codes defined the relationship between African Americans and white Southerners—laying out exactly what rights newly emancipated slaves were entitled to.

The continued dependence on an agricultural economy and the loss of the dependable labor pool provided by slavery forced the South to look for a replacement, while the freedmen did not have the necessary capital to develop an independent farming system. As a result, legal slavery was replaced throughout the South with the economic bondage known as sharecropping. Included in this chapter is a typical contractual agreement between a landowner and a sharecropper.

The Radical Republicans reacted quickly to the legal and economic changes being made in the South. Unlike the executive branch, which believed a quick and expedient readmission of the South to the Union was possible, these legislators thought that the white South was insufficiently repentant for the war and deserved punishment. They attempted to institute their own plans for Reconstruction, which included federal protection for the freedmen. The Fourteenth Amendment was intended guarantee the political rights of the freedmen and punish southerners who had actively participated in the war. Congress secured ratification by threatening the South with no national representation if they did not ratify the amendment and if freedmen were denied the right to vote.

During the period in which the federal government controlled the south, some white Southerners sought extralegal ways to maintain control. Among the organizations that developed was the Ku Klux Klan, a quasi-secret society dedicated to using violence to intimidate and influence the political actions of the freedmen. The last document in this chapter is a collection of statements made by former slaves looking back on their experiences with the Klan. Pierce Harper recalled that if freedmen, ". . . made good money an' had a good farm de Ku Klux'd come and murder you." The Klan, powerful throughout the South, intimidated and terrorized African Americans who tried to live out the promise of freedom.

Study Questions

1. How was the relationship between white and black societies defined by the Black Codes?

2. What privileges did freedmen gain and lose in the Black Codes?

3. Did the freedmen have any alternative to the sharecropping system?

4. Under the sharecropping system, had the freedmen replaced their legal slavery with economic slavery?

5. Why didn't the Fourteenth Amendment ensure the political enfranchisement of the freedmen?

6. According to the testimony of the former slaves how did the Ku Klux Klan intimidate and threaten their existence?

Mississippi Black Code (1865)

The Mississippi Black Codes are an example of the manner by which the old order was maintained in the South while African Americans were given limited new rights. Many in the North and the Republicans in Congress were alarmed by the black codes. Reaction to the codes helped to radicalize Congress and catalyzed its attempt to seize control of Reconstruction from the president.[*]

The Civil Rights of Freedmen in Mississippi

Section 1. Be it enacted by the legislature of the State of Mississippi, That all freedmen, free Negroes, and mulattoes may sue and be sued, implead and be

---

[*] From *Mississippi, Laws of the State . . .* , 1865 (Jackson, Miss., 1896), 82–86.

impleaded in all the courts of law and equity of this state, and may acquire personal property and choses in action, by descent or purchase, any may dispose of the same, in the same manner, and to the same extent that white persons may: Provided that the provisions of this section shall not be so construed as to allow any freedman, free Negro, or mulatto to rent or lease any lands or tenements, except in incorporated town or cities in which places the corporate authorities shall control the same.

Sec. 2. Be it further enacted, That all freedmen, free Negroes, and mulattoes may intermarry with each other, in the same manner and under the same regulations that are provided by law for white persons: Provided, that the clerk of probate shall keep separate records of the same.

Sec. 3. Be it further enacted, That all freedmen, free Negroes, and mulattoes, who do now and have heretofore lived and cohabited together as husband and wife shall be taken and held in law as legally married, and the issue shall be taken and held as legitimate for all purposes. That it shall not be lawful for any freedman, free Negro, or mulatto to intermarry with any white person; nor for any white person to intermarry with any freedman, free Negro, or mulatto; any person who shall so intermarry shall be deemed guilty of felony and, on conviction thereof, shall be confined in the state penitentiary for life; and those shall be deemed freedmen, free Negroes, and mulattoes who are of pure Negro blood, and those descended from a Negro to the third generation inclusive, though one ancestor of each generation may have been a white person.

Sec. 4. Be it further enacted, That in addition to cases in which freedmen, free Negroes, and mulattoes are now by law competent witnesses, freedmen, free Negroes, or mulattoes shall be competent in civil cases when a party or parties to the suit, either plaintiff or plaintiffs, defendant or defendants, also in cases where freedmen, free Negroes, and mulattoes is or are either plaintiff or plaintiffs, defendant or defendants, and a white person or white persons is or are the opposing party or parties, plaintiff or plaintiffs, defendant or defendants. They shall also be competent witnesses in all criminal prosecutions where the crime charged is alleged to have been committed by a white person upon or against the person or property of a freedman, free Negro, or mulatto: Provided that in all cases said witnesses shall be examined in open court on the stand, except, however, they may be examined before the grand jury, and shall in all cases be subject to the rules and tests of the common law as to competency and credibility.

Sec. 5. Be it further enacted, That every freedman, free Negro, and mulatto shall, on the second Monday of January, one thousand eight hundred and sixty-six, and annually thereafter, have a lawful home or employment. . . .

Sec. 6. Be it further enacted, That all contracts for labor made with freedmen, free Negroes, and mulattoes for a longer period than one month shall be in writing and in duplicate, attested and read to said freedman, free Negro, or mulatto, by a beat, city or county officers, or two disinterested white persons of the country in which the labor is to be performed, of which each party shall have one; and said contracts shall be taken and held as entire contracts, and if the laborer shall quit the service of the employer, before expiration of his term of service, without good cause, he shall forfeit his wages for that year, up to the time of quitting.

Sec. 7.   Be it further enacted, That every civil officer shall, and every person may, arrest and carry back to his or her legal employer any freedman, free Negro, or mulatto who shall have quit the service of his or her employer before the expiration of his or her term of service without good cause, and said officer and person shall be entitled to receive for arresting and carrying back every deserting employee aforesaid, the sum of five dollars, and ten cents per mile from the place of arrest to the place of delivery, and the same shall be paid by the employer, and held as a set-off for so much against the wages of said deserting employee.

Sec. 8.   Be it further enacted, That upon affidavit made by the employer of any freedman, free Negro, or mulatto, or other credible person, before any justice of the peace or member of the board of police, that any freedman, free Negro, or mulatto, legally employed by said employer, has illegally deserted said employment, such justice of the peace or member of the board of police shall issue his warrant or warrants, returnable before himself, or other such officer, directed to any sheriff, constable, or special deputy, commanding him to arrest said deserter and return him or her to said employer, and the like proceedings shall be had as provided in the preceding section. . . .

Sec. 9.   Be it further enacted, That if any person shall persuade or attempt to persuade, entice, or cause any freedman, free Negro, or mulatto to desert from the legal employment of any person, before the expiration of his or her term of service, or shall knowingly employ any such deserting freedman, free Negro, or mulatto, or shall knowingly give or sell to any such deserting freedman, free Negro, or mulatto, any food, raiment, or other thing, he or she shall be guilty of a misdemeanor and, upon conviction, shall be fined not less than twenty-five dollars and not more then two hundred dollars and the costs, and, if said fine and costs shall not be immediately paid, the court shall sentence said convict to not exceeding two months' imprisonment in the county jail, and he or she shall moreover be liable to the party injured in damages: . . . .

Sec. 10.   Be it further enacted, That it shall be lawful for any freedman, free Negro, or mulatto to charge any white person, freedman, free Negro, or mulatto, by affidavit, with any criminal offense against his or her person or property and upon such affidavit the proper process shall be issued and executed as if said affidavit was made by a white person, and it shall be lawful for any freedman, free Negro, or mulatto, in any action, suit, or controversy pending, or about to be instituted, in any court of law or equity of this state, to make all needful and lawful affidavits, as shall be necessary for the institution, prosecution, or defense of such suit or controversy.

Sec. 11. Be it further enacted, That the penal laws of this state, in all cases not otherwise specially provided for, shall apply and extend to all freedmen, free Negroes, and mulattoes. . . .

Approved November 25, 1865

A Sharecrop Contract (1882)

This is a typical contractual agreement between a landowner and sharecropper. The system ensured that the sharecropper remained poor and in debt to the owner and that the sharecropper might never become an independent farmer.*

To every one applying to rent land upon shares, the following conditions must be read, and agreed to.

To every 30 and 35 acres, I agree to furnish the team, plow, and farming implements, except cotton planters, and I do not agree to furnish a cart to every cropper. The croppers are to have half of the cotton, corn, and fodder (and peas and pumpkins and potatoes if any are planted) if the following conditions are complied with, but—if not—they are to have only two-fifths ($^2/_5$). Croppers are to have no part or interest in the cotton seed raised from the crop planted and worked by them. No vine crops of any description, that is, no watermelons, muskmelons, . . . squashes or anything of that kind, except peas and pumpkins, and potatoes, are to be planted in the cotton or corn. All must work under my direction. All plantation work to be done by the croppers. My part of the crop to be housed by them, and the fodder and oats to be hauled and put in the house. All the cotton must be topped about 1st August. If any cropper fails from any cause to save all the fodder from his crop, I am to have enough fodder to make it equal to one-half of the whole if the whole amount of fodder had been saved.

For every mule or horse furnished by me there must be 1000 good sized rails. . . hauled, and the fence repaired as far as they will go, the fence to be torn down and put up from the bottom if I so direct. All croppers to haul rails and work on fence whenever I may order. Rails to be split when I may say. Each cropper to clean out every ditch in his crop, and where a ditch runs between two croppers, the cleaning out of that ditch is to be divided equally between them. Every ditch bank in the crop must be shrubbed down and cleaned off before the crop is planted and must be cut down every time the land is worked with his hoe and when the crop is "laid by," the ditch

* From *Grimes Family Papers* (#3357), 1882. Held in the Southern Historical Collection University of North Carolina, Chapel Hill.

banks must be left clean of bushes, weeds, and seeds. The cleaning out of all ditches must be done by the first of October. The rails must be split and the fence repaired before corn is planted.

Each cropper must keep in good repair all bridges in his crop or over ditches that he has to clean out and when a bridge needs repairing that is outside of all their crops, then any one that I call on must repair it.

Fence jams to be done as ditch banks. If any cotton is planted on the land outside of the plantation fence, I am to have three-fourths of all the cotton made in those patches, that is to say, no cotton must be planted by croppers in their home patches.

All croppers must clean out stable and fill them with straw, and haul straw in front of stable whenever I direct. All the cotton must be manured, and enough fertilizer must be brought to manure each crop highly, the croppers to pay for one-half of all manure bought, the quantity to be purchased for each crop must be left to me.

No cropper is to work off the plantation when there is any work to be done on the land he has rented, or when his work is needed by me or other croppers. Trees to be cut down on Orchard, house field, & Evanson fences, leaving such as I may designate.

Road field is to be planted from the very edge of the ditch to the fence, and all the land to be planted close up to the ditches and fences. No stock of any kind belonging to croppers to run in the plantation after crops are gathered.

If the fence should be blown down, or if trees should fall on the fence outside of the land planted by any of the croppers, any one or all that I may call upon must put it up and repair it. Every cropper must feed or have fed, the team he works, Saturday nights, Sundays, and every morning before going to work, beginning to feed his team (morning, noon, and night every day in the week) on the day he rents and feeding it to including the 31st day of December. If any cropper shall from any cause fail to repair his fence as far as 1000 rails will go, or shall fail to clean out any part of his ditches, or shall fail to leave his ditch banks, any part of them, well shrubbed and clean when his crop is laid by, or shall fail to clean out stables, fill them up and haul straw in front of them whenever he is told, he shall have only two-fifths ($^2/_5$) of the cotton, corn, fodder, peas, and pumpkins made on the land he cultivates.

If any cropper shall fail to feed his team Saturday nights, all day Sunday and all the rest of the week, morning/noon, and night, for every time he so fails he must pay me five cents.

No corn or cotton stalks must be burned, but must be cut down, cut up and plowed in. Nothing must be burned off the land except when it is impossible to plow it in.

Every cropper must be responsible for all gear and farming implements placed in his hands, and if not returned must be paid for unless it is worn out by use.

Croppers must sow & plow in oats and haul them to the crib, but must have no part of them. Nothing to be sold from their crops, nor fodder nor corn to be carried out of the fields until my rent is all paid, and all amounts they owe me and for which I am responsible are paid in full.

I am to gin & pack all the cotton and charge every cropper an eighteenth of his part, the cropper to furnish his part of the bagging, ties, & twine.

The sale of every cropper's part of the cotton to be made by me when and where I choose to sell, and after deducting all they owe me and all sums that I may be responsible for on their accounts, to pay them their half of the net proceeds. Work of every description, particularly the work on fences and ditches, to be done to my satisfaction, and must be done over until I am satisfied that it is done as it should be.

No wood to burn, nor light wood, nor poles, nor timber for boards, nor wood for any purpose whatever must be gotten above the house occupied by Henry Beasley—nor must any trees be cut down nor any wood used for any purpose, except for firewood, without my permission.

The Fourteenth Amendment (1868)

> The Fourteenth Amendment, designed to protect the rights of freedmen and grant them the right to vote, was proposed by the Radical Republicans in Congress. President Andrew Johnson and the Democrats campaigned against the amendment (and the Radical Republicans), arguing that it represented a step toward black equality and that it would change congressional representation by eliminating the three-fifths provision. It was ratified only after Congress made readmission of southern states dependent on their ratification. Women, like Susan B. Anthony and Elizabeth Cady Stanton, campaigned against the amendment because it did not grant suffrage to women.

Sec. 1. All persons born or naturalized in the United States, and subject to the jurisdiction thereof, are citizens of the United States and of the State wherein they reside. No State shall make or enforce any law which shall abridge the privileges or immunities of citizens of the United States; nor shall any State deprive any person of life, liberty, or property, without due process of law; nor deny to any person within its jurisdiction the equal protection of the laws.

Sec. 2. Representatives shall be apportioned among the several States according to their respective numbers, counting the whole number of persons in each State, excluding Indians not taxed. But when the right to vote at any election for the choice of electors for President and Vice President of the United States, Representatives in Congress, the Executive and Judicial officers of a State, or the members of the Legislature thereof, is denied to any of the male inhabitants of such State, being twenty-one years of age, and citizens of the United States, or in any way abridged, except for participation in rebellion, or other crime, the basis of representation therein shall be reduced in the proportion which the number of such male citizens shall bear to the whole number of male citizens twenty-one years of age in such State.

Sec. 3. No person shall be a Senator or Representative in Congress, or elector of President and Vice President, or hold any office, civil or military, under the United States, or under any State, who, having previously taken an oath, as a member of Congress, or as an officer of the United States, or as a member of any State legislature, or as an executive or judicial officer of any State, to support the Constitution of the United States, shall have engaged in insurrection or rebellion against the same, or given aid or comfort to the enemies thereof. But Congress may by a vote of two-thirds of each House, remove such disability.

Sec. 4. The validity of the public debt of the United States, authorized by law, including debts incurred for payment of pensions and bounties for services in suppressing insurrection or rebellion, shall not be questioned. But neither the United States nor any State shall assume or pay any debt or obligation incurred in aid of insurrection or rebellion against the united States, or any claim for the loss or emancipation of any slave; but all such debts, obligations and claims shall be held illegal and void.

Sec. 5. The Congress shall have power to enforce, by appropriate legislation, the provisions of this article.

The Victims of the Ku Klux Klan (1935)

These statements are from a collection of oral histories collected from former slaves under the New Deal's WPA Writers Project. They describe in detail some of the tactics of the Klan, whose goal, according to U.S. President Ulysses S. Grant, was "to reduce the colored people to a condition closely allied to that of slavery."*

Pierce Harper

After de colored people was considered free an' turned loose de Klu Klux broke out. Some of de colored people commenced to farming like I tol' you an' all de ol' stock dey could pick up after de Yankees left dey took an' took care of. If you got so you made good money an' had a good farm de Klu Klux'd come an' murder you. De gov'ment built de colored people school houses an' de Klu Klux went to work an' burn 'em down. Dey'd go to de jails an' take de colored men out an' knock der brains out an' break der necks an' throw 'em in de river.

Der was a man dat dey taken, his name was Jim Freeman. Dey taken him an' destroyed his stuff an' him 'cause he was making some money. Hung him on a tree in his front yard, right in front of his cabin. Der was some young men who went to de schools de gov'ment opened for de colored folks. Some white widder woman said someone had stole something she own', so dey put these young fellers in jail 'cause dey suspicioned 'em. De Klu Kluxes went to de jail an' took 'em out an' kill 'em. Dat happened de second year after de War.

After de Klu Kluxes got so strong de colored men got together an' made a complaint before de law. De Gov'nor told de law to give 'em de ol' guns in de commissary what de Southern soldiers had use, so dey issued de col'red men old muskets an' told 'em to protect theirselves.

De colored men got together an' organized the 'Malicy [Militia]. Dey had leaders like regular soldiers, men dat led 'em right on. Dey didn't meet 'cept when dey heard de Klu Kluxes was coming to get some of de colored folks. Den de one who knowed dat tol' de leader an' he went 'round an' told de others when an' where dey's meet. Den dey was ready for 'em. Dey's hide in de cabins an' when de Klu Kluxes come dere dey was. Den's when dey found out who a lot of de Klu Kluxes was, 'cause a lot of 'em was killed. Dey wore dem long sheets an' you couldn't tell who dey was. Dey even covered der horses up so you couldn't tell who dey belong to. Men you thought was your friend was Klu Kluxes. You deal wit' em in de stores in de day time an' at night dey come out to your house an' kill you.

Sue Craft

My teacher's name Dunlap—a white teacher teachin' de cullud. De Ku Klux whupped him fo' teachin' us. I saw de Ku Klux ridin' a heap dem days. Dey had hoods pulled ovah der faces. One time dey come to our house twict. Fus' time dey come quiet. It was right 'fore de 'lection o' Grant jus' after slavery. It was fus' time cullud people 'lowed t' vote. Dey ast my father was he goint to vote for Grant. He tell 'em he don' know he goin' vote. After 'lection day come back, whoopin' an' hollerin. Dey shoot out de winder lights. It was 'cause my father voted for Grant. Dey broke de do' open. My father was a settin' on de bed. I 'member he had a shot gun in his han'. Well, de broke de do' down, an' then father he shoot, an' dey scattered all ovah de fence.

Morgan Ray

. . . I heard a lot about the Klu Klux, but it warn't till long afterwards dat I evah see 'em. It was one night after de work of de day was done and I was takin' a walk near where I worked. Suddenly I heard the hoof beats of horses and I natcherly wuz curious and waited beside the road to see what was coming'. I saw a company of men hooded and wearin' what looked like sheets. Dey had a young cullud man as der prisoner. I wuz too skairt to say anything or ask any questions. I just went on my sweet way. Later I found out dey acclaimed de prisoner had assulted a white woman. Dey strung him up when he wouldn't confess, and shot him full of holes and threw his body in de pond.

15

Expansion and Conflict in the West

Westward expansion was an important part of America's development in the late nineteenth century. Spurred by cheap land and delivered by continent-spanning railroads, settlers from the East and abroad poured into the Great Plains to farm or ranch the prairie or otherwise make their fortunes. This expansion had dramatic effects on the Native Americans already living in the West, many of whom had been relocated there from their ancestral homelands further east.

Even after the Civil War, Native Americans still dominated much of the western United States. But by 1877, the buffalo had been decimated, and increasing numbers of settlers, ranchers, and railroaders encroached onto Indian land. Whites pressured Indians, often with blatant disregard for old treaties, onto reservations where they would be "reformed" under strict discipline. Native American groups who resisted were to be "killed off."

The reservation system devastated many Native American groups by destroying the patterns of tribal life but the Dawes Act was even more insidious. Inspired in part by the national attention Helen Hunt Jackson's *A Century of Dishonor* (1881) drew to the Indians' plight, the act, passed in 1887, set the course for federal Native American policy for the next century. It stipulated that Native Americans acquire land individually, rather tribally, in the hopes of simultaneously fostering a tradition of private land ownership and destroying the power of the Native American political organizations. In exchange, Native Americans would become citizens and would gain outright ownership of their land after twenty-five years. Native Americans lost approximately 60 percent of their lands in the twenty years after the passage of the Dawes Act.

Years following the passage of the Dawes Act also saw a religious revitalization movement called the Ghost Dance spread through the Native American communities of the West— terrifying whites, who had long tried to prevent Native Americans from gathering in large numbers to mark religious observances. The Sioux, a hunting people who had been driven onto a small territory in North Dakota, were touched by the Ghost Dance movement in 1890. Led by a medicine man who promised them that they would be reborn in a world without whites, where everyone was young and buffalo plentiful, they began to "dance in the snow" and act "wild" and "crazy"—shocking the military officers near the reservation.

The Sioux also figured prominently in a milestone confrontation between whites and Indians. In December 1890 a melee occurred when Indian Affairs agents, sent to arrest Sitting Bull, the Sioux leader famous for having crushed Custer, from his camp. Sitting Bull was killed, along with six agents and eight Indians. In the days following, numerous Sioux groups gathered at Wounded Knee Creek, including various Ghost Dance followers and others intimidated by earlier U.S. military actions. A standoff ensued, continuing until December 29 when a group of Sioux under Chief Big Foot were ordered to disarm and in the process of doing so a shot was fired by a "half crazy" Indian. In the massacre that followed, 25 agents were killed along with 150 Indians, 18 of whom were children. One of the documents included here, from Black Elk, is an eyewitness account from the Sioux side. The next is from President Benjamin Harrison's account of the massacre, and his description of the progress on Indian relations in general.

The next series of documents in this chapter covers the settlement of the West from the white perspective. Frederick Jackson Turner's piece has great historiographical significance; in it he argued that the frontier shaped and created the essential American character, a character defined by individualism and democratic values. Turner's thesis found a resonance in the 1890s, when America's own continental frontier was "closing" and the country was beginning to expand toward Asia and Latin America.

Farming life on the frontier was incredibly uncertain and difficult. In the first wave of frontier settlement, from 1879 to the early 1890s, thousands of families moved out onto the Great Plains—some from the East Coast and others from Germany, Britain, Scandinavia, and Eastern Europe. Life was difficult and survival was tenuous—many settlers left the plains for the East. The selection here, from a novel of the 1920s by O. E. Rolevaag, describes the difficulty women in particular faced in adjusting to a lonely landscape.

Discontent with farming life in the West was not only internalized: increasingly, after depressions in the 1880s and 1890s, farmers in the West and in the South organized into political organizations to improve their social and economic status. They formed farmer's alliances, cooperatives, and public schools. In 1892 the Populist Party was formed as an independent third party fielding a candidate in the presidential election. In general, Populists were isolated farmers (like the farmer and his wife in *The Giants in the Earth*) who were disenchanted and disengaged from traditional party politics and social structures. The platform of the Populist Party, included here, reflects this in its calls for a reform of the nation's political and social systems, including government takeover of the railroads, banks, and telephone and telegraph systems. Although the Populist presidential candidate, James B. Weaver, gained only 8.5 percent of the popular vote, Populists had sufficiently strong support in rural areas in the South and the West to elect a number of governors from the party.

Study Questions

1. Examine Helen Hunt Jackson's argument that individual property rights would help bring "salvation" to Native Americans. What are her assumptions about Native American character?

2. Analyze Black Elk's statement that "I was not sorry for the women and children. It was better for them to be happy in the other world, and I wanted to be there."

3. Contrast President Harrison's and Black Elk's descriptions of the Wounded Knee Massacre.

4. How does Frederick Jackson Turner's thesis fit into the ideology of manifest destiny discussed in Chapter 11?

5. Compare Turner's concept of what it means to be an American with Crèvecoeur's.

6. Considering the other documents in this chapter, is Turner's thesis that the frontier helped create and foster American democracy realistic?

7. Compare the selection from *Giants in the Earth* describing Beret's desolation with the selection in Chapter 11 from the diary and journals of Elizabeth Greer. Describe the conflicts between expectations and reality.

8. Discuss the expansionist attitude toward the environment. Consider Turner's ideas on the effects of the American environment on the American character, Rolvaag's literary description of prairie isolation, and the Omaha platform's position on land rights.

9. Analyze the Omaha Platform in terms of who benefited from each resolution. Which were aimed at urban voters, which at rural or western constituencies?

Helen Hunt Jackson, from *A Century of Dishonor* (1881)

Helen Hunt Jackson's *A Century of Dishonor* brought national attention to the plight of Native Americans when it was published in 1881. Jackson, a Massachusetts native who had traveled to California, describes in particular the plight of the California Indians, who had seen 90 percent of their population die from war and disease in the years after the gold rush.*

---

* From Helen Hunt Jackson, *A Century of Dishonor* (New York, 1881).

There are within the limits of the United States between two hundred and fifty and three hundred thousand Indians, exclusive of those in Alaska. The names of the different tribes and bands, as entered in the statistical table so the Indian Office Reports, number nearly three hundred. One of the most careful estimates which have been made of their numbers and localities gives them as follows: "In Minnesota and States east of the Mississippi, about 32,500; in Nebraska, Kansas, and the Indian Territory, 70,650; in the Territories of Dakota, Montana, Wyoming, and Idaho, 65,000; in Nevada and the Territories of Colorado, New Mexico, Utah, and Arizona, 84,000; and on the Pacific slope, 48,000."

Of these, 130,000 are self-supporting on their own reservations, "receiving nothing from the Government except interest on their own moneys, or annuities granted them in consideration of the cession of their lands to the United States."

. . . Of the remainder, 84,000 are partially supported by the Government—the interest money due them and their annuities, as provided by treaty, being inadequate to their subsistence on the reservations where they are confined. . . .

There are about 55,000 who never visit an agency, over whom the Government does not pretend to have either control or care. These 55,000 "subsist by hunting, fishing, on roots, nuts, berries, etc., and by begging and stealing"; and this also seems to dispose of the accusation that the Indian will not "work for a living." There remains a small portion, about 31,000, that are entirely subsisted by the Government.

There is not among these three hundred bands of Indians one which has not suffered cruelly at the hands either of the Government or of white settlers. The poorer, the more insignificant, the more helpless the band, the more certain the cruelty and outrage to which they have been subjected. This is especially true of the bands on the Pacific slope. These Indians found themselves of a sudden surrounded by and caught up in the great influx of gold-seeking settlers, as helpless creatures on a shore are caught up in a tidal wave. There was not time for the Government to make treaties; not even time for communities to make laws. The tale of the wrongs, the oppressions, the murders of the Pacific-slope Indians in the last thirty years would be a volume by itself, and is too monstrous to be believed.

It makes little difference, however, where one opens the record of the history of the Indians; every page and every year has its dark stain. The story of one tribe is the story of all, varied only differences of time and place; but neither time nor place makes any difference in the main facts. Colorado is as greedy and unjust in 1880 as was Georgia in 1830, and Ohio in 1795; and the United States Government breaks promises now as deftly as then, and with an added ingenuity from long practice.

One of its strongest supports in so doing is the wide-spread sentiment among the people of dislike to the Indian, of impatience with his presence as a "barrier to civilization" and distrust of it as a possible danger. The old tales of the frontier life, with its horrors of Indian warfare, have gradually, by two or three generations' telling, produced in the average mind something like an hereditary instinct of questioning and unreasoning aversion which it is almost impossible to dislodge or soften. . . .

President after president has appointed commission after commission to inquire into and report upon Indian affairs, and to make suggestions as to the best methods of managing them. The reports are filled with eloquent statements of wrongs done to the

Indians, of perfidies on the part of the Government; they counsel, as earnestly as words can, a trial of the simple and unperplexing expedients of telling truth, keeping promises, making fair bargains, dealing justly in all ways and all things. These reports are bound up with the Government's Annual Reports, and that is the end of them. . . .

The history of the Government connections with the Indians is a shameful record of broken treaties and unfulfilled promises. The history of the border white man's connection with the Indians is a sickening record of murder, outrage, robbery, and wrongs committed by the former, as the rule, and occasional savage outbreaks and unspeakably barbarous deeds of retaliation by the latter, as the exception.

Taught by the Government that they had rights entitled to respect, when those rights have been assailed by the rapacity of the white man, the arm which should have been raised to protect them has ever been ready to sustain the aggressor.

The testimony of some of the highest military officers of the United States is on record to the effect that, in our Indian wars, almost without exception, the first aggressions have been made by the white man. . . . Every crime committed by a white man against an Indian is concealed and palliated. Every offense committed by an Indian against a white man is borne on the wings of the post or the telegraph to the remotest corner of the land, clothed with all the horrors which the reality or imagination can throw around it. Against such influences as these are the people of the United States need to be warned.

To assume that it would be easy, or by any one sudden stroke of legislative policy possible, to undo the mischief and hurt of the long past, set the Indian policy of the country right for the future, and make the Indians at once safe and happy, is the blunder of a hasty and uninformed judgment. The notion which seems to be growing more prevalent, that simply to make all Indians at once citizens of the United States would be a sovereign and instantaneous panacea for all their ills and all the Government's perplexities, is a very inconsiderate one. To administer complete citizenship of a sudden, all round, to all Indians, barbarous and civilized alike, would be as grotesque a blunder as to dose them all round with any one medicine, irrespective of the symptoms and needs of their diseases. It would kill more than it would cure. Nevertheless, it is true, as was well stated by one of the superintendents of Indian Affairs in 1857, that, "so long as they are not citizens of the United States, their rights of property must remain insecure against invasion. The doors of the federal tribunals being barred against them while wards and dependents, they can only partially exercise the rights of free government, or give to those who make, execute, and construe the few laws they are allowed to enact, dignity sufficient to make them respectable. While they continue individually to gather the crumbs that fall from the table of the United States, idleness, improvidence, and indebtedness will be the rule, and industry, thrift, and freedom from debt the exception. The utter absence of individual title to particular lands deprives every one among them of the chief incentive to labor and exertion—the very mainspring on which the prosperity of a people depends."

All judicious plans and measures for their safety and salvation must embody provisions for their becoming citizens as fast as they are fit, and must protect them till then in every right and particular in which our laws protect other "persons" who are not citizens. . . .

However great perplexity and difficulty there may be in the details of any and every plan possible for doing at this late day anything like justice to the Indian, however, hard it may be for good statesmen and good men to agree upon the things that ought to be done, there certainly is, or ought to be, no perplexity whatever, on difficulty whatever, in agreeing upon certain things that ought not to be done, and which must cease to be done before the first steps can be taken toward righting the wrongs, curing the ills, and wiping out the disgrace to us of the present conditions of our Indians.

Cheating, robbing, breaking promises—these three are clearly things which must cease to be done. One more thing, also, and that is the refusal of the protection of the law to the Indian's rights of property, "of life, liberty, and the pursuit of happiness."

When these four things have ceased to be done, time, statesmanship, philanthropy, and Christianity can slowly and surely do the rest. Till these four things have ceased to be done, statesmanship and philanthropy alike must work in vain, and even Christianity can reap but small harvest.

Black Elk, Account of the Wounded Knee Massacre (1890)

There were a number of long-standing issues at Wounded Knee that contributed to the tension on the reservation prior to the massacre. In the bad crop years of 1889 and 1890, the U.S. government failed to provide the full amount of food, agricultural implements and seeds, clothing, and supplies mandated by its treaty with the Indians. Many, including Black Elk, criticized the violent reaction of the Indian Agents, many of whom were inexperienced, and some of whom were remnants of Custer's Seventh Cavalry, crushed by Sitting Bull just fourteen years before at the Little Big Horn. Black Elk, a young man in 1890, describes the tragedy at Wounded Knee in this excerpt from his autobiography, *Black Elk Speaks*.[*]

It was about this time that bad news came to us from the north. We heard that some policemen from Standing Rock had gone to arrest Sitting Bull on Grand River, and that he would not let them take him; so there was a fight, and they killed him.

It was now near the end of the Moon of Popping Trees, and I was twenty-seven years old [December 1890]. We heard that Big Foot was coming down from the

---

[*] Reprinted from *Black Elk Speaks*, by John G. Neihardt, by permission of the University of Nebraska Press. Copyright 1932, 1959, 1972, by John G. Neihardt. Copyright © 1961 by John G. Neihardt Trust.

Badlands with nearly four hundred people. Some of these were from Sitting Bull's band. They had run away when Sitting Bull was killed, and joined Big Foot on Good River. There were only about a hundred warriors in this band, and all the others were women and children and some old men. They were all starving and freezing, and Big Foot was so sick that they had to bring him along in a pony drag. They had all run away to hide in the Badlands, and they were coming in now because they were starving and freezing. Soldiers were over there looking for them. The soldiers had everything and were not freezing and starving. Near Porcupine Butte the soldiers came up to the Big Foots, and they surrendered and went along with the soldiers to Wounded Knee Creek.

It was in the evening when we heard that the Big Foots were camped over there with the soldiers, about fifteen miles by the old road from where we were. It was the next morning [December 29, 1890] that something terrible happened.

That evening before it happened, I went in to Pine Ridge and heard these things, and while I was there, soldiers started for where the Big Foots were. These made about five hundred soldiers that were there next morning. When I saw them starting I felt that something terrible was going to happen. That night I could hardly sleep at all. I walked around most of the night.

In the morning I went out after my horses, and while I was out I heard shooting off toward the east, and I knew from the sound that it must be wagon-guns [cannon] going off. The sounds went right through my body, and I felt that something terrible would happen. . . . [He donned his ghost shirt, and armed only with a bow, mounted his pony and rode in the direction of the shooting, and was joined on the way by others.]

In a little while we had come to the top of the ridge where, looking to the east, you can see for the first time the monument and the burying ground on the little hill where the church is. That is where the terrible thing started. Just south of the burying ground on the little hill a deep dry gulch runs about east and west, very crooked, and it rises westward to nearly the top of the ridge where we were. It had no name, but the Wasichus [white men] sometimes called Battle Creek now. We stopped on the ridge not far from the head of the dry gulch. Wagon guns were still going off over there on the little hill, and they were going off again where they hit among the gulch. There was much shooting down yonder, and there were many cries, and we could see calvarymen scattered over the hills ahead of us. Calvarymen were riding along the gulch and shooting into it, where the women and children were running away and trying to hide in the gullies and the stunted pines. . . .

We followed down along the dry gulch, and what we saw was terrible. Dead and wounded women and children and little babies were scattered all along there where they had been trying to run away. The soldiers had followed along the gulch, as they ran, and murdered them in there. Sometimes they were in heaps because they had huddled together, and some were scattered all along. Sometimes bunches of them had been killed and torn to pieces where the wagon guns hit them. I saw a little baby trying to suck its mother, but she was bloody and dead.

There were two little boys at one place in this gulch. They had guns and they had been killing soldiers all by themselves. We could see the soldiers they had killed. The boys were all alone there, and they were not hurt. These were very brave little boys.

When we drove the soldiers back, they dug themselves in, and we were not enough people to drive them out from there. In the evening they marched off up Wounded Knee Creek, and then we saw all that they had done there.

Men and women and children were heaped and scattered all over the flat at the bottom of the little hill where the soldiers had their wagon-guns, and westward up the dry gulch all the way to the high ridge, the dead women and children and babies were scattered.

When I saw this I wished that I had died too, but I was not sorry for the women and children. It was better for them to be happy in the other world, and I wanted to be there too. But before I went there I wanted to have revenge. I thought there might be a day, and we should have revenge.

In the morning the soldiers began to take all the guns away from the Big Foots, who were camped in the flat below the little hill where the monument and burying ground are now. The people had stacked most of their guns, and even their knives, by the teepee where Big Foot was lying sick. Soldiers were on the little hill and all around, and there were soldiers across the dry gulch to the south and over east along Wounded Knee Creek too. The people were nearly surrounded, and the wagon-guns were pointed at them.

It was a good winter day when all this happened. The sun was shining. But after the soldiers marched away from their dirty work, a heavy snow began to fall. The wind came up in the night. There was a big blizzard, and it grew very cold. The snow drifted deep in the crooked gulch, and it was one long grave of butchered women and children and babies, who had never done any harm and were only trying to run away.

Benjamin Harrison, Report on Wounded Knee Massacre and the Decrease in Indian Land Acreage (1891)

The following is an excerpt from President Benjamin Harrison's annual message, delivered December 9, 1891, in which he describes the Wounded Knee Massacre and the progress of the program to decrease Native American land acreage.*

The outbreak among the Sioux which occurred in December last is as to its causes and incidents fully reported upon by the War Department and the Department of the

---

* From 3rd Annual Message, President Benjamin Harrison, December 9, 1891.

Interior. That these Indians had some just complaints, especially in the matter of the reduction of the appropriation for rations and in the delays attending the enactment of laws to enable the Department to perform the engagements entered into with them, is probably true; but the Sioux tribes are naturally warlike and turbulent, and their warriors were excited by their medicine men and chiefs, who preached the coming of an Indian messiah who was to give them power to destroy their enemies. In view of the alarm that prevailed among the white settlers near the reservation and of the fatal consequences that would have resulted from an Indian incursion, I placed at the disposal of General Miles, commanding the Division of the Missouri, all such forces as we thought by him to be required. He is entitled to the credit of having given thorough protection to the settlers and of bringing the hostiles into subjection with the least possible loss of life. . . .

Since March 4, 1889, about 23,000,000 acres have been separated from Indian reservations and added to the public domain for the use of those who desired to secure free homes under our beneficent laws. It is difficult to estimate the increase of wealth which will result from the conversion of these waste lands into farms, but it is more difficult to estimate the betterment which will result to the families that have found renewed hope and courage in the ownership of a home and the assurance of a comfortable subsistence under free and healthful conditions. It is also gratifying to be able to feel, as we may, that this work has proceeded upon lines of justice toward the Indian, and that he may now, if he will, secure to himself the good influences of a settled habitation, the fruits of industry, and the security of citizenship.

Frederick Jackson Turner, "The Significance of the Frontier in American History" (1893)

Frederick Jackson Turner was one of a new group of professionally trained historians (he had been trained at Johns Hopkins). His essay argued the colonization of the American west formed the American character. His thesis was often used to describe the necessity of American expansion beyond the Pacific Ocean.*

Up to our own day American history has been in a large degree the history of the colonization of the Great West. The existence of an area of free land, continuous recession, and the advance of American settlements westward, explain American development.

---

* From Frederick Jackson Turner, *The Frontier in American History* (New York: Henry Holt and Company, 1921).

Behind institutions, behind constitutional forms and modifications lie the vital forces that call these organs into life and shape them to meet changing conditions. The peculiarity of American institutions is, the fact that they have been compelled to adapt themselves to the changes of an expanding people—to the changes involved in crossing a continent, this winning a wilderness, and in developing at each area of this progress out of the primitive economic and political conditions of the frontier into the complexity of city life. . . .

Thus American development has exhibited not merely advance along a single line, but a return to primitive conditions on a continually advancing frontier line, and a new development for that area. American social development has been continually beginning over again on the frontier. This perennial rebirth, this fluidity of American life, this expansion westward with its new opportunities, its continuous touch with the simplicity of primitive society, furnish the forces dominating American character. The true point of view in the history of this nation is not the Atlantic coast, it is the West. . . .

The frontier is the line of most rapid and effective Americanization. The wilderness masters the colonist. It finds him a European in dress, industries, tools, modes of travel, and thought. It takes him from the railroad car and puts him in the birch canoe. It strips off the garments of civilization and arrays him in the hunting shirt and the moccasin. It puts him in the log cabin of the Cherokee and Iroquois and runs and Indian palisade around him. Before long he has gone to planting Indian corn and plowing with a sharp stick; he shouts the war cry and takes the scalp in orthodox Indian fashion. In short, at the frontier the environment is at first too strong for the man. He must accept the conditions which it furnishes, or perish, and so he fits himself into the Indian clearings and follows the Indian trails. Little by little he transforms the wilderness but the outcome is not the old Europe, not simply the development of Germanic germs, any more than the first phenomenon was a case of reversion to the Germanic mark. The fact is, that here is a new product that is American. At first, the frontier was the Atlantic coast. It was the frontier of Europe in a very real sense. Moving westward, the frontier became more and more American. As successive terminal moraines result from successive glaciations, so each frontier leaves its traces behind it, and when it becomes a settled area the region still partakes of the frontier characteristics. Thus the advance of the frontier has meant a steady movement away from the influence of Europe, a steady growth of independence on American lines. And to study this advance, the men who grew up under these conditions, and the political, economic, and social results of its, is to study the really American part of our history. . . .

Since the days when the fleet of Columbus sailed into the waters of the New World, America has been another name for opportunity, and the people of the United States have taken their tone form the incessant expansion which has not only been open but has been forced upon them. He would be a rash prophet who should assert that the expansive character has now entirely ceased. Movement has been its dominant fact, and unless this training has no effect upon a people, the American energy will continually demand a wider field for its exercise. But never again will such gifts of free land offer themselves. For a moment, at the frontier, the bonds of custom are broken and unrestraint is triumphant. There is not *tabula rasa*. The stubborn American environment is there with its imperious summons to accept its conditions; the inherited ways of doing things are also there; and yet, in spite of environment, and in spite of custom, each frontier did indeed furnish a new field of opportunity, a gate of escape from the bondage of the past; and freshness and confidence, and scorn of older society, impatience of its restrains and its ideas, and indifference to its lessons, have accompanied the frontier. What the Mediterranean Sea was to the Greeks, breaking the bond of custom, offering new experiences, calling out new institutions and activities, that, and more, the ever retreating frontier has been to the United States directly, and to the nations of Europe more remotely. And now, four centuries from the discovery of America, at the end of a hundred years of life under the Constitution, the frontier has gone, and with its going has closed the first period in American history.

O. E. Rolvaag, *Giants in the Earth* (1927)

This selection is taken from O. E. Rolvaag's novel *Giants in the Earth*, which describes the isolation and desperation on the Great Plains. The protagonist in this passage, Beret, the wife of a Norwegian farmer, eventually descends into madness and death.*

In a certain sense, she had to admit to herself, it was lovely up here. The broad expanse stretching away endlessly in every direction, seemed almost like the ocean—especially now, when darkness was falling. It reminded her strongly of the sea, and yet it was very different. . . . This formless prairie had no heart that beat, no waves that sang, no soul that could be touched . . . or cared. . . .

The infinitude surrounding her on every hand might not have been so oppressive, might even have brought her a measure of peace, if it had not been for the deep silence, which lay heavier here than in a church. Indeed, what was there to break it? She had passed beyond the outposts of civilization; the nearest dwelling places of men were far away. Here no warbling of birds rose on the air, no buzzing of insects sounded; even the wind had died away; the waving blades of grass that trembled to the faintest breath now stood erect and quiet, as if listening, in the great hush of the evening. . . . All along the way, coming out, she had noticed this strange thing; the stillness had grown deeper, the silence more depressing, the farther west they journeyed; it must have been over two weeks now since she had heard a bird sing! Had they traveled into some nameless, abandoned region? Could no living thing exist out here, in the empty, desolate, endless wastes of green and blue? . . . How could existence go on, she thought, desperately? If life is to thrive and endure, it must at least have something to hide behind! . . .

The children were playing boisterously a little way off. What a terrible noise they made! But she had better let them keep on with their play, as long as they were happy. . . . She sat perfectly quiet, thinking of the long, oh, so interminably long march that they would have to make, back to the place where human beings dwelt. It would be small hardship for her, of course, sitting in the wagon; but she pitied Per Hansa and the boys—and then the poor oxen! . . . He certainly would soon find out for himself that a home for men and women and children could never be established in this wilderness. . . . And how could she bring new life into the world out here! . . .

Slowly her thoughts began to centre on her husband; they grew warm and tender as they dwelt on him. She trembled as they came. . . .

But only for a brief while. As her eyes darted nervously here and there, flitting from object to object and trying to pierce the purple dimness that was steadily closing in, a sense of desolation so profound settled upon her that she seemed unable to think at all. It would not do to gaze any longer at the terror out there, where everything was turning to grim and awful darkness. . . . She threw herself back in the grass and looked up into the heavens. But darkness and infinitude lay there, also—the sense of utter desolation still remained. . . . Suddenly, for the first time, she realized the full extent of her loneliness, the dreadful nature of the fate that had overtaken her. Lying there on her back, and staring up into the quiet sky across which the shadows of night were imperceptibly creeping, she went over in her mind every step of their wanderings, every mile of the distance they had traveled since they had left home. . . .

Winter was ever tightening its grip. The drifting snow flew wildly under a low sky, and stirred up the whole universe into a whirling mass; it swept the plain like the giant broom of a witch, churning up a flurry so thick that people could scarcely open their eyes.

As soon as the weather cleared icy gusts drove through every chink and cranny, leaving white frost behind; people's breaths hung frozen in the air the moment it was out of the mouth; if one touched iron, a piece of skin would be torn away.

At intervals a day of bright sunshine came. Then the whole vast plain flittered with the flashing brilliance of diamonds; the glare was so strong that it burnt the sight; the eyes saw blackness where there was nothing but shining white. . . . .

But no sooner had they reached America than the west-fever had smitten the old settlements like a plague. Such a thing had never happened before in the history of mankind; people were intoxicated by bewildering visions; they spoke dazedly, as though under the force of a spell. . . . "Go west! . . . Go west, folks! . . . The farther west, the better the land!". . . Men beheld in feverish dreams the endless plains, teeming with fruitfulness, glowing, out there where day sank into night—a Beulah Land of corn and wine! . . . She had never dreamed that the good Lord would let such folly loose among men. Were it only the young people who had been caught by the plague, she would not have wondered; but the old had been taken even worse. . . . "Now we're bound west?" said the young. . . . "Wait a minute—we're going along with you!" cried the old, and followed after. . . . Human beings gathered together, in small companies and large—took whatever was movable along, and left the old homestead without as much as a sigh! Ever westward led the course, to where the sun glowed in matchless glory as it sank at night; people drifted about in a sort of delirium, like sea birds in mating time; then they flew toward the sunset, in small flocks, and large—always toward Sunset Land. . . . Now she saw it clearly: here on the trackless plains, the thousand-year-old hunger of the poor after human happiness had been unloosed!

The Omaha Platform of the Populist Party (1892)

This is a selection from the Populist Party platform, drafted at their national convention in Omaha, Nebraska, where the party nominated James B. Weaver for president. The Populists, mostly small farmers in the South and West, attempted to broaden their base in their platform, trying to appeal in particular to urban workers.*

Preamble

The conditions which surround us best justify our cooperation; we meet in the midst of a nation brought to the verge of moral, political, and material ruin. Corruption dominates the ballot-box, the Legislatures, the Congress, and touches even the ermine of the bench. The people are demoralized; most of the States have been compelled to isolate the voters at the polling places to prevent universal intimidation and bribery. The newspapers are largely subsidized or muzzled, public opinion silenced, business prostrated, homes covered with mortgages, labor impoverished, and the land concentrating in the hands of capitalists. The urban workmen are denied the right to organize for self-protection, imported pauperized labor beats down their wages, a hireling standing army, unrecognized by our laws, is established to shoot them down, and they are rapidly degenerating into European conditions. The fruits of the toil of millions are boldly stolen to build up colossal fortunes for a few, unprecedented in the history of mankind and the possessors of these, in turn, despise the Republic and endanger liberty. From the same prolific womb of governmental injustice we breed the two great classes—tramps and millionaires. . . .

Assembled on the anniversary of the birthday of the nation, and filled with the spirit of the grand general and chief who established our independence, we seek to restore the government of the Republic to the hands of the "plain people," with which class it

---

* From the Omaha Platform, Edward McPherson, *A Handbook of Politics for 1892* (Da Capo Press).

originated. We assert our purposes to be identical with the purposes of the National Constitution; to form a more perfect union and establish justice, insure domestic tranquillity, provide for the common defense, promote the general welfare, and secure the blessings of liberty for ourselves and our posterity. . . .

Platform

We declare, therefore—

First.—That the union of the labor forces of the United States this day consummated shall be permanent and perpetual; may its spirit enter into all hearts for the salvation of the Republic and the uplifting of mankind.

Second.—Wealth belongs to him who creates it, and every dollar taken from industry without an equivalent is robbery. "If any will not work, neither shall he eat." The interests of rural and civil labor are the same; their enemies are identical.

Third.—We believe that the time has come when the railroad corporations will either own the people or the people must own the railroads. . . .

FINANCE.—We demand a national currency, safe, sound, and flexible issued by the general government only, a full legal tender for all debts, public and private. . . .

1. We demand free and unlimited coinage of silver and gold at the present legal ratio of 16 to 1.

2. We demand that the amount of circulating medium be speedily increased to not less than $50 per capita.

3. We demand a graduated income tax.

4. We believe that the money of the country should be kept as much as possible in the hands of the people, and hence we demand that all State and national revenues shall be limited to the necessary expenses of the government, economically and honestly administered.

5. We demand that postal savings banks be established by the government for the safe deposit of the earnings of the people and to facilitate exchange.

TRANSPORTATION.—Transportation being a means of exchange and a public necessity, the government should own and operate the railroads in the interest of the people. The telegraph and telephone, like the post-office system, being a necessity for the transmission of news, should be owned and operated by the government in the interest of the people.

LAND.—The land, including all the natural sources of wealth, is the heritage of the people, and should not be monopolized for speculative purposes, and alien ownership of land should be prohibited. All land now held by railroads and other corporations in excess of their actual needs, and all lands now owned by aliens should be reclaimed by the government and held for actual settlers only.

Expressions of Sentiments

1. RESOLVED, That we demand a free ballot, and a fair count of all elections, and pledge ourselves to secure it to every legal voter without Federal intervention, through the adoption by the States of the unperverted Australian or secret ballot system.

2. RESOLVED, That the revenue derived from a graduated income tax should be applied to the reduction of the burden of taxation now levied upon the domestic industries of this country.

3. RESOLVED, That we pledge our support to fair and liberal pensions to ex-Union soldiers and sailors.

4. RESOLVED, That we condemn the fallacy of protecting American labor under the present system, which opens our ports to the pauper and criminal classes of the world and crowds out our wage-earners; and we denounce the present ineffective laws against contract labor, and demand the further restriction of undesirable emigration.

5. RESOLVED, That we cordially sympathize with the efforts of organized workingmen to shorten the hours of labor, and demand a rigid enforcement of the existing eight-hour law on Government work, and ask that a penalty clause be added to the said law.

6. RESOLVED, That we regard the maintenance of a large standing army of mercenaries, known as the Pinkerton system, as a menace to our liberties, and we demand its abolition. . . .

7. RESOLVED, That we commend to the favorable consideration of the people and the reform press the legislative system known as the initiative and referendum.

8. RESOLVED, That we favor a constitutional provision limiting the office of President and Vice-President to one term, and providing for the election of Senators of the United States by a direct vote of the people.

9. RESOLVED, That we oppose any subsidy or national aid to any private corporation for any purpose.

16

The Wealth of a Nation

Rapid industrial expansion in the last quarter of the nineteenth century led to an explosion of economic growth, which in turn dramatically reshaped American society. By the end of the century the United States had become the foremost industrial power in the world and had transformed itself from an agrarian, homogeneous society into an urban, industrial, and heterogeneous power. The new America delivered prosperity and progress for some citizens, but many others never reaped the rewards of change. This chapter examines both sides of the transformation of American society.

During this period a group of businessmen rose to prominence—men like Andrew Carnegie, John D. Rockefeller, and J. Pierpont Morgan—and enormous money and power was concentrated in their hands. Using shrewd business techniques, including monopolies and trusts, they built up personal fortunes and corporations that dominated the national economy. In "The Gospel of Wealth," Andrew Carnegie, a steel magnate and the nation's most famous rags-to-riches story, provided a rationale for the accumulation and distribution of wealth.

American intellectuals, on the other hand, often responded suspiciously to the new order. Mark Twain, one of the leading novelist of the times, viewed industrial America with disdain and despair. Much of his work idealized America's agrarian past while harshly criticizing the new American society. In the except from *The Gilded Age* included here, Twain describes a harsh, materialistic industrial world.

Edward Bellamy, author of the best-selling *Looking Backward: 2000–1887*, described a utopia in the year 2000, where, under the direction of the national government, all people lived in prosperity and had an equal share in a new society. Although his utopia was similar in many ways to socialism, Bellamy called his utopian system "nationalism"—appealing to the new nationalism of industrializing and imperialistic America. Bellamy's book was a huge success; its publisher, Houghton Mifflin, proudly proclaimed, "Of only one other book have 300,000 copies been printed within two years of its publication." (*Uncle Tom's Cabin* was the other.) *Looking Backward* furthermore inspired the formation of over 150 Nationalist Clubs throughout the country, their purpose being to turn Bellamy's ideas into reality.

The working people who provided the labor that made businessmen like Andrew Carnegie wealthy became increasingly active after the Civil War. Strikes, some of which were led by unions like the Knights of Labor, the International Ladies' Garment Workers Union, the Western Federation of Miners, and the American Federation of Labor, became increasingly common as workers tried to gain additional on-the-job rights and fair wages. The last document in this chapter is an excerpt from the autobiography of a great radical labor-union organizer Mary Harris, better known as Mother Jones, describing her efforts to publicize child labor in the mining industry.

Study Questions

1. Does the "Gospel of Wealth" reinforce the concepts of social Darwinism?

2. According to Twain, who bore the cost of the relationship between business and government?

3. What trends evident by the late nineteenth century did Bellamy regard as harbingers of the future? How did this contribute to the credibility of his book? To what extent might this account for the book's extraordinary popularity?

4. Who did Mother Jones blame the sufferings of the mill children on? What might Carnegie's reaction have been?

Andrew Carnegie, from "The Gospel of Wealth" (1889)

Written in 1889 for *The North American Review*, this piece justified the fortunes made by industrialists like Carnegie and provided a model for the distribution of their wealth. Carnegie believed laissez-faire economics were tied to social responsibility. Carnegie was born in Scotland and worked in the United States as a messenger for Western Union and a bobbin boy before, through shrewd salesmanship and investment, he became the head of Carnegie Steel Company, which, after it was sold to J. P. Morgan, became United States Steel.*

The problem of our age is the proper administration of wealth, that the ties of brotherhood may still bind together the rich and poor in harmonious relationship. The conditions of human life have not only been changed, but revolutionized, within the

---

* From Andrew Carnegie, "Wealth," *North American Review*, 1889.

past few hundred years. In former days there was little difference between the dwelling, dress, food, and environment of the chief and those of his retainers. . . . The contrast between the palace of the millionaire and the cottage of the laborer with us to-day measures the change which has come with civilization. This change, however, is not to be deplored, but welcomed as highly beneficial. It is well, say, essential, for the progress of the race that the houses of some should be homes for all that is highest and best in literature and the arts, and for all the refinements of civilization, rather than that none should be so. Much better this great irregularity than universal squalor. Without wealth there can be no Meccenas.

. . . to-day the world obtains commodities of excellent quality at prices which even the preceding generation would have deemed incredible. In the commercial world similar causes have produced similar results, and the race is benefited thereby. The poor enjoy what the rich could not before afford. What were the luxuries have become the necessaries of life. . . .

Objections to the foundations upon which society is based are not in order, because the condition of the race is better with these than it has been with any other which has been tried. . . . No evil, but good, has come to the race from the accumulation of wealth by those who have had the ability and energy to produce it. . . .

We start, then, with a condition of affairs under which the best interests of the race are promoted, but which inevitably gives wealth to the few. . . . What is the proper mode of administering wealth after the laws upon which civilization is founded have thrown it into the hands of the few? . . .

There are but three modes in which surplus wealth can be disposed of. It can be left to the families of the decedents; or it can be bequeathed for public purposes; or, finally, it can be administered by its possessors during their lives. . . .

There remains, then, only one mode of suing great fortunes; but in this we have the true antidote for the temporary unequal distribution of wealth, the reconciliation of the rich and the poor—a reign of harmony, another ideal, differing, indeed, from that of the Communist in requiring only the further evolution of existing conditions, not the total overthrow of our civilization. It is founded upon the most intense Individualism. . . . Under its sway we shall have an ideal State, in which the surplus wealth of the few will become, in the best sense, property of the many, because administering for the common good; and this wealth, passes through the hands of the few, can be made much more potent force for the elevation of our race than if distributed in small sums to the people themselves. Even the poorest can be made to see this, and to agree that great sums gathered by some of their fellow-citizens—spent for public purposes, from which masses reap the principal benefit, are more valuable to them than if scattered among themselves in trifling amounts through the course of many years.

If we consider the results which flow from the Cooper Institute, for instance. . . , and compare these with those who would have ensured for the good of the man form an equal sum distributed by Mr. Cooper in his lifetime in the form of wages, which the highest form of distributing, being work done and not for charity, we can estimate of the possibilities for the improvement of the race which lie embedded in the present law of the accumulation of wealth. . . .

This, then, is held to be the duty of the man of wealth: To set an example of modest, unostentatious living, shunning display or extravagance; to provide moderately for the legitimate wants of those dependent upon him; and, after doing so, to consider all surplus revenues which come to him simply as trust funds, which he is called upon to administer, and strictly bound as a matter of duty to administer in the manner which, in his judgment, is best calculated to produce the most beneficial results for the community—the man of wealth thus becoming the mere trustee and agent for his poorer brethren, bringing to their service his superior wisdom, experience, and ability to administer, doing for them better than they would or could do for them selves. . . .

In bestowing charity, the main consideration should be to help those who will help themselves; to provide part of the means by which those who desire to improve may do so; to give those who desire to rise the aids by which they may rise; to assist, but rarely or never to do all. Neither the individual nor the race is improved by alms giving. Those worthy of assistance, except in rare cases, seldom require assistance. . . .

The rich man is thus almost restricted to following the examples of Peter Cooper, Enoch Pratt of Baltimore, Mr. Pratt of Brooklyn, Senator Stanford, and others, who know that the best means of benefiting the community is to place within its reach the ladders upon which the aspiring can rise—free libraries, parks, and means of recreation, by which men are helped in body and mind; works of art, certain to give pleasure and improve the general condition of the people; in this manner returning their surplus wealth to the mass of their fellows in the forms best calculated to do them lasting good.

Thus is the problem of rich and poor to be solved. The laws of accumulation will be left free, the laws of distribution free. Individualism will continue, but the millionaire will be but a trustee for the poor, intrusted for a season with a great part of the increased wealth of the community, but administering it for the community far better than if could or would have done for itself. The best minds will thus have reached a stage in the development of the race in which it is clearly seen that there is no mode of disposing of surplus wealth creditable to thoughtful and earnest men into whose hands it flows, save by using it year by year for the general good. . . .

Such, in my opinion, is the true gospel concerning wealth, obedience to which is destined some day to solve the problem of the rich and the poor, and to bring "Peace on earth, among men good will."

Mark Twain, from *The Gilded Age* (1873)

In this excerpt from his satirical *The Gilded* Age, Twain skewers the speculators and new values of the late nineteenth century. In this piece, the main character, Colonial Beriah Sellers, is the typical get-rich-quick speculator. Harry Brierly is a young engineer who discovers the monetary relationship between the company and the government.[*]

He called, with official importance in his mien, at No.—Wall Street, where a great gilt sign betokened the presence of the headquarters of the "Columbus River Slackwater Navigation Company." He entered and gave a dressy porter his card, and was requested to wait a moment in a sort of anteroom. The porter returned in a minute, and asked whom he would like to see?

"The president of the company, of course."

"He is busy with some gentlemen, sir; says he will be done with them directly."

That a copper-plate card with "Engineer—Chief" on it should be received with such tranquillity as this, annoyed Mr. Brierly not a little.

"Good morning, sir; take a seat—take a seat."

"Thank you, sir," said Harry, throwing as much chill into his manner as his ruffled dignity prompted.

"We perceive by your reports and the reports of the chief superintendent, that you have been making gratifying progress with the work. We are all very much pleased."

"Indeed? We did not discover it from your letters—which we have not received; nor by the treatment our drafts have met with—which were not honored; nor by the reception of any part of the appropriation, no part of it having come to hand."

"Why, my dear Mr. Brierly, there must be some mistake. I am sure we wrote you and also Mr. Sellers, recently—when my clerk comes he will show copies—letters informing you of the ten per cent. assessment."

"Oh, certainly, we got those letters. But what we wanted was money to carry on the work—money to pay the men."

"Certainly, certainly—true enough—but we credited you both for a large part of your assessments—I am sure that was in our letters."

"Of course that was in—I remember that."

"Ah, very well, then. Now we begin to understand each other."

"Well, I don't see that we do. There's two months' wages due the men, and—"

"How? Haven't you paid the men?"

"Paid them! How are we going to pay them when you don't honor our drafts?"

"Why, my dear sir, I cannot see how you can find an fault with us. I am sure we have acted in a perfectly straightforward business way. Now let us look at the thing a moment. You subscribed for one hundred shares of the capital stock, at one thousand dollars a share, I believe?"

"Yes, sir, I did."

"And Mr. Sellers took a like amount?"

"Yes, sir."

---

[*] From Samuel Clemens [Mark Twain] and Charles Dudley Warner, *The Gilded Age: A Tale of Today* (Hartford: American Publishing Company, 1874), 250–257, 260–261.

"Very well. No concern can get along without money. We levied a ten per cent. assessment. It was the original understanding that you and Mr. Sellers were to have the positions you now hold, with salaries of six hundred dollars a month each, while in active service. You were duly elected to these places, and you accepted them.

"Certainly."

"Very well. You were given your instructions and put to work. By your reports it appears that you have expended the sum of $9,640 upon the said work. Two months' salary to you two officers amounts altogether to $2,400—about one-eighth of your ten per cent. assessment, you see; which leaves you in debt to the company for the other seven-eighths of the assessment—viz., something over $8,000 apiece. Now, instead of requiring you to forward this aggregate of $16,000 or $17,000 to New York, the company voted unanimously to let you pay it over to the contractors, laborers from time to time, and give you credit on the books for it. And they did it without a murmur, too, for they were pleased with the progress you had made, and were glad to pay you that little compliment—and a very neat one it was, too, I am sure. The work you did fell short of $10,000, a trifle. Let me see—$9,640 from $20,000—salary $2,400 added—ah, yes, the balance due the company from yourself and Mr. Sellers is $7,960, which I will take the responsibility of allowing to stand for the present, unless you prefer to draw a check now, and thus—"

"Confound it, do you mean to say that instead of the company owing us $2,400, we owe the company $7,960?"

Edward Bellamy, from *Looking Backward* (1888)

Bellamy's *Looking Backward* is the story of Julian West, a wealthy young Bostonian who enters a hypnotic sleep in 1887 and awakes 113 years later. In the society to which he awakens, the squalor of Boston's slums has been replaced by "a great city," made up of "miles of broad streets, shaded by trees and lined with fine buildings." The injustice of the nineteenth century's industrial system has given way to a socialist utopia, while its business monopolies evolved into one great trust, taken over by the nation. "Credit cards" gave each citizen an equal share of the goods created by the new society. The collective society eradicated crime, poverty, war, and advertising—all without violence. Less appealing or arduous tasks are filled voluntarily; because people filling them work shorter hours and under good conditions. The key to Bellamy's book was its inclusion of most of the reform ideas of his generation and the presentation of a society based on such ideas in a nonthreatening form. The following excerpt describes

Julian West before he falls into his sleep and later, having the future described to him by Dr. Leete, his affable guide. *

I myself was rich and also educated, and possessed, therefore, all the elements of happiness enjoyed by the most fortunate in that age. Living in luxury, and occupied only with the pursuit of the pleasures and refinements of life, I derived the means of my support from the labor of others, rendering no sort of service in return. My parents and grand-parents lived in the same way, and I expected that my descendants, if I had any, would enjoy a like easy existence.

. . . This mystery of use without consumption, of warmth without combustion, seems like magic, but was merely an ingenious application of the art now happily lost but carried to a great perfection by your ancestors, of shifting the burden of one's support on the shoulders of others. The man who had accomplished this, and it was the end all sought, was said to live on the income of his investments. . . . I shall only stop now to say that interest on investments was a species of tax in perpetuity upon the product of those engaged in industry which a person possessing or inheriting money was able to levy. . . .

* * * * *

"I would give a great deal for just one glimpse of the Boston of your day," replied Dr. Leete. "No doubt, as you imply, the cities of that period were rather shabby affairs. If you had the taste to make them splendid, which I would not be so rude as to question, the general poverty resulting from your extraordinary industrial system would not have given you the means. Moreover, the excessive individualism which then prevailed was inconsistent with much public spirit. What little wealth you had seems almost wholly to have been lavished in private luxury. Nowadays, on the contrary, there is no destination of the surplus wealth so popular as the adornment of the city, which all enjoy in equal degree." . . .

* * * * *

"As no such thing as the labor question is known nowadays," replied Dr. Leete, "and there is no way in which it could arise, I suppose we may claim to have solved it. . . . The solution came as the result of a process of industrial evolution which could not have terminated otherwise. All that society had to do was to recognize and cooperate with that evolution, when its tendency had become unmistakable." . . .

"Meanwhile, without being in the smallest degree checked by the clamor against it, the absorption of business by ever larger monopolies continued. In the United States there was not, after the beginning of the last quarter of the century, any opportunity whatever for individual enterprise in any important field of industry, unless backed by great capital. During the last decade of the century, such small businesses as still remained were fast-failing survivals of a past epoch. . . . The railroads had gone on

---

* From E. Bellamy, *Looking Backward* (New York: Modern Library, 1951).

combining till a few great syndicates controlled every rail in the land. In manufactories, every important staple was controlled by a syndicate. These syndicates, pools, trusts, or whatever their name, fixed prices and crushed all competition except when combinations as vast as themselves arose. Then a struggle, resulting in still greater consolidation, ensued.

"...The movement toward the conduct of business by larger and larger aggregations of capital, the tendency toward monopolies, which had been so desperately and vainly resisted, was recognized at last, in its true significance, as a process which only needed to complete its logical evolution to open a golden future to humanity.

"Early in the last century the evolution was completed by the final consolidation of the entire capital of the nation. The industry and commerce of the country, ceasing to be conducted by a set of irresponsible corporations and syndicates of private persons at their caprice and for their profit, were intrusted to a single syndicate representing the people, to be conducted in the common interest for the common profit. The nation, that is to say, organized as the one great business corporation in which all other corporations were absorbed. . . ."

Mother Jones, "The March of the Mill Children" (1903)

Mother Jones was especially active in the mine-workers' strikes of the 1890s. By the time of this excerpt, she was already over 60, and a strike veteran. One of her concerns was the exploitation of children. In this public-relations marvel, Jones marched mill children (many of whom had missing digits and other work-related deformities), from Pennsylvania to President Theodore Roosevelt's home in Long Island, New York. Her work contributed to the passage of protective legislation for children in Pennsylvania.[*]

In the spring of 1903 I went to Kensington, Pennsylvania, where seventy-five thousand textile workers were on strike. Of this number at least ten thousand were little children. The workers were striking for more pay and shorter hours. Every day little children came into Union Headquarters, some with their hands off, some with the thumb missing, some with their fingers off at the knuckle. They were stooped little things, round shouldered and skinny. Many of them were not over ten years of age, although the state law prohibited their working before they were twelve years of age.

---

[*] Reprinted from Mary Harris, *The Autobiography of Mother Jones*, 3d ed. (Chicago: Charles H. Kerr Publishing Company, 1977).

The law was poorly enforced and the mothers of these children often swore falsely as to their children's age. In a single block in Kensington, fourteen women, mothers of twenty-two children all under twelve, explained it was a question of starvation or perjury. That the fathers had been killed or maimed at the mines.

I asked the newspapermen why they didn't publish the facts about child labor in Pennsylvania. They said they couldn't because the mill owners had stock in the papers.

"Well, I've got stock in these little children," said I, "and I'll arrange a little publicity."

We assembled a number of boys and girls one morning in Independence Park, and from there were arranged to parade with banners to the courthouse where we would hold a meeting.

A great crowd gathered in the public square in front of the city hall. I put the little boys with their fingers off and hands crushed and maimed on a platform. I held up their mutilated hands and showed them to the crowd, and made the statement that Philadelphia's mansions were built on the broken bones, the quivering hearts and drooping heads of these children. That their little lives went out to make wealth for others. That neither state nor city officials paid any attention to these wrongs. That they did not care that these children were to be the future citizens of the nation. . . .

I called upon the millionaire manufacturers to cease their moral murders, and I cried to the officials in the open windows opposite, "Someday the workers will take possession of your city hall, and when we do, no child will be sacrificed on the altar of profit."

The reporters quoted my statement that Philadelphia mansions were built on the broken bones and quivering hearts of children. The Philadelphia papers and the New York papers got into a squabble with each other over the question. The universities discussed it. Preachers began talking. That was what I wanted. Public attention on the subject of child labor.

The matter quieted down for a while and I concluded the people needed stirring up again. . . . I asked some of the parents if they would let me have their little boys and girls for a week or ten days, promising to bring them back safe and sound. They consented. A man named Sweeny was marshall for our "army." A few men and women went with me to help with the children. They were on strike and I thought they might as well have a little recreation.

The children carried knapsacks on their backs in which was a knife and fork, a tin cup and a plate. We took along a wash boiler in which to cook the food on the road. One little fellow had a drum and another had a fife. That was our band. We carried banners that said, "We want more schools and less hospitals." "We want time to play." "Prosperity is here. Where is ours!"

We started from Philadelphia where we held a great mass meeting. I decided to go with the children to see President Roosevelt to ask him to have Congress pass a law prohibiting the exploitation of childhood. I thought that President Roosevelt might see these mill children and compare them with his own little ones who were spending the summer on the seashore at Oyster Bay. . . .

The children were very happy, having plenty to eat, taking baths in the brooks and rivers every day. I thought when the strike is over and they go back to the mills, they will never have another holiday like this. All along the line of the march the farmers drove out to meet us with wagon loads of fruit and vegetables. Their wives brought the children clothes and money. The interurban trainmen would stop their trains and give us free rides.

We were on the outskirts of New Trenton, New Jersey, cooking our lunch in the wash boiler, when the conductor on the interurban car stopped and told us the police were coming to notify us that we could not enter the town. There were mills in the town and the mill owners didn't like our coming.

I said, "All right, the police will be just in time for lunch."

Sure enough, the police came and we invited them to dine with us. They looked at the little gathering of children with their tin plates and cups around the wash boiler. They just smiled and spoke kindly to the children, and said nothing at all about not going into the city.

We went in, held our meeting, and it was the wives of the police who took the little children and cared for them that night, sending them back in the morning with a nice lunch rolled up in paper napkins.

Everywhere we had meetings, showing up with living children, the horrors of child labor. . . .

I called on the mayor of Princeton and asked for permission to speak opposite the campus of the University. I said I wanted to speak on higher education. The mayor gave me permission. A great crowd gathered, professors and students and the people; and I told them that the rich robbed these little children of any education of the lowest order, that they might send their sons and daughters to places of higher education. . . . And I showed those professors children in our army who could scarcely read or write because they were working ten hours a day in the silk mills of Pennsylvania.

"Here's a text book on economics," I said, pointing to a little chap, James Ashworth, who was ten years old and who was stooped over like an old man from carrying bundles of yarn that weighed seventy-five pounds. "He gets three dollars a week." . . .

I sent a committee over to the New York Chief of Police, Ebstein, asking for permission to march up Fourth Avenue to Madison Square, where I wanted to hold a meeting. The chief refused and forbade our entrance to the city.

I went over myself to New York and saw Mayor Seth Low. The mayor was most courteous but he said he would have to support the police commissioner. I asked him what the reason was for refusing us entrance to the city, and he said that we were not citizens of New York.

"Oh, I think we will clear that up, Mr. Mayor," I said. "Permit me to call your attention to an incident which took place in this nation just a year ago. A piece of rotten royalty came over here from Germany, called Prince Henry. The Congress of the United States voted $45,000 to fill that fellow's stomach for three weeks and to entertain him. His brother was getting $4,000,000 in dividends out of the blood of the workers in this country. Was he a citizen of this land?"

"And it was reported, Mr. Mayor, that you and all the officials of New York and the University Club entertained that chap." And I repeated, "Was he a citizen of New York?"

"No, Mother," said the mayor, "he was not." . . .

"Well, Mr. Mayor, these are the little citizens of the nation and they also produce its wealth. Aren't we entitled to enter your city?" . . .

We marched to Twentieth Street. I told an immense crowd of the horrors of child labor in the mills around the anthracite region, and I showed them some of the children. I showed them Eddie Dunphy, a little fellow of twelve, whose job it was to sit all day on a high stool, handing in the right thread to another worker. Eleven hours a day he sat on the high stool with dangerous machinery all about him. All day long, winter and summer, spring and fall, for three dollars a week.

And then I showed them Gussie Rangnew, a little girl from whom all the childhood had gone. Her face was like an old woman's. Gussie packed stockings in a factory, eleven hours a day for a few cents a day.

We raised a lot of money for the strikers, and hundreds of friends offered their homes to the little ones while we were in the city.

The next day we went to Coney Island at the invitation of Mr. Bostick, who owned the wild animal show. The children had a wonderful time such as they never had in all their lives. After the exhibition of the trained animals, Mr. Bostick let me speak to the audience. . . . Right in front were the empty iron cages of the animals. I put my little children in the cages and they clung to the iron bars while I talked. . . .

"Fifty years ago there was a cry against slavery, and men gave up their lives to stop the selling of black children on the block. Today the white child is sold for two dollars a week to the manufacturers. Fifty years ago the black babies were sold C.O.D. Today the white baby is sold on the installment plan. . . .

"The trouble is that no one in Washington cares. I saw our legislators in one hour pass three bills for the relief of the railways, but when labor cries for aid for the children they will not listen.

"I asked a man in prison once how he happened to be there, and he said he had stolen a pair of shoes. I told him if he had stolen a railroad he would be a United States Senator.

"We are told that every American boy has the chance of being president. I tell you that these little boys in the iron cages would sell their chance any day for good square meals and a chance to play."

The next day we left Coney Island for Manhattan Beach to visit Senator Platt, who had made an appointment to see me at nine o'clock in the morning. The children got stuck in the sandbanks and I had a time cleaning the sand off the littlest ones. So we started to walk on the railroad track. I was told it was private property and we had to get off. Finally a saloon keeper showed us a shortcut into the sacred grounds of the hotel, and suddenly the army appeared in the lobby. The little fellows played "Hail, hail, the gang's all here" on their fifes and drums, and Senator Platt, when he saw the little army, ran away through the back door to New York.

I asked the manager if he would give the children breakfast, and charge it up to the Senator, as we had an invitation to breakfast that morning with him. He gave us a private room and he gave those children a breakfast as they had never had in all their lives. I had breakfast too, and a reporter from one of the Hearst papers and I charged it all up to Senator Platt.

We marched down to Oyster Bay, but the President refused to see us and he would not answer my letters. But our march had done its work. We had drawn the attention of the nation to the crime of child labor. And while the strike of the textile workers in Kensington was lost and the children driven back to work, not long afterward the Pennsylvania legislature passed a child labor law that sent thousands of children home from the mills, and kept thousands of others from entering the factory until they were fourteen years of age.

17

Divisions in the New South

Not all Americans and not all regions of America shared in the explosive economic growth of the Gilded Age. The South, in particular, was largely bypassed. Much of its population remained marginalized, none more so than former slaves who lived under the yoke of overt prejudice, poverty, and institutionalized segregation. Already shaped by slavery, in the years following the Civil War relations between whites and African Americans deteriorated further. Lynchings were commonplace, while Jim Crow laws legislating segregation blanketed the South. In 1896, the Supreme Court declared in *Plessy v. Ferguson* that "separate but equal" facilities for the races did not violate the Fourteenth Amendment's clause mandating equal protection under the law for all citizens.

The African-American community had divergent responses to these developments. Booker T. Washington, a former slave and the founder of the Tuskegee Institute in Alabama, argued that African Americans would only make their way to freedom and success through hard work and self-help. In his Atlanta Exposition address, reprinted here, Washington declared his loyalty to the Southern economic system and his acceptance of the status of African Americans. His speech was well received by its white audience.

W. E. B. Du Bois was a Massachusetts-raised African American who had received his Ph.D. from Harvard University and was one of the founders of the National Association for the Advancement of Colored People (NAACP). Du Bois argued that African Americans needed to fight to win equal justice, that an educated black elite (the "talented tenth") should lead blacks (in the United States and in Africa) to freedom, and that Booker T. Washington's accommodation strategy set back the African-American cause.

Leading the fight against Jim Crow and lynching in the South was Ida B. Wells-Barnett, a journalist and newspaper editor in Memphis, Tennessee. After three successful grocery-store owners were lynched in 1892, Wells-Barnett began to campaign against lynching and to write about the culture of the South. Her accounts of lynching and racism in the South gained her a national audience. Like W. E. B. Du Bois, she disagreed with Booker T. Washington and was among the first women to join the NAACP. Later in life, she broke with the NAACP, considering it too timid, and supported the controversial Marcus Garvey and his calls for black pride, if not his back-to-Africa movement.

Study Questions

1. How different were the ultimate goals of Washington and Du Bois? Is there a difference between their long-and-short term goals?

2. Did Washington really propose exchanging black political rights for economic rights?

3. Analyze Wells-Barnett's critique of lynching and her call to arms. She did not support Washington, but in what ways are her calls for action and her critique of society different from those of Du Bois.

From *Plessy v. Ferguson* (1896)

This infamous court decision upheld the constitutionality of segregation in public accommodations. The case was brought by Homer A. Plessy, a young mixed-race carpenter from Louisiana, who challenged a Louisiana law that segregated trains for "the comfort of passengers." Segregation was not common during the Reconstruction and post-Reconstruction periods of the 1870s and 1880s, but laws like that challenged by Plessy in Louisiana were passed after a Supreme Court ruling in 1883 ruled that private individuals could not be punished for racial discrimination.*

This case turns upon the constitutionality of an act of the general assembly of the state of Louisiana, passed in 1890, providing for separate railway carriages for the white and colored races. . . .

The constitutionality of this act is attacked upon the ground that it conflicts both with the 13th Amendment of the Constitution, abolishing slavery, and the 14th Amendment, which prohibits certain restrictive legislation on the part of the states.

---

* From *Plessy vs. Ferguson*, Supreme Court, 163, 537 (1896).

1. That it does not conflict with the 13th Amendment, which abolished slavery and involuntary servitude, except as a punishment for crime, is too clear for argument. . . . Indeed, we do not understand that the 13th Amendment is strenuously relied upon by the plaintiff. . . .

The object of the [14th] amendment was undoubtedly to enforce the absolute equality of the two races before the law, but in the nature of things it could not have been intended to abolish distinctions based upon color, or to enforce social, as distinguished from political, equality, or a commingling of the two races upon terms unsatisfactory to either. Laws permitting, and even requiring their separation in places where they are liable to be brought into contact do not necessarily imply the inferiority of either race to the other, and have been generally, if not universally, recognized as within the competency of the state legislatures in the exercise of their police power. . . .

We consider the underlying fallacy of the plaintiff's argument to consist in the assumption that the enforced separation of the two races stamps the colored race with a badge of inferiority. If this be so, it is not by reason of anything found in the act, but solely because the colored race chooses to put that construction upon it. . . .

The argument also assumes that social prejudice may be overcome by legislation, and that equal rights cannot be secured to the Negro except by an enforced commingling of the two races. We cannot accept this proposition. If the two races are to meet on terms of social equality, it must be the result of natural affinities, a mutual appreciation of each other's merits and a voluntary consent of individuals. . . . Legislation is powerless to eradicate racial instincts or abolish distinctions based upon physical differences and the attempt to do so can only result in accentuating the difficulties of the present situation. If the civil and political right of both races be equal, one cannot be inferior to the other civilly or politically. If one race be inferior to the other socially, the Constitution of the United States cannot put them upon the same plane.

Booker T. Washington, Atlanta Exposition Address (1895)

Booker T. Washington, the dominant black leader of the late nineteenth century, believed that blacks needed to accommodate themselves to white prejudices, at least temporarily, and concentrate on self-improvement. Because of these beliefs, he was considered by whites to be a moderate, "reasonable" black leader. But while in public he minimized the importance of civil and political rights, behind the scenes he lobbied against discriminatory measures and financed test cases in the courts. Washington was born a slave and taught himself to read; eventually he worked his way through the Hampton Institute. In 1881, he became the head of the Tuskegee Institute. This document, drawn from a speech delivered by Washington at the Cotton State Exposition of Industry and the Arts is famous for its presentation of the "Atlanta compromise" approach to race relations. The exhibition, held in Atlanta in 1895, was designed to encourage diversification of the southern economy. The publishers and bankers who organized it invited Washington to address the mostly white gathering almost as an afterthought. Nevertheless, his speech received overwhelming approval, garnering favorable responses from such diverse sources as the editor of the *Atlanta Constitution* and President Grover Cleveland.*

... Ignorant and inexperienced, it is not strange that in the first years of our new life we began at the top instead of at the bottom; that a seat in Congress or the state legislature was more sought than real estate or industrial skill; that the political convention or stump speaking had more attractions than starting a dairy farm or truck garden.

A ship lost at sea for many days suddenly sighted a friendly vessel. From the mast of the unfortunate vessel was seen a signal, "Water, water; we die of thirst!" The answer from the friendly vessel at once came back, "Cast down your bucket where you are." ... The captain of the distressed vessel, at last heeding the injunction, cast down his bucket, and it came up full of fresh, sparkling water.... To those of my race who underestimate the importance of cultivating friendly relations with the southern white man, who is their next-door neighbor, I would say: "Cast down your bucket where you are"—cast it down in making friends in every manly way of the people of all races by whom we are surrounded.

Cast it down in agriculture, mechanics, in commerce, in domestic service, and in the professions.... Our greatest danger is that in the great leap from slavery to freedom we may overlook the fact that the masses of us are to live by the productions of our hands, and fail to keep in mind that we shall prosper in proportion as we learn to dignify and glorify common labour, and put brains and skill into the common occupations of life.... No race can prosper till it learns that there is as much dignity in tilling a field as in writing a poem. It is at the bottom of life we must begin, and not at the top.

To those of the white race who look to the incoming of those of foreign birth and strange tongue and habits for the prosperity of the South, were I permitted I would repeat what I say to my own race, "Cast down your bucket where you are." Cast it down among the eight millions of Negroes whose habits you know, whose fidelity and love you have tested in days when to have proved treacherous meant the ruin of your firesides. Cast down your bucket among these people who have, without strikes and

---

*From Booker T. Washington's Atlanta Exposition Address (1895) reprinted in R. Twombly, *Blacks in White America Since 1865* (New York: David McKay, 1971).

labour wars, tilled your fields, cleared your forests, built your railroads and cities, and brought forth treasures from the bowels of the earth. . . . Casting down your bucket among my people . . . you will find that they will buy your surplus land, make blossom the waste places in your fields, and run your factories. While doing this, you can be sure in the future, as in the past, that you and your families will be surrounded by the most patient, faithful, law-abiding, and unresentful people that the world has seen. . . . In all things that are purely social we can be as separate as the finders, yet one as the hand in all things essential to mutual progress. . . .

The wisest among my race understand that the agitation of questions of social equality is the extremest folly, and that progress in the enjoyment of all the privileges that will come to us must be the result of severe and constant struggle rather than of artificial forcing. No race that has anything to contribute to the markets of the world is long in any degree ostracized. It is important and right that all privileges of the law be ours, but it is vastly more important that we be prepared for the exercise of these privileges. The opportunity to earn a dollar in a factory just now is worth infinitely more than the opportunity to spend a dollar in an opera-house.

W. E. B. Du Bois, from "Of Mr. Booker T. Washington and Others" (1903)

W. E. B. Du Bois was a Massachusetts native who received his Ph.D. from Harvard University in 1895 and made a career as a teacher at Atlanta University. He believed that if blacks prepared themselves only to be farmers, mechanics, and domestics, as Booker T. Washington advised, they would remain forever in such occupations. Du Bois was one of the founders of the Niagara Movement and was a founding member of the National Association for the Advancement of Colored People (NAACP). and agitated for political rights and higher education for blacks. This document is from "Of Mr. Booker T. Washington and Others," one of the essays in his *The Souls of Black Folk* (1903). In it, Du Bois argues that Washington's approach contributed to the loss of political rights, the erection of caste barriers, and the diversion of funds from academic education for talented blacks.[*]

---

[*] From W. E. B. Du Bois, "Of Mr. Booker T. Washington and Others" (1903) reprinted in W. E. B. Du Bois *Souls of Black Folk* (New York: New American Library, 1969).

Easily the most striking thing in the history of the American Negro since 1876 is the ascendancy of Mr. Booker T. Washington. . . . His programme of industrial education, conciliation of the South, and submission and silence as to civil and political rights was not wholly original. . . . But Mr. Washington first indissolubly linked these things; he . . . changed it from a by-path into a veritable Way of Life. . . .

Mr. Washington represents in Negro thought the old attitude of adjustment and submission; but adjustment at such a peculiar time as to make his programme unique. This is an age of unusual economic development, and Mr. Washington's programme naturally takes an economic cast, becoming a gospel of Work and Money to such an extent as apparently almost completely to overshadow the higher aims of life. . . . Mr. Washington's programme practically accepts the alleged inferiority of the Negro races. . . . In the history of nearly all other races and peoples the doctrine preached at such crises has been that manly self-respect is worth more than lands and houses, and that a people who voluntarily surrender such respect, or cease striving for it, are not worth civilizing.

. . . Mr. Washington distinctly asks that black people give up, at least for the present, three things,—

First, political power.

Second, insistence on civil rights.

Third, higher education of Negro youth,

. . . The question then comes: Is it possible, and probable, that nine millions of men can make effective progress in economic lines if they are deprived of political rights, made a servile caste, and allowed only the most meagre chance for developing their exceptional men? If history and reason give any distinct answer to these questions, it is an emphatic No. . . .

. . . while it is a great truth to say that the Negro must strive and strive mightily to help himself, it is equally true that unless his striving be not simply seconded, but rather aroused and encouraged, by the initiative of the richer and wiser environing group, he cannot hope for great success.

. . . So far as Mr. Washington preaches Thrift, Patience, and Industrial Training for the masses, we must hold up his hands and strive with him, rejoicing in his honors and glorying in the strength of this Joshua called of God and of man to lead the headless host. But so far as Mr. Washington apologizes for injustice, North or South, does not rightly value the privilege and duty of voting, belittles the emasculating effects of caste distinctions, and opposes the higher training and ambition of our brighter minds,—so far as he, the South, or the Nation, does this, we must unceasingly and firmly oppose them.

Ida B. Wells-Barnett, from *A Red Record* (1895)

In the South, lynching was considered to be proper punishment for African-American men accused of raping white women. However, as Wells-Barnett's research into lynching revealed, many victims of lynching committed no transgression but being black and financially independent. Wells-Barnett wrote editorials for her Memphis paper, the *Free Speech,* criticizing the myth of southern white-female purity and even suggested that white women might be sexually attracted to black men. Soon after these editorials, the offices of *Free Speech* were burned and threats were made against Wells-Barnett's life. She did not return to the South for thirty years. The following selection from Wells-Barnett's autobiography, *A Red Record,* describes her early editorials and her work against lynching.[*]

A word as to the charge itself. In considering the third reason assigned by the Southern white people for the butchery of blacks, the question must be asked, what the white man means when he charges the black man with rape. Does he mean the crime which the statutes of the states describe as such? Not by any means. With the Southern white man, any misalliance existing between a white woman and a colored man is a sufficient foundation for the charge of rape. The southern white man says that it is impossible for a voluntary alliance to exist between a white woman and a colored man, and therefore, the fact of an alliance is a proof of force. In numerous instances where colored men have been lynched on the charge of rape, it was positively known at the time of lynching, and indisputably proven after the victim's death, that the relationship sustained between the man and the woman was voluntary and clandestine, and that in no court of law could even the charge of assault have been successfully maintained.

It was for the assertion of this fact, in the defense of her own race, that the writer hereof became an exile; her property destroyed and her return to her home forbidden under penalty of death, for writing the following editorial which was printed in her paper, the *Free Speech*, in Memphis, Tenn., May 21, 1892:

"Eight Negroes lynched since last issue of the *Free Speech:* one at Little Rock, Ark., last Saturday morning where the citizens broke (?) into the penitentiary and got their man; three near Anniston, Ala., one near New Orleans; and three at Clarksville, Ga.; the last three for killing a white man, and five on the same old racket—the new alarm about raping white women. The same programme of hanging, then shooting bullets into the lifeless bodies was carried out to the letter. Nobody in this section of the country believes in the old threadbare lie that Negro men rape white women. If

[*] From Ida Wells-Barnett, *A Red Record* (Chicago: Donohue & Henneberry, 1895), 8–15.

Southern white men are not careful, they will overreach themselves and public sentiment will have a reaction; a conclusion will then be reached which will be very damaging to the moral reputation of their women."

But threats cannot suppress the truth, and while the Negro suffers the soul deformity, resultant from two and a half centuries of slavery, he is no more guilty of this vilest of all vile charges than the white man who would blacken his name.

During all the years of slavery, no such charge was ever made, not even during the dark days of the rebellion. . . . While the master was away fighting to forge the fetters upon the slave, he left his wife and children with no protectors save the Negroes themselves. . . .

Likewise during the period of alleged "insurrection," and alarming "race riots," it never occurred to the white man that his wife and children were in danger of assault. Nor in the Reconstruction era, when the hue and cry was against "Negro Domination," was there ever a thought that the domination would ever contaminate a fireside or strike toward the virtue of womanhood. . . .

It is not the purpose of this defense to say one word against the white women of the South. Such need not be said, but it is their misfortune that the . . . white men of that section . . . to justify their own barbarism . . . assume a chivalry which they do not possess. True chivalry respects all womanhood, and no one who reads the record, as it is written in the faces of the million mulattos in the South, will for a minute conceive that the southern white man had a very chivalrous regard for the honor due the women of his race, or respect for the womanhood which circumstances placed in his power. . . . Virtue knows no color line, and the chivalry which depends on complexion of skin and texture of hair can command no honest respect.

When emancipation came to the Negroes . . . from every nook and corner of the North, brave young white women . . . left their cultured homes, their happy associations and their lives of ease, and with heroic determination went to the South to carry light and truth to the benighted blacks. . . . They became the social outlaws in the South. The peculiar sensitiveness of the southern white men for women, never shed its protecting influence about them. No friendly word from their own race cheered them in their work; no hospitable doors gave them the companionship like that from which they had come. No chivalrous white man doffed his hat in honor or respect. They were "Nigger teachers"—unpardonable offenders in the social ethics of the South, and were insulted, persecuted and ostracized, not by Negroes, but by the white manhood which boasts of its chivalry toward women.

And yet these northern women worked on, year after year. . . . Threading their way through dense forests, working in schoolhouses, in the cabin and in the church, thrown at all times and in all places among the unfortunate and lowly Negroes, whom they had come to find and to serve, these northern women, thousands and thousands of them, have spent more than a quarter of a century in giving the colored people their splendid lessons for home and heart and soul. Without protection, save that which innocence gives to every good woman, they went about their work, fearing no assault and suffering none. Their chivalrous protectors were hundreds of miles away in their northern homes, and yet they never feared any "great dark-faced mobs." . . . They never complained of assaults, and no mob was ever called into existence to avenge crimes against them. Before the world adjudges the Negro a moral monster, a vicious assailant of womanhood and a menace to the sacred precincts of home, the colored people ask the consideration of the silent record of gratitude, respect, protection and devotion of the millions of the race in the South, to the thousands of northern white women who have served as teachers and missionaries since the war. . . .

These pages are written in no spirit of vindictiveness. . . . We plead not for the colored people alone, but for all victims of the terrible injustice which puts men and women to death without form of law. During the year 1894, there were 132 persons executed in the United States by due form of law, while in the same year, 197 persons were put to death by mobs, who gave the victims no opportunity to make a lawful defense. No comment need be made upon a condition of public sentiment responsible for such alarming results.

18

Huddled Masses

Between 1860 and 1920, more than 25 million hopeful immigrants arrived in the United States, drawn by the promise of opportunity, the growing American economy's need for cheap labor, and economic instability in Europe and Asia. Along with many rural Americans they flocked to cities like New York, Chicago, Pittsburgh, and St. Louis. These immigrants arriving on American shores provided a stark contrast to those who had preceded them in the earlier part of the century: The "old" immigration, prior to 1890, was from northern and western Europe—places like England, Germany, and Ireland; the "new" immigrants came from eastern and Southern Europe—places like Russia, Poland, Italy, and Greece—as well as other lands including China and Mexico. These new immigrants, often unskilled workers and in many cases temporary, settled in urban neighborhoods and profoundly transformed the American city.

The work most immigrants found in the newly industrialized United States was poorly paid and dangerous. Furthermore, for many families economic survival meant that everyone had to work, including children. The first selection in this chapter, "Children in the Coal Mines," is an excerpt from a book on child labor by the reformer John Spargo and describes the life of child miners.

The transition to America was very difficult for many immigrants, and two documents in this chapter portray some of the problems they faced. Letters to the *Jewish Daily Forward*, a Yiddish-language newspaper in New York, describe some of the difficulties faced by Jewish immigrants. Unlike many other immigrants, Jews often entered America in family groups, and the letters to the *Forward* describe some of the hardships they encountered as they tried to maintain Old World values and family ties in a new and alien land. Asian immigrants, mostly Chinese men working on the railroad, were concentrated on the West Coast, but increasingly, Asians, like Lee Chew in this chapter, made their way to East Coast urban hubs.

Even more than other groups, Asians were the focus of incredible nativistic hostility. Mobs attacked Chinese workers on the West Coast, and their immigration was cut off in the Chinese Exclusion Act of 1882. But all immigrants were at risk for attack, as a wave of nativism swept the United States in the 1880s driven by anti-Catholicism and fear of job loss to newer, cheaper workers. The American

Protective Association gained widespread popularity for its anti-Catholic, anti-immigrant stance. Included here, as the last document in this chapter, is the secret oath of this organization.

Study Questions

1. Compare Spargo's account of child labor with Mother Jones's in Chapter 16.

2. According to the letters from "A Bintel Brief," what difficulties did Jewish immigrants face in the New World?

3. Compare the experiences of the Jewish and Chinese immigrants. What similarities and differences were there?

4. Why did the American Protective Association fear Catholic immigrants?

John Spargo, From *The Bitter Cry of Children* (1906)

This selection describes the plight of children working in coal mines. Children were often put to work by their parents as a way of keeping the family out of poverty, and for employers, child labor was inexpensive and children were often thought to be more adept at detailed work. They thus were widely used in the textile and mining industries. Child labor outraged middle-class native-born reformers who sentimentalized childhood.*

Work in the coal breakers is exceedingly hard and dangerous. Crouched over the chutes, the boys sit hour after hour, picking out the pieces of slate and other refuse from the coal as it rushes past to the washers. From the cramped position they have to assume, most of them become more or less deformed and bent-backed like old men. When a boy has been working for some time and begins to get round-shouldered, his fellows say that "He's got his boy to carry around whenever he goes."

The coal is hard, and accidents to the hands, such as cut, broken, or crushed fingers, are common among the boys. Sometimes there is a worse accident: a terrified shriek is heard, and a boy is mangled and torn in the machinery, or disappears in the chute to be picked out later smothered and dead. Clouds of dust fill the breakers and are inhaled by the boys, laying the foundations for asthma and miners' consumption.

---

*From John Spargo, *The Bitter Cry of Children* (New York: Macmillan, 1906), 163–165.

I once stood in a breaker for half an hour and tried to do the work a twelve-year-old boy was doing day after day, for ten hours at a stretch, for sixty cents a day. The gloom of the breaker appalled me. Outside the sun shone brightly, the air was pellucid, and the birds sang in chorus with the trees and the rivers. Within the breaker there was blackness, clouds of deadly dust enfolded everything, the harsh, grinding roar of the machinery and the ceaseless rushing of coal through the chutes filled the ears. I tried to pick out the pieces of slate from the hurrying stream of coal, often missing them; my hands were bruised and cut in a few minutes; I was covered from head to foot with coal dust, and for many hours afterwards I was expectorating some of the small particles of anthracite I had swallowed.

I could not do that work and live, but there were boys of ten and twelve years of age doing it for fifty and sixty cents a day. Some of them had never been inside of a school; few of them could read a child's primer. True, some of them attended the night schools, but after working ten hours in the breaker the educational results from attending school were practically nil. "We goes fer a good time, an' we keeps de guys wot's dere hoppin' all de time," said little Owen Jones, whose work I had been trying to do. . . .

As I stood in that breaker I thought of the reply of the small boy to Robert Owen [British social reformer]. Visiting an English coal mine one day, Owen asked a twelve-year-old if he knew God. The boy stared vacantly at his questioner: "God?" he said, "God? No, I don't. He must work in some other mine." It was hard to realize amid the danger and din and blackness of that Pennsylvania breaker that such a thing as belief in a great All-good God existed.

From the breakers the boys graduate to the mine depths, where they become door tenders, switch boys, or mule drivers. Here, far below the surface, work is still more dangerous. At fourteen and fifteen the boys assume the same risks as the men, and are surrounded by the same perils. Nor is it in Pennsylvania only that these conditions exist. In the bituminous mines of West Virginia, boys of nine or ten are frequently employed. I met one little fellow ten years old in Mt. Carbon, W. Va., last year, who was employed as a "trap boy." Think of what it means to be a trap boy at ten years of age. It means to sit alone in a dark mine passage hour after hour, with no human soul near; to see no living creature except the mules as they pass with their loads, or a rat or two seeking to share one's meal; to stand in water or mud that covers the ankles, chilled to the marrow by the cold draughts that rush in when you open the trap door for the mules to pass through; to work for fourteen hours—waiting—opening and shutting a door—then waiting again—for sixty cents; to reach the surface when all is wrapped in the mantle of night, and to fall to the earth exhausted and have to be carried away to the nearest "shack" to be revived before it is possible to walk to the farther shack called "home." Boys twelve years of age may be legally employed in the mines of West Virginia, by day or by night, and for as many hours as the employers care to make them toil or their bodies will stand the strain. Where the disregard of child life is such that this may be done openly and with legal sanction, it is easy to believe what miners have again and again told me—that there are hundreds of little boys of nine and ten years of age employed in the coal mines of this state.

Letters to the *Jewish Daily Forward* (1906–1907)

The *Jewish Daily Forward* was a Yiddish-language newspaper serving New York's Jewish immigrant community. In 1906, the *Forward*'s editor, Abraham Cahan, began a column called "A Bintel Brief" meaning "a bundle of letters." Cahan wrote not only the responses, but some of the letters too. The bulk of the letters in the early years of the column came from young, newly arrived immigrants. Some dealt with personal problems: love, jealously, intermarriage, affairs between boarders and the married women in whose homes they lived. Others were about poverty, unemployment, and sweatshops. All provide a glimpse of the process of adjustment to life in America.*

Dear Editor,

I am a Russian revolutionist and a freethinker. Here in America I became acquainted with a girl who is also a freethinker. We decided to marry, but the problem is that she has Orthodox parents, and for their sake we must have a religious ceremony. If we refuse the ceremony we will be cut off from them forever. Her parents also want me to go to the synagogue with them before the wedding, and I don't know what to do. Therefore I ask you to advise me how to act.

Respectfully, J. B.

ANSWER:

The advice is that there are times when it pays to give in to old parents and not grieve them. It depends on the circumstances. When one can get along with kindness it is better not to break off relations with the parents.

* * * * *

---

* Letters to the *Jewish Daily Forward* from *A Bintel Brief*, Isaac Metzker ed. (Garden City, New York: Doubleday, 1971). Copyright © 1971 by Isaac Metzker. Forward and notes copyright © 1971 Doubleday, a division of Bantam, Doubleday, Dell Publishing Group, Inc. Used by permission of Doubleday, a division of Bantam, Doubleday, Dell Publishing Group, Inc.

Worthy Editor,

Allow me a little space in your newspaper and, I beg you, give me some advice as to what to do.

There are seven people in our family—parents and five children. I am the oldest child, and a fourteen-year-old girl. We have been in the country two years and my father, who is a frail man, is the only one working to support the whole family.

I go to school, where I do very well. But since times are hard now and my father earned only five dollars this week, I began to talk about giving up my studies and going to work in order to help my father as much as possible. But my mother didn't ever want to hear of it. She wants me to continue my education. She even went out and spent ten dollars on winter clothes for me. But I didn't enjoy the clothes, because I think I am doing the wrong thing. Instead of bringing something into the house, my parents have to spend money on me.

I have a lot of compassion for my parents. My mother is now pregnant, but she still has to take care of the three boarders we have in the house. Mother and Father work very hard and they want to keep me in school.

I am writing to you without their knowledge, and I beg you to tell me how to act. Hoping you can advise me, I remain,

Your reader,

ANSWER:

The advice to the girl is that she should obey her parents and further her education, because in that way she will be able to give them greater satisfaction than if she went out to work.

* * * * *

Worthy Editor,

I was born in America and my parents gave me a good education. I . . . finished high school, completed a course in bookkeeping and got a good job. I have many friends, and several boys have already proposed to me. Recently I went to visit my parents' home town in Russian Poland. My mother's family in Europe had invited my parents to a wedding, but instead of going themselves, they sent me. . . . I had a good time. Our European family, like my parents, are quite well off and they treated me well. The indulged me in everything and I stayed with them six months.

It was lively in the town. . . . [T]hey all accepted me warmly, looked up to me—after all, I was a citizen of the free land, America. Among the social leaders of the community was an intelligent young man, a friend of my uncle's, who took me to various gatherings and affairs.

He was very attentive, and after a short while he declared his love for me in a long letter. . . .

As my love for him grew, however, I wrote to my parents about him, and then we became officially engaged.

A few months later we both went to my parents in the States and they received him like their own son. My bridegroom immediately began to learn English and tried to adjust to the new life. Yet when I introduced him to my friends they looked at him with disappointment. "This 'greenhorn' is your fiancee?" they asked. I told them what a big role he played in his town, how everyone respected him, but they looked at me as if I were crazy and scoffed at my words.

At first I thought, Let them laugh, when they get better acquainted with him they'll talk differently. In time, though, I was affected by their talk and began to think, like them, that he really was a "greenhorn" and acted like one.

In short, my love for him is cooling off gradually. I'm suffering terribly because my feelings for him are changing. In Europe, where everyone admired him and all the girls envied me, he looked different. But, here, I see before me another person.

I haven't the courage to tell him, and I can't even talk about it to my parents. He still loves me with all his heart, and I don't know what to do. I choke it all up inside myself, and I beg you to help me with advice in my desperate situation.

Respectfully,

A Worried Reader

ANSWER:

The writer would make a grave mistake if she were to separate from her bridegroom now. She must not lose her common sense and be influenced by the foolish opinions of her friends who divided the world into "greenhorns" and real Americans.

We can assure the writer that her bridegroom will learn English quickly. He will know American history and literature as well as her friends do, and be a better American than they. She should be proud of his love and laugh at those who call him "greenhorn."

Lee Chew, *Life of a Chinese Immigrant* (1903)

The following selection is from a biography of a Chinese immigrant commissioned by the reformist journal *The Independent.* Note that Chew arrived in the United States before the Chinese Exclusion Act of 1882, and was therefore dictating this as a middle-aged man. Chew was involved in many of the jobs associated with Chinese immigrants during this period—mining, laundry, and railroad construction.*

The village where I was born is situated in the province of Canton, on one of the banks of the Si-Kiang River. It is called a village, altho it is really as big as a city, for there are about 5,000 men in it over eighteen years of age—women and children and even youths are not counted in our villages. . . .

. . . I heard about the American foreign devils, that they were false, having made a treaty by which it was agreed that they could freely come to China, and the Chinese as freely go to their country. After this treaty was made China opened its doors to them and then they broke the treaty that they had asked for by shutting the Chinese out of their country. . . .

The man had gone away from our village a poor boy. Now he returned with unlimited wealth, which he had obtained in the country of the American wizards. After many amazing adventures he had become a merchant in a city called Mott Street, so it was said. . . .

Having made his wealth among the barbarians this man had faithfully returned to pour it out among his tribesmen, and he is living in our village now very happy, and a pillar of strength to the poor.

The wealth of this man filled my mind with the idea that I, too, would like to go to the country of the wizards and gain some of their wealth, and after a long time my father consented, and gave me his blessing, and my mother took leave of me with tears, while my grandfather laid his hand upon my head and told me to remember and live up to the admonitions of the Sages, to avoid gambling, bad women and men of evil minds, and so to govern my conduct that when I died my ancestors might rejoice to welcome me as a guest on high.

My father gave me $100, and I went to Hong Kong with five other boys from our place and we got steerage passage on a steamer, paying $50 each. . . .

. . . Of the great power of these people I saw many signs. The engines that moved the ship were wonderful monsters, strong enough to lift mountains. When I got to San Francisco, which was before the passage of the Exclusion act, I was half starved,

---

* From *The Independent*, 54 (2818), February 19, 1903, 417–423.

because I was afraid to eat the provisions of the barbarians, but a few days' living in the Chinese quarter made me happy again. . . .

The Chinese laundryman does not learn his trade in China; there are no laundries in China. . . . All the Chinese laundrymen here were taught in the first place by American women just as I was taught.

When I went to work for that American family I could not speak a word of English, and I did not know anything about house work. The family consisted of husband, wife and two children. They were very good to me and paid me $3.50 a week, of which I could save $3. . . .

In six months I had learned how to do the work of our house quite well, and I was getting $5 a week and board, and putting away about $4.25 a week. I had also learned some English, and by going to a Sunday school I learned more English and something about Jesus, who was a great Sage, and whose precepts are like those of Kong-foo-tsze.

It was twenty years ago when I came to this country, and I worked for two years as a servant, getting at least $35 a month. I sent money home to comfort my parents. . . .

When I first opened a laundry it was in company with a partner, who had been in the business for some years. We went to a town about 500 miles inland, where a railroad was building. We got a board shanty and worked for the men employed by the railroads. . . .

We were three years with the railroad, and then went to the mines, where we made plenty of money in gold dust, but had a hard time, for many of the miners were wild men who carried revolvers and after drinking would come into our place to shoot and steal shirts, for which we had to pay. One of these men hit his head hard against a flat iron and all the miners came and broke our laundry, chasing us out of town. They were going to hang us. We lost all our property and $365 in money, which a member of the mob must have found.

Luckily most of our money was in the hands of Chinese bankers in San Francisco. I drew $500 and went East to Chicago, where I had a laundry for three years, during which I increased my capital to $2,500. After that I was four years in Detroit. I went home to China in 1897, but returned in 1898, and began a laundry business in Buffalo.

The ordinary laundry shop is generally divided into three rooms. In front is the room where the customers are received, behind that a bedroom and in the back the work shop, which is also the dining room and kitchen. The stove and cooking utensils are the same as those of the Americans. . . .

I have found out, during my residence in this country, that much of the Chinese prejudice against Americans is unfounded, and I no longer put faith in the wild tales that were told about them in our village, tho some of the Chinese, who have been here twenty years and who are learned men, still believe that there is no marriage in this country, that the land is infested with demons and that all the people are given over to general wickedness.

I know better. Americans are not all bad, nor are they wicked wizards. Still, they have their faults, and their treatment of us is outrageous. . . .

The reason why so many Chinese go into the laundry business in this country is because it requires little capital and is one of the few opportunities that are open. . . .

There is no reason for the prejudice against the Chinese. The cheap labor cry was always a falsehood. Their labor was never cheap, and is not cheap now. It has always commanded the highest market price. But the trouble is that the Chinese are such excellent and faithful workers that bosses will have no others when they can get them. If you look at men working on the street you will find an overseer for every four or five of them. That watching is not necessary for Chinese. They work as well when left to themselves as they do when some one is looking at them. . . .

The Secret Oath of the American Protective Association (1893)

> The American Protective Association was one of the largest and most powerful anti-immigrant and anti-Catholic organizations of the late nineteenth century, claiming more than a million members by 1896. Taking its cue and beliefs from anti-Catholic biases perpetuated in Europe since the Inquisition and the Protestant Reformation it arose, in part, as a nativist response to the large numbers of immigrants from Catholic countries and spread rumors that Catholics intended to slaughter non-Catholics and that Catholic elected officials discriminated against non-Catholic job applicants and citizens.*

I do most solemnly promise and swear that I will always, to the utmost of my ability, labor, plead, and wage a continuous warfare against ignorance and fanaticism; that I will use my utmost power to strike the shackles and chains of blind obedience to the Roman Catholic Church from the hampered and bound consciences of a priest-ridden and church-oppressed people; that I will never allow anyone, a member of the Roman Catholic Church, to become a member of this order, I knowing him to be such; that I will use my influence to promote the interest of all Protestants everywhere in the world that I may be; that I will not employ a Roman Catholic in any capacity, if I can procure the services of a Protestant.

I furthermore promise and swear that I will not aid in building or maintaining, by my resources, any Roman Catholic church or institution of their sect or creed whatsoever, but will do all in my power to retard and break down the power of the Pope, in this country or any other; that I will not enter into any controversy with a Roman Catholic

---

* From *Documents of American Catholic History* ed. T. Ellis, (Wilmington DE: Michael Glazier, Inc., 1956), 500–501. A Bruce Publishing Company.

upon the subject of this order, nor will I enter into any agreement with a Roman Catholic to strike or create a disturbance whereby the Catholic employees may undermine and substitute their Protestant co-workers; that in all grievances I will seek only Protestants, and counsel with them to the exclusion of all Roman Catholics, and will not make known to them anything of any nature matured at such conferences.

I furthermore promise and swear that I will not countenance the nomination, in any caucus or convention, of a Roman Catholic for any office in the gift of the American people, and that I will not vote for, or counsel others to vote for, any Roman Catholic, but will vote only for a Protestant, so far as may lie in my power (should there be two Roman Catholics in opposite tickets, I will erase the name on the ticket I vote); that I will at all times endeavor to place the political positions of this government in the hands of Protestants, to the entire exclusion of the Roman Catholic Church, of the members thereof, and the mandate of the Pope.

To all of which I do most solemnly promise and swear, so help me God.

Amen.

19

City Life

Cities were transformed in the late nineteenth century as new transportation technologies—subways, trolleys, and cable cars—expanded the urban environment. New transportation fostered the growth of new residential areas outside the confines of the city proper. With the growth of such suburbs, rich and poor no longer lived side by side. While the rich and the emergent middle class escaped the cities, the poor—overwhelmingly new immigrants and African Americans—were sequestered in neighborhoods filled with crime, substandard services, and disease. The development of these essentially new cities led to a new urban culture and new political systems while the cities' concentrations of poverty inspired new attempts to reform the desperate conditions. This chapter examines these aspects of urban life in the late nineteenth century.

In poor sections of cities like New York, Chicago, and Philadelphia, thousands of families packed into overcrowded tenements. Sanitation was virtually nonexistent, and manure and mud filled city streets while disease—smallpox, diphtheria, and yellow fever—ran rampant. Included here are two descriptions of city life in New York City, one by a New York City Health Commissioner and the other by one of the founders of the Children's Aid Society. These pieces describe not only the horrors of urban life, but also some of the motivations and biases of the reformers, in city government and private charities, who tried to improve the urban environment.

Immigration and urban growth coincided with and often encouraged the development of new systems of political organization in the United States. Most significant among these developments was the machine system. Machine bosses promised services (turkeys at Christmas, money in a time of need, shoes for children, and the like) in exchange for votes and controlled the infrastructure of the city. Bosses accepted bribes from, among others, prostitutes and saloon owners, appointed their friends and family members to city jobs, and siphoned off as much as they could from city coffers for themselves and their blocs. But although they were corrupt, bosses weren't simply thieves: they also provided some valuable social services to their constituents in an era when government did little to help the poor. Two documents in this chapter, from the social reformer and muckraker Lincoln Steffens and from a selection of conversations with a ward boss, reveal the different motivations and perceptions of boss politics.

City growth, improved transportation, and a nascent leisure class helped spawn new forms of urban nightlife and entertainment. Jazz clubs, professional baseball teams, parks, and nickelodeons sprang up to occupy the leisure time of working- and middle-class Americans, radically altering social life in the new urban centers of industrial America. Large populations, more leisure time, new modes of transportation were all factors in the creation of entertainment centers like Coney Island in New York. A prototype for other cities, Coney Island provided an array of inexpensive ways for people to enjoy themselves.

Study Questions

1. Does Brace's selection reveal any Social Darwinist biases? What assumptions does he betray about the American character?

2. Compare Brace's and Waring's hypotheses on the origins of urban problems.

3. Is Plunkitt right about Steffens? If so, to what extent and why?

4. Elsewhere in *The Shame of the Cities*, Steffens excoriates kickbacks and other forms of corruption. To be sure, much of the money went to leaders like Plunkitt. Too often, however, reformers ignored the fact that some of the money went to provide services. Why did reformers fail to wean voters from the machines?

5. Is Steffens's analogy between voters in Philadelphia and blacks in the South apt? If so, why? If not, why not?

6. Comment on the description of women in "Bathing at Coney Island."

Charles Loring Brace, "The Life of the Street Rats" (1872)

"The Life of the Street Rats" is a description of the lives of the urban poor in New York City, from a book titled *The Dangerous Classes Of New York and Twenty Years Among Them*, written by the early reformer and founder of the Children's Aid Society Charles Loring Brace.*

---

* From Charles Loring Brace "The Life of the Street Rats," in *The Dangerous Classes of New York and Twenty Years Among Them* (New York, 1872).

. . . The intensity of the American temperament is felt in every fibre of these children of poverty and vice. Their crimes have the unrestrained and sanguinary character of a race accustomed to overcome all obstacles. They rifle a bank, where English thieves pick a pocket; they murder, where European proletaires cudgel or fight with fists; in a riot, they begin what seems about to be the sacking of a city, where English rioters would merely batter policemen, or smash lamps. The "dangerous classes" of New York are mainly American-born, but the children of Irish and German immigrants. . . . .

There are thousands on thousands in New York who have no assignable home, and "flirt" from attic to attic, and cellar to cellar; there are other thousands more or less connected with criminal enterprises; and still other tens of thousands, poor, hard-pressed, and depending for daily bread on the day's earnings, swarming in tenement-houses, who behold the gilded rewards of toil all about them, but are never permitted to touch them.

All these great masses of destitute, miserable, and criminal persons believe that for ages the rich have had all the good things of life, while to them have been left the evil things. Capital to them is the tyrant.

Let but Law lift its hand from them for a season, or let the civilizing influences of American life fail to reach them, and, if the opportunity offered, we should see an explosion from this class which might leave this city in ashes and blood.

Seventeen years ago, my attention had been called to the extraordinarily degraded condition of the children in a district lying on the west side of the city, between Seventeenth and Nineteenth Streets, and the Seventh and Tenth Avenues. A certain block, called "Misery Row," in Tenth Avenue, was the main seed-bed of crime and poverty in the quarter, and was also invariably a "fever-nest." Here the poor obtained wretched rooms at a comparatively low rent; these they sub-let, and thus, in little, crowded, close tenements, were herded men, women and children of all ages. The parents were invariably given to hard drinking, and the children were sent out to beg or to steal. Besides them, other children, who were orphans, or who had run away from drunkards' homes, or had been working on the canal-boats that discharged on the docks near by, drifted into the quarter, as if attracted by the atmosphere of crime and laziness that prevailed in the neighborhood. These slept around the breweries of the ward, or on the hay-barges, or in the old sheds of Eighteenth and Nineteenth Streets. They were mere children, and kept life together by all sorts of street-jobs—helping the brewery laborers, blackening boots, sweeping sidewalks, "smashing baggages" (as they called it), and the like. Herding together, they soon began to form an unconscious society for vagrancy and idleness. Finding that work brought but poor pay, they tried shorter roads to getting money by petty [sic] thefts, in which they were very adroit. Even if they earned a considerable sum by a lucky day's job, they quickly spent it in gambling, or for some folly.

The police soon knew them as "street-rats"; but, like the rats, they were too quick and cunning to be often caught in their petty plunderings, so they gnawed away at the foundations of society undisturbed.

George Waring, Sanitary Conditions in New York (1897)

The following is an analysis of conditions in New York City by a New York City sanitation commissioner. Writing in 1897, twenty years after Charles Loring Brace, George Waring argues that improved sanitary conditions were made possible by the breakdown of the boss system in New York.*

Before 1895 the streets were almost universally in a filthy state. In wet weather they were covered with slime, and in dry weather the air was filled with dust. Artificial sprinkling in summer converted the dust into mud, and the drying winds changed the mud to powder. Rubbish of all kinds, garbage, and ashes lay neglected in the streets, and in the hot weather the city stank with the emanations of putrefying organic matter. It was not always possible to see the pavement, because of the dirt that covered it. One expert, a former contractor of street-cleaning, told me that West Broadway could not be cleaned, because it was so coated with grease from wagon-axles; it was really coated with slimy mud. The sewer inlets were clogged with refuse. Dirty paper was prevalent everywhere, and black rottenness was seen and smelled on every hand.

The practice of standing unharnessed trucks and wagons in the public streets was well-nigh universal in all except the main thoroughfares and the better residence districts. The Board of Health made an enumeration of vehicles so standing on Sunday, counting twenty-five thousand on a portion of one side of the city; they reached the conclusion that there were in all more than sixty thousand. These trucks not only restricted traffic and made complete street-cleaning practically impossible, but they were harbors of vice and crime. Thieves and highwaymen made them their dens, toughs caroused in them, both sexes resorted to them, and they were used for the vilest purposes, until they became, both figuratively and literally, a stench in the nostrils of the people. In the crowded districts they were a veritable nocturnal hell. Against all this the poor people were powerless to get relief. The highest city officials, after feeble attempts at removal, declared that New York was so peculiarly constructed (having no alleys through which the rear of the lots could be reached) that its commerce could not be carried on unless this privilege were given to its truckmen; in short, the removal of the trucks was "an impossibility" . . .

The condition of the streets, of the force, and of the stock was the fault of no man and of no set of men. It was the fault of the system. The department was throttled by partisan control—so throttled it could neither do good work, command its own respect and that of the pubic, nor maintain its material in good order. It was run as an adjunct of a political organization. In that capacity it was a marked success. It paid fat tribute;

---

* From George W. Waring, Jr., *Street Cleaning* (New York: Doubleday and McClure, 1897), 13–31.

it fed thousands of voters, and it gave power and influence to hundreds of political leaders. It had this appointed function, and it performed it well. . . .

New York is now thoroughly clean in every part, the empty vehicles are gone. . . . "Clean streets" means much more than the casual observer is apt to think It has justly been said that "cleanliness is catching," and clean streets are leading to clean hallways and stair cases and cleaner living-rooms. . . .

Few realize the many minor ways in which the work of the department has benefited the people at large. For example, there is far less injury from dust to clothing, to furniture, and to goods in shops; mud is not tracked from the streets on to the sidewalks, and thence into the houses; boots require far less cleaning; the wearing of overshoes has been largely abandoned; wet feet and bedraggled skirts are mainly things of the past; and children now make free use of a playground of streets which were formerly impossible to them. "Scratches," a skin disease of horses due to mud and slush, used to entail very serious cost on truckmen and liverymen. It is now almost unknown. Horses used to "pick up a nail" with alarming frequency, and this caused great loss of service, and, like scratches made the bill of the veterinary surgeon a serious matter. There are practically no nails now to be found in the streets.

The great, the almost inestimable, beneficial effect of the work of the department is showing the large reduction of the death-rate and in the less keenly realized but still more important reduction in the sick-rate. As compared with the average death-rate of 26.78 of 1882–94, that of 1895 was 23.10, that of 1896 was 21.52, and that of the first half of 1897 was 19.63. If this latter figure is maintained throughout the year, there will have been fifteen thousand fewer deaths than there would have been had the average rate of the thirteen previous years prevailed. The report of the Board of Health for 1896, basing its calculations on diarrheal diseases July, August, and September, in the filthiest wards, in the most crowded wards, and in the remainder of the city, shows a very marked reduction in all, and the largest reduction in the first two classes.

Lincoln Steffens, from *The Shame of the Cities* (1904)

Lincoln Steffens, author of *The Shame of the Cities*, was among the most famous of the muckraking journalists. *The Shame of the Cities* was from a series of articles on municipal corruption Steffens wrote for *McClure's* magazine in 1902 and 1903. In them he reflected the disgust reformers felt for the machines and their methods of politics.*

---

* From Lincloln Steffens *The Shame of the Cities* (New York: Hill & Wang, 1957).

The Philadelphia machine isn't the best. It isn't sound, and I doubt if it would stand in New York or Chicago. The enduring strength of the typical American political machine is that it is a natural growth—a sucker, but deep-rooted in the people. The New Yorkers vote for Tammany Hall. The Philadelphians do not vote; they are disfranchised, and their disfranchisement is one anchor of the foundation of the Philadelphia organization.

This is no figure of speech. The honest citizens of Philadelphia have no more rights at the polls than the negroes down South. Nor do they fight very hard for this basic privilege. You can arouse their Republican ire by talking about the black Republican votes lost in the Southern States by white Democratic intimidation, but if you remind the average Philadelphian that he is in the same position, he will look startled, then say, "That's so, that's literally true, only I never thought of it in just that way." And it is literally true.

The machine controls the whole process of voting, and practices fraud at every stage. The assessor's list is the voting list, and the assessor is the machine's man. . . . The assessor pads the list with the names of dead dogs, children, and non-existent persons. One newspaper printed the picture of a dog, another that of a little four-year-old negro boy, down on such a list. A ring orator in a speech resenting sneers at his ward as "low down" reminded his hearers that that was the ward of Independence Hall, and naming over signers of the Declaration of Independence, he closed his highest flight of eloquence with the statement that "these men, the fathers of American liberty, voted down here once. And," he added, with a catching grin, "they vote here yet." Rudolph Blankenburg, a persistent fighter for the right and the use of the right to vote (and, by the way, an immigrant), sent out just before one election a registered letter to each voter on the rolls of a certain selected division. Sixty-three per cent were returned marked "not at," "removed," "deceased," etc. From one four-story house where forty-four voters were addressed, eighteen letters came back undelivered; from another of forty-eight voters, came back forty-one letters; from another sixty-one out of sixty-two; from another, forty-four out of forty-seven. Six houses in one division were assessed at one hundred and seventy-two voters, more than the votes cast in the previous election in any one of two hundred entire divisions.

The repeating is done boldly, for the machine controls the election officers, often choosing them from among the fraudulent names; and when no one appears to serve, assigning the heeler ready for the expected vacancy. The police are forbidden by law to stand within thirty feet of the polls, but they are at the box and they are there to see that the machine's orders are obeyed and that repeaters whom they help to furnish are permitted to vote without "intimidation" on the names they, the police, have supplied. . . .

William T. Riordon, from *Plunkitt of Tammany Hall* (1905)

This is an excerpt from William L. Riordon's *Plunkitt of Tammany Hall,* a collection of conversations Riordon allegedly had with George Washington Plunkitt, a Tammany ward boss. Plunkitt's transportation and general-contracting business thrived through his connections with Tammany bosses from Tweed through Murphy. Plunkitt distinguished between "honest graft," which he argued was the oil that kept the machine running, and "dishonest graft."[*]

"Everybody is talkin' these days about Tammany men growin' rich on graft, but nobody thinks of drawin' the distinction between honest graft and dishonest graft. There's all the difference in the world between the two. Yes, many of our men have grown rich in politics. I have myself. I've made a big fortune out of the game, and I'm gettin' richer every day, but I've not gone in for dishonest graft—blackmailin' gamblers, saloon-keepers, disorderly people, etc.—and neither has any of the men who have made big fortunes in politics.

"There's an honest graft, and I'm an example of how it works. I might sum up the whole thing by sayin': 'I seen my opportunities and I took 'em.'

"Just let me explain my examples. My party's in power in the city, and it's goin' to undertake a lot of public improvements. Well, I'm tipped off, say, that they're going to lay out a new park at a certain place.

"I see my opportunity and I take it. I go to that place and I buy up all the land I can in the neighborhood. Then the board of this or that makes its plan public, and there is a rush to get my land, which nobody cared particular for before.

"Ain't it perfectly honest to charge a good price and make a profit on my investment and foresight? Of course it is. Well, that's honest graft. . . .

". . . It's just like lookin' ahead in Wall Street or in the coffee or cotton market.

". . . Now, let me tell you that most politicians who are accused of robbin the city get rich the same way.

"They didn't steal a dollar from the city treasury. They just seen their opportunities and took them. That is why, when a reform administration comes in and spends a half million dollars in tryin' to find the public robberies they talk about in the campaign, they don't find them.

"The books are always all right. The money in the city treasury is all right. Everything is all right All they can show is that the Tammany heads of departments looked after their friends, within the law, and gave them what opportunities they could to make honest graft. . . .

---

[*] From W. Riordan, *Plunkitt of Tammany Hall* (New York: McClure, Phillips & Co., 1905).

"I've been readin' a book by Lincoln Steffens on *The Shame of the Cities*. Steffens means well but, like all reformers, he don't know how to make distinctions. He can't see no difference between honest graft and dishonest graft and, consequent, he gets things all mixed up. There's the biggest kind of a difference between political looters and politicians who make a fortune out of politics by keepin' their eyes wide open. The looter goes in for himself alone without considerin' his organization or his city. The politician looks after his own interests, the organization's interests, and the city's interests all at the same time. . . ."

Richard K. Fox, from *Coney Island Frolics* (1883)

Coney Island, a beach off the coast of New York City, featured an amusement park and beach resort built with the working- and middle-class communities of the city in mind. It was a place where social conventions were loosened—men could take off their ties—and patrons could revel in immediate satisfaction and fun. This selection is from an instruction manual or travel guide to Coney Island, *Coney Island Frolics: How New York's Gay Girls and Jolly Boys Enjoy Themselves by the Sea*.[*]

There are various ways of bathing at Coney Island. You can go in at the West End, where they give you a tumbledown closet like a sentry box stuck up in the sand, or at the great hotels where more or less approach to genuine comfort is afforded. The pier, too, is fitted up with extensive bathing houses, and altogether no one who wants a dip in the briny and has a quarter to pay for it need to go without it.

If a man is troubled with illusions concerning the female form divine and wishes to be rid of those illusions he should go to Coney Island and closely watch the thousands of women who bathe there every Sunday.

A woman, or at least most women, in bathing undergoes a transformation that is really wonderful. They waltz into the bathing-rooms clad in all the paraphernalia that most gladdens the feminine heart. The hair is gracefully dressed, and appears most abundant; the face is decorated with all that elaborate detail which defies description by one uninitiated in the mysteries of the boudoir; the form is moulded by the milliner to distracting elegance of proportion, and the feet appear aristocratically slender and are arched in French boots.

---

[*] From Richard K. Fox, *Bathing at Coney Island, Coney Island Frolics: How New York's Gay Girls and Jolly Boys Enjoy Themselves by the Sea* (New York: Police Gazette 1883).

Thus they appear as they sail past the gaping crowds of men, who make Coney Island a loafing place on Sundays. They seek out their individual dressing-rooms and disappear. Somewhere inside of an hour, they make their appearance ready for the briny surf. If it were not for the men who accompany them it would be impossible to recognize them as the same persons who but a little while ago entered those diminutive rooms. . . .

The broad amphitheatre at Manhattan Beach built at the water's edge is often filled with spectators. Many pay admission fees to witness the feats of swimmers, the clumsiness of beginners and the ludicrous mishaps of the never-absent stout persons. Under the bathinghouse is a sixty horse-power engine. It rinses and washes the suits for the bathers, and its steady puffing is an odd accompaniment to the merry shouts of the bathers and the noise of the shifting crowd ashore. . . .

A person who intends to bathe at Manhattan or Brighton Beach first buys a ticket and deposits it in a box such as is placed in every elevated railroad station. If he carries valuables he may have them deposited without extra charge in a safe that weighs seven tons and has one thousand compartments. He encloses them in an envelope and seals it. Then he writes his name partly on the flap of the envelope and partly on the envelope itself. For this envelope he receives a metal check attached to an elastic string, in order that he may wear it about his neck while bathing. This check has been taken from one of the compartments of the safe which bears the same number as the check. Into the same compartment the sealed envelope is put. When the bather returns from the surf he must return the check and must write his name on a piece of paper. This signature is compared with the one on the envelope. Should the bather report that his check has been lost or stolen his signature is deemed a sufficient warrant for the return of the valuables. The safe has double doors in front and behind. Each drawer may be drawn out from either side. When the throng presses six men may be employed at this safe.

20

The American Flag Around the Globe

As its economy steadily grew and it filled in the continent in the decades after the Civil War, America began to turn its expansionist energies abroad. Business groups sought a foreign policy that would support their interests, while many Americans believed that it was America's manifest destiny to spread American civilization over the globe. Leading political figures were concerned that unless the United States expanded, European powers would continue to dominate around the world. This chapter is an overview of the different ideologies and critiques of American imperialism.

The Spanish-American War marked the emergence of the United States as a world power. In this "splendid little war," the United States fought for the liberation of Cuba from what was seen as tyrannical Spanish rule. American victory brought on a national debate about the morality of additional expansion and involvement elsewhere, particularly in the Philippines.

Some Americans considered it the duty of America as a Christian nation to dominate the world and spread "civilization" throughout. Josiah Strong, one of the voices in this chapter, was a Congregationalist minister and one of the foremost advocates of missionary expansionism.

Other Americans, like Indiana Senator Albert Beveridge, also believed in an expansionist foreign policy but for different reasons. Beveridge, in particular, believed that the United States needed to expand in order to dominate world markets because, in his words, "the trade of the world must and should be ours." American industries were producing more goods than the American market could absorb and the overseas market was necessary, in his eyes, to support the American economy. In this selection from Beveridge's famous "The March of the Flag," the senator argued for keeping the Philippines.

On the other hand, many people, particularly intellectuals, opposed this so-called American imperialism. William Graham Sumner, a sociologist at Yale known as a leading advocate of social Darwinism, argued that acquiring colonies was anti-American and that it could do great harm American society. But among the most outspoken opponents of imperialism was Mark Twain. The excerpt printed here, from Twain's autobiography, concerns the struggle in the Philippines, which proved bloody and costly: over 100,000 Americans served there, of whom 4,000 were wounded while 20,000 Filipinos were killed and perhaps 200,000 died of disease and starvation.

The final decision about the Philippines rested with President William McKinley. The last document explains his reasons for keeping the Philippines—which he did, a decision that led to the war there and the expansion of the American empire into the South Pacific.

Study Questions

1. According to Josiah Strong, why must the United States become a world power? How steeped in social Darwinism is his thesis?

2. Did Strong, Beveridge, and Sumner rely upon the doctrine of social Darwinism to support their arguments?

3. What does Twain have to say about the legitimacy of America's Christianizing mission?

4. Americans made a distinction between European imperialism and America's activities in the Philippines. Does Twain recognize the legitimacy of this distinction? Does Sumner?

5. On what grounds does Sumner base his opposition to American imperialism?

6. What racial assumptions do the authors in this chapter share? Where do they differ?

7. What assumptions about American uniqueness do the authors in this chapter share? Where do they differ?

8. How might President McKinley's audience (expansionist Methodist ministers and missionaries) have influenced his speech?

Josiah Strong, from *Our Country* (1885)

Strong, like others, believed the Anglo-Saxon people were superior to non-Christian, non-white peoples, and that it was the responsibility of the United States to spread its way of life. *Our Country* is the articulation of so-called missionary expansionism.*

---

* From Josiah Strong, *Our Country Its Possible Future and Its Present Crisis* (New York: Baker & Taylor, 1885), 159–161, 165, 170, 178–180.

Every race which has deeply impressed itself on the human family has been the representative of some great idea—one or more—which had given direction to the nation's life and form to its civilization. Among the Egyptians this seminal idea was life, among the Persians it was light, among the Hebrews it was purity, among the Greeks it was beauty, among the Romans it was law. The Anglo-Saxon is the representative of two great ideas, which are closely related. One of them is that of civil liberty. Nearly all of the civil liberty in the world is enjoyed by Anglo-Saxons: the English, the British colonists, and the people of the United States. ". . ." The noblest races have always been lovers of liberty. That love ran strong in early German blood, and has profoundly influenced the institutions of all the branches of the great German family; but it was left for the Anglo-Saxon branch fully to recognize the right of the individual to himself, and formally to declare it the foundation stone of government."

The other great idea of which the Anglo-Saxon is the exponent is that of a pure spiritual Christianity." It was no accident that the great reformation of the sixteenth century originated among a Teutonic, rather than a Latin people. It was the fire of liberty burning in the Saxon heart that flamed up against the absolutism of the Pope. . . ."

It is not necessary to argue to those for whom I write that the two great needs of mankind, that all men may be lifted up into the light of the highest Christian civilization, are, first, a pure, spiritual Christianity, and, second, civil liberty." Without controversy, these are the forces which, in the past, have contributed most to the elevation of the human race, and they must continue to be, in the future, the most efficient ministers to its progress." It follows, then, that the Anglo-Saxon, as the great representative of these two ideas, the depositary [sic] of these two greatest blessings, sustains peculiar relations to the world's future, is divinely commissioned to be, in a peculiar sense, his brother's keeper. . . .

There can be no reasonable doubt that North America is to be the great home of the Anglo-Saxon, the principal seat of his power, the center of his life and influence. Not only does it constitute seven-elevenths of his possessions, but this empire is unsevered, while the remaining four-elevenths are fragmentary and scattered over the earth. Australia will have a great population; but its disadvantages, as compared with North America, are too manifest to need mention. Our continent has room and resources and climate, it lies in the pathway of the nations, it belongs to the zone of power, and already, among Anglo-Saxons, do we lead in population and wealth.

Mr. Darwin is not only disposed to see, in the superior vigor of our people, an illustration of his favorite theory of natural selection, but even intimates that the world's history thus far has been simply preparatory for our future, and tributary to it. He says: "There is apparently much truth in the belief that the wonderful progress of the United States, as well as the character of the people, are the results of natural selection; for the more energetic, restless, and courageous men from all parts of Europe have emigrated during the last ten or twelve generations to that great country, and have there succeeded best. . . ."

. . . The time is coming when the pressure of population on the means of subsistence will be felt there as it is now felt in Europe and Asia. Then will the world enter upon a new stage of its history—the final competition of races, for which the

Anglo-Saxon is being schooled. Long before the thousands millions are here, the mighty centrifugal tendency, inherent in this stock and strengthened in the United States, will assert itself. Then this race of unequaled energy, with all the majesty of numbers and the might of wealth behind it—the representative, let us hope, of the largest liberty, the purest Christianity, the highest civilization—having developed peculiarly aggressive traits calculated to impress its institutions upon mankind, will spread itself over the earth. If I read not amiss, this powerful race will move down upon Mexico, down upon Central and South America, out upon the islands of the sea, over upon Africa and beyond. And can anyone doubt that the result of this competition of races will be the "survival of the fittest"? . . .

In my own mind, there is no doubt that the Anglo-Saxon is to exercise the commanding influence in the world's future; but the exact nature of that influence is, as yet, undetermined. How far his civilization will be materialistic and atheistic, and how long it will take thoroughly to Christianize and sweeten it, how rapidly he will hasten the coming of the kingdom wherein dwelleth righteousness, or how many ages he may retard it, is still uncertain; but it is now being swiftly determined. . . .

Notwithstanding the great perils which threaten it, I cannot think our civilization will perish; but I believe it is fully in the hand of the Christians of the United States, during the next fifteen or twenty years, to hasten or retard the coming of Christ's kingdom in the world by hundreds, and perhaps thousands, of years. We of this generation and nation occupy the Gibraltar of the ages which command the world's future.

Albert Beveridge, "The March of the Flag" (1898)

Albert Beveridge, a Republican senator from Indiana, was one of the leading spokesmen for a strongly expansionist foreign policy. In this address, which was widely read during the period, Beveridge merged prevalent opinions about America's civilizing mission with its economic destiny.*

It is a noble land that God has given us; a land that can feed and clothe the world; a land whose coastlines would enclose half the countries of Europe; a land set like a sentinel between the two imperial oceans of the globe, a greater England with a nobler destiny.

* From "The March of the Flag," printed in the *Indianapolis Journal*, September 17, 1898. From Albert J. Beveridge, *The Meaning of Times* (Indianapolis: Bobbs-Merrill, 1908), 47–49, 56–57.

It is a mighty people that He has planted on this soil; a people sprung from the most masterful blood of history; a people perpetually revitalized by the virile, man-producing working folk of all the earth; a people imperial by virtue of their power, by right of their institutions, by authority of their Heaven-directed purposes—the propagandists and not the misers of liberty.

It is a glorious history our God has bestowed upon His chosen people; a history heroic with faith in our mission and our future; a history of statesmen who flung the boundaries of the Republic out into unexplored lands and savage wilderness; a history of soldiers who carried the flag across blazing deserts and through the ranks of hostile mountains, even to the gates of sunset; a history of a multiplying people who overran a continent in half a century; a history of prophets who saw the consequences of evils inherited from the past and of martyrs who died to save us from them; a history divinely logical, in the process of whose tremendous seasoning we find ourselves to-day.

Therefore, in this campaign, the question is larger than a party question. It is an American question. It is a world question. Shall the American people continue their march toward the commercial supremacy of the world? Shall free institutions broaden their blessed reign as the children of liberty wax in strength, until the empire of our principles is established over the hearts of all mankind?

Have we no mission to perform, no duty to discharge to our fellowman? Has God endowed us with gifts beyond our deserts and marked us as the people of His peculiar favor, merely to rot in our own selfishness, as men and nations must, who take cowardice for their companion and self for their deity—as China has, as India has, as Egypt has?

Shall we be as the man who had one talent and hid it, or as he who had ten talents and use them until they grew to riches? And shall we reap the reward that waits on our discharge of our high duty; shall we occupy new markets for what our farmers raise, our factories make, our merchants sell—aye, and, please God, new markets for what our ships shall carry?

Hawaii is ours, Puerto Rico is to be ours; at the prayer of her people Cuba finally will be ours; in the islands of the East, even to the gates of Asia, coaling stations are to be ours at the very least; the flag of a liberal government is to float over the Philippines, and may it be the banner that Taylor unfurled in Texas and Frémont carried to the coast.

The Opposition tells us that we ought not to govern a people without their consent. I answer, The rule of liberty that all just government derives its authority from the consent of the governed, applies only to those who are capable of self-government. We govern the Indians without their consent, we govern our territories without their consent, we govern our children without their consent. How do they know that our government would be without their consent? Would not the people of the Philippines prefer the just, human, civilizing government of this Republic to the savage, bloody rule of pillage and extortion from which we have rescued them?

And, regardless of this formula of words made only for enlightened, self-governing people, do we owe no duty to the world? Shall we turn these peoples back to the reeking hands from which we have taken them? Shall we abandon them, with

Germany, England, Japan, hungering for them? Shall we save them from those nations, to give them a self-rule of tragedy? . . . Then, like men and not like children, let us on to our tasks, our mission, and our destiny.

Wonderfully has God guided us. Yonder at Bunker Hill and Yorktown His providence was above us. At New Orleans and on ensanguined seas His hand sustained us. Abraham Lincoln was His minister and His was the altar of freedom the Nation's soldiers set up on a hundred battle-fields. His power directed Dewey in the East and delivered the Spanish fleet into our hands, as He delivered the elder Armada into the hands of our English sires two centuries ago. The American people can not use a dishonest medium of exchange; it is ours to set the world its example of right and honor. We can not fly from our world duties; it is ours to execute the purpose of a fate that has driven us to be greater than our small intentions. we can not retreat from any soil where Providence has unfurled our banner; it is ours to save that soil for liberty and civilization.

William Graham Sumner, from "On Empire and the Philippines" (1898)

"On Empire and the Philippines," the essay from which this extract comes, was written in 1898 and was published in Sumner's *War and Other Essays.* Known as a social Darwinist, Sumner was also an ardent anti-imperialist. After entering Yale as a student in 1859, Sumner studied abroad after graduation, and returned to teach at his alma mater until his death in 1910.*

There is not a civilized nation that does not talk about its civilizing mission just as grandly as we do. The English, who really have more to boast of it in this respect than anybody else, talk least about it, but the Phariseeism with which they correct and instruct other people has made them hated all over the globe. The French believe themselves the guardians of the highest and purest culture, and that the eyes of all mankind are fixed on Paris, whence they expect oracles of thought and taste. The Germans regard themselves as charged with a mission, especially to us Americans, to save us from egoism and materialism. The Russians, in their books and newspapers, talk about the civilizing mission of Russian in language that might be translated from some of the finest paragraphs of our imperialistic newspapers.

The first principle of Mohammedanism is that we Christians are dogs and infidels, fit only to be enslaved or butchered by Moslems. It is a corollary that wherever

---

* From William Graham Sumner, *War and Other Essays* (Ayer Co. Publications, Inc., 1911).

Mohammedanism extends it carries, in the belief of its votaries, the highest blessings, and that the whole human race would be enormously elevated if Mohammedanism should supplant Christianity everywhere.

To come, last, to Spain, the Spaniards have, for centuries, considered themselves the most zealous and self-sacrificing Christians, especially charged by the Almighty, on this account, to spread the true religion and civilization over the globe. They think themselves free and noble, leaders in refinement and the sentiments of personal honor, and they despise us as sordid money-grabbers and heretics. I could bring you passages from peninsular authors of the first rank about the grand role of Spain and Portugal in spreading freedom and truth.

Now each nation laughs at all the others when it observes these manifestations of national vanity. You may rely upon it that they are all ridiculous by virtue of these pretensions, including ourselves. The point is that each of them repudiates the standards of the others, and the outlying nations, which are to be civilized, hate all the standards of civilized men.

We assume that what we like and practice, and what we think better, must come as a welcome blessing to Spanish-Americans and Filipinos. This is grossly and obviously untrue. They hate our ways. They are hostile to our ideas. Our religion, language, institutions, and manners offend them. They like their own ways, and if we appear amongst them as rulers, there will be social discord in all the great departments of social interest. The most important thing which we shall inherit from the Spaniards will be the task of suppressing rebellions.

If the United States takes out of the hands of Spain her mission, on the ground that Spain is not executing it well, and if this nation in its turn attempts to be schoolmistress to others, it will shrivel up into the same vanity and self-conceit of which Spain now presents an example. To read our current literature one would think that we were already well on the way to it.

Now, the great reason why all these enterprises which begin by saying to somebody else, "We know what is good for you better than you know yourself and we are going to make you do it," are false and wrong is that they violate liberty; or, to turn the same statement into other words, the reason why liberty, of which we Americans talk so much, is a good thing is that it means leaving people to live out their own lives in their own way, while we do the same!

"If we believe in liberty, as an American principle, why do we not stand by it? Why are we going to throw it away to enter upon a Spanish policy of dominion and regulation? "

Mark Twain, "Incident in the Philippines" (1924)

This is an excerpt from Mark Twain's autobiography, a haphazard affair undertaken in 1906 but unprinted until Twain's manuscripts

were compiled by A. B. Paine and published in 1924. In this piece
Twain reported some of the horrors reported from the Philippines,
where American soldiers responded to a guerrilla war by
destroying property, attacking civilians, and raping Filipino women.*

. . . This incident burst upon the world last Friday in an official cablegram from the
commander of our forces in the Philippines to our government at Washington. The
substance of it was as follows:

A tribe of Moros, dark-skinned savages, had fortified themselves in the bowl of an
extinct crater not many miles from Jolo; and as they were hostiles, and bitter against us
because we have been trying for eight years to take their liberties away from them,
their presence in that position was a menace. Our commander, General Leonard Wood,
ordered a reconnaissance [*sic*]. It was found that the Moros numbered six hundred,
counting women and children; that their crater bowl was in the summit of a peak or
mountain twenty-two hundred feet above sea level, and very difficult of access for
Christian troops and artillery. . . . Our troops climbed the heights by devious and
difficult trails, and even took some artillery with them. . . . [When they] arrived at the
rim of the crater, the battle began. Our soldiers numbered five hundred and forty. They
were assisted by auxiliaries consisting of a detachment of native constabulary in our
pay—their numbers not given—and by a naval detachment, whose numbers are not
stated. But apparently the contending parties were about equal as to number—six
hundred men on our side, on the edge of the bowl; six hundred men, women, and
children in the bottom of the bowl. Depth of the bowl, 50 feet.

General Wood's order was, "Kill or capture the six hundred."

The battle began—it is officially called by that name—our forces firing down into
the crater with their artillery and their deadly small arms of precision; the savages
furiously returning the fire, probably with brickbats—though this is merely a surmise
of mine, as the weapons used by the savages are not nominated in the cablegram.
Heretofore the Moros have used knives and clubs mainly; also ineffectual trade-
muskets when they had any.

The official report stated that the battle was fought with prodigious energy on both
sides during a day and a half, and that it ended with a complete victory for the
American arms. The completeness of the victory is established by this fact: that of the
six hundred Moros not one was left alive. The brilliancy of the victory is established
by this other fact, to wit: that of our six hundred heroes only fifteen lost their lives.

General Wood was present and looking on. His order had been, "Kill or capture
those savages." Apparently our little army considered that the "or" left them authorized
to kill or capture according to taste, and that their taste had remained what it has been
for eight years, in our army out there—the taste of Christian butchers. . . .

Let us now consider two or three details of our military history. In one of the great
battles of the Civil War ten per cent of the forces engaged on the two sides were killed
and wounded. At Waterloo, where four hundred thousand men were present on the two

---

* Fromexcerpts Mark Twain's "Autobiography" (1899) from Maxwell Geismar ed., *Mark Twain and the
Three R's* (Indianapolis: Bobbs-Merrill, 1979).

sides, fifty thousand fell, killed and wounded, in five hours, leaving three hundred and fifty sound and all right for further adventures. Eight years ago, when the pathetic comedy called the Cuban War was played, we summoned two hundred and fifty thousand men. We fought a number of showy battles, and when the war was over we had lost two hundred sixty-eight men out of our two hundred and fifty thousand, in killed and wounded in the field, and just fourteen times as many by the gallantry of the army doctors in the hospitals and camps. We did not exterminate the Spaniards—far from it. In each engagement we left an average of two per cent of the enemy killed or crippled on the field.

Contrast these things with the great statistics which have arrived from that Moro crater! There, with six hundred engaged on each side, we lost fifteen men killed outright, and we had thirty-two wounded. . . . "The enemy numbered six hundred—including women and children"—and "we abolished them utterly, leaving not even a baby alive to cry for its dead mother." This is incomparably the greatest victory that was ever achieved by the Christian soldiers of the United States.

William McKinley, "Decision on the Philippines" (1900)

In this speech to a group of ministers, the president outlined his rationale for deciding to annex the Philippines, paying the Spanish (under duress) $20 million for the privilege. It was a difficult decision, and a decision that determined the path of American foreign policy for much of the next century.*

When next I realized that the Philippines had dropped into our laps, I confess I did not know what to do with them. I sought counsel from all sides—Democrats as well as Republicans—but got little help. I thought first we would take only Manila; then Luzon; then other islands, perhaps, also.

I walked the floor of the White House night after night until midnight; and I am not ashamed to tell you, gentlemen, that I went down on my knees and prayed to Almighty God for light and guidance more than one night. And one night late it came to me this way—I don't know how it was, but it came:

(1)   That we could not give them back to Spain—that would be cowardly and dishonorable;

(2)   That we could not turn them over to France or Germany, our commercial rivals in the Orient—that would be bad business and discreditable;

---

* This document is a report of an interview with McKinley at the White House, November 21, 1899, written by one of the interviewers and confirmed by others present. Published in *The Christian Advocate*, January 22, 1903, it is here cited from C. S. Olcott, *The Life of William McKinley* (1916), vol. 2, 110–111.

(3)   That we could not leave them to themselves—they were unfit for self-government, and they would soon have anarchy and misrule worse then Spain's was; and

(4)   That there was nothing left for us to do but to take them all, and to educate the Filipinos, and uplift and civilize and Christianize them and by God's grace do the very best we could by them, as our fellow men for whom Christ also died.

And then I went to bed and went to sleep, and slept soundly, and the next morning I sent for the chief engineer of the War Department (our map-maker), and I told him to put the Philippines on the map of the United States (pointing to a large map on the wall of his office), and there they are and there they will stay while I am President!

21

Reforming the American Nation

Earlier chapters have illustrated the contributions of progressive reformers on the state and local levels: the muckraker Lincoln Steffens wrote against political machines; Mother Jones protested child labor; Ida B. Wells-Barnett agitated against the practice of lynching; Charles Loring Brace called attention to living conditions in the cities; and John Spargo wrote about children in the coal mines. This chapter focuses on progressivism and the changes it wrought on the national political system.

The Progressive movement established the framework for American liberalism and changed the relationship between government and society, making government the agent of change aimed at improving Americans' quality of life. Using terms like "regulate," "bring order," and "make more efficient," the progressive agenda focused on solutions for problems created by the new economic order and urban growth.

The presidency of Theodore Roosevelt catapulted the Progressive movement onto the national political scene. Roosevelt's strong support for the movement brought it popularity and publicity—never more so than in 1912 when, after losing the Republican nomination to William Taft, the current president, Roosevelt walked out of the Republican convention and established the Progressive Party. In the presidential campaign that followed, two of the candidates—Roosevelt, who had been president from 1902 to 1908, and Woodrow Wilson, a former president of Princeton University and governor of New Jersey—ran on strongly progressive platforms.

Wilson and Roosevelt debated how to deal with the most pressing problem of the new century, economic concentration of wealth and industrial power. Selections in this chapter contrast Roosevelt's and Wilson's visions for the role of federal government and the appropriate use of its power.

At the 1912 Progressive Party convention in Chicago, which nominated Roosevelt, Jane Addams seconded his nomination while a banner reading "Votes for Women" hung in the auditorium. Women's groups had been actively campaigning for suffrage since the Seneca Falls convention of 1848, but had gained the vote only in a few western states. By the early 1900s, women's rights groups became increasingly more militant and successful, as new leadership connected the vote to the reform movement. If women were to protect themselves against industrial overwork, rape, and prostitution, and continue "urban housekeeping"—cleaning up cities and closing down saloons—and if newly arrived immigrants could vote, certainly women deserved the right to vote. Two selections in this chapter describe the rationales for women suffrage, which was only granted with the passage of the Nineteenth Amendment in 1920, after militant protests during World War I.

Study Questions

1. Compare the visions of the role of federal government in the New Nationalism and New Freedom. Which approach most accurately reflected the economic realities of the late nineteenth and early twentieth centuries? Which most accurately anticipated the future?

2. Why did Wilson mention George W. Perkin's involvement with the Progressive Party? What was Wilson implying by doing so?

3. What was Roosevelt's answer to Wilson's charge that the New Nationalism would lead to the "time when the combined power of high finance would be greater than the power of the government"?

4. Analyze the arguments for women's suffrage presented in this chapter. From their arguments about women's role in the political process, would one expect suffragists like Addams and the NAWSA to be proponents of a more active or more limited government?

Theodore Roosevelt, from *The New Nationalism* (1910)

In this speech, delivered at Osawatomie, Kansas, in 1910, Roosevelt outlined the ideas which would become the basis of his 1912 presidential campaign. He expounded on his vision of a "new nationalism," which recognized the inevitability of economic concentration and called on government to regulate the new economic structures and to become the "steward of public welfare."*

Practical equality of opportunity for all citizens, when we achieve it, will have two great results. First, every man will have a fair chance to make of himself all that in him lies; to reach the highest point to which his capacities, unassisted by special privilege

---

* From Theodore Roosevelt, *The New Nationalism*, 1910.

of his own and unhampered by the special privilege of others, can carry him, and to get for himself and his family substantially what he has earned. Second, equality of opportunity means that the commonwealth will get from every citizen the highest service of which he is capable. No man who carries the burden of the special privileges of another can give to the commonwealth that service to which it is fairly entitled. . . .

Now, this means that our government, national and state, must be freed from the sinister influence or control of special interests. Exactly as the special interests of cotton and slavery threatened our political integrity before the Civil War, so now the great special business interests too often control and corrupt the men and methods of government for their own profit. We must drive the special interests out of politics. That is one of our tasks today. . . .

The true friend of property, the true conservative, is he who insists that property shall be the servant and not the master of the commonwealth; who insists that the creature of man's making shall be the servant and not the master of the man who made it. The citizens of the United States must effectively control the mighty commercial forces which they have themselves called into being. . . .

It has become entirely clear that we must have government supervision of the capitalization, not only of the public service corporations, including, particularly, railways, but of all corporations doing an interstate business. I do not wish to see the nation forced into the ownership of the railways if it can possibly be avoided, and the only alternative is thoroughgoing and effective regulation, which shall be based on a full knowledge of all the facts, including a physical valuation of property. . . .

Combinations in industry are the result of an imperative economic law which cannot be repealed by political legislation. The effort at prohibiting all combination has substantially failed. The way out lies, not in attempting to prevent such combinations, but in completely controlling them in the interest of the public welfare.

Woodrow Wilson, from *The New Freedom* (1913)

This excerpt is from Woodrow Wilson's book published after the campaign, *The New Freedom: A Call for the Emancipation of the Generous Energies of a People.* Wilson believed federal power should be controlled and limited.[*]

The doctrine that monopoly is inevitable and that the only course open to the people of the United States is to submit to and regulate it found a champion during the campaign

---

[*] From Woodrow Wilson, *The New Freedom: A Call for the Emancipation of the Generous Energies of a People*, 1913.

of 1912 in the new party or branch of the Republican Party, founded under the leadership of Mr. Roosevelt, with the conspicuous aid,—I mention him with no satirical intention, but merely to set the facts down accurately,—of Mr. George W. Perkins, organizer of the Steel Trust and the Harvester Trust, and with the support of patriotic, conscientious and high-minded men and women of the land. The fact that its acceptance of monopoly was a feature of the new party platform from which the attention of the generous and just was diverted by the charm of a social program of great attractiveness to all concerned for the amelioration of the lot of those who suffer wrong and privation, and the further fact that, even so, the platform was repudiated by the majority of the nation, render it no less necessary to reflect on the party in the country's history. It may be useful, in order to relieve of the minds of many from an error of no small magnitude, to consider now, the heat of a presidential contest being past, exactly what it was that Mr. Roosevelt proposed.

Mr. Roosevelt attached to his platform some very splendid suggestions as to noble enterprises which we ought to undertake for the uplift of the human race; . . . If you have read the trust plank in that platform as often as I have read it, you have found it very long, but very tolerant. It did not anywhere condemn monopoly, except in words; its essential meaning was that the trusts have been bad and must be made to be good. You know that Mr. Roosevelt long ago classified trusts for us as good and bad, and he said that he was afraid only of the bad ones. Now he does not desire that there should be any more of the bad ones, but proposes that they should all be made good by discipline, directly applied by a commission of executive appointment. All he explicitly complains of is lack of publicity and lack of fairness; not the exercise of power, for throughout that plank the power of the great corporations is accepted as the inevitable consequence of the modern organization of industry. All that it is proposed to do is to take them under control and deregulation.

The fundamental part of such a program is that the trusts shall be recognized as a permanent part of our economic order, and that the government shall try to make trusts the ministers, the instruments, through which the life of this country shall be justly and happily developed on its industrial side. . . .

Shall we try to get the grip of monopoly away from our lives, or shall we not? Shall we withhold our hand and say monopoly is inevitable, that all we can do is to regulate it? Shall we say that all we can do is to put government in competition with monopoly and try its strength against it? Shall we admit that the creature of our own hands is stronger than we are? We have been dreading all along the time when the combined power of high finance would be greater than the power of the government.

Jane Addams, "Ballot Necessary for Women" (1906)

In this newspaper editorial from 1906, Jane Addams, the founder of Hull House and a famed reformer and progressive, wrote in favor of women's suffrage. Like many other women suffragists in her period, she connected the vote for women with theories that women's ability nurture home and family would extend into the political sphere.*

Insanitary housing, poisonous sewage, contaminated water, infant mortality, the spread of contagion, adulterated food, impure milk, smoke-laden air, ill-ventilated factories, dangerous occupations, juvenile crime, unwholesome crowding, prostitution and drunkenness are the enemies which the modern cities must face and overcome would they survive. Logically, its electorate should be made up of those who can bear a valiant part in this arduous contest, those who in the past have at least attempted to care for children, to clean houses, to prepare foods, to isolate the family from oral dangers, those who have traditionally taken care of that side of life which inevitably becomes the subject of municipal consideration and control as soon as the population is congested. To test the elector's fitness to deal with this situation by his ability to bear arms is absurd. These problems must be solved, if they are solved at all, not from the military point of view, not even from the industrial point of view, but from a third which is rapidly developing in all the great cities of the world—the human welfare point of view.

National American Woman Suffrage Association, Mother's Day Letter (1912)

The National American Woman Suffrage Association (NAWSA) was formed in 1890 from the merger of two organizations, founded by Elizabeth Cady Stanton and Susan B. Anthony respectively in 1869. Under the leadership of Carrie Chapman Catt, membership in the organization rose to two million. Catt's organization was relatively mainstream, especially in contrast the militant National

---

* From Jane Addams, "Jane Addams Declares Ballot for Women Made Necessary by Changed Conditions," *Chicago Sunday Record-Herald*, April 1, 1906.

Woman's Party, which adopted radical tactics including hunger
strikes, demonstrations, and pickets.[*]

Dear Sir:

"Mother's Day" is becoming more and more observed in the churches of our land,
and many clergymen on that day are delivering special sermons, calling attention to the
Mother's influence in the Home. . . .

In view of the fact that in the moral and social reform work of the churches, the
Mothers and Women of the churches are seeking to correct serious evils that exist in
our cities as a menace to the morals of their children outside the home, and in view of
the fact that churchwomen are finding that much of their effort is ineffective and of no
value, because they are denied the weapon of Christian warfare, the ballot . . . we ask
of you, will you not in justice to the Mothers of your church choose for your topic on
"Mother's Day" some subject bearing on "The need of the Mother's influence in the
State?"

Women are recognized as the most religious, the most moral and the most sober
portion of the American people. Why deny them a voice in public affairs when we give
it for the asking to every ignorant foreigner who comes to our shores?

The women have always been the mainstay and chief supporters of the churches,
and in their struggle for their civil liberty. Should not their clergymen or Christian
brothers sympathize with them and "Remember those in bonds as bound with them"
and help them in their struggle? On behalf of the church work committee representing
Christian Mothers in every State in the Union, I would be pleased to know if you will
be one to raise your voice on "Mother's Day" in favor of the extension of the Mother's
influence in our land "to help those women that labored with you in the Gospel?"

---

[*] From "Report of the Church Work Committee," *Proceedings of the Forty-Fourth Annual Convention of
the National American Woman Suffrage Association* (New York: National American Woman Suffrage
Association, 1912), 55–57.

22

America at War

When war broke out in 1914, Americans thought that Europe had gone mad. President Wilson, who had been elected because of his domestic policies, found himself forced to develop a foreign policy—one that would keep the United States out of the conflict. Wilson believed he could accomplish this if the United States remained completely neutral. In the 1916 presidential campaign he ran on a platform that promised "Peace, Prosperity and Progress," but just one year later, after peace negotiations failed and the Germans resumed unrestricted submarine warfare, Wilson asked the Congress for a declaration of war against Germany.

Some Americans, including Wilson, considered the war an extension of the progressive reform movement. The president promised the war would "make the world safe for democracy" and insisted that it was a moral crusade. Helping Wilson was the Committee on Public Information, headed by George Creel, which through speeches, pamphlets, posters, and movies exhorted Americans to support the war effort. This patriotic hysteria was often militantly racist, anti-German, and anti-immigrant. The Boy Scouts pamphlet included in this chapter was written in part by the Committee on Public Information and depicts some of the zeal and militancy of the war effort.

The Creel Committee and the passage of the Espionage and Sedition Acts helped create a domestic environment in which dissent was associated with treason. Socialists, labor activists, pacifists, and all those who questioned the war could be subject to imprisonment. Eugene Debs, the former Socialist presidential candidate, was sentenced to ten years in prison for his opposition to the war. Socialist newspapers were banned; union organizers and pacifists were attacked by mobs or hanged in effigy. The government, and large numbers of the American public, demanded unquestioning patriotism. The selection included here from the memoirs of Secretary of War Newton Baker describes his concerns about the treatment of German-Americans.

While patriotism ran high, the United States entered the war in 1917 unprepared for military action. The American doughboy quickly learned that Sherman had been right: war was indeed hell. In the enclosed selection from Eugene Kennedy's diary, a white soldier describes the horrors of life on the front lines in France. More than 200,000 black soldiers fought in World War I, in segregated units. Most, as Kennedy recalls in his diary, were not allowed into combat and were employed as servants, laborers, and drivers. Still, many African-American leaders, including W. E. B. Du Bois, thought that black participation in the war would lead to a narrowing of the color line and even political equality. In the speech included here, the Reverend Francis Grimke expresses his hope that the struggle for democracy in Europe would lead to an increase in racial equality at home.

Long before the war ended, Wilson began to plan the peace—a peace that he hoped would lead to a better society. In his Fourteen Points, Wilson presented a plan that would make the world "fit and safe to live in." He presented his points at the Paris peace conference, but the resulting Versailles treaty, calling for extensive German war reparations and a German declaration of war guilt, ran counter his Wilson's plan. Wilson hoped to improve upon the Versailles treaty through his League of Nations, an organization founded to negotiate international disputes. The League was rejected by Congress in 1920 and Wilson ended his presidency an enfeebled, partially paralyzed man.

Study Questions

1. In the Boy Scout pamphlet, who was the "enemy from within"? Connect the propaganda in this pamphlet with other examples of nativist thinking from earlier chapters.

2. Could the attacks against German-Americans, Socialists, pacifists, and other groups within the United States have been prevented? How did Baker's thinking fall in line with Wilson's thoughts about government expressed in the excerpt from *The New Freedom* in the previous chapter?

3. Comment on ethnic stereotypes evident in Eugene Kennedy's diary.

4. Why did Grimke hope that African Americans would gain from their participation in the war? Why did he place a special burden on the returning soldiers?

5. Were Wilson's Fourteen Points addressed to preventing war or establishing a new world order?

Boy Scouts of America from, "Boy Scouts Support the War Effort" (1917)

This is a selection from a pamphlet published by the Boy Scouts of America. The pamphlet encourages vigilantism and loyalty checks, among other "patriotic" measures. Many Americans became formal or informal loyalty enforcers during the World War I and many individuals were sent to prison for published or unpublished criticisms of the war efforts or Wilson's policies. The Boy Scouts played an important role on the home front, which included planting vegetable gardens and recycling.*

To the Members of the Boy Scouts of America!

Attention, Scouts! We are again called upon to do active service for our country! Every one of the 285,661 Scouts and 76,957 Scout Officials has been summoned by President Woodrow Wilson, Commander-in-Chief of the Army and Navy, to serve as a dispatch bearer from the Government at Washington to the American people all over the country. The prompt, enthusiastic, and hearty response of every one of us has been pledged by our [Scout] President, Mr. Livingstone. Our splendid record of accomplishments in war activities promises full success in this new job.

This patriotic service will be rendered under the slogan: "EVERY SCOUT TO BOOST AMERICA" AS A GOVERNMENT DISPATCH BEARER. The World War is for liberty and democracy.

America has long been recognized as the leader among nations standing for liberty and democracy. American entered the war as a sacred duty to uphold the principles of liberty and democracy.

As a democracy, our country faces great danger—not so much from submarines, battleships and armies, because, thanks to our allies, our enemies have apparently little chance of reaching our shores.

Our danger is from within. Our enemies have representatives everywhere; they tell lies; they mispresent the truth; they deceive our own people; they are a real menace to our country.

Already we have seen how poor Russia has been made to suffer because her people do not know the truth. Representatives of the enemy have been very effective in their deceitful efforts to make trouble for the Government.

Fortunately here in America our people are better educated—they want the truth. Our President recognized the justice and wisdom of this demand when in the early stages of the war he created the Committee on Public Information. He knew that the Government would need the confidence, enthusiasm and willing service of every man and woman, every boy and girl in the nation. He knew that the only possible way to create a genuine feeling of partnership between the people and its representatives in Washington was to take the people into his confidence by full, frank statements concerning the reasons for our entering the war, the various steps taken during the war and the ultimate aims of the war.

Neither the President as Commander-in-Chief, nor our army and navy by land and sea, can alone win the war. At this moment the best defense that America has is an enlightened and loyal citizenship. Therefore, we as scouts are going to have the opportunity of rendering real patriotic service under our slogan.

---

* From a pamphlet entitled Committee on Public Information, Boy Scouts of America, 1917.

"EVERY SCOUT TO BOOST AMERICA" AS A GOVERNMENT DISPATCH BEARER.

Here is where our service begins. We are to help spread the facts about America and America's part in the World War. We are to fight lies with truth.

We are to help create public opinion "just as effective in helping to bring victory as ships and guns," to stir patriotism, the great force behind the ships and guns. Isn't that a challenge for every loyal Scout?

"EVERY SCOUT TO BOOST AMERICA" AS A GOVERNMENT DISPATCH BEARER: HOW?

As Mr. George Creel, the Chairman of the Committee on Public Information, says in his letter, scouts are to serve as direct special representatives of the Committee on Public Information to keep the people informed about the War and its causes and progress. The Committee has already prepared a number of special pamphlets and other will be prepared. It places upon the members of the Boy Scouts of America the responsibility of putting the information in these pamphlets in homes of the American people. Every Scout will be furnished a credential card by his Scoutmaster. Under the direction of our leaders, the Boy Scouts of America are to serve as an intelligence division of the citizens' army, always prepared and alert to respond to any call which may come from the President of the United States and the Committee on Public Information at Washington.

... Each Scoutmaster is to be furnished with a complete set of all of the government publications, in order that all of the members of his troop may be completely informed. Each scout and scout official is expected to seize every opportunity to serve the Committee on Public Information by making available authoritative information. It is up to the Boy Scouts to see that as many people as possible have an intelligent understanding of any and all facts incident to our present national crisis and the World War. . . .

PAMPHLETS NOW READY FOR CIRCULATION

Note:—A set will be sent to every Scoutmaster. You will need to know what is in these pamphlets so as to act as a serviceable bureau of information and be able to give each person the particular intelligence he seeks.

Newton D. Baker, "The Treatment of German-Americans" (1918)

This selection is taken from the wartime writings of the secretary of war. In this piece, Baker expressed concern about the treatment of German-Americans and argued that the government was not responsible for nativist actions.[*]

[*] From Frederick Palmer, *Newton D. Baker*, vol. 2 (Dodd, Mead & Company, 1931), 162–163.

The spirit of the country seems unusually good, but there is a growing frenzy of suspicion and hostility toward disloyalty. I am afraid we are going to have a good many instances of people roughly treated on very slight evidence of disloyalty. Already a number of men and some women have been "tarred and feathered," and a portion of the press is urging with great vehemence more strenuous efforts at detection and punishment. This usually takes the form of advocating "drum-head courts-martial" and "being stood up against a wall and shot," which are perhaps none too bad for real traitors, but are very suggestive of summary discipline to arouse mob spirit, which unhappily does not take time to weigh evidence.

In Cleveland a few days ago a foreign-looking man got into a street car and, taking a seat, noticed pasted in the window next to him a Liberty Loan poster, which he immediately tore down, tore into small bits, and stamped under his feet. The people in the car surged around him with the demand that he be lynched, when a Secret Service man showed his badge and placed him under arrest, taking him in a car to the police station, where he was searched and found to have two Liberty Bonds in his pocket and to be a non-English Pole. When an interpreter was procured, it was discovered that the circular which he had destroyed had had on it a picture of the German Emperor, which had so infuriated the fellow that he destroyed the circular to show his vehement hatred of the common enemy. As he was unable to speak a single word of English, he would undoubtedly have been hanged but for the intervention and entirely accidental presence of the Secret Service agent.

I am afraid the grave danger in this sort of thing, apart from its injustice, is that the German Government will adopt retaliatory measures. While the Government of the United States is not only responsible for these things, but very zealously trying to prevent them, the German Government draws no fine distinctions.

Eugene Kennedy, A "Doughboy" Describes the Fighting Front (1918)

This selection from the dairy of Eugene Kennedy describes life on the front lines in Europe. American soldiers were often poorly equipped and ill-fed, as this doughboy reports.[*]

Thursday, September 12, 1918

Hiked through dark woods. No light allowed, guided by holding on the pack of the man ahead. Stumbled through underbrush for about half mile into an open field where

[*] From the diary of Eugene Kennedy. Courtesy of Eugene Kennedy Collection, Hoover Institution on War, Revolution, and Peace, Stanford University.

we waited in soaking rain until about 10:00 P.M. We then started on our hike to the St. Mihiel front, arriving on the crest of a hill at 1:00 A.M. I saw a sight which I shall never forget. It was the zero hour and in one instant the entire front as far as the eye could reach in either direction was a sheet of flame while the heavy artillery made the earth quake. The barrage was so intense that for a time we could not make out whether the Americans or Germans were putting it over. After timing the interval between flash and report we knew that the heaviest artillery was less than a mile away and consequently it was ours. We waded through pools and mud across open lots into a woods on a hill and had to pitch tents in mud. Blankets all wet and we are soaked to the skin. Have carried full pack from 10:00 P.M. to 2:00 A.M., without a rest. . . . Despite the cannonading I slept until 8:00 A.M. and awoke to find every discharge of 14-inch artillery shaking our tent like a leaf. Remarkable how we could sleep. No breakfast. . . . The doughboys had gone over the top at 5:00 A.M. and the French were shelling the back areas toward Metz. . . . Firing is incessant, so is rain. See an air battle just before turning in.

Friday, September 13, 1918

Called at 3:00 A.M. Struck tents and started to hike at 5:00 A.M. with full packs and a pick. Put on gas mask at alert position and hiked about five miles to St. Jean, where we unslung full packs and went on about four miles further with short packs and picks. Passed several batteries and saw many dead horses who gave out at start of push. Our doughboys are still shoving and "Jerry" is dropping so many shells on road into no man's land that we stayed back in field and made no effort to repair shell-torn road. Plenty of German prisoners being brought back. . . . Guns booming all the time. . . .

Thursday, October 17, 1918

Struck tents at 8:00 A.M. and moved about four miles to Chatel. Pitched tents on a side hill so steep that we had to cut steps to ascend. Worked like hell to shovel out a spot to pitch tent on. Just across the valley in front of us about two hundred yards distant, there had occurred an explosion due to a mine planted by the "Bosche" [Germans] and set with a time fuse. It had blown two men (French), two horses, and the wagon into fragments. . . . Arriving on the scene we found Quinn ransacking the wagon. It was full of grub. We each loaded a burlap bag with cans of condensed milk, peas, lobster, salmon, and bread. I started back . . . when suddenly another mine exploded, the biggest I ever saw. Rocks and dirt flew sky high. Quinn was hit in the knee and had to go to hospital. . . . At 6:00 P.M. each of our four platoons left camp in units to go up front and throw three foot and one artillery bridge across the Aire River. On way to river we were heavily shelled and gassed. . . . We put a bridge across 75-foot span. . . . Third platoon men had to get into water and swim or stand in water to their necks. The toughest job we had so far. . . .

Monday, October 21, 1918

Fragment from shell struck mess-kit on my back. . . . Equipment, both American and German, thrown everywhere, especially Hun helmets and belts of machine gunners. . . . Went scouting . . . for narrow-gauge rails to replace the ones "Jerry" spoiled before evacuating. Negro engineers working on railroad same as at St. Mihiel, that's all they are good for. . . .

Friday, November 1, 1918

Started out at 4:00 A.M. The drive is on. Fritz is coming back at us. Machine guns cracking, flares and Verry lights, artillery from both sides. A real war and we are walking right into the zone, ducking shells all the way. The artillery is nerve racking and we don't know from which angle "Jerry" will fire next. Halted behind shelter of railroad track just outside of Grand Pre after being forced back off main road by shell fire. Trees splintered like toothpicks. Machine gunners on top of railroad bank. . . . "Jerry" drove Ewell and me into a two-by-four shell hole, snipers' bullets close.

Sunday, November 3, 1918

Many dead Germans along the road. One heap on a manure pile. . . . Devastation everywhere. Our barrage has rooted up the entire territory like a ploughed field. Dead horses galore, many of them have a hind quarter cut off—the Huns need food. Dead men here and there. The sight I enjoy better than a dead German is to see heaps of them. Rain again. Couldn't keep rain out of our faces and it was pouring hard. Got up at midnight and drove stakes to secure shelter-half over us, pulled our wet blankets out of mud and made the bed all over again. Slept like a log with all my equipment in the open. One hundred forty-two planes sighted in evening.

Sunday, November 10, 1918

First day off in over two months. . . . Took a bath and we were issued new underwear but the cooties [lice] got there first. . . . The papers show a picture of the Kaiser entitled "William the Lost," and stating that he had abdicated. Had a good dinner. Rumor at night that armistice was signed. Some fellows discharged their arms in the courtyard, but most of us were too well pleased with dry bunk to get up.

F. J. Grimke, "Address of Welcome to the Men Who Have Returned from the Battlefront" (1919)

While blacks enlisted to fight for freedom in Europe, they faced segregation in the armed forces and discrimination at home. The

Reverend Francis J. Grimke of Washington, D.C., was bitterly aware of this contradiction. This address was delivered to African-American soldiers returning home to Washington in 1919.*

Young gentlemen, I am glad to welcome you home again after months of absence in a foreign land in obedience to the call of your country—glad that you have returned to us without any serious casualties.

I am sure you have acquitted yourself well; that in the record that you have made for yourselves, during your absence from home, there is nothing to be ashamed of, nothing that will reflect any discredit upon the race with which you are identified. . . .

While you were away you had the opportunity of coming in contact with another than the American type of white man; and through that contact you have learned what it is to be treated as a man, regardless of the color of your skin or race identity. Unfortunately you had to go away from home to receive a man's treatment, to breathe the pure, bracing air of liberty, equality, fraternity. And, while it was with no intention of bringing to you that knowledge, of putting you where you could get that kind of experience, but simply because they couldn't very well get along without you, I am glad nevertheless, that you were sent. You know now that the mean, contemptible spirit of race prejudice that curses this land is not the spirit of other lands; you know now what it is to be treated as a man. And, one of the things that I am particularly hoping for, now that you have had this experience, is that you have come back determined, as never before, to keep up the struggle for our rights until, here in these United States, in this boasted land of the free and home of the brave, every man, regardless of the color of his skin, shall be accorded a man's treatment.

Your trip will be of very little value to the race in this country unless you have come back with the love of liberty, equality, fraternity burning in your souls. . . . In the struggle that is before us, you can do a great deal in helping to better conditions. You, who gave up everything—home, friends, relatives—you who took your lives in your hands and went forth to lay them, a willing sacrifice upon the altar of your country and in the interest of democracy throughout the world, have a right to speak—to speak with authority; and that right you must exercise.

We, who remained at home, followed you while you were away, with the deepest interest; and, our hearts burned with indignation when tidings came to us, as it did from time to time, of the manner in which you were treated by those over you, from whom you had every reason, in view of the circumstances that took you abroad and what it was costing you, to expect decent, humane treatment, instead of the treatment that was accorded you. The physical hardships, incident to a soldier's life in times of war, are trying enough, are hard enough to bear—and, during this world war, on the other side of the water, I understand they were unusually hard. To add to these the insults, the studied insults that were heaped upon you, and for no reason except that

---

* From the writings of F. J. Brimke from *A Documentary History of the Negro People in the United States, 1910–1933*. ed. Herbert Aptheker (Secaucus, New Jersey: Citadel, 1977).

you were colored, is so shocking that were it not for positive evidence, it would be almost unbelievable. . . .

I know of nothing that sets forth this cursed American race prejudice in a more odious, execrable light than the treatment of our colored soldiers in this great world struggle that has been going on, by the very government that ought to have shielded them from the brutes that were over them. . . .

If it was worth going abroad to make the world safe for democracy, it is equally worth laboring no less earnestly to make it safe at home. We shall be greatly disappointed if you do not do this—if you fail to do your part.

Woodrow Wilson, The Fourteen Points (1918)

Included here are Wilson's Fourteen Points, presented as a speech to Congress on January 8, 1918, designed to make the world safe for all people and formulate the agenda for postwar peace negotiations.*

It will be our wish and purpose that the processes of peace, when they are begun, shall be absolutely open and that they shall involve and permit henceforth no secret understandings of any kind. The day of conquest and aggrandizement is gone by; so is also the day of secret covenants entered into in the interest of particular governments and likely at some unlooked-for moment to upset the peace of the world. . . .

We entered this war because violations of right had occurred which touched us to the quick and made the life of our own people impossible unless they were corrected and the world secure once for all against their recurrence.

What we demand in this war, therefore, is nothing peculiar to ourselves. It is that the world be made fit and safe to live in; and particularly that it be made safe for every peace-loving nation which, like our own, wishes to live its own life, determine its own institutions, be assured of justice and fair dealing by the other peoples of the world as against force and selfish aggressions.

All the peoples of the world are in effect partners in this interest, and for our own part we see very clearly that unless justice be done to others it will not be done to us. The program of the world's peace, therefore, is our program; and that program, the only possible program, as we see it, is this:

1. Open covenants of peace, openly arrived at, after which there shall be no private international understandings of any kind but diplomacy shall proceed always frankly and in the public view.

---

* Woodrow Wilson, *Message to Congress*, January 8, 1918.

2. Absolute freedom of navigation upon the seas, outside territorial waters, alike in peace and in war, except as the seas may be closed in whole or in part by international action for the enforcement of international covenants.

3. The removal, so far as possible, of all economic barriers and the establishment of an equality of trade conditions among all the nations consenting to the peace and associating themselves for its maintenance.

4. Adequate guarantees given and taken that national armaments will be reduced to the lowest points consistent with domestic safety.

5. A free, open-minded, and absolutely impartial adjustment of all colonial claims, based upon a strict observance of the principle that in determining all such questions of sovereignty the interests of the populations concerned must have equal weight with the equitable claims of the government whose title is to be determined.

6. The evacuation of all Russian territory and such a settlement of all questions affecting Russia as will secure the best and freest cooperation of the other nations of the world in obtaining for her an unhampered and unembarrassed opportunity for the independent determination of her own political development and national policy and assure her of a sincere welcome into the society of free nations under institutions of her own choosing; and, more than a welcome, assistance also of every kind that she may need and may herself desire. The treatment accorded Russian by her sister nations in the months to come will be the acid test of their good will, of their comprehension of her needs as distinguished from their own interests, and of their intelligent and unselfish sympathy.

7. Belgium, the whole world will agree, must be evacuated and restored, without any attempt to limit the sovereignty which she enjoys in common with all other free nations. No other single act will serve as this will serve to restore confidence among the nations in the laws which they have themselves set and determined for the government of their relations with one another. Without this healing act the whole structure and validity of international law is forever impaired.

8. All French territory should be freed and the invaded portions restored, and the wrong done to France by Prussia in 1871 in the matter of Alsace-Lorraine, which has unsettled the peace of the world for nearly fifty years, should be righted, in order that peace may once more be made secure in the interest of all.

9. A readjustment of the frontiers of Italy should be affected along clearly recognizable lines of nationality.

10. The peoples of Austria-Hungary, whose place among the nations we wish to see safeguarded and assured, should be accorded the freest opportunity of autonomous development.

11. Rumania, Serbia, and Montenegro should be evacuated; occupied territories restored; Serbia accorded free and secure access to the sea; and the relations of the several Balkan states to one another determined by friendly counsel along historically established lines of allegiance and nationality; and international guarantees of the political and economic independence and territorial integrity of the several Balkan states should be entered into.

12. The Turkish portions of the present Ottoman Empire should be assured a secure sovereignty, but the other nationalities which are now under Turkish rule should be assured an undoubted security of life and an absolutely unmolested opportunity of autonomous development, and the Dardanelles should be permanently opened as a free passage to the ships and commerce of all nations under international guarantees.

13. An independent Polish state should be erected which should include the territories inhabited by indisputably Polish populations, which should be assured a free and secure access to the sea, and whose political and economic independence and territorial integrity should be guaranteed by international covenant.

14. A general association of nations must be formed under specific covenants for the purpose of affording mutual guarantees of political independence and territorial integrity to great and small states alike.

In regard to these essential rectifications of wrong and assertions of right we feel ourselves to be intimate partners of all the governments and peoples associated together against the imperialists. We cannot be separated in interest or divided in purpose. We stand together until the end. . . .

An evident principle runs through the whole program I have outlined. It is the principle of justice to all peoples and nationalities, and their right to live on equal terms of liberty and safety with one another, whether they be strong or weak.

Unless this principle be made its foundation no part of the structure of international justice can stand. The people of the United States could act upon no other principle; and to the vindication of this principle they are ready to devote their lives, their honor, and everything that they possess. The moral climax of this the culminating and final war for human liberty has come, and they are ready to put their own strength, their own highest purpose, their own integrity and devotion to the test.

23

The New Decade

The 1920s were a decade of growing middle-class affluence and cultural conflict. As technology like the automobile, electricity, and running water became available to more Americans and improved their daily lives, the new society of the 1920s was becoming increasingly intolerant, xenophobic, and racist. The youth, freedom, and consumerism trumpeted by advertising and mass culture and most visibly represented by the automobile and city life often strained against America's rural roots and deep-seated fears of rapid change. The Ku Klux Klan expanded (most notably in urban areas) while the passage of Prohibition indicated that many believed that morality could be legislated.

In the early 1920s, Congress, bowing to nativist pressure, moved to restrict or even bar immigration. The 1924 Comprehensive Immigration Law, included here, banned all immigration from Asia (Chinese immigration had already been banned in 1880 and Japanese immigration in 1908) and limited immigration from southern and eastern Europe. To a great extent, Mexican and African-Americans workers filled the labor shortages caused by these immigration restriction.

Another sign of the intolerance and racism of the 1920s was the famous Sacco and Vanzetti case, in which two Italian anarchists were tried and executed for the murder of a guard during a Massachusetts robbery. Whether they were actually guilty is still unclear, but the trial became an international symbol of the bigotry and paranoia inspired by political radicals. The court statement of Bartolomeo Vanzetti is a sometimes eloquent critique of the society that permitted his conviction.

Women gained the vote just as World War I ended and entered the 1920s with their legal rights expanding and their social role changing. Increasingly, women attended college and worked outside the home; divorce laws were liberalized. Most famously, the 1920s saw the advent of the so-called New Woman and the flapper—a liberated woman who embraced sex, short skirts, and smoking. Yet simultaneously the 1920s saw a reemphasis of the importance of women's fulfillment in the home and marriage—rather than in the workplace. Women were still clustered in "women's jobs" and the number of women in professions dropped. In an article from *Harper's* excerpted here, Dorothy Dunbar Bromley describes some of the transformations in gender roles in the 1920s.

As America transformed from a primarily industrial society into a consumer society, advertising enjoyed an explosive renaissance. The goods that drove the economy of the 1920s—automobiles, radios, washing machines, vacuum cleaners, sewing machines, and telephones—were not unquestionable necessities of life. Not only did advertising have to convince a consumer to buy a particular brand of product, it often needed to create a demand for the product itself.

Advertisers accomplished this by associating products with social correctness and sexual fulfillment. Advertising for Listerine mouthwash demonstrates this. While earlier ads for Listerine touted the product as a germ killer and "topical antiseptic," Listerine by the 1920s promised to eliminate "halitosis," a term for bad breath unearthed in an obscure British medical journal. A Listerine ad from 1922 told a sad tale:

> She was a beautiful girl and talented too. She had the advantages of education and better clothes than most girls of her set. She possessed that culture and poise that travel brings. Yet in the one pursuit that stands foremost in the mind of every girl and woman—marriage— she was a failure.

The reason for her failure, of course, was halitosis. This ad, and others included here, exposes both the power of advertisement and the gender roles re-emphasized in the 1920s.

Study Questions

1. Why did Americans want to restrict immigration in the 1920s? Why was 1890 used as the base year to determine quotas? Which countries benefited from the law? Which suffered? Which countries are missing from the table altogether?

2. Vanzetti describes a backlash against foreigners and against "slackers." Dorothy Dunbar Bromley suggests that women in earlier times would have gotten farther had they relied on their "ability." Technology made some jobs easier and women and ethnic minorities continued to move into low-status positions in the 1920s. Discuss changing attitudes these developments provoked.

3. How do Dorothy Dunbar Bromley's objectives differ from those in the Declaration of Sentiments? Would Bromley have agreed with the Listerine advertisement that marriage was the "pursuit . . . foremost in the mind of every girl and woman"?

4. On what fears particular to the 1920s does the furniture advertisement play? What forces drew "young people" out of the house? How likely was a new living-room set to counteract those forces? Why might this ad have been effective?

5. Both advertisements in this chapter play on the guilt of the consumer. To which parent is the ad for flashlight batteries addressed? Why?

Comprehensive Immigration Law (1924)

This act limited immigration to two percent of those born in any given foreign country in the United States in 1890. In 1927 an even more restrictive law limited immigration to around 150,000 per year. (By contrast, between 1840 and 1920, on average, a half a million immigrants had entered the country per year.) Despite the act's stringency, immigration laws were not enforced strictly: in order to prevent labor shortages in the Southwest, Mexican workers were encouraged to cross the border to work in the United States.[*]

By the President of the United States of America

A Proclamation

Whereas it is provided in the act of Congress approved May 26, 1924, entitled "An act to limit the immigration of aliens into the United States, and for other purposes" that "The annual quota of any nationality shall be two per centum of the number of foreign-born individuals of such nationality resident in continental Untied States as determined by the United States Census of 1890, but the minimum quota of any nationality shall be 100 (Sec. 11 a). . . .

"The Secretary of State, the Secretary of Commerce, and the Secretary of Labor, jointly, shall, as soon as feasible after the enactment of this act, prepare a statement showing the number of individuals of the various nationalities resident in continental United States as determined by the United States Census of 1890, which statement shall be the population basis for the purposes of subdivision (a) of section 11 (Sec. 12 b).

"Such officials shall, jointly, report annually to the President the quota of each nationality under subdivision (a) of section 11, together with the statements, estimates, and revisions provided for in this section. The President shall proclaim and make known the quotas so reported". (Sec. 12 e).

Now, therefore I, Calvin Coolidge, President of the United States of America acting under and by virtue of the power in me vested by the aforesaid act of Congress, do hereby proclaim and make known that on and after July 1, 1924, and throughout the fiscal year 1924–1925, the quota of each nationality provided in said act shall be as follows:

---

[*] From U.S. Bureau of Immigration, *Annual Report of the Commissioner-General of Immigration, 1924* (Washington, D.C.: Government Printing Office, 1924), 24 ff.

COUNTRY OR AREA OF BIRTH
QUOTA 1924–1925

Afghanistan— 100
Albania— 100
Andorra— 100
Arabian peninsula (1, 2)— 100
Armenia— 124
Australia, including Papua, Tasmania, and all islands appertaining to Australia (3, 4)— 121
Austria— 785
Belgium (5)— 512
Bhutan— 100
Bulgaria— 100
Cameroon (proposed British mandate)— 100
Cameroon (French mandate)— 100
China— 100
Czechoslovakia— 3,073
Danzig, Free City of— 228
Denmark (5, 6)— 2,789
Egypt— 100
Estonia— 124
Ethiopia (Abyssinia)— 100
Finland— 170
France (1, 5, 6)— 3,954
Germany— 51,227
Great Britain and Northern Ireland (1, 3, 5, 6)— 34,007
Greece— 100
Hungary— 473
Iceland— 100
India (3)— 100
Iraq (Mesopotamia)— 100
Irish Free State (3)— 28,567
Italy, including Rhodes, Dodecanesia, and Castellorizzo (5)— 3,845
Japan— 100
Latvia—142
Liberia— 100
Liechtenstein— 100

Lithuania— 344
Luxemburg— 100
Monaco— 100
Morocco (French and Spanish Zones and Tangier)— 100
Muscat (Oman)— 100
Nauru (proposed British mandate) (4)— 100
Nepal— 100
Netherlands (1, 5, 6)— 1648
New Zealand (including appertaining islands (3, 4)— 100
Norway (5)— 6,453
New Guinea, and other Pacific Islands under proposed Australian mandate (4)— 100
Palestine (with Trans-Jordan, proposed British mandate)— 100
Persia (1)— 100
Poland— 5,982
Portugal (1, 5)— 503
Ruanda and Urundi (Belgium mandate)— 100
Rumania— 603
Russia, European and Asiatic (1)— 2,248
Samoa, Western (4) (proposed mandate of New Zealand)— 100
San Marino— 100
Siam— 100
South Africa, Union of (3)— 100
South West Africa (proposed mandate of Union of South Africa)— 100
Spain (5)— 131
Sweden— 9,561
Switzerland— 2,081
Syria and The Lebanon (French mandate)— 100
Tanganyika (proposed British mandate)— 100
Togoland (proposed British mandate)— 100
Togoland (French mandate)— 100
Turkey— 100
Yap and other Pacific islands (under Japanese mandate) (4)— 100
Yugoslavia— 671

GENERAL NOTE.—The immigration quotas assigned to the various countries and quota-areas should not be regarded as having any political significance whatever, or as involving recognition of new governments, or of new boundaries, or of transfers of territory except as the United States Government has already made such recognition in a formal and official manner. . . . Calvin Coolidge.

Bartolomeo Vanzetti, Court Statement (1927)

In 1920, Nicola Sacco and Bartolomeo Vanzetti were arrested for killing a guard during the robbery of a shoe factory in South Braintree, Massachusetts. With their conviction, based on what some considered flimsy evidence, the two Italian anarchists became symbols and causes célèbres for liberals across the globe. Nevertheless, after several appeals Sacco and Vanzetti were condemned to death and were executed in the electric chair.[*]

Now, I should say that I am not only innocent of all these things, not only have I never committed a real crime in my life—though some sins but not crimes—not only have I struggled all my life to eliminate crimes, the crimes that the officials and the official moral condemns, but also the crime that the official moral and the official law sanctions and sanctifies—the exploitation and the oppression of the man by the man, and if there is a reason why I am here as a guilty man, if there is a reason why you in a few minutes can doom me, it is this reason and none else. . . .

We were tried during a time that has now passed into history. I mean by that, a time when there was a hysteria of resentment and hate against the people of our principles, against the foreigner, against slackers. . . .

Well, I have already said that I not only am not guilty . . . but I never commit a crime in my life—I have never stole and I have never killed and I have never spilt blood, and I have fought against crime and I have fought and have sacrificed myself even to eliminate the crimes the law and the church legitimate and sanctify.

This is what I say: I would not wish to a dog or to a snake, to the most low and misfortunate creature of the earth—I would not wish to any of them what I have had to suffer for things that I am not guilty of. But my conviction is that I have suffered for things I am guilty of. I am suffering because I am a radical and indeed I am a radical; I have suffered because I was an Italian, and indeed I am an Italian; I have suffered more for my family and for my beloved than for myself; but I am so convinced to be right that if you could execute me two times, and if I could be reborn two other times, I would live again to do what I have done already.

I have finished. Thank you.

---

[*] Reprinted from *The Sacco-Vanzetti Case* (New York: Henry Holt, 1929), vol. 5, 4896–4904.

Dorothy Dunbar Bromley, From "Feminist: New Style" (1927)

Women's roles and place in society were changing in the 1920s: More women than ever worked outside the home; some women—typified by the flapper—flouted convention and bobbed their hair, smoked cigarettes, and trimmed their skirts. Dorothy Dunbar Bromley was an unabashed optimist who rejected collective women's activism, believing women could fulfill their individual destinies through a new style of combining work, marriage, and family.*

Is it not high time that we laid [bare] the ghost of the so-called feminist?

"Feminism" has become a term of opprobrium to the modern young woman. For the word suggests the old school of fighting feminists who wore flat heels and had very little feminine charm. Indeed, if a blundering male assumes that a young woman is a feminist simply because she happens to have a job or a profession of her own, she will be highly—and quite justifiably—insulted. Yet she and her kind can hardly be dubbed "old-fashioned" women. What *are* they, then? . . .

The constantly increasing group of young women in their twenties and thirties, the truly modern ones, admit that a full life calls for marriage and children, as well as a career. These women, if they launch upon marriage, are keen to make a success of it and an art of child rearing. But *at the same time* they are moved by an inescapable inner compulsion to be individuals in their own right. And in this era of simplified housekeeping they see their opportunity, for it is obvious that a woman who plans intelligently can salvage some time for her own pursuits. Furthermore, they are convinced that they will be better wives and mothers for the breath they gain from functioning outside the home. . . .

In brief, Feminist—New Style reasons that if she is economically independent, and if she has, to boot, a vital interest in some work of her own, she will have given as few hostages to Fate as it is humanly possible to give. Love may die, and children may grow up, but one's work goes on forever. . . .

Fourth Tenet. Nor has she become hostile to the other sex in the course of her struggle to orient herself. On the contrary, she frankly likes men and is grateful to more than a few for the encouragement and help they have given her.

In the business and professional worlds, for instance, Feminist—New Style has observed that more and more men are coming to accord women as much responsibility as they show themselves able to carry. She and her generation have never found it necessary to bludgeon their way, and she is inclined to think that certain of the pioneers would have got farther if they had relied on their ability, rather than on their militant methods. To tell the truth, she enjoys working with men, more than with women, for their methods are more direct and their view larger, and she finds that she can deal with them on a basis of frank comradeship.

Fifth Tenet. By the same corollary, Feminist—New Style professes no loyalty to women *en masse*, although she staunchly believes in individual women. Surveying her sex as a whole, she finds their actions petty, their range of interests narrow, their talk trivial and repetitious. As for those who set themselves up as leaders of the sex, they are either strident creatures of so little ability and balance that they have won no chance to "express themselves" (to use their own hackneyed phrase) in a man-made world; or they are brilliant, restless individuals who too often battle for women's rights for the sake of personal glory.

Sixth Tenet. There is, however, one thing which Feminist—New Style envies Frenchwoman, and that is their sense of "chic." Indeed, she is so far removed from the early feminists that she is altogether baffled by the psychology which led some of them to abjure men in the same voice with which they aped them. Certainly their vanity must have been anaesthetized, she tells herself, as she pictures them with their short hair, so different from her own shingle, and dressed in their own unflattering mannish clothes—quite the antithesis of her own boyish effects which are subtly designed to set off feminine charms.

Seventh Tenet. Empty slogans seem to Feminist—New Style just as bad taste as masculine dress and manners. They serve only to prolong the war between the sexes and to prevent women from learning to think straight. Take these, for instance, "Keep your maiden name." "Come out of the kitchen." "Never darn a sock." After all, what's in a name or in a sock? Madame Curie managed to become one of the world's geniuses even though she suffered the terrible handicap of bearing her husband's name, and it is altogether likely that she darned a sock or two of Monsieur Curie's when there was no servant at hand to do it.

Finally, Feminist—New Style proclaims that men and children shall no longer circumscribe her world, although they may constitute a large part of it. She is intensely self-conscious, whereas the feminists were intensely sex-conscious. Aware of possessing a mind, she takes a keen pleasure in using that mind for some definite purpose; and also in learning to think clearly and cogently against a background of historical and scientific knowledge. She aspires to understand the meaning of the twentieth century, as she sees it expressed in the skyscrapers, the rapid pace of city life, the expressionistic drama, the abstract conceptions of art, the new music, the Joycean novel. She knows that it is her American, her twentieth-century birthright to emerge from creature of instinct into a full-fledged individual who is capable of molding her own life. And in this respect she holds that she is becoming man's equal. . . .

Advertisements (1925, 1927)

Aside from selling sex appeal and conformity, advertising used powerful emotions, like fear and guilt to sell products. Scott Tissue, for example, ran a campaign to warn the public that harsh toilet paper caused irritation that was "not only a source of discomfort but also a possible seat of infection." One ad showed a woman in a hospital bed with concerned friends hovering by her bedside. Another showed a team of surgeons preparing to operate on a victim of harsh toilet paper. The advertisements included here play on fear like this as well as guilt and shame induced by failing to use or own the right products.

Advertisement for Berkey & Gay Furniture Company (1925)

Do they know Your son at MALUCIO's?

There's a hole in the door at Malucio's. Ring the bell and a pair of eyes will look coldly out at you. If you are known you will get in. Malucio has to be careful.

There have been riotous nights at Malucio's. Tragic nights, too. But somehow the fat little man has managed to avoid the law.

Almost every town has its Malucio's. Some, brightly disguised as cabarets—others, mere back street filling stations for pocket flasks.

But every Malucio will tell you the same thing. His best customers are not the ne'er-do-wells of other years. They are the young people—frequently, the best young people of the town.

Malucio has put one over on the American home. Ultimately he will be driven out. Until then THE HOME MUST BID MORE INTELLIGENTLY FOR MALUCIO'S BUSINESS.

There are many reasons why it is profitable and wise to furnish the home attractively, but one of these, and not the least, is—Malucio's.

The younger generation is sensitive to beauty, princely proud, and will not entertain in homes of which it is secretly ashamed.

But make your rooms attractive, appeal to the vaulting pride of youth, and you may worry that much less about Malucio's—and the other modern frivolities that his name symbolizes.

A guest room smartly and tastefully furnished—a refined and attractive dining room—will more than hold their own against the tinsel cheapness of Malucio's.

Nor is good furniture any longer a luxury for the favored few. THE PRESCOTT suite shown above, for instance, is a moderately priced pattern, conforming in every detail to the finest Berkey & Gay standards.

In style, in the selection of rare and beautiful woods, and in the rich texture of the finish and hand decorating, it reveals the skill of craftsmen long expert in the art of quality furniture making.

The PRESCOTT is typical of values now on display at the store of your local Berkey & Gay dealer. Depend on his showing you furniture in which you may take deep pride—beautiful, well built, luxuriously finished, and moderately priced.

There is a Berkey & Gay pattern suited to every home—an infinite variety of styles at prices ranging all the way from $350 to $6,000.

Advertisement for Eveready Flashlight and Battery (1927)

The Song that STOPPED!

A child of five skipped down the garden path and laughed because the sky was blue. "Jane," called her mother from the kitchen window, "come here and help me bake your birthday cake." Little feet sped. "Don't fall," her mother warned.

Jane stood in the kitchen door and wrinkled her nose in joy. Her gingham dress was luminous against the sun. What a child! Dr. and Mrs. Wentworth cherished Jane.

"Go down to the cellar and get mother some preserves . . . the kind you like."

"The preserves are in the cellar," she chanted, making a progress twice around the kitchen. "Heigh-ho a-derry-o, the preserves are . . ." her voice grew fainter as she danced off. " . . . in the . . ."

The thread of song snapped. A soft *thud-thud*. Fear fluttered Mrs. Wentworth's heart. She rushed to the cellar door.

"Mother!" . . . a child screaming in pain. Mrs. Wentworth saw a little morsel of girlhood lying in a heap of gingham and yellow hair at the bottom of the dark stairs.

The sky is still blue. But there will be no birthday party tomorrow. An ambulance clanged up to Dr. Wentworth's house today. Jane's leg is broken.

If a flashlight had been hanging on a hook at the head of the cellar stairs, this little tragedy would have been averted. If Jane had been taught to use a flashlight as carefully as her father, Dr. Wentworth, had taught her to use a tooth-brush, a life need not have been endangered.

An Eveready Flashlight is always a convenience and often a life-saver. Keep one about the house, in the car; and take one with you wherever you go. Keep it supplied with fresh Eveready Batteries—the longest-lasting flashlight batteries made. Eveready Flashlights, $1.00 up.

NATIONAL CARBON CO., INC. EVEREADY FLASHLIGHTS & BATTERIES

A THOUSAND THINGS MAY HAPPEN IN THE DARK

24

Hard Times

The 1929 stock-market crash was the catalyst for the worst depression in the nation's history. By the presidential election of 1932, 25 percent of the American workforce had lost their jobs, while per capita incomes had been halved. Franklin Delano Roosevelt won the presidency by appealing to the "forgotten man" and attacking rich businessmen. His New Deal programs did not end the depression, but perhaps more significantly, they did restore national confidence and faith in government.

Some felt that the New Deal programs did not go far enough. Huey Long and Father Charles Coughlin led populist protest movements attacking the New Deal for not doing enough for the common man. Coughlin, a Detroit radio personality, blamed the depression on a conspiracy of bankers and Jewish businessmen. His anti-Semitism struck a chord with many desperate for scapegoats. Meanwhile, Long, the governor and senator from Louisiana, promised a guaranteed income for all Americans and vowed to aggressively tax the rich.

The depression did not affect everyone in the same way. Stories of middle-class people losing their homes, wealthy children being pulled from boarding schools, and the working class finding themselves on the streets did not represent the full range of experience during the Great Depression. Many people, for instance, noticed little change in their daily lives. The very poor continued to live a squalid existence, while a number of middle-class people, particularly those with secure and relatively stable incomes, could afford services once out of their reach. African-Americans received few benefits from New Deal legislation and were often the last hired and first fired when times got tough. A letter to President Roosevelt and selections from Studs Turkel's *Hard Times* describe the difficulties of the depression in the words of those who lived through it.

Study Questions

1. Why would the public feel a renewed sense of confidence after Roosevelt's First Inaugural Address? Did it give a plan of action to end the depression?

2. How did Coughlin feel about banks? How would he change the banking system? How does his approach differ from Roosevelt's? What does he think about Roosevelt's banking legislation?

3. How does Long propose to "share our wealth"? What is the difference between his proposals and Roosevelt's "soak the rich" tax? Of what New Deal program in particular is Long critical?

4. Given the events of the early 1930s, what in particular about the proposals put forward by Coughlin and Long would appeal to their listeners?

5. What reasons did Roosevelt, Couglin, and Long respectively give for the depression? Who did they blame it on? Compare and contrast their solutions.

6. Why didn't minorities receive the full benefits of the legislation passed during the New Deal?

7. What kinds of occupations were likely to have either benefited from the depression or to have maintained their positions? To what factors does Benton attribute his firm's success? Why did Clifford Burke notice little change in his life?

Franklin D. Roosevelt, First Inaugural Address (1932)

Roosevelt's First Inaugural Address is very familiar and oft-quoted. It was gauged to reassure the American people, to remind them of their unique heritage, the primary task of government, and the spirit that had made the nation great.[*]

I am certain that my fellow Americans expect that on my induction into the Presidency I will address them with a candor and a decision which the present situation of our Nation impels. This is preeminently the time to speak the truth, the whole truth, frankly and boldly. Nor need we shrink from honestly facing conditions in our country today. This great Nation will endure as it has endured, will revive and will prosper. So, first of all, let me assert my firm belief that the only thing we have to fear is fear itself— nameless, unreasoning, unjustified terror which paralyzes needed efforts to convert retreat into advance. In every dark hour of our national life a leadership of frankness and vigor has met with that understanding and support of the people themselves which is essential to victory. I am convinced that you will again give that support to leadership in these critical days.

---

[*] From Franklin D. Roosevelt, *Inaugural Address*, March 4, 1933.

In such a spirit on my part and on yours we face our common difficulties. They concern, thank God, only material things. Values have shrunken to fantastic levels; taxes have risen; our ability to pay has fallen; government of all kinds is faced by serious curtailment of income; the means of exchange are frozen in the currents of trade; the withered leaves of industrial enterprise lie on every side; farmers find no markets for their produce; the savings of many years in thousands of families are gone.

More important, a host of unemployed citizens face the grim problem of existence, and an equally great number toil with little return. Only a foolish optimist can deny the dark reality of the movement.

Yet our distress comes from no failure or substance. We are stricken by no plague of locusts. Compared with the perils which our forefathers conquered because they believed and were not afraid, we have still much to be thankful for. Nature still offers her bounty and human efforts have multiplied it. Plenty is at our doorstep, but a generous use of it languishes in the very sight of the supply. Primarily this is because rulers of the exchange of mankind's goods have failed through their own stubbornness and their own incompetence, have admitted their failure, and have abdicated. Practices of the unscrupulous money changers stand indicted in the court of public opinion, rejected by the hearts and minds of men.

True they have tried, but their efforts have been cast in the pattern of an outworn tradition. Faced by failure of credit they have proposed only the lending of more money. Stripped of the lure of profit by which to induce our people to follow their leadership, they have resorted to exhortations, pleading tearfully for restored confidence. They have known only the rules of a generation of self-seekers. They have no vision, and when there is no vision the people perish.

The money changers have fled from their high seats in the temple of our civilization. We may now restore that temple to the ancient truths. The measure of the restoration lies in the extent to which we apply social values more noble than mere monetary profit.

Happiness lies not in the mere possession of money; it lies in the joy of achievement, in the thrill of creative effort. The joy and moral stimulation of work no longer must be forgotten in the mad chase of evanescent profits. These dark days will be worth all they cost us if they teach us that our true destiny is not to be ministered unto but to minister to ourselves and to our fellow men.

Recognition of the falsity of material wealth as the standard of success goes hand in hand with the abandonment of the false belief that public office and high political position are to be valued only by the standards of pride of place and personal profit; and there must be an end to a conduct in banking and in business which too often has given to a sacred trust the likeness of callous and selfish wrongdoing. Small wonder that confidence languishes, for it thrives only on honesty, on honor, on the sacredness of obligations, on faithful protection, on unselfish performance; without them it cannot live.

Restoration calls, however not for changes in ethics alone. This Nation asks for action, and action now.

Our greatest primary task is to put people to work. This is no unsolvable problem if we face it wisely and courageously. It can be accomplished in part by direct recruiting by the Government itself, treating the task as we would treat the emergency of a war, but at the same time, through this employment, accomplishing greatly needed projects to stimulate and reorganize the use of our natural resources.

Hand in hand with this we must frankly recognize the overbalance of population in our industrial centers and, by engaging on a national scale in a redistribution, endeavor to provide a better use of the land for those best fitted for the land. The task can be helped by definite efforts to raise the values of agricultural products and with this the power to purchase the output of our cities. It can be helped by preventing realistically the tragedy of the growing loss through foreclosure of our small homes and our farms. It can be helped by insistence that the Federal, State, and local governments act forthwith on the demand that their cost be drastically reduced. It can be helped by the unifying of relief activities which today are often scattered, uneconomical, and unequal. It can be helped by national planning for and supervision of all forms of transportation and of communications and other utilities which have a definitely public character. There are many ways in which it can be helped but it can never be helped merely by talking about it. We must act and act quickly.

Finally, in our progress toward a resumption of work we require two safeguards against a return of the evils of the old order: there must be a strict supervision of all banking an credits and investments, so that there will be an end to speculation with other people's money; and there must be provision for an adequate but sound currency.

These are the lines of attack. I shall presently urge upon a new Congress, in special session, detailed measures for their fulfillment, and I shall seek the immediate assistance of the several States.

Through this program of action we address ourselves to putting our own national house in order and making income balance outgo. Our international trade relations, though vastly important, are in point of time and necessity secondary to the establishment of a sound national economy. I favor as a practical policy the putting of first things first. I shall spare no effort to restore world trade by international economic readjustment, but the emergency at home cannot wait on that accomplishment.

The basic thought that guides these specific means of national recovery is not narrowly nationalistic. It is the insistence as a first consideration, upon the interdependence of the various elements in and parts of the United States—a recognition of the old and permanently important manifestation of the American spirit of the pioneer. It is the way to recovery. It is the immediate way. It is the strongest assurance that the recovery will endure.

In the field of world policy I would dedicate this Nation to the policy of the good neighbor—the neighbor who respects his obligations and respects the sanctity of his agreements in and with a world of neighbors.

If I read the temper of our people correctly, we now realize as we have never realized before our interdependence on each other; that we cannot merely take but we must give as well; that if we are to go forward, we must move as a trained and loyal army willing to sacrifice for the good of a common discipline, because without such discipline no progress is made, no leadership becomes effective. We are, I know, ready and willing to submit our lives and property to such discipline, because it makes possible a leadership which aims at a larger good. This I propose to offer, pledging that the larger purpose will bind upon us all as a sacred obligation with a unity of duty hitherto evoked only in time of armed strife.

With this pledge taken, I assume unhesitatingly the leadership of this great army of our people dedicated to a disciplined attack upon our common problems.

Action in this image and to this end is feasible under the form of government which we have inherited from our ancestors. Our Constitution is so simple and practical that it is possible always to meet extraordinary needs by changes in emphasis and arrangement without loss of essential form. That is why our constitutional system has proved itself the most superbly enduring political mechanism the modern world has produced. It has met every stress of vast expansion of territory, of foreign wars, of bitter internal strife, of world relations.

It is to be hoped that the normal balance of Executive and legislative authority may be wholly adequate to meet the unprecedented task before us. But it may be that an unprecedented demand and need for undelayed action may call for temporary departure from that normal balance of public procedure.

I am prepared under my constitutional duty to recommend the measures that a stricken Nation in the midst of a stricken world may require. These measures, or such other measures as the Congress may build out of its experience and wisdom, I shall seek, within my constitutional authority to bring to speedy adoption.

But in the event that the Congress shall fail to take one of these two courses and in the event that the national emergency is still critical, I shall not evade the clear course of duty that will then confront me. I shall ask the Congress for the one remaining instrument to meet the crisis—broad Executive power to wage a war against the emergency, as great as the power that would be given to me if we were in fact invaded by a foreign foe.

For the trust reposed in me I will return the courage and the devotion that befit the time. I can do no less.

We face the arduous days that lie before us in the warm courage of national unity; with the clear consciousness of seeking old and precious moral values; with the clear satisfaction that comes from the stern performance of duty by old and young alike. We aim at the assurance of a rounded and permanent national life.

We do not distrust the future of essential democracy. The people of the United States have not failed. In their need they have registered a mandate that they want direct, vigorous action. They have asked for discipline and direction under leadership. They have made me the present instrument of their wishes. In the spirit of the gift I take it.

In this dedication of a Nation we humbly ask the blessing of God. May He protect each and every one of us. May He guide me in the days to come.

Huey Long, "Share Our Wealth" (1935)

The charismatic Huey Long was elected governor of Louisiana in 1928, owing in large measure to his "Share Our Wealth" philosophy, which provided services to the poor, built hospitals and schools, and granted awesome powers to Long himself. In 1930 he became a U.S. Senator and, critical of Roosevelt, had ambitions to run for president before he was killed in 1935. His Share Our Wealth Society had more than 4.6 million members. This circular was addressed "To Members and Well-Wishers of the Share Our Wealth Society" and was placed in the *Congressional Record* in 1935.*

Here is the whole sum and substance of the Share Our Wealth movement:

1. Every family to be furnished by the government a homestead allowance, free of debt, of not less than one-third the average family wealth of the country, which means, at the lowest, that every family shall have the reasonable comforts of life up to a value of from $5,000 to $6,000: No person to have a fortune of more than 100 to 300 times the average family fortune, which means that the limit to fortune is between $1,500,000 and $5,000,000, with annual capital levy taxes imposed on all above $1,000,000.

2. The yearly income of every family shall be not less than one-third of the average family income, which means that, according to the estimates of the statisticians of the U.S. Government and Wall Street, no family's annual income would be less than from $2,000 to $2,500: No yearly income shall be allowed to any person larger than from 100 to 300 times the size of the average family income, which means that no person would be allowed to earn in any year more than $600,000 to $1,800,000, all to be subject to present income tax laws.

3. To limit or regulate the hours of work to such an extent as to prevent over-production; the most modern and efficient machinery would be encouraged so that as much would be produced as possible so as to satisfy all demands of the people, but also to allow the maximum time to the workers for recreation, convenience, education, and luxuries of life.

4. An old-age pension to the persons over 60.

---

* From Huey Long, "To The Members and Well-Wishers of the Share Our Wealth Society," *Congressional Record*, 1935 (Washington D.C.: U.S. Government Printing Office, 1935).

5. To balance agricultural production with what can be consumed according to the laws of God, which includes the preserving and storing of surplus commodities to be paid for and held by the Government for emergencies when such are needed. Please bear in mind, however, that when the people of America have had money to buy things they needed, we have never had a surplus of any commodity. This plan of God does not call for destroying any of the things raised to eat or wear, nor does it countenance whole destruction of hogs, cattle or milk.

6. To pay the veterans of our wars what we owe them and to care for their disabled.

7. Education and training for all children to be equal in opportunity in all schools, colleges, universities, and other institutions for training in the professions and vocations of life; to be regulated on the capacity of children to learn, and not on the ability of parents to pay the costs. Training for life's work to be as much universal and thorough for all walks in life as has been the training in the arts of killing.

8. The raising of revenues and taxes for the support of this program to come from the reduction of swollen fortunes from the top, as well as for the support of public works to give employment whenever there may be any slackening necessary in private enterprise.

Father Charles E. Coughlin, "A Third Party" (1936)

Father Charles E. Couglin was a Roman Catholic priest and radio host from Detroit whose radio program was heard by between 30 and 45 million people. With rhetoric bordering on the fascist, Coughlin denounced Jews, communists, and the Roosevelt administration. This document is from a Coughlin speech given in 1936 entitled "A Third Party." The speech advocated support of the Union Party, a coalition of Townsendites, Coughlinites, and the remnants of Huey Long's movement.*

By 1932 a new era of production had come into full bloom. It was represented by the motor car, the tractor and power lathe, which enables the laborer to produce wealth ten times more rapidly than was possible for his ancestors. Within the short expanse of 150 years the problem of production had been solved, due to the ingenuity of men like Arkwright and his loom, Fulton and his steam engine, and Edison and his dynamo. These and a thousand other benefactors of mankind made it possible for the teeming

---

* From Christopher Hollis, "Fr. Coughlin, A Third Party," *London Tablet*, 9 September 1936.

millions of people throughout the world to transfer speedily the raw materials into the thousand necessities and conveniences which fall under the common name of wealth.

Thus, with the advent of our scientific era, with its far-flung fields, its spacious factories, its humming motors, its thundering locomotives, its highly trained mechanics, it is inconceivable how such a thing as a so-called depression should blight the lives of an entire nation when there was a plenitude of everything surrounding us, only to be withheld from us because the so-called leaders of high finance persisted in clinging to an outworn theory of privately issued money, the medium through which wealth is distributed.

I challenged this private control and creation of money because it was alien to our Constitution, which says "Congress shall have the right to coin and regulate the value of money." I challenged this system of permitting a small group of private citizens to create money and credit out of nothing, to issue it into circulation through loans and to demand that borrowers repay them with money which represented real goods, real labor and real service. I advocated that it be replaced by the American system— namely, that the creation and control of money and credit are the rights of the people through their democratic government. . . .

No man in modern times received such plaudits from the poor as did Franklin Roosevelt when he promised to drive the money changers from the temple—the money changers who had clipped the coins of wages, who had manufactured spurious money and who had brought proud America to her knees.

March 4, 1933! I shall never forget the inaugural address, which seemed to re-echo the very words of Christ Himself as He actually drove the money changers from the temple.

The thrill that was mine was yours. Through dim clouds of the depression this man Roosevelt was, as it were, a new savior of his people! . . .

Such were our hopes in the springtime of 1933.

My friends, what have we witnessed as the finger of time turned the pages of the calendar? Nineteen hundred and thirty-three and the National Recovery Act which multiplied profits for the monopolists; 1934 and the AAA which raised the price of foodstuffs by throwing back God's best gifts into His face; 1935 and the Banking Act which rewarded the exploiters of the poor, the Federal Reserve bankers and their associates, by handing over to them the temple from which they were to have been cast! . . .

Alas! The temple still remains the private property of the money changers. The golden key has been handed over to them for safekeeping—the key which now is fashioned in the shape of a double cross.

Mrs. Henry Weddington, Letter to President Roosevelt (1938)

Although prominent African Americans, including Mary McLeon Bethune, the director of Negro activities at the National Youth Administration, found a sometimes-sympathetic ear in Franklin Roosevelt, African Americans were routinely discriminated against in federal New Deal programs, which supported segregation and discriminated against blacks. As Mrs. Weddington describes, African Americans were often the poorest of the poor, and discrimination and outright racism made the depression even more difficult for them.*

Dear President Roosevelt:

I really don't know exactly how to begin this letter to you. Perhaps I should first tell you who I am. I am a young married woman. I am a Negro. . . . I believe that you are familiar with the labor situation among the Negroes, but I want you to know how I and many of us feel about it and what we expect of you.

My husband is working for the W.P.A. doing skilled labor. Before he started on this we were on relief for three months. We were three months trying to get relief. While trying to obtain relief I lost my unborn child. I believe if I had sufficient food this would not have happened. My husband was perfectly willing to work but could not find it. Now I am pregnant again. He is working at Tilden Tech. School where there are more white than colored. Every month more than one hundred persons are given private employment and not one of them are colored. It isn't that the colored men are not as skilled as the white, it is the fact that they are black and therefore must not get ahead.

We are citizens just as much or more than the majority of this country. . . . We are just as intelligent as they. This is supposed to be a free country regardless of color, creed or race but still we are slaves. . . . Won't you help us? I'm sure you can. I admire you and have very much confidence in you. I believe you are a real Christian and non-prejudiced. I have never doubted that you would be elected again. I believe you can and must do something about the labor conditions of the Negro.

Why must our men fight and die for their country when it won't even given them a job that they are fitted for? They would much rather fight and die for their families or race. Before it is over many of them might. We did not ask to be brought here as slaves, nor did we ask to be born black. We are real citizens of this land and must and will be

---

* Reprinted from *Black Women in White America*, ed. Gerda Lerner (New York: Pantheon, 1972), 300–302.

recognized as such! . . . If you are a real Christian you can not stand by and let these conditions exist.

My husband is young, intelligent and very depressed over this situation. We want to live, not merely exist from day to day, but to live as you or any human being desires to do. We want our unborn children to have an equal chance as the white. We don't want them to suffer as we are doing now because of race prejudice. My husband is 22 and I am 18 years of age. We want to own just a comfortable home by the time he reaches his early thirties. Is that asking too much? But how can we do that when the $26 he makes every two weeks don't hardly last the two weeks it should. I can manage money rather well but still we don't have the sufficient amount of food or clothes to keep us warm. . . . I would appreciate it very much if you would give this letter some consideration and give me an answer. I realize that you are a very busy person and have many problems but please give this problem a little thought also.

I will close thanking you in advance.

Sincerely and hopefully yours

Mrs. Henry Weddington

Studs Terkel, from *Hard Times* (1986)

This selection is taken from Studs Terkel's collection of oral histories of people who experienced the Great Depression. The first interview is with William Benton, who began the advertising agency of Benton & Bowles with his friend Chester Bowles in 1929. Benton went on to become a United States senator from Connecticut, assistant secretary of state, vice president of the University of Chicago, publisher of the *Encyclopedia Britannica*, governor of Connecticut, and American ambassador to India. The next interview is with Clifford Burke, a black man who, when Terkel interviewed him, was living on a pension. During the depression, he worked on and off as a teamster in a lumberyard and also made money hustling pool. It was a point of pride that he never applied for PWA or WPA.[*]

---

[*] From Studs Terkel *Hard Times* (New York: Pantheon, 1986).

William Benton, "In all catastrophes, there is the potential of benefit."

I left Chicago in June of '29, just a few months before the Crash. Chester Bowles and I started in business with seventeen hundred square feet, just the two of us and a couple of girls. July 15, 1929 this was the very day of the all-time peak on the stock market.

As I solicited business, my chart was kind of a cross. The left-hand line started at the top corner and ended in the bottom right-hand corner. That was the stock market index. The other line was Benton & Bowles. It started at the bottom left-hand corner and ended in the top right-hand corner. A cross. As the stock market plummeted into oblivion, Benton & Bowles went up into stardom. When I sold the agency in 1935, it was the single biggest office in the world. And the most profitable office.

My friend, Beardsley Ruml, was advocate of the theory: progress through catastrophe. In all catastrophes, there is the potential of benefit. I benefited out of the Depression. Others did, too. I suppose the people who sold red ink, red pencils, and red crayons benefited.

I was only twenty-nine, and Bowles was only twenty-eight. When things are prosperous, big clients are not likely to listen to young men or to new ideas. In 1929, most of your Wall Street manipulators called it The New Era. They felt it was the start of a perpetual boom that would carry us on and on forever to new plateaus. . . .

Benton & Bowles plunged into radio in a big way for our clients.

We didn't know the Depression was going on. Except that our clients' products were plummeting, and they were willing to talk to us about new ideas. They wouldn't have let us in the door if times were good. So the Depression benefited me. My income doubled every year. When I left Benton & Bowles, it must have been close to half a million dollars. That's the kind of money great motion picture stars weren't earning. That was 1935. The Depression just passed me right over.

Clifford Burke, "The Negro was born in depression."

The Negro was born in depression. It didn't mean too much to him. The Great American Depression, as you call it. The best he could be is a janitor or a porter or shoeshine boy. It only became official when it hit the white man. If you can tell me the difference between the depression today and the Depression of 1932 for a black man, I'd like to know it. Now, it's worse, because of the prices. Know the rents they're payin' out here? I hate to tell ya.

We had one big advantage. Our wives, they could go to the store and get a bag of beans or a sack of flour and a piece of fat meat, and they could cook this. And we could eat it. Steak? A steak would kick in my stomach like a mule in a tin stable. Now you take the white fella, he couldn't do this. His wife would tell him: Look, if you can't do any better than this, I'm gonna leave you. I seen it happen. He couldn't stand bringing home beans instead of steak and capon. And he couldn't stand the idea of going on relief like a Negro.

You take a fella had a job paying him $60, and here I am making $25. If I go home taking beans to my wife, we'll eat it. It isn't exactly what we want, but we'll eat it. The white man that's been making big money, he's taking beans home, his wife'll say: Get out. [Laughs.]

Why did these big wheels kill themselves? They weren't able to live up to the standards they were accustomed to, and they got ashamed in front of their women. You see, you can tell anybody a lie, and he'll agree with you. But you start layin' down the facts of real life, he won't accept it. The American white man has been superior so long, he can't figure out why he should come down.

I remember a friend of mine, he didn't know he was a Negro. I mean he acted like he never knew it. He got tied downtown with some stock. He blew about twenty thousand. He came home and drank a bottle of poison. A bottle of iodine or something like that. It was a rarity to hear a Negro killing himself over a financial situation. He might have killed himself over some woman. Or getting in a fight. But when it came to the financial end of it, there were so few who had anything. [Laughs.]

25

Peace and War

World War II catapulted the United States into the international arena after several decades of relative isolation. When the war began in 1939, America was forced to rethink its global responsibilities and relationships and narrow its comfortable distance from world events. Rumors that the Germans were building an atomic bomb added to the pressure to act. Franklin Roosevelt, restrained by the neutrality acts and popular isolationism and pacifism, was not able to do very much to aid the British or the French.

However, by January 1941, when Roosevelt delivered his State of the Union address after winning reelection for an unprecedented third term, war seemed imminent. In his address (reprinted here) Roosevelt warned the nation of the threat posed by fascism in Germany, Italy, and Japan. He also proposed his Lend-Lease program, designed to circumvent the neutrality acts, through which the United States would "lend" munitions to England without expecting payment in return. Lend-Lease passed Congress, in March, and American involvement in the war escalated until we formally entered the war following the attack on Pearl Harbor in December of 1941.

On the heels of the depression's upheavals, World War II brought further dramatic changes to American society. Foremost among these was that a critical shortage in the labor supply for war production allowed American women to enter the workforce in unprecedented numbers; by the end of the war, nineteen million women had gone to work outside the home, many at jobs that had been traditionally closed to them. Two interviews included in this chapter describe the experiences of some of these women, who were collectively nicknamed "Rosie the Riviters" after a popular song.

While American women, and to a lesser extent blacks, made significant gains in the 1940s, no group in American society suffered more from World War II than Japanese Americans. The American government, acting on racial hatred and irrational rumors, interned over 110,000 Japanese Americans—most of whom were American citizens—in "relocation centers" in the American West. Japanese Americans lost their homes, property, and businesses and were humiliated and ill-treated in the camps. The selection here from an interview with Ben Yorita, who was confined to one of these concentration camps, describes some of the indignities and injustices of his internment.

Study Questions

1. Why did Einstein's letter spur President Roosevelt into action? Why might Einstein have regretted sending the letter?

2. Compare the Four Freedoms speech to Wilson's Fourteen Points. Was Roosevelt as idealistic as Wilson? What were Roosevelt's long-term objectives?

3. Did American women benefit from World War II? How did women's traditional roles change during the war? Why did the women whose stories are included in this chapter go to work?

4. Many of the interviews in this chapter were collected in the 1970s and 1980s. How might the subject's memories have been clouded over the years or influenced by the passage of time? See in particular the last paragraph of "A Woman Remembers the War" and the first paragraph of Ben Yorita's account.

5. The women whose wartime experiences are recounted in this chapter both worked before the war. Was this unusual? Might this have influenced their decision to work in defense plants? If so, how? How might the kind of work they did before the war have an impact on how they regarded their wartime jobs?

6. Does Ben Yorita express bitterness for what happened to him during the war? How might the evacuation have broken down the culture, families, and traditions of the Japanese American community?

Albert Einstein, Letter to President Roosevelt (1939)

This letter from Albert Einstein warned Franklin Roosevelt that German researchers were close to making an atomic bomb. Inspired by Einstein (and his fellow scientists), Roosevelt organized a secret project (known later as the Manhattan project), to ensure that the United States had a bomb before Germany. In later life, Albert Einstein, committed to peace, regretted sending this letter.[*]

---

[*] Reprinted from Otton Nathan and Heinz Noren, eds. *Einstein on Peace* (New York: Simon and Schuster, 1960), 290.

Albert Einstein
Old Grove Rd.
Nassau Point
Peconic, Long Island

August 2nd, 1939

F. D. Roosevelt,
President of the United States,
White House
Washington, D. C.

Sir:

Some recent work by E. Fermi and L. Szilard, which has been communicated to me in manuscript, leads me to expect that the element uranium may be turned into a new and important source of energy in the immediate future. Certain aspects of the situation which has arisen seem to call for watchfulness and, if necessary, quick action on the part of the Administration. I believe therefore that it is my duty to bring to your attention the following facts and recommendations:

In the course of the last four months it has been made probable—through the work of Joliot in France as well as Fermi and Szilard in America—that it may become possible to set up a nuclear chain reaction in a large mass of uranium, by which vast amount of power and large quantities of new radium-like elements would be generated. Now it appears almost certain that this could be achieved in the immediate future.

This new phenomenon would also lead to the construction of bombs, and it is conceivable—though much less certain—that extremely powerful bombs of a new type may thus be constructed. A single bomb of this type, carried by boat and exploded in a port, might very well destroy the whole port together with some of the surrounding territory. However, such bombs might very well prove to be too heavy for transportation by air.

The United States has only very poor ores of uranium in moderate quantities. There is some good ore in Canada and the former Czechoslovakia, while the most important source of uranium is the Belgian Congo.

In view of this situation you may think it desirable to have some permanent contact maintained between the Administration and the group of physicists working on chain reactions in America. One possible way of achieving this might be for you to entrust with this task a person who has your confidence and who could perhaps serve in an inofficial capacity. His task might comprise the following:

a) to approach Government Departments, keep them informed of the further development, and put forward recommendations for Government action, giving particular attention to the problem of securing a supply of uranium ore for the United States:

b) to speed up the experimental work, which is at present being carried on within the limits of the budgets of University laboratories, by providing funds, if such funds be required, through his contacts with private persons who are willing to make contributions for this cause, and perhaps also by obtaining the co-operation of industrial laboratories which have the necessary equipment.

I understand that Germany has actually stopped the sale of uranium from the Czechoslovakian mines which she has taken over. That she should have taken such early action might perhaps be understood on the ground that the son of the German Under-Secretary of State, von Weizsacker, is attached to the Kaiser-Wilhelm-Institut in Berlin where some of the American work on uranium is now being repeated.

Yours very truly,

[signed] Albert Einstein

Franklin D. Roosevelt, The Four Freedoms (1941)

This selection from Roosevelt's annual address to Congress is his argument for American involvement in the war, tied to his Lend-Lease act which provided military supplies for England. Many Americans, including the famous aviator Charles Lindbergh, were isolationist and pacifist and believed intervention would be futile and that the United States should remain uninvolved in European wars.*

Armed defense of democratic existence is now being gallantly waged in four continents. If that defense fails, all the population and all the resources of Europe, Asia, Africa and Australasia will be dominated by the conquerors. The total of those populations and their resources . . . greatly exceeds the sum total of the population and the resources of the whole of the Western Hemisphere—many times over.

In times like these it is immature—and incidentally untrue—for anybody to brag that an unprepared America, single-handed, and with one hand tied behind its back, can hold off the whole world.

* From Franklin D. Roosevelt, "Annual Message to Congress," January 6, 1941, *Congressional Record*, 77th Cong. 1st sess., LXXXVII, pt. I, 45–47.

No realistic American can expect from a dictator's peace international generosity, or return of true independence, or world disarmament, or freedom of expression, or freedom of religion—or even good business. . . .

The need of the moment is that our actions and our policy should be devoted primarily—almost exclusively—to meeting this foreign peril. For all our domestic problems are now a part of the great emergency.

Just as our national policy in internal affairs has been based upon a decent respect for the rights and the dignity of all our fellow men within our gates, so our national policy in foreign affairs has been based on a decent respect for the rights and dignity of all nations, large and small. And the justice of morality must and will win in the end.

Our national policy is this:

First, by an impressive expression of the public will and without regard to partisanship, we are committed to all-inclusive national defense.

Second, by an impressive expression of the public will and without regard to partisanship, we are committed to full support of all those resolute peoples, everywhere, who are resisting aggression and are thereby keeping war away from our hemisphere. By this support, we express our determination that the democratic cause shall prevail, and we strengthen the defense and security of our own nation.

Third, by an impressive expression of the public will and without regard to partisanship, we are committed to the proposition that principles of morality and considerations for our own security will never permit us to acquiesce in a peace dictated by aggressors and sponsored by appeasers. We know that enduring peace cannot be bought at the cost of other people's freedom. . . .

I also ask this Congress for authority and for funds sufficient to manufacture additional munitions and war supplies of many kinds, to be turned over to those nations which are now in actual war with aggressor nations.

Our most useful and immediate role is to act as an arsenal for them as well as for ourselves. They do not need man power. They do need billions of dollars' worth of the weapons of defense. . . .

Let us say to the democracies, "We Americans are vitally concerned in your defense of freedom. We are putting forth our energies, our resources, and our organizing powers to give you the strength to regain and maintain a free world. We shall send you, in ever-increasing numbers, ships, planes, tanks, guns. This is our purpose and our pledge." . . .

There is nothing mysterious about the foundations of a healthy and strong democracy. The basic things expected by our people of their political and economic systems are simple.

They are:

> Equality of opportunity for youth and for others.
> Jobs for those who can work.
> Security for those who need it.
> The ending of special privilege for the few.
> The preservation of civil liberties for all.
> The enjoyment of the fruits of scientific progress in a wider and constantly rising standard of living.

These are the simple and basic things that must never be lost sight of in the turmoil and unbelievable complexity of our modern world. The inner and abiding strength of our economic and political systems is dependent upon the degree to which they fulfill these expectations. . . .

In the future days, which we seek to make secure, we look forward to a world founded upon four essential human freedoms.

The first is freedom of speech and expression everywhere in the world.

The second is freedom of every person to worship God in his own way everywhere in the world.

The third is freedom from want, which, translated into world terms, means economic understandings which will secure to every nation a healthy peacetime life for its inhabitants everywhere in the world.

The fourth is freedom from fear—which, translated into world terms, means a world-wide reduction of armaments to such a point and in such a thorough fashion that no nation will be in a position to commit an act of physical aggression against any neighbor—anywhere in the world.

That is no vision of a distant millennium. It is a definite basis for a kind of world attainable in our own time and generation. That kind of world is the very antithesis of the so-called new order of tyranny which the dictators seek to create with the crash of a bomb.

To that new order we oppose the greater conception—the moral order. A good society is able to face schemes of world domination and foreign revolutions alike without fear.

Since the beginning of our American history we have been engaged in change—in a perpetual peaceful revolution—a revolution which goes on steadily, quietly adjusting itself to changing conditions—without the concentration camp or the quicklime in the ditch. The world order which we seek is the cooperation of free countries, working together in a friendly, civilized society.

Fanny Christina Hill, "The Black Woman Has Worked All of Her Life" (1979)

This interview with Fanny Christina Hill is taken from a series of interviews performed by Sherna Berger Gluck in 1979. Hill was born in Texas in 1918; her father was a farmer and her mother worked as a domestic servant. Like many African Americans, Gluck migrated from the South to California, where she worked as a live-in domestic, returning to Texas for a short time to get married. After her husband went into the service, Hill got a job at North American Aviation. Unlike many women who were fired after

the war, Hill continued to work at North American (which later
became Rockwell International) until her retirement.*

My father was supposed to have been a farmer, but he just got by by doing a little bit
of nothing. Some men are like that. Mama went to work and supported us the best she
could. There were times we wouldn't have anything to eat if Mama hadn't gone to
work. That's why you talk about women liberation and women go out to work? The
black woman has worked all of her life and she really was the first one to go out to
work and know how to make ends meet, because it was forced on her. . . .

Negroes rented rooms quite a bit. It was a wonderful thing, 'cause it made it
possible for you to come and stay without a problem. My sister and I was rooming
with this lady and we was paying six dollars a week, which was good money, because
she was renting the house for only twenty-six dollars a month. She had another girl
living on the back porch and she was charging her three dollars. So you get the idea.

We were accustomed to shacking up with each other. We had to live like that
because that was the only way to survive. Negroes, as a rule, are accustomed to a lot of
people around. They have lived like that from slavery time on. We figured out how to
get along with each other. . . .

But they had to fight [to get jobs at North American]. They fought hand, tooth,
and nail to get in there. And the first five or six Negroes who went in there, they were
well educated, but they started them off as janitors. After they once got their foot in the
door and was there for three months—you work for three months before they say
you're hired—then they had to start fighting all over again to get off of that broom and
get something decent. And some of them did.

But they'd always give that Negro man the worst part of everything. See, the jobs
have already been tested and tried out before they ever get into the department, and
they know what's good about them and what's bad about them. They always managed
to give the worst one to the Negro. The only reason why the women fared better was
they just couldn't quite give the woman as tough a job that they gave the men. But
sometimes they did.

I can't exactly tell you what a tough job would be, but it's just like putting that
caster on that little stand there. Let's face it, now you know that's light and you can lift
that real easy, but there are other jobs twice as heavy as that. See, the larger the hole is,
the thicker the drill, which would take you longer. So you know that's a tougher job.
Okay, so they'd have the Negro doing that tough drilling. But when they got to the
place where they figured out to get a drill press to drill with—which would be easier—
they gave it to a white person. So they just practiced that and still do, right down to this
day. I just don't know if it will ever get straight.

* From Interview with Fanny Christina Hill from Sherna Berger Gluck, *Rosie the Riveter Revisited* (New
York: Macmillan, 1987). Excerpted with permission of Twayne Publishers, an imprint of Macmillan
Publishing Company. Copyright © 1987 by Sherna Berger Gluck.

There were some departments, they didn't even allow a black person to walk through there let alone work in there. Some of the white people did not want to work with the Negro.

A Woman Remembers the War (1984)

This selection is taken from a collection of interviews by Mark Harris, Franklin Mitchell, and Steven Schecter published as *The Homefront: America During World War II* in 1984. It describes the wartime experiences of a white woman working in war industries in California.*

When the war started I was twenty-six, unmarried, and working as a cosmetics clerk in a drugstore in Los Angeles. I was running the whole department, handling the inventory and all that. It seemed asinine, though, to be selling lipstick when the country was at war. I felt that I was capable of doing something more than that toward the war effort.

There was also a big difference between my salary and those in defense work. I was making something like twenty-two, twenty-four dollars a week in the drugstore. You could earn a much greater amount of money for your labor in defense plants. Also it interested me. There was a certain curiosity about meeting that kind of challenge, and here was an opportunity to do that, for there were more and more openings for women.

So I went to two or three plants and took their tests. And they all told me I had absolutely no mechanical ability. I said, "I don't believe that." So I went to another plant, A.D.E.I. I was interviewed and got the job. This particular plant made the hydraulic-valve system for the B-17. And where did they put women? In the burr room. You sat at a workbench, which was essentially like a picnic table, with a bunch of other women, and you worked grinding and sanding machine parts to make them smooth. That's what you did all day long. It was very mechanical and it was very boring. There were about thirty women in the burr room, and it was like being in a beauty shop every day. I couldn't stand the inane talk. So when they asked me if I would like to work someplace else in the shop, I said I very much would.

They started training me. I went to a blueprint class and learned how to use a micrometer and how to draw tools out of the tool crib and everything else. Then one day they said, "Okay, how would you like to go into the machine shop?"

I said, "Terrific."

And they said, "Now, Adele, it's going to be a real challenge, because you'll be the only woman in the machine shop." I thought to myself, well, that's going to be fun, all those guys and Adele in the machine shop. So the foreman took me over there. It was a big room, with a high ceiling and fluorescent lights, and it was very noisy. I walked in there, in my overalls, and suddenly all the machines stopped and every guy in the shop just turned around and looked at me. It took, I think, two weeks before anyone even talked to me. The discrimination was indescribable. They wanted to kill me.

My attitude was, "Okay, you bastards, I'm going to prove to you I can do anything you can do, and maybe better than some of you." And that's exactly the way it turned out. I used to do the rework on the pieces that the guy on the shift before me had screwed up. I finally got assigned to nothing but rework.

Later they taught me to run an automatic screwing machine. It's a big mother, and it took a lot of strength just to throw that thing into gear. They probably thought I wasn't going to be able to do it. But I was determined to succeed. As a matter of fact, I developed the most fantastic biceps from throwing that machine into gear. Even today I still have a little of that muscle left.

Anyway, eventually some of the men became very friendly, particularly the older ones, the ones in their late forties or fifties. They were journeymen tool and die makers and were so skilled that they could work anywhere at very high salaries. They were sort of fatherly, protective. They weren't threatened by me. The younger men, I think, were.

Our plant was an open shop, and the International Association of Machinists was trying to unionize the workers. I joined them and worked to try to get the union in the plant. I proselytized for the union during lunch hour, and I had a big altercation with the management over that. The employers and my lead man and foreman called me into the office and said, "We have a right to fire you."

I said, "on what basis? I work as well or better than anybody else in the shop except the journeymen."

They said, "No, not because of that. Because you're talking for the union on company property. You're not allowed to do that."

I said, "Well, that's just too bad, because I can't get off the grounds here. You won't allow us to leave the grounds during lunch hour. And you don't pay me for my lunch hour, so that time doesn't belong to you, so you can't tell me what to do." And they backed down.

I had one experience at the plant that really made me work for the union. One day while I was burring I had an accident and ripped some cartilage out of my hand. It wasn't serious, but it looked kind of messy. They had to take me over to the industrial hospital to get my hand sutured. I came back and couldn't work for a day or two because my hand was all bandaged. It wasn't serious, but it was awkward. When I got my paycheck, I saw that they had docked me for time that I was in the industrial hospital. When I saw that I was really mad.

It's ironic that when the union finally got into the plant, they had me transferred out. They were anxious to get rid of me because after we got them in I went to a few meetings and complained about it being a Jim Crow union. So they arranged for me to have a higher rating instead of a worker's rating. This allowed me to make twenty-five cents an hour more, and I got transferred to another plant. By this time I was married. When I became pregnant I worked for about three months more, then I quit.

For me defense work was the beginning of my emancipation as a woman. For the first time in my life I found out that I could do something with my hands besides bake a pie. I found out that I had manual dexterity and the mentality to read blueprints and gauges, and to be inquisitive enough about things to develop skills other than the conventional roles that women had at that time. I had the consciousness-raising experience of being the only woman in this machine shop and having the mantle of challenge laid down by the men, which stimulated my competitiveness and forced me to prove myself. This, plus working in the union, gave me a lot of self-confidence.

Ben Yorita, Memories of the Internment Camp (1981)

This selection from an interview in the 1980s with a Japanese-American man describes his evacuation to a concentration camp in the West. Yorita, an American citizen, and his family lost much of their property during the internment. Japanese Americans were not compensated for their losses until 1988.[*]

Students weren't as aware of national politics then as they are now, and Japanese Americans were actually apolitical then. Our parents couldn't vote, so we simply weren't interested in politics because there was nothing we could do about it if we were.

There were two reasons we were living in the ghettos: Birds of a feather flock together and we had all the traditional aspects of Japanese life—Japanese restaurants, baths, and so forth; and discrimination forced us together. The dominant society prevented us from going elsewhere.

Right after Pearl Harbor we had no idea what was going to happen, but toward the end of December we started hearing rumors and talk of the evacuation started. We could tell from what we read in the newspapers and the propaganda they were printing—guys like Henry McLemore, who said he hated all Japs and that we should be rounded up, gave us the idea of how strong feelings were against us. So we were expecting something and the evacuation was no great surprise.

. . . Once the evacuation was decided, we were told we had about a month to get rid of our property or do whatever we wanted to do with it. That was a rough time for my brother, who was running a print shop my parents owned. We were still in debt on

[*] Excerpted from Archie Satterfield, *The Home Front: An Oral History of the War Years in America* (Chicago: Playboy Press, 1981), 330–338. Copyright © 1981 by Archie Satterfield. Used by permission.

it and we didn't know what to do with all the equipment. . . . We sold the equipment through newspaper classified ads: "Evacuating: Household goods for sale." Second-hand dealers and everybody else came in and bought our refrigerator, the piano, and I had a whole bunch of books I sold for $5, which was one of my personal losses. We had to sell our car, and the whole thing was very sad. By the way it was the first time we had ever had a refrigerator and it had to be sold after only a few months.

We could take only what we could carry, and most of us were carrying two suitcases or duffel bags. The rest of our stuff that we couldn't sell was stored in the Buddhist church my mother belonged to. When we came back, thieves had broken in and stolen almost everything of value from the church.

. . . They took all of us down to the Puyallup fairgrounds, Camp Harmony, and everything had been thrown together in haste. They had converted some of the display and exhibit areas into rooms and had put up some barracks on the parking lot. . . . .

They had also built barbed-wire fences around the camp with a tower on each corner with military personnel and machine guns, rifles, and searchlights. It was terrifying because we didn't know what was going to happen to us. We didn't know where we were going and we were just doing what we were told. No questions asked. If you get an order, you go ahead and do it.

. . . There was no fraternization, no contact with the military or any Caucasian except when we were processed into the camp. . . .

There was no privacy whatsoever in the latrines and showers, and it was humiliating for the women because they were much more modest then than today. It wasn't so bad for the men because they were accustomed to open latrines and showers. . . .

From Camp Harmony on, the family structure was broken down. Children ran everywhere they wanted to in the camp, and parents lost their authority. We could eat in any mess hall we wanted, and kids began ignoring their parents and wandering wherever they pleased.

Eventually they boarded us on army trucks and took us to trains to be transported to the camps inland. We had been in Camp Harmony from May until September. . . .

When we got to Twin Falls, we were loaded onto trucks again, and we looked around and all we could see was that vast desert with nothing but sagebrush. When the trucks started rolling, it was dusty, and the camp itself wasn't completed yet. The barracks had been built and the kitchen facilities were there, but the laundry room, showers, and latrines were not finished. They had taken a bulldozer in the good old American style and leveled the terrain and then built the camp. When the wind blew, it was dusty and we had to wear face masks to go to the dining hall. When winter came and it rained, the dust turned into gumbo mud. Until the latrines were finished, we had to use outhouses.

The administrators were civilians and they tried to organize us into a chain of command to make the camp function. Each block of barracks was told to appoint a representative, who were called block managers. Of course we called them the Blockheads.

When winter came, it was very cold and I began withdrawing my savings to buy clothes because we had none that was suitable for that climate. Montgomery Ward and

Sears Roebuck did a landslide business from the camps because we ordered our shoes and warm clothing from them. The people who didn't have savings suffered quite a bit until the camp distributed navy pea coats. Then everybody in camp was wearing oversize pea coats because we were such small people. Other than army blankets, I don't remember any other clothing issues.

The barracks were just single-wall construction and the only insulation was tar paper nailed on the outside, and they never were improved. The larger rooms had potbellied stoves, and we all slept on army cots. Only the people over sixty years old were able to get metal cots, which had a bit more spring to them than the army cots, which were just stationary hammocks.

These camps were technically relocation centers and there was no effort to hold us in them, but they didn't try actively to relocate us until much later. On my own initiative I tried to get out as soon as I could, and started writing letters to friends around the country. I found a friend in Salt Lake City who agreed to sponsor me for room and board, and he got his boss to agree to hire me. I got out in May 1943, which was earlier than most. In fact, I was one of the first to leave Minidoka.

. . . I got on the bus with my suitcase, all by myself, my first time in the outside world, and paid my fare and began looking for a seat, then this old guy said: "Hey, Tokyo, sit next to me."

I thought, Oh, my God, Tokyo! I sat next to him and he was a friendly old guy who meant well.

26

The Cold War at Home and Abroad

At the end of World War II, only two nations possessed the military and economic power to assume positions of leadership. For both the United States and the Soviet Union, the war colored their actions in the period immediately following. Neither nation wanted to suffer the horrors of war again. The Soviets began to surround themselves with a barrier of buffer states—Czechoslovakia, North Korea, and East Germany were among the first—in order to protect themselves, while the United States, responding aggressively to the Soviets' expansion, adopted a policy of "containment" (as articulated in George Kennan's famous telegram from the U.S. embassy in Moscow).

Each nation perceived the other as a threat to world peace and its own national security. By 1947, with most of Eastern Europe under the control of the communists, President Harry Truman had come to believe that an "Iron Curtain," as Winston Churchill described it, had descended on Eastern Europe and would soon also move southward. In Turkey and Greece, British-supported governments appeared to be falling under Soviet pressure as their British military and economic support dried up. Communists fought against monarchists in Greece and the Soviets vied for control of the passage from the Black Sea to the Mediterranean in Turkey. In response Truman argued that America should step in where Britain had left off, and furthermore act to stem the spread of communism and Soviet power anywhere else in the world. This so-called Truman Doctrine would exert enormous influence on American foreign policy for many years to come.

The Truman Doctrine was not the only policy through which the United States sought to counter Soviet global influence. Perhaps the most successful American program of the postwar period was formulated by Secretary of State George Marshall. The economic problems of Western Europe worried Marshall; like Truman, he feared that economic instability would lead to political turmoil and provide new political opportunities for the communists. Thus the rapid economic recovery of Europe was crucial, and the Marshall Plan was constructed to provide massive economic assistance to Western Europe. Part of its ingenuity was that the plan was designed not only to fuel European recovery but also to create markets for American goods. Approved by

Congress, the Marshall Plan sent $15 billion in economic assistance to American allies in Europe.

The Cold War pervaded all aspects of American life but was particularly trenchant in domestic politics. Aggressive anticommunist rhetoric fostered paranoias and suspicions on anyone who was not "red, white, and blue." In political debates, Republicans were quick to accuse the Democrats of being "soft on communism." Some even believed that Roosevelt had given Eastern Europe to the Soviet Union at the Yalta conference. And in 1947, Truman established the Federal Employee Loyalty probe—an investigation into the patriotism of all federal employees.

In this climate of suspicion and fear the House on Un-American Activities Committee began a series of hearings focusing on the loyalty of the entertainment community. Over a four-year period, scores of Hollywood writers, directors, actors and actresses were asked to testify about the infiltration of communists into the industry. Some, most notably the Hollywood Ten, refused to testify and were sent to prison. For years afterward, suspected communists were virtually unable to work in the film community. The selection included here, from the testimony of future president Ronald Reagan, outlines the Screen Actors Guild's cooperation with HUAC in eradicating suspected communists from the film community and illuminates some of the tactics of the House committee.

The HUAC hearings encouraged Americans to see communist influence and conspiracy in myriad institutions. This paranoia was intensified in the red scare led by Senator Joseph R. McCarthy. In his speeches and in hearings he led from 1950 to 1954, McCarthy fanned the flames of national fear, by inspecting libraries, subpoenaing witnesses, and in the end, attacking army leaders in a fervent effort to root out communists. The selection included here is from the very beginning of McCarthy's short-lived fame; it is the first instance in which he hints at the presence of communists in the State Department.

Study Questions

1. How did the Truman Doctrine define American foreign policy and America's role in world affairs? How did Truman divide the world into good and evil?

2. What did Truman and Marshall consider the role of foreign aid in foreign policy?

3. Did Marshall and Truman exaggerate the threats to national security?

4. Why was Hollywood a target of the House Un-American Activities Committee?

5. How does McCarthy make his anticommunism seem populist in his Wheeling speech?

Harry S Truman, The Truman Doctrine (1947)

> World War II left Europe economically devastated and politically unstable. Early in 1947, it appeared that Turkey and Greece would fall under Soviet influence. In this famous speech, Truman outlines his support for a policy of aggressive containment of the Soviet Union not only in Turkey and Greece, but all over the world. In the words of his secretary of state, Dean Acheson, the Truman administration worried that "like apples in a barrel infected by one rotten one, the corruption of Greece would infect Iran and all of the east."*

At the present moment in world history nearly every nation must choose between alternative ways of life. The choice is too often not a free one.

One way of life is based upon the will of the majority, and is distinguished by free institutions, representative government, free elections, guaranties of individual liberty, freedom of speech and religion, and freedom from political oppression.

The second way of life is based upon the will of a minority forcibly imposed upon the majority. It relies upon terror and oppression, a controlled press and radio, fixed elections, and the suppression of personal freedoms.

I believe that it must be the policy of the United States to support free peoples who are resisting attempted subjugation by armed minorities or by outside pressures.

I believe that we must assist free peoples to work out their own destinies in their own way.

I believe that our help should be primarily through economic and financial aid, which is essential to economic stability and orderly political processes.

The world is not static, and the status quo is not sacred. But we cannot allow changes in the status quo in violation of the Charter of the United Nations by such methods as coercion, or by such subterfuges as political infiltration. In helping free and independent nations to maintain their freedom, the United States will be giving effect to the principles of the Charter of the United Nations. . . .

The seeds of totalitarian regimes are nurtured by misery and want. They spread and grow in the evil soil of poverty and strife. They reach their full growth when the hope of a people for a better life has died.

We must keep that hope alive.

The free peoples of the world look to us for support in maintaining their freedoms.

If we falter in our leadership, we may endanger the peace of the world—and we shall surely endanger the welfare of our own Nation.

---

* From Harry S Truman, "Speech, March 12, 1947," in *Public Papers of the Presidents, Harry S Truman, 1947* (Washington, D.C.: U.S. Government Printing Office, 1963), 176–180.

George Marshall, The Marshall Plan (1947)

In this speech, delivered at the Harvard University commencement in 1947, Secretary of State Marshall articulated a plan for American aid to Europe. The plan was designed to fill the power vacuum in Europe and to help Europe reconstruct itself after the devastation of war. Marshall even extended the promise of aid to the Soviet-dominated countries of Eastern Europe. The program was remarkably successful and by the early 1950s the Western European economy was much recovered.[*]

The truth of the matter is that Europe's requirements for the next three or four years of foreign food and other essential products—principally from America—are so much greater than her present ability to pay that she must have substantial additional help or face economic, social, and political deterioration of a very grave character. . . .

Aside from the demoralizing effect on the world at large and the possibilities of disturbances arising as a result of the desperation of the people concerned, the consequences of the economy of the United States should be apparent to all. It is logical that the United States should do whatever it is able to do to assist in the return of normal economic health in the world, without which there can be no political stability and no assured peace. Our policy is directed not against any country or doctrine but against hunger, poverty, desperation, and chaos. Its purpose should be the revival of a working economy in the world so as to permit the emergence of political and social conditions in which free institutions can exist.

Such assistance, I am convinced, must not be on a piecemeal basis as various crises develop. Any assistance that this Government may render in the future should provide a cure rather than a mere palliative. Any government that is willing to assist in the task of recovery will find full cooperation, I am sure, on the part of the United States Government. Any government which maneuvers to block the recovery of other countries cannot expect help from us. Furthermore, governments, political parties, or groups which seek to perpetuate human misery in order to profit there from politically or otherwise will encounter the opposition of the United States.

It is already evident that, before the United States Government can proceed much further in its efforts to alleviate the situation and help start the European world on its way to recovery, there must be some agreement among the countries of Europe as to the requirements of the situation and the part those countries themselves will take in order to give proper effect to whatever action might be undertaken by this Government.

---

[*] From George Marshall, Speech of June 5, 1947, *Department of State Bulletin* 16 (June 15, 1947), 1159–1160.

It would be neither fitting nor efficacious for this Government to undertake to draw up unilaterally a program designed to place Europe on its feet economically. This is the business of the Europeans. The initiative, I think, must come from Europe. The role of this country should consist of friendly aid in the drafting of a European program and of later support of such a program so far as it may be practical for us to do so. The program should be a joint one, agreed to by a number, if not all, European nations.

Ronald Reagan, Testimony Before the House Un-American Activities Committee (1947)

Ronald Reagan testified in front of the House Un-American Activities Committee in his capacity as President of the Screen Actors Guild. This selection reveals that he believed that there was a "subversive" element in Hollywood—although he is reluctant to name names. Other Hollywood stars, including Frank Sinatra, denounced the HUAC hearings. *

The Committee met at 10:30 A.M. [October 23, 1947], the Honorable J. Parnell Thomas (Chairman) presiding.

THE CHAIRMAN: The record will show that Mr. McDowell, Mr. Vail, Mr. Nixon, and Mr. Thomas are present. A Subcommittee is sitting.

Staff members present: Mr. Robert E. Stripling, Chief Investigator; Messrs. Louis J. Russell, H. A. Smith, and Robert B. Gatson, Investigators; and Mr. Benjamin Mandel, Director of Research.

MR. STRIPLING: When and where were you born, Mr. Reagan?

MR. REAGAN: Tampico, Illinois, February 6, 1911.

MR. STRIPLING: What is your present occupation?

MR. REAGAN: Motion-picture actor.

MR. STRIPLING: How long have you been engaged in that profession?

---

* From U.S. House Committee on Un-American Activities, *Hearing before the Committee on Un-American Activities*, 1947.

MR. REAGAN: Since June 1937, with a brief interlude of three and a half years—that at the time didn't seem very brief.

MR. STRIPLING: What period was that?

MR. REAGAN: That was during the late war.

MR. STRIPLING: What branch of the service were you in?

MR. REAGAN: Well, sir, I had been for several years in the Reserve as an officer in the United States Calvary, but I was assigned to the Air Corp.

MR. STRIPLING: Are you the president of the guild at the present time?

MR. REAGAN: Yes, sir. . . .

MR. STRIPLING: As a member of the board of directors, as president of the Screen Actors Guild, and as an active member, have you at any time observed or noted within the organization a clique of either Communists or Fascists who were attempting to exert influence or pressure on the guild?

MR. REAGAN: Well, sir, my testimony must be very similar to that of Mr. [George] Murphy and Mr. [Robert] Montgomery. There has been a small group within the Screen Actors Guild which has consistently opposed the policy of the guild board and officers of the guild, as evidenced by the vote on various issues. That small clique referred to has been suspected of more or less following the tactics that we associated with the Communist Party.

MR. STRIPLING: Would you refer to them as a disruptive influence within the guild?

MR. REAGAN: I would say that at times they have attempted to be a disruptive influence.

MR. STRIPLING: You have no knowledge yourself as to whether or not any of them are members of the Communist Party?

MR. REAGAN: No, sir, I have no investigative force, or anything, and I do not know.

MR. STRIPLING: Has it ever been reported to you that certain members of the guild were Communists?

MR. REAGAN: Yes, sir, I have heard different discussions and some of them tagged as Communists.

MR. STRIPLING: Would you say that this clique has attempted to dominate the guild?

MR. REAGAN: Well, sir, by attempting to put over their own particular views on various issues. . . .

MR. STRIPLING: Mr. Reagan, there has been testimony to the effect here that numerous Communist-front organizations have been set up in Hollywood. Have you ever been solicited to join any of those organizations or any organization which you consider to be a Communist-front organization?

MR. REAGAN: Well, sir, I have received literature from an organization called the Committee for a Far-Eastern Democratic Policy. I don't know whether it is Communist or not. I only know that I didn't like their views and as a result I didn't want to have anything to do with them. . . .

MR. STRIPLING: Would you say from your observation that this is typical of the tactics or strategy of the Communists, to solicit and use the names of prominent people to either raise money or gain support.

MR. REAGAN: I think it is in keeping with their tactics, yes, sir.

MR. STRIPLING: Do you think there is anything democratic about those tactics?

MR. REAGAN: I do not, sir.

MR. STRIPLING: Mr. Reagan, what is your feeling about what steps should be taken to rid the motion-picture industry of any Communist influences?

MR. REAGAN: Well, sir, ninety-nine percent of us are pretty well aware of what is going on, and I think, within the bounds of our democratic rights and never once stepping over the rights given us by democracy, we have done a pretty good job in our business of keeping those people's activities curtailed. After all, we must recognize them at present as a political party. On that basis we have exposed their lies when we came across them, we have opposed their propaganda, and I can certainly testify that in the case of the Screen Actors Guild we have been eminently successful in preventing them from, with their usual tactics, trying to run a majority of an organization with a well-organized minority. In opposing those people, the best thing to do is make democracy work. . . .

Sir, I detest, I abhor their philosophy, but I detest more than that their tactics, which are those of the fifth column, and are dishonest, but at the same time I never as a citizen want to see our country become urged, by either fear or resentment of this group that we ever compromise with any of our democratic principles through that fear or resentment. I still think that democracy can do it.

Joseph R. McCarthy, from Speech Delivered to the Women's Club of Wheeling, West Virginia (1950)

This speech, delivered in February 1950 and addressed to the Women's Club of Wheeling, West Virginia, gained Senator McCarthy national attention. Initially, McCarthy claimed he could identify 205 known Communists in the State Department; in this version of the speech, submitted into the *Congressional Record*, he has reduced the number to 57. McCarthy's speech attacks in particular the state department, then headed by Dean Acheson. Acheson was one of McCarthy's favorite victims, in part because of his relationship with Alger Hiss (a former State Department official later accused of spying for the Soviet Union and convicted of perjury). McCarthy later called Acheson and his predecessor, George Marshall (then secretary of defense), leaders or "executioners" in a "great conspiracy" directed by Moscow intended to "diminish the United States."*

Five years after a world war has been one, men's hearts should anticipate a long peace, and men's minds should be free from the heavy weight that comes from war. But this is not such a period—for this is not a period of peace. This is a time of the "cold war." This is a time when all the world is split into two vast, increasingly hostile armed camps. . . .

The reason why we find ourselves in a position of impotency is not because our only powerful potential enemy has sent men to invade our shores, but rather because of the traitorous actions of those who have been treated so well by this Nation. It has not been the less fortunate or members of minority groups who have been selling this Nation out, but rather those who have had all the benefits that the wealthiest nation on earth has to offer—the finest homes, the finest college education, and the finest jobs in Government.

This is glaringly true in the State Department. There the bright young men who are born with silver spoons in their mouths are the ones who have been the worst. . . . In my opinion, the State Department, which is one of the most important government departments, is thoroughly infested with Communists.

I have in my hand 57 cases of individuals who would appear to be either card carrying members or certainly loyal to the Communist Party, but who nevertheless are still helping to shape our foreign policy. . . .

---

* From Joseph McCarthy, Remarks, *Congressional Record,* 81st Congress, 1st sess, 1951, 6556–603.

As you know, very recently the Secretary of State proclaimed his loyalty to a man guilty of what has always been considered as the most abominable of all crimes—of being a traitor to the people who gave him a position of great trust. The Secretary of State in attempting to justify his continued devotion to the man who sold out the Christian world to the atheistic world, referred to Christ's Sermon on the Mount as a justification and reason therefor, and the reaction of the American people to this would have made the heart of Abraham Lincoln happy.

When this pompous diplomat in striped pants, with a phony British accent, proclaimed to the American people that Christ on the Mount endorsed communism, high treason, and a betrayal of a sacred trust, the blasphemy was so great that it awakened the dormant indignation of the American people.

He has lighted the spark which is resulting in a moral uprising and will end only when the whole sorry mess of twisted, warped thinkers are swept from the national scene so that we may have a new birth of national honesty and decency in government.

27

Liberty for All

African Americans entered the postwar era with expectations of an end to segregation and racial equality. The New Deal and the war had increased employment opportunities for African Americans; during the war millions of blacks moved north and west to cities like New York, Los Angeles, Detroit, and Chicago to work in wartime industries. They established roots, and friends and family often followed to take advantage of the jobs created by the expanding American economy. While racism still prevailed throughout the nation—Jim Crow still held fast in the South and *de facto* segregation and discrimination marked life in the North—social currents made increased opportunity and equality for African Americans inevitable.

In 1947, Jackie Robinson became the first African American to play major-league baseball and in 1948, President Harry Truman put an end to segregation in the armed services. The most significant event however, was the Supreme Court's landmark 1954 *Brown v. Board of Education* decision. Culminating a three-year legal struggle led by the NAACP, the Court's decision rejected segregated schools as "inherently unequal."

Until the 1950s, blacks' struggle for Civil Rights concentrated on challenging segregation's legal bases through the courts. In the 1950s, though, it became a more populist cause. The Civil Rights movement of the 1950s, characterized by boycotts, peaceful protests, and attempts to secure voting rights and put an end to segregation, began a new, more activist phase of the struggle for opportunity and equality. The Montgomery, Alabama, bus boycott precipitated by Rosa Parks traditionally marks the beginning of this phase of the Civil Rights era. It also marks the emergence of Martin Luther King, Jr., as the spokesperson and primary figurehead for the movement.

After the successful Montgomery boycott, King organized the Southern Christian Leadership Conference (SCLC) in 1957. The SCLC and King advocated nonviolent direct action as a means of winning equality for black Americans. The Student Nonviolent Coordinating Committee (SNCC), formed in 1960 as a somewhat more militant offshoot of the SCLC, grew out of the SCLC's marches and sit-ins. It directed its energies into voter registration drives in the Deep South, where it met with entrenched and violent resistance. Such confrontations convinced some that nonviolence would not work. For while many had adopted nonviolence as an effective tool, they did not share the deep moral and religious commitment to it held by King, and others. As the fifties became the sixties, many SNCC field workers began to question not just the tactic of nonviolence but also the goal of integration.

By the time of the March on Washington in 1963, SNCC was thoroughly disillusioned with the Kennedy administration, which had demonstrated only lukewarm support for Civil Rights and had failed to protect Civil Rights workers in the South. King's famous "I have a dream" speech and John Lewis's speech, both delivered at the march, emphasize nonviolence and have a religious orientation. They were out of step with a growing number of people within SNCC.

After the assassination of President John F. Kennedy, who had supported the march on Washington but been unable to move the important Civil Rights bill through Congress, Lyndon Johnson passed the Civil Rights Act of 1964 prohibiting discrimination on the basis of race. A year later, the Voting Rights Act authorized the federal government to protect the rights of African Americans to vote.

Change was easy to legislate but very difficult to effect. Even after the March on Washington and the passage of the Civil Rights and Voting Rights Acts, racism and inequity remained causing some within the Civil Rights movement to become impatient with the pace and the method of change. After a group of SNCC-organized African American activists offering themselves as an alternative to the all-white Mississippi delegation—the Freedom Democratic Party—were not seated at the 1964 Democratic National Convention in Atlantic City, increasing numbers of activists became disillusioned with traditional political action. Stokley Carmichael and the Black Panthers, for example, began to advocate black power and black pride, echoing the call for black separatism championed by Malcolm X and the Black Muslims. The final document in this chapter is from Stokely Charmichael's *Black Power* in which he rejects the integrationist Civil Rights movement.

Study Questions

1. President Dwight Eisenhower is reported as commenting that "I personally think the [*Brown v. Board of Education*] decision was wrong" and that the "hearts of men" can't be changed with decisions. How might Justice Warren answer this charge? Discuss the Court's activism in this case.

2. Discuss Jo Ann Gibson Robinson's telling of the Rosa Parks story. Does she describe the bus boycott as a spontaneous uprising or a well thought out protest? Why might she choose to describe it one way or another? Why might women be involved in the protest?

3. In what way were King's tactics and SNCC's tactics particularly appropriate to their goals? In what way do Carmichael's tactics match his goals? In what ways are Carmichael's tactics appropriate to his different goals?

4. Who was King's intended audience? John Lewis's? Carmichael's?

5. Compare Lewis's speech with the SNCC's Statement of Purpose. What changes in tone do you observe? Does the change in tone represent any change in basic tactics or goals?

6. What in Lewis's speech do you think so disturbed other Civil Rights leaders? Why do you think they wanted Lewis to soften his speech?

7. Discuss the changes in attitude from SNCC's Statement of Purpose to Carmichael's *Black Power*. What might account for those changes?

Brown v. Board of Education (1954)

This landmark Supreme Court decision was the outcome of three years of litigation by the father of Linda Brown, an elementary school student from Topeka, Kansas. In this decision, the Court declared segregated schools unconstitutional. In subsequent decisions, it ruled that schools be desegregated with "all deliberate speed." Somewhat reluctantly, President Dwight Eisenhower oversaw the process in the South in the 1950s, which culminated in the dramatic desegregation of the Little Rock, Arkansas, high school in 1957 under the protection of the National Guard.*

Mr. Chief Justice Warren delivered the opinion of the Court

These cases come to us from the States of Kansas, South Carolina, Virginia, and Delaware. They are premised on different facts and different local conditions, but a common legal question justifies their consideration together in this consolidated opinion.

In each of the cases, minors of the Negro race, through their legal representatives, seek the aid of the courts in obtaining admission to the public schools of their community on a nonsegregated basis. In each instance, they had been denied admission to schools attended by white children under laws requiring or permitting segregation according to race. This segregation was alleged to deprive the plaintiffs of the equal protection of the laws under the Fourteenth Amendment. In each of the cases other than the Delaware case, a three-judge federal district court denied relief to the plaintiffs on the so-called "separate but equal" doctrine announced by this Court in *Plessy v. Ferguson*, 163 U.S. 537. Under that doctrine, equality of treatment is accorded when the races are provided substantially equal facilities, even though these facilities be separate. In the Delaware case, the Supreme Court of Delaware adhered to

---

* From NAACP Legal Defense and Education Fund, Inc., "Summary of Argument," in the Supreme Court of the United States *Brown v. Board of Education of Topeka*, 347 U.S. 483 (1954).

that doctrine, but ordered that the plaintiffs be admitted to the white schools because of their superiority to the Negro schools.

The plaintiffs contended that segregated public schools are not "equal" and cannot be made "equal," and that hence they are deprived of the equal protection of the laws. . . .

In the first cases in this Court construing the Fourteenth Amendment, decided shortly after its adoption, the Court interpreted it as proscribing all state-imposed discriminations against the Negro race. The doctrine of "separate but equal" did not make its appearance in this Court until 1896 in the case of *Plessy v. Ferguson, supra,* involving not education but transportation. American courts have since labored with the doctrine for over half a century. In this Court, there have been six cases involving the "separate but equal" doctrine in the field of public education. . . . In none of these cases was it necessary to examine the doctrine to grant relief to the Negro plaintiff. And in *Sweatt v. Painter* . . . the Court expressly reserved decision on the question of whether *Plessy v. Ferguson* should be held inapplicable to public education.

In the instant cases, that question is directly presented. Here, unlike *Sweatt v. Painter*, there are findings below that the Negro and white schools involved have been equalized, or are being equalized, with respect to buildings, curricula, qualifications and salaries of teachers, and other "tangible" factors. Our decision, therefore, cannot turn on merely a comparison of these tangible factors in the Negro and white schools involved in each of the cases. We must look instead to the effect of segregation itself on public education.

In approaching this problem, we cannot turn the clock back to 1868 when the Amendment was adopted, or even to 1896 when *Plessy v. Ferguson* was written. We must consider public education in the light of its full development and its present place in American life throughout the Nation. Only in this way can it be determined if segregation in public schools deprives these plaintiffs of the equal protection of the laws.

Today, education is perhaps the most important function of state and local governments. Compulsory school attendance laws and the great expenditures for education both demonstrate our recognition of the importance of education to our democratic society. It is required in the performance of our most basic public responsibilities, even service in the armed forces. It is the very foundation of good citizenship. Today it is a principal instrument in awakening the child to cultural values, in preparing him for later professional training, and in helping him to adjust normally to his environment. In these days, it is doubtful that any child may reasonably be expected to succeed in life if he is denied the opportunity of an education. Such an opportunity, where the state has undertaken to provide it, is a right which must be made available to all on equal terms.

We come then to the question presented: Does segregation of children in public schools solely on the basis of race, even though the physical facilities and other "tangible" factors may be equal, deprive the children of the minority group of equal education opportunities? We believe that it does.

In *Sweatt v. Painter* . . . in finding that a segregated law school for Negroes could not provide them equal education opportunities, the Court relied in large part on "those qualities which are incapable of objective measurement but which make for greatness in a law school." In *McLaurin v. Oklahoma State Regents* . . . the Court, in requiring that a Negro admitted to a white graduate school be treated like all other students, again resorted to intangible considerations: ". . . his ability to study, to engage in discussions and exchange views with other students, and in general, to learn his profession." Such considerations apply with added force to children in grade and high schools. To separate them from others of similar age and qualifications solely because of their race generates a feeling of inferiority as to their status in the community that may affect their hearts and minds in a way unlikely ever to be undone. The effect of this separation on their educational opportunities was well stated by a finding in the Kansas case by a court which nevertheless felt compelled to rule against the Negro plaintiffs:

Segregation of white and colored children in public schools has a detrimental effect upon the colored children. The impact is greater when it has the sanction of the law; for the policy of separating the races is usually interpreted as denoting the inferiority of the Negro group. A sense of inferiority affects the motivation of a child to learn. Segregation with the sanction of law, therefore, has a tendency to retard the education and mental development of negro children and to deprive them of some of the benefits they would receive in a racial[ly] integrated school system.

Whatever may have been the extent of psychological knowledge at the time of *Plessy v. Ferguson*, this finding is amply supported by modern authority. Any language in *Plessy v. Ferguson* contrary to this finding is rejected.

We conclude that in the field of public education the doctrine of "separate but equal" has no place. Separate educational facilities are inherently unequal. Therefore, we hold that the plaintiffs and others similarly situated for whom the actions have been brought are, by reason of the segregation complained of, deprived of the equal protection of the laws guaranteed by the Fourteenth Amendment. This disposition makes unnecessary any discussion whether such segregation also violates the Due Process Clause of the Fourteenth Amendment.

Jo Ann Gibson Robinson, The Montgomery Bus Boycott (1955)

In this memoir, Jo Ann Gibson Robinson recalls her role in the Montgomery, Alabama, bus boycott begun by Rosa Parks, a seamstress and member of the NAACP. Women, like Parks and Robinson, were actively involved in the southern Civil Rights Movement.[*]

[*] From Jo Ann Gibson Robinson, *The Montgomery Bus Boycott and the Women Who Started It: The Memoir of Jo Ann Gibson Robinson*, ed. David J. Garrow (Knoxville: University of Tennessee Press, 1987), 43–45.

In the afternoon of Thursday, December 1, [1955] a prominent black woman named Mrs. Rosa Parks was arrested for refusing to vacate her seat for a white man. Mrs. Parks was a medium-sized, cultured mulatto woman; a civic and religious worker; quiet unassuming, and pleasant in manner and appearance; dignified and reserved; of high morals and a strong character. She was—and still is, for she lives to tell the story—respected in all black circles. By trade she was a seamstress, adept and competent in her work.

Tired from work, Mrs. Parks boarded a bus. The "reserved seats" were partially filled, but the seats just behind the reserved section were vacant, and Mrs. Parks sat down in one. It was during the busy evening rush hour. More black and white passengers boarded the bus, and soon all the reserved seats were occupied. The driver demanded that Mrs. Parks get up and surrender her seat to a white man, but she was tired from her work. She remained seated. In a few minutes, police summoned by the driver appeared, placed Mrs. Parks under arrest and took her to jail.

It was the first time the soft-spoken, middle-aged woman had been arrested. She maintained her decorum and poise, and the word of her arrest spread. Mr. E. D. Nixon, a longtime stalwart of our NAACP branch, along with liberal white attorney Clifford Durr and his wife Virginia, went to the jail and obtained Mrs. Parks's release on bond. Her trial was scheduled for Monday, December 5, 1955.

The news traveled like wildfire into every black home. Telephones jangled; people congregated on street corners and in homes and talked. But nothing was done. A numbing helplessness seemed to paralyze everyone. Very few stayed off the buses the rest of that day or the next. There was fear, discontent, and uncertainty. Everyone seemed to wait for someone to *do* something, but nobody made a move. For that day and a half, black Americans rode the buses as before, as if nothing had happened. They were sullen and uncommunicative, but they rode the buses. There was a silent, tension-filled waiting. For blacks were not talking loudly in public places—they were quiet, sullen, waiting. Just waiting!

Thursday evening came and went. Thursday night was far spent, when, at about 11:30 P.M., I sat in my peaceful, single-family dwelling on a side street. I was thinking about the situation. Lost in thought, I was startled by the telephone's ring. Black attorney Fred Gray, who had been out of town all day, had just gotten back and was returning the phone message I had left him about Mrs. Parks's arrest. Attorney Gray, though a very young man, had been one of my most active colleagues in our previous meetings with bus company officials and Commissioner Birmingham. A Montgomery native who had attended Alabama State and been one of my students, Fred Gray had gone on to law school in Ohio before returning to his hometown to open a practice with the only other black lawyer in Montgomery, Charles Langford.

Fred Gray and his wife Bernice were good friends of mine, and we talked often. In addition to being a lawyer, Gray was a trained, ordained minister of the gospel, actively serving as assistant pastor of Holt Street Church of Christ.

Tonight his voice on the phone was very short and to the point. Fred was shocked by the news of Mrs. Parks's arrest. I informed him that I already was thinking that the WPC [Women's Political Council] should distribute thousands of notices calling for all bus riders to stay off the buses on Monday, the day of Mrs. Parks's trial. "Are you ready?" he asked. Without hesitation, I assured him that we were. With that he hung up, and I went to work.

I made some notes on the back of an envelope: "The Women's Political Council will not wait for Mrs. Parks's consent to call for a boycott of city buses. On Friday, December 2, 1955, the women of Montgomery will call for a boycott to take place on Monday, December 5."

Student Nonviolent Coordinating Committee, Statement of Purpose (1960)

The Statement of Purpose of the SNCC (pronounced "snick"), was adopted at a conference held at Shaw University in April 1960. The statement was adopted at the insistence of James Lawson, a former theology student at Vanderbilt University and one of the leaders of the Nashville student movement.

We affirm the philosophical or religious ideal of nonviolence as the foundation of our purpose, the presupposition of our faith, and the manner of our action. Nonviolence as it grows from Judaic-Christian tradition seeks a social order of justice permeated by love. Integration of human endeavor represents the crucial first step toward such a society.

Through nonviolence, courage displaces fear; love transforms hate. Acceptance dissipates prejudice; hope ends despair. Peace dominates war; faith reconciles doubt. Mutual regard cancels enmity. Justice for all overthrows injustice. The redemptive community supersedes systems of gross social immorality.

Love is the central motif of nonviolence. Love is the force by which God binds man to Himself and man to man. Such love goes to the extreme; it remains loving and forgiving even in the midst of hostility. It matches the capacity of evil to inflict suffering with an even more enduring capacity to absorb evil, all the while persisting in love.

By appealing to conscience and standing on the moral nature of human existence, nonviolence nurtures the atmosphere in which reconciliation and justice become actual possibilities.

Martin Luther King, Jr., "I Have a Dream" (1963)

In this powerful speech delivered to an audience of more than
200,000 people gathered at the Washington Monument, Martin
Luther King, Jr., proclaimed his faith in the future when the ideals of
the Declaration of Independence would be realized.*

Five score years ago, a great American, in whose symbolic shadow we stand, signed
the Emancipation Proclamation. This momentous decree came as a great beacon light
of hope to millions of Negro salves who had been seared in the flames of withering
injustice. It came as a joyous daybreak to end the long night of captivity.

But one hundred years later, we must face the tragic fact that the Negro is still not
free. One hundred years later, the Negro lives on a lonely island of poverty in the midst
of a vast ocean of material prosperity. One hundred years later the Negro is still
languished in the corners of American society and finds himself an exile in his own
land. So we have come here today to dramatize an appalling condition.

In a sense we have come to our nation's Capital to cash a check. When the
architects of our republic wrote the magnificent words of the Constitution and the
Declaration of Independence, they were signing a promissory note to which every
American was to fall heir. This note was a promise that all men would be guaranteed
the unalienable rights of life, liberty, and the pursuit of happiness. . . .

But there is something that I must say to my people who stand on the warm
threshold which leads to this palace of justice. In the process of gaining our rightful
place we must not be guilty of wrongful deeds. Let us not seek to satisfy our thirst for
freedom by drinking from the cup of bitterness and hatred. We must forever conduct
our struggle on the high plane of dignity and discipline. We must not allow our
creative protest to degenerate into physical violence. Again and again we must rise to
the majestic heights of meeting physical force with soul force. The marvelous new
militancy which has engulfed the Negro community must not lead us to a distrust of all
white people, for many of our white brothers, as evidenced by their presence here
today, have come to realize that their destiny is tied up with our destiny and their
freedom is inextricably bound to our freedom. We cannot walk alone.

And as we walk, we must make the pledge that we shall march ahead. We cannot
turn back. There are those who are asking the devotees of civil rights, "When will you
be satisfied?" We can never be satisfied as long as the Negro is the victim of the
unspeakable horrors of police brutality. We can never be satisfied as long as our
bodies, heavy with the fatigue of travel, cannot gain lodging in the motels of the
highways and the hotels of the cities. We cannot be satisfied as long as the Negro's

---

basic mobility is from a smaller ghetto to a larger one. We can never be satisfied as long as a Negro in Mississippi cannot vote and a Negro in New York believes he has nothing for which to vote. No, no we are not satisfied, and we will not be satisfied until justice rolls down like waters and righteousness like a mighty stream. . . .

I say to you today, my friends, that in spite of the difficulties and frustrations of the moment I still have a dream. It is a dream deeply rooted in the American dream.

I have a dream that one day this nation will rise up and live out the true meaning of its creed: "We hold these truths to be self-evident; that all men are created equal."

I have a dream that one day on the red hills of Georgia the sons of former slaves and the sons of former slave owners will be able to sit down together at the table of brotherhood.

I have a dream that one day even the state of Mississippi, a desert state sweltering with the heat of injustice and oppression, will be transformed into an oasis of freedom and justice.

I have a dream that my four little children will one day live in a nation where they will not be judged by the color of their skin but by the content of their character.

I have a dream today.

I have a dream that one day the state of Alabama, whose governor's lips are presently dripping with the words of interposition and nullification, will be transformed into a situation where little black boys and black girls will be able to join hands with little white boys and white girls and walk together as brothers and sisters.

I have a dream today.

I have a dream that one day every valley shall be exalted, every hill and mountain shall be made low, the rough places will be made plains, and the crooked places will be made straight, and the glory of the Lord shall be revealed, and all flesh shall see it together.

John Lewis, Address at the March on Washington (1963)

Lewis's speech, delivered at the 1963 March on Washington, reflected some of the anger and disillusionment felt by the SNCC. A group of Civil Rights leaders, including Martin Luther King, Jr., Ralph Abernathy, Bayard Rustin, and A. Philip Randolph, persuaded Lewis to modify the speech. The real irony was not that Lewis delivered a toned-down version of his speech but that even Lewis's original draft did not represent the dominant sensibility of SNCC. Lewis's emphasis on nonviolence and his religious orientation (he had been a student at the American Baptist Theological Seminary) were out of step with a growing number of people within SNCC.

We march today for jobs and freedom, but we have nothing to be proud of, for hundreds and thousands of our brothers are not here—they have no money for their transportation, for they are receiving starvation wages . . . or no wages, at all.

In good conscience, we cannot support the Administration's civil rights bill, for it is too little, and too late. There's not one thing in the bill that will protect our people from police brutality.

The voting section of the bill will not help the thousands of citizens who want to vote. . . .

What is in the bill that will protect the homeless and starving people of this nation? What is there in this bill to ensure the equality of a maid who earns $5.00 a week in the home of a family whose income is $100,000 a year?

The bill will not protect young children and old women from police dogs and fire hoses for engaging in peaceful demonstrations. . . .

For the first time in 100 years this nation is being awakened to the fact that segregation is evil and it must be destroyed in all forms. Our presence today proves that we have been aroused to the point of action.

We are now involved in a serious revolution. This nation is still a place of cheap political leaders who build their careers on immoral compromise and ally themselves with open forms of political, economic, and social exploitation. . . . The party of Kennedy is also the party of Eastland. The party of Javits is also the party of Goldwater. Where is our party?

I want to know—which side is the federal government on?

The revolution is at hand, and we must free ourselves of the chains of political and economic slavery. The non-violent revolution is saying, "We will not wait for the courts to act, for we have been waiting hundreds of years. We will not wait for the President, nor the Justice Department, nor Congress, but we will take matters into our own hands, and create a great source of power, outside of any national structure that could and would assure us victory." . . . We cannot be patient, we do not want to be free gradually, we want our freedom, and we want it now. We can not depend on any political party, for both the Democrats and Republicans have betrayed the basic principles of the Declaration of Independence. . . .

The revolution is a serious one. Mr. Kennedy is trying to take the revolution out of the streets and put it in the courts. Listen, Mr. Kennedy, listen. Mr. Congressman, listen, fellow citizens—the black masses are on the march for jobs and freedom, and we must say to the politicians that there won't be a "cooling-off period."

We won't stop now. All of the forces of Eastland, Barnett, and Wallace won't stop this revolution. The next time we march, we won't march on Washington, but will march through the South, through the Heart of Dixie, the way Sherman did—nonviolently. We will make the action of the past few months look petty. And I say to you, WAKE UP AMERICA!

The Civil Rights Act of 1964

The Civil Rights Act was passed, in President Lyndon Johnson's words, as "a memorial" to President Kennedy. The act made racial discrimination illegal and granted the Justice Department broad enforcement powers. However, it was not until the next year, when the Voting Right Act was passed, that African Americans' right to register to vote was explicitly protected by the federal government.*

TITLE I

Voting Rights

Sec. 101 (2). No person acting under color of law shall—

(A) in determining whether any individual is qualified under State law or laws to vote in any Federal election, apply any standard, practice, or procedure different form the standards, practices, or procedures applied under such law or laws to other individuals within the same county, parish, or similar political subdivision who have been found by State officials to be qualified to vote; . . . .

(C) employ any literacy test as a qualification for voting in any Federal election unless (i) such test is administered to each individual wholly in writing; and (ii) a certified copy of the test and of the answers given by the individual is furnished to him within twenty-five days of the submission of his request made within the period of time during which records and papers are required to be retained and preserved pursuant to Title III of the Civil Rights Act of 1960. . . .

TITLE II

Injunctive Relief Against Discrimination in Places of Public Accommodation

Sec. 201. (a) All persons shall be entitled to the full and equal enjoyment of the goods, services, facilities, privileges, advantages, and accommodations of any place of public accommodation, as defined in this section, without discrimination or segregation on the ground of race, color, religion, or national origin.

(b) Each of the following establishments which serves the public is a place of public accommodation within the meaning of this title if its operations affect commerce, or if discrimination or segregation by it is supported by State action:

(1) any inn, motel, or other establishment which provides lodging to transient guests, other than an establishment located within a building which contains not more than five rooms for rent or hire and which is actually occupied by the proprietor of such establishment as his residence;

---

* 78 U.S. Statutes at Large, 2241 ff. Public law 88–352.

(2)   any restaurant, cafeteria, lunch room, lunch counter, soda fountain, or other activity principally engaged in selling food for consumption on the premises. . . .

(3) any motion picture house, theater, concert hall, sports arena, stadium, or other place of exhibition or entertainment. . . .

(d) Discrimination or segregation by an establishment is supported by State action within the meaning of this title if such discrimination or segregation (1) is carried on under color of any law, statute, ordinance, or regulation; or (2) is carried on under color of any custom or usage required or enforced by officials of the State or political subdivision thereof. . . .

Sec. 202. All persons shall be entitled to be free, at any establishment or place, from discrimination or segregation of any kind on the ground of race, color, religion, or national origin, if such discrimination or segregation is or purports to be required by any law, statute, ordinance, regulation, rule, or order of a State or any agency or political subdivision thereof. . . .

Sec. 206. (a) Whenever the Attorney General has reasonable cause to believe that any person or group of persons is engaged in a pattern of practice of resistance to the full enjoyment of any of the rights secured by this title, the Attorney General may bring a civil action in the appropriate district court of the United States by filing with it a complaint . . . requesting such preventive relief, including an application for a permanent or temporary injunction, restraining order or other order against the person or persons responsible for such pattern or practice, as he deems necessary to insure the full enjoyment of the rights herein described.

TITLE IV

Nondiscrimination in Federally Assisted Programs

Sec. 601. No person in the United States shall, on the ground of race, color, or national origin, be excluded from participation in, be denied the benefits of, or be subjected to discrimination under any program or activity receiving Federal financial assistance.

Stokely Carmichael and Chrles Hamilton, from *Black Power* (1967)

Stokely Carmichael was a member of SNCC and was elected its chairman in 1966. In this passage from his book written with Charles Hamilton, *Black Power*, he rejected the tactics and the goals of the mainstream Civil Rights movement.*

---

* From Stokely Carmichael and Charles Hamilton, *Black Power* (New York: Vintage, 1967).

The advocates of Black Power reject the old slogans and meaningless rhetoric of previous years in the civil rights struggle. The language of yesterday is indeed irrelevant: progress, non-violence, integration, fear of "white backlash," coalition. . . .

One of the tragedies of the struggle against racism is that up to this point there has been no national organization which could speak to the growing militancy of young black people in the urban ghettos and the black-belt South. There has been only a "civil rights" movement, whose tone of voice was adapted to an audience of middle-class whites. It served as a sort of buffer zone between that audience and angry young blacks. It claimed to speak for the needs of a community, but it did not speak in the tone of that community. None of its so-called leaders could go into a rioting community and be listened to. In a sense, the blame must be shared—along with the mass media—by those leaders for what happened in Watts, Harlem, Chicago, Cleveland, and other places. Each time the black people in those cities saw Dr. Martin Luther King get slapped they became angry. When they saw little black girls bombed to death in a church and civil rights workers ambushed and murdered, they were angrier; and when nothing happened, they were steaming mad. We had nothing to offer that they could see, except to go out and be beaten again. We helped to build their frustration.

We had only the old language of love and suffering. And in most places—that is, from the liberals and middle class—we got back the old language of patience and progress. . . .

Such language, along with admonitions to remain non-violent and fear the white backlash, convinced some that that course was the only course to follow. It misled some into believing that a black minority could bow its head and get whipped into a meaningful position of power. The very notion is absurd. . . .

There are many who still sincerely believe in that approach. From our viewpoint, rampaging white mobs and white night-riders must be made to understand that their days of free head-whipping are over. Black people should and must fight back. Nothing more quickly repels someone bent on destroying you than the unequivocal message: "O.K., fool, make your move, and run the same risk I run—of dying."

Next we deal with the term "integration." According to its advocates, social justice will be accomplished by "integrating the Negro into the mainstream institutions of the society from which he has been traditionally excluded." This concept is based on the assumption that there is nothing of value in the black community and that little of value could be created among black people. The thing to do is to siphon off the "acceptable" black people into the surrounding middle-class white community.

The goals of integrationists are middle-class goals, articulated primarily by a small group of Negroes with middle-class aspirations or status. . . .

Secondly, while color blindness may be a sound goal ultimately, we must realize that race is an overwhelming fact of life in this historical period. There is no black man in the country who can live "simply as a man." His blackness is an ever-present fact of this racist society, whether he recognizes it or not. It is unlikely that this or the next generation will witness the time when race will no longer be relevant in the conduct of public affairs and in public policy decision-making. . . .

"Integration" as a goal today speaks to the problem of blackness not only in an unrealistic way but also in a despicable way. It is based on complete acceptance of the fact that in order to have a decent house or education, black people must move into a white neighborhood or send their children to a white school. This reinforces, among both black and white, the idea that "white" is automatically superior and "black" is by definition inferior. For this reason, "integration" is a subterfuge for the maintenance of white supremacy.

28

Cuba, Vietnam, and the Crisis of Authority

Foreign policy—centered on and dictated by the Cold War and the Vietnam war—dominated the presidency from 1960 to 1976. While significant changes occurred in domestic life, global issues occupied center stage in the administrations of Kennedy, Johnson, Nixon, and Ford and proved to be the downfall of Johnson. This was a generation of presidents who remembered the lessons of World War II.

American policy in Southeast Asia was based on the domino theory, the foundation of which lay in American fears of unchecked aggression and its consequences. American involvement in Southeast Asia and in Vietnam in particular dated back to the Eisenhower administration. Under the leadership of communist Ho Chi Minh, nationalist rebels had been fighting from the puppet regime dominated by France, the country's former colonial ruler. But despite fears that a victory for the communists would signify an expansion of the Soviets' influence, Eisenhower refused to commit American ground troops to the aid of the French at the battle of Dien Bien in 1954, predicting that it would involve the U.S. in a war impossible to win. A few years later, however, after the French withdrawal and the division of Vietnam into North and South, the Eisenhower administration began plying the South Vietnam's anticommunist government with aid, military advisors, and equipment in an attempt to stave off a communist takeover by the North. Eisenhower's reaction to Dien Bien Phu, excerpted here, provides an unhappy foreshadowing of American involvement in Vietnam.

While President Kennedy continued Eisenhower's low-level involvement in Vietnam, his defining Cold War moment came in a standoff with the Soviets over Cuba. JFK's handling of Cuba has alternately been described as his greatest triumph and his greatest blunder. Whatever the case, it was often seen to be the closest that the United States and Soviet Union came to making the Cold War a hot one. The Bay of Pigs invasion, in April of 1961, was certainly a failure. In this invasion, 2,000 Cuban exiles were sent to invade Cuba, where they were quickly forced to give up their arms. The Cuban Missile Crisis, in October of the following year, occurred after the Soviet

Union planned to move missiles onto Cuban soil. Kennedy, acting aggressively, announced that the navy would turn back the Soviet ships bringing weapons to Cuba and that all work on the missile bases must be stopped. After a few days of tension, the Soviets capitulated, leading to a softening of the tense relationship between the two countries.

Meanwhile, in Vietnam, American involvement gradually escalated between the Eisenhower years and Kennedy's assassination in 1963. The number of military advisors, for example, grew from some 675 to 16,000. But it was not until shortly after the Kennedy assassination that the U.S. became a major player in Vietnam. President Johnson declared that he wouldn't be the president who lost in Vietnam and dramatically increased American military presence. If there was an "official" beginning to the Vietnam war, it would have to be the Gulf of Tonkin incident—a supposed attack on an American destroyer in the Gulf of Tonkin in northern Vietnam.

The Gulf of Tonkin incident provided Johnson with an ideal entree into Vietnam. In response to it, the number of American troops in country rose to 530,000. But meanwhile, domestic opposition to America's role in the war became increasingly vocal and strident. Hundreds of thousands marched on New York and Washington to protest the war. Students were active in antiwar protests (although many of them had student draft deferments) and four were killed at anti-ROTC demonstrations at Kent State University in Ohio in May 1970. Such opposition was not without merit, for after the Tet offensive in 1968, it became apparent to many that the United States could not win the war. And in the following year, the full scope of the war's brutality became clear when the My Lai massacre, in which women and children were slaughtered, was publicized. Bowing to domestic pressures, Richard Nixon in 1968 pledged to "Vietnamize" the war and pull U.S. troops out. A few days before his reelection in 1972, his secretary of state, Henry Kissinger, announced that "peace was at hand." Peace was declared, but anti-government opposition and a withering of trust in public officials was still in the air. American involvement in Vietnam continued until 1975.

Study Questions

1. What were Eisenhower's primary concerns in considering the situation at Dien Bien Phu and deciding whether or not to commit American forces to aid the French?

2. Consider Eisenhower's statement that "if we were to put one combat soldier into Indochina, then our entire prestige would be at stake, not only in that area but throughout the world." Under John Kennedy, American soldiers began to assume combat roles. What were the consequences?

3. Was Kennedy correct that the missiles in Cuba "add to an already clear and present danger"? Do the discussions in the Excomm bear out that assertion?

4. If Robert McNamara was correct and the missiles in Cuba posed a political, rather than a military, problem, were the solutions discussed appropriate? In the meeting Kennedy and his advisors discussed a tactical air strike, a massive air strike, an invasion, and eventually a blockade. What option or options did they not discuss?

5. How does the Tonkin Gulf Resolution lead to the extension of the powers of the executive branch? What is the relationship between the resolution and the passage of the War Powers Act?

6. What arguments does Bill Clinton have against the draft? According to the Clinton letter, what alternatives to the war were students taking?

Dwight D. Eisenhower, Decision Not to Intervene at Dien Bien Phu (1954)

Initially, Eisenhower considered coming to the aid of the French at Dien Bien Phu. However, he insisted that in order to obtain American assistance, the French had to internationalize the war and to promise freedom for Laos, Cambodia, and Vietnam if and when the communists were defeated. The French would not agree to Eisenhower's terms, so Eisenhower refused to commit American forces. The first document is from a letter Eisenhower wrote on April 26, 1954 to Alfred Gruenther, who was on Eisenhower's staff during World War II, served as Ike's chief of staff at NATO, and later was himself Supreme Allied Commander of NATO forces. The second document is an excerpt from a letter Eisenhower wrote to Swede Hazlett, a boyhood friend, with whom Eisenhower corresponded in long, frank, and revealing letters. This letter was written the day after the letter to Gruenther. The third document comes from the diary kept by James C. Hagerty, Eisenhower's press secretary. The excerpt is from the entry for April 26, 1954.

Dwight D. Eisenhower to Alfred Gruenther, April 26, 1954

As you know, you and I started more than three years ago trying to convince the French that they could not win the Indo-China war and particularly could not get real American support in that region unless they would unequivocally pledge independence to the Associated States upon the achievement of military victory. Along with this—indeed as a corollary to it—this administration has been arguing that no Western power can go to Asia militarily, except as one of a concert of powers, which concert must include local Asiatic peoples.

To contemplate anything else is to lay ourselves open to the charge of imperialism and colonialism or—at the very least—of objectionable paternalism. Even, therefore, if we could by some sudden stroke assure the saving of the Dien Bien Phu garrison, I think that under the conditions proposed by the French, the free world would lose more than it would gain.

Dwight D. Eisenhower to Swede Hazlett, April 27, 1954

In my last letter I remember that I mentioned Dien Bien Phu. It still holds out and while the situation looked particularly desperate during the past week, there now appears to be a slight improvement and the place may hold on for another week or ten days. The general situation in Southeast Asia, which is rather dramatically epitomized by the Dien Bien Phu battle, is a complicated one that has been a long time developing. . . .

For more than three years I have been urging upon successive French governments the advisability of finding some way of "internationalizing" the war; such action would be proof to all the world and particularly to the Viet Namese that France's purpose is not colonial in character but is to defeat Communism in the region and to give the natives their freedom. The reply has always been vague, containing references to national prestige, Constitutional limitations, inevitable effects upon the Moroccan and Tunisian peoples, and dissertations on plain political difficulties and battles within the French Parliament. The result has been that the French have failed entirely to produce any enthusiasm on the part of the Vietnamese for participation in the war. . . .

In any event, any nation that intervenes in a civil war can scarcely expect to win unless the side in whose favor it intervenes possesses a high morale based upon a war purpose or cause in which it believes. The French have used weasel words in promising independence and through this one reason as much as anything else, have suffered reverses that have been really inexcusable.

James C. Hagerty, Diary, Monday, April 26, 1954

Indochina. The President said that the French "are weary as hell." He said that it didn't look as though Dienbienphu could hold out for more than a week and would fall possibly sooner. Reported that the British thought that the French were not putting out as much as they could, but that he did not necessarily agree with their viewpoint. "The French go up and down every day—they are very volatile. They think they are a great power one day and they feel sorry for themselves the next day." The President said that if we were to put one combat soldier into Indochina, then our entire prestige would be at stake, not only in that area but throughout the world. . . . The President said the situation looked very grim this morning, but that he and Dulles were doing everything they could to get the free countries to act in concert. In addition, he said "there are plenty of people in Asia, and we can train them to fight well. I don't see any reason for American ground troops to be committed in Indochina, don't think we need it, but we can train their forces and it may be necessary for us eventually to use some of our planes or aircraft carriers off the coast and some of our fighting craft we have in that area for support."

John F. Kennedy, Cuban Missile Address (1962)

This is an excerpt from the television address President Kennedy gave on October 22, 1962, to the American people, letting them know about the security threat posed by the Soviets in Cuba and his willingness to take strong aggressive action against it. It is interesting to note that while all this transpired the Soviet Union already had missiles stationed in Siberia which were within range of the West Coast and that the United States had missiles in Europe that were certainly within range of the Soviet Union's major population centers.*

Good evening, my fellow citizens. This Government, as promised, has maintained the closest surveillance of the Soviet military build-up on the island of Cuba. Within the past week unmistakable evidence has established the fact that a series of offensive missile sites is now in preparation on that imprisoned island. The purposes of these bases can be none other than to provide a nuclear strike capability against the Western Hemisphere.

Upon receiving the first preliminary hard information of this nature last Tuesday morning [October 16] at 9:00 A.M., I directed that our surveillance be stepped up. And now having confirmed and completed our evaluation of the evidence and our decision on a course of action, this Government feels obliged to report this new crisis to you in fullest detail.

The characteristics of these new missile sites indicate two distinct types of installations. Several of them include medium-range ballistic missiles capable of carrying a nuclear warhead for a distance of more than 1,000 nautical miles. Each of these missiles, in short, is capable of striking Washington, D.C., the Panama Canal, Cape Canaveral, Mexico City, or any other city in the southeastern part of the United States, in Central America, or in the Caribbean area.

Additional sites not yet completed appear to be designed for intermediate-range ballistic missiles capable of traveling more than twice as far—and thus capable of striking most of the major cities in the Western Hemisphere, ranging as far north as

---

* From *The Public Papers of the Presidents, John F. Kennedy, 1962* (Washington, D.C.: Government Printing Office, 1963).

Hudson Bay, Canada, and as far south as Lima, Peru. In addition, jet bombers, capable of carrying nuclear weapons, are now being uncrated and assembled in Cuba, while the necessary air bases are being prepared.

This urgent transformation of Cuba into an important strategic base—by the presence of these large, long-range, and clearly offensive weapons of sudden mass destruction—constitutes an explicit threat to the peace and security of all the Americas, in flagrant and deliberate defiance of the Rio Pact of 1947, the traditions of this nation and Hemisphere, the Joint Resolution of the Eighty-seventh Congress, the Charter of the United Nations, and my own public warnings to the Soviets on September 4 and 13.

This action also contradicts the repeated assurances of Soviet spokesmen, both publicly and privately delivered, that the arms build-up in Cuba would retain its original defensive character and that the Soviet Union had no need or desire to station strategic missiles on the territory of any other nation. . . .

In that sense missiles in Cuba add to an already clear and present danger— although it should be noted the nations of Latin America have never previously been subjected to a potential nuclear threat.

But this secret, swift, and extraordinary build-up of Communist missiles—in an area well known to have a special and historical relationship to the United States and the nations of the Western Hemisphere, in violation of Soviet assurances, and in defiance of American and hemispheric policy—this sudden, clandestine decision to station strategic weapons for the first time outside of Soviet soil—is a deliberately provocative and unjustifiable change in the status quo which cannot be accepted by this country if our courage and our commitments are ever to be trusted again by either friend or foe.

Transcript of Excomm Meeting (1962)

This is an excerpt from the transcript of one of President Kennedy's Executive Committee (Excomm) meetings on October 16, 1962. Kennedy secretly taped the proceedings of these, and other, meetings during his presidency. Present at the meeting are Secretary of Defense Robert S. McNamara; Robert F. Kennedy, the president's brother and the U.S. Attorney General; McGeorge Bundy, a national security affairs officer; and various other national security advisors and defense department officials.*

* From the documentary holdings of the Kennedy Library in Boston, Mass.

BUNDY: But, the, uh, question I would like to ask is, quite aside from what we've said—and we're very hard-locked into it, I know—What is the strategic impact on the position of the United States of MRBMs [medium-range ballistic missiles] in Cuba? How gravely does it change the strategic balance?

MCNAMARA: Mac, I asked the Chiefs that this afternoon, in effect. And they said, substantially. My own personal view is not at all.

BUNDY: Not so much.

MCNAMARA: And, I think this is an important element here. . . .

* * * * *

[discussion of the psychological impact of Soviet weapons in Cuba]

DOUGLAS DILLON: Yeah. That is the point.

EDWIN M. MARTIN: Yeah. The psychological factor of our having taken it.

DILLON: Taken it, that's the best.

RFK: Well, and the fact that if you go there, we're gonna fire it.

JFK: What's that again, Ed? What are you saying?

MARTIN: Well, it's a psychological factor that we have sat back and let 'em do it to us, that is more important than the direct threat . . .

JFK: [unintelligible] I said we weren't going to.

MARTIN: [unintelligible]

BUNDY(?): That's something we could manage.

JFK: Last month I said we weren't going to.

[laughter]

JFK: Last month I should have said . . .

[UNIDENTIFIED]: Well . . .

JFK: . . . that we don't care. But when we said we were not going to and they go ahead and do it, and then we do nothing, then . . .

[UNIDENTIFIED]: That's right.

JFK: . . . I would think that our risks increase. Oh, I agree. What difference does it make? They've got enough to blow us up now anyway. I think it's just a question of . . . After all this is a political struggle as much as military. . . .

* * * * *

[McNamara advocates examining political response—"We haven't discussed it fully today."]

MCNAMARA: I, I, I'll be quite frank. I don't think there is a military problem here. This is my answer to Mac's question. . . .

BUNDY: That's my honest [judgment(?)].

MCNAMARA: . . . and therefore, and I've gone through this today, and I asked myself, Well what is it then if it isn't a military problem? Well, it's just exactly this problem, that, that, uh, if Cuba should possess a capacity to carry out offensive actions against the U.S., the U.S. would act.

[UNIDENTIFIED]: That's right.

[UNIDENTIFIED]: That's right.

MCNAMARA: Now, it's that problem, this . . .

[UNIDENTIFIED]: You can't get around that one.

MCNAMARA: . . . this is a domestic political problem. . . .

[McNamara suggested blockade and 24-hour surveillance. George Ball pointed out that 24-hour surveillance has holes—can't monitor during darkness.]

MCNAMARA: Oh, well, it's really the, yes, it isn't the surveillance, it's the ultimatum that is . . .

BALL (?): Yeah.

MCNAMARA: . . . the key part of this.

BALL (?): Yeah.

MCNAMARA: And what I tried to do was develop a little package that meets the action requirement of the paragraph I read.

[UNIDENTIFIED]: Yeah.

MCNAMARA: Because, as I suggested, I don't believe it's primarily a military problem. It's primarily a, a domestic, political problem.

The Tonkin Gulf Incident (1964)

In August 1964, President Lyndon Johnson declared that an American destroyer had been fired upon while sailing in international waters in the Gulf of Tonkin off northern Vietnam. Not until later was it revealed that the destroyer had really been in North Vietnamese territorial waters—just thirty miles from shore—assisting South Vietnamese soldiers. Included here are the text of Johnson's message to Congress requesting support for increased involvement and the Congress's resolution granting it, which passed in the House 416–0 and the Senate 88–2.*

President Johnson's Message to Congress

Last night I announced to the American people that North Vietnamese regime had conducted further deliberate attacks against US. naval vessels operating in international waters, and that I had therefore directed air action against gunboats and supporting facilities used in these hostile operations. This air action has now been carried out with substantial damage to the boats and facilities. Two US. aircraft were lost in the action.

After consultation with the leaders of both parties in the Congress, I further announced a decision to ask the Congress for a resolution expressing the unity and determination of the United States in supporting freedom and in protecting peace in southeast Asia.

These latest actions of the North Vietnamese regime have given a new and grave turn to the already serious situation in southeast Asia. Our commitments in that area are well known to the Congress. They were first made in 1954 by President Eisenhower. They were further defined in the Southeast Asia Collective Defense Treaty approved by the Senate in February 1955.

This treaty with its accompanying protocol obligates the United States and other members to act in accordance with their constitutional processes to meet Communist aggression against any of the parties or protocol states.

Our policy in southeast Asia has been consistent and unchanged since 1954. I summarized it on June 2 in our simple propositions:

1. America keeps her word. Here as elsewhere, we must and shall honor our commitments.

2. The issue is the future of southeast Asia as a whole. A threat to any nation in that region is a threat to all, and a threat to us.

---

* President Johnson's Message to Congress, and Joint Resolution of Congress, H. J. Res. 1145 *Department of State Bulletin,* August 24, 1964.

3. Our purpose is peace. We have no military, political, or territorial ambitions in the area.

4. This is not just a jungle war, but a struggle for freedom on every front of human activity. Our military and economic assistance to South Vietnam and Laos in particular has the purpose of helping these countries to repel aggression and strengthen their independence.

The threat to the free nations of southeast Asia has long been clear. The North Vietnamese regime has constantly sought to take over South Vietnam and Laos. This Communist regime has violated the Geneva accords for Vietnam. It has systematically conducted a campaign of subversion, which included the direction, training, and supply of personnel and arms for the conduct of guerrilla warfare in South Vietnamese territory. In Laos, the North Vietnamese regime has maintained military forces, used Laotian territory for infiltration into South Vietnam, and most recently carried out combat operations—all in direct violation of the Geneva agreements of 1962.

In recent months, the actions of the North Vietnamese regime have become steadily more threatening. . . .

As President of the United States I have concluded that I should now ask the Congress, on its part, to join in affirming the national determination that all such attacks will be met, and that the United States will continue in its basic policy of assisting the free nations of the area to defend their freedom.

As I have repeatedly made clear, the United States intends no rashness, and seeks no wider war. We must make it clear to all that the United States is united in its determination to bring about the end of Communist subversion and aggression in the area. We seek the full and effective restoration of the international agreements signed in Geneva in 1954, with respect to South Vietnam, and again in Geneva in 1962, with respect to Laos. . . .

Joint Resolution of Congress

To promote the maintenance of international peace and security in southeast Asia.

Whereas naval units of the Communist regime in Vietnam, in violation of the principles of the Charter of the United Nations and of international law, have deliberately and repeatedly attacked United States naval vessels lawfully present in international waters, and have thereby created a serious threat to international peace; and

Whereas these attacks are part of a deliberate and systematic campaign of aggression that the Communist regime in North Vietnam has been waging against its neighbors and the nations joined with them in the collective defense of their freedom; and

Whereas the United States is assisting the peoples of southeast Asia to protect their freedom and has no territorial, military or political ambitions in that area, but desires only that these peoples should be left in peace to work out their own destinies in their own way; Now, therefore, be it

Resolved by the Senate and House of Representatives of the United States of America in Congress assembled, that the Congress approves and supports the determination of the President, as Commander in Chief, to take all necessary measures to repel any armed attack against the forces of the United States and to prevent further aggression.

SEC. 2. The United States regards as vital to its national interest and to world peace the maintenance of international peace and security in southeast Asia. Consonant with the Constitution of the United States and the Charter of the United Nations and in accordance with its obligations under the Southeast Asia Collective Defense Treaty, the United States is, therefore, prepared, as the President determines, to take all necessary steps, including the use of armed force, to assist any member or protocol state of the Southeast Asia Collective Defense Treaty requesting assistance in defense of its freedom.

SEC. 3. This resolution shall expire when the President shall determine that the peace and security of the area is reasonably assured by international conditions created by action of the United Nations or otherwise, except that it may be terminated earlier by concurrent resolution of the Congress.

Bill Clinton, Letter to Colonel Holmes (1969)

Like many other Americans, Bill Clinton opposed the Vietnam war. Some, including Muhammad Ali, actively resisted the draft—some so far as going to jail or fleeing to Canada. Although reforms were attempted, the conscription process was unfair—college students were granted educational deferments and the less privileged, particularly African Americans and Hispanics, were dramatically overrepresented in combat. Bill Clinton enrolled in the University of Arkansas's ROTC program, planning on becoming commissioned upon his return from his Rhodes scholarship at Oxford. His ROTC commander, Lt. Colonel Eugene Holmes, sent a deferment to Clinton's draft board based on that information. The following December, Clinton sent this letter to Holmes. It has been reprinted numerous times—often as part of an argument for Clinton's cowardice and lack of patriotism, but it is reprinted here as an example of the student argument against the war in Vietnam. Note that Clinton wrote this letter just a month after the disclosure of American atrocities at My Lai and massive protest demonstrations in Washington D.C.*

---

* Reprinted from the Associated Press, February 3, 1992. Used by permission.

December 3, 1969

Dear Colonel Holmes,

I am sorry to be so long in writing. I know I promised to let you hear from me at least once a month, and from now on you will, but I have had to have some time to think about this first letter. Almost daily since my return to England I have thought about writing about what I want to and ought to say.

First, I want to thank you, not just for saving me from the draft, but for being so kind and decent to me last summer, when I was as low as I have ever been. One thing which made the bond we struck in good faith somewhat palatable to me was my high regard for you personally. In retrospect, it seems that the admiration might not have been mutual had you known a little more about me, about my political beliefs and activities. At least you might have thought me more fit for the draft than for R.O.T.C.

Let me try to explain. As you know, I worked for two years in a very minor position on the Senate Foreign Relations Committee. I did it for the experience and the salary but also for the opportunity, however small, of working every day against a war I opposed and despised with a depth of feeling I had reserved solely for racism in America before Vietnam. I did not take the matter lightly but studied it carefully, and there was a time when not many people had more information about Vietnam at hand than I did.

I have written and spoken and marched against the war. One of the national organizers of the Vietnam Moratorium is a close friend of mine. After I left Arkansas last summer, I went to Washington to work in the national headquarters of the Moratorium, then to England to organize the Americans here for demonstrations Oct. 15 and Nov. 16.

Interlocked with the war is the draft issue, which I did not begin to consider separately until early 1968. For a law seminar at Georgetown I wrote a paper on the legal arguments for and against allowing, within the Selective Service System, the classification of selective conscientious objection, for those opposed to participation in a particular war, not simply to "participation in war in any form."

From my work I came to believe that the draft system itself is illegitimate. No government really rooted in limited, parliamentary democracy should have the power to make its citizens fight and kill and die in a war they may oppose, a war which even possibly may be wrong, a war which, in any case, does not involve immediately the peace and freedom of the nation.

The draft was justified in World War II because the life of the people collectively was at stake. Individuals had to fight, if the nation was to survive, for the lives of their countrymen and their way of life. Vietnam is no such case. Nor was Korea an example, where, in my opinion, certain military action was justified but the draft was not, for the reasons stated above.

Because of my opposition to the draft and the war, I am in great sympathy with those who are not willing to fight, kill, and maybe die for their country (i.e. the particular policy of a particular government) right or wrong. Two of my friends at Oxford are conscientious objectors. I wrote a letter of recommendation for one of them to his Mississippi draft board, a letter which I am more proud of than anything else I wrote at Oxford last year. One of my roommates is a draft resister who is under possible indictment and may never be able to go home again. He is one of the bravest, best men I know. His country needs men like him more than they know. That he is considered a criminal is an obscenity.

The decision not to be a resister and the related subsequent decisions were the most difficult of my life. I decided to accept the draft in spite of my beliefs for one reason: to maintain my political viability within the system. For years I have worked to prepare myself for a political life characterized by both practical political ability and concern for rapid social progress. It is a life I still feel compelled to try to lead. I do not think our system of government is by definition corrupt, however dangerous and inadequate it has been in recent years. (The society may be corrupt, but that is not the same thing, and it is true we are all finished anyway.)

When the draft came, despite political convictions, I was having a hard time facing the prospect of fighting a war I had been fighting against, and that is why I contacted you. R.O.T.C. was the one way left in which I could possibly, but not positively, avoid both Vietnam and resistance. Going on with my education, even coming back to England, played no part in my decision to join R.O.T.C. I am back here, and would have been at Arkansas Law School because there is nothing else I can do. In fact, I would like to have been able to take a year out perhaps to teach in a small college or work on some community action project and in the process to decide whether to attend law school or graduate school and how to begin putting what I have learned to use.

But the particulars of my personal life are not nearly as important to me as the principles involved. After I signed the R.O.T.C. letter of intent I began to wonder whether the compromise I had made with myself was not more objectionable than the draft would have been, because I had no interest in the R.O.T.C. program in itself and all I seemed to have done was to protect myself from physical harm. Also, I began to think I had deceived you, not by lies—there were none—but by failing to tell you all the things I'm writing now. I doubt that I had the mental coherence to articulate them then.

At that time, after we had made our agreement and you had sent my I-D deferment to my draft board, the anguish and loss of my self-regard and self-confidence really set in. I hardly slept for weeks and kept going by eating compulsively and reading until exhaustion brought sleep. Finally, on Sept. 12 I stayed up all night writing a letter to the chairman of my draft board, saying basically what is in the preceding paragraph, thanking him for trying to help in a case where he really couldn't, and stating that I couldn't do the R.O.T.C. after all and would he please draft me as soon as possible.

I never mailed the letter, but I did carry it on me every day until I got on the plane to return to England. I didn't mail the letter because I didn't see, in the end, how my going in the army and maybe going to Vietnam would achieve anything except a feeling that I had punished myself and gotten what I deserved. So I came back to England to try to make something of this second year of my Rhodes scholarship.

And that is where I am now, writing to you because you have been good to me and have a right to know what I think and feel. I am writing too in the hope that my telling this one story will help you to understand more clearly how so many fine people have come to find themselves still loving their country but loathing the military, to which you and other good men have devoted years, lifetimes, of the best service you could give. To many of us, it is no longer clear what is clear, the conclusion is likely to be illegal.

Forgive the length of this letter. There was much to say. There is still a lot to be said, but it can wait. Please say hello to Col. Jones for me.

Merry Christmas.

Sincerely,

Bill Clinton

29

Dreams of a Great Society

The 1960s opened on a hopeful note of change and expectation. John F. Kennedy's election brought a promise of a new society—a New Frontier, as he put it, where the country could resolve its problems at home and provide leadership abroad. It was an era of activists—an activist presidency, growth of activist government, and a generation of young people increasingly (sometimes radically) involved with the political process.

John Kennedy and his successor, Lyndon Johnson, shared a vision of government working to jump-start the economy, alleviate poverty, and end racial discrimination. During his administration Kennedy was unable to get much of his social legislation—including the first major Civil Rights bill since Reconstruction—through Congress. But following Kennedy's assassination in Dallas in 1963, Lyndon Johnson pushed through Congress an aggressive series of legislative initiatives called the Great Society plan, which included anti-poverty programs, the Job Corps, Medicare (medical care for senior citizens), the Voting Rights Act, Head Start, minimum-wage laws, the National Foundations for the Arts and Humanities, a new immigration act, and Medicaid (medical care for the poor).

Voices against America's status quo were heard throughout the 1960s and 1970s, as students, African Americans, Latinos, and women demanded to be politically, economically and socially enfranchised. Students (like Bill Clinton in chapter 28) became active in the free-speech movements and protested against the war in Vietnam, among others issues, and staged marches, strikes, and university takeovers. African Americans (as previously discussed in chapter 27) radicalized, especially after riots in Watts in 1965, New York and Chicago in 1966, and Newark in 1967, and the murder of Martin Luther King, Jr., in 1968. Mexican Americans began to organize in the West, and in 1965, under the leadership of César Chávez, staged an important strike against grape farmers, demanding higher wages, union recognition, and improved working conditions. Women, who were slighted and marginalized in both the student and Civil Rights movements, began to organize groups to promote equality between the sexes, including fighting for an Equal Rights Amendment, changes in divorce laws and laws concerning rape and domestic violence, the legalization of abortion, and easier access to child care.

Study Questions

1. In his inaugural speech does John Kennedy carry on the tradition of the Progressive movement and the New Deal? Does he promise an activist government? In this context, how does "ask not what your country can do for you, ask what you can do for your country" fit in?

2. Was the Great Society the apex of twentieth-century American liberalism?

3. Was NOW a militant organization? What issues was NOW primarily concerned with?

4. What issues dominate the Port Huron Statement?

5. What long-term goals did César Chávez have for his organization?

John F. Kennedy, Inaugural Address (1961)

In many ways, John Kennedy, his young wife Jackie, and their two small children personified the New Frontier and the hopes of a new, postwar America. This speech, with its now famous lines, has itself symbolized the Kennedy legacy—which, after his assassination in November of 1963—unified a generation.[*]

My fellow citizens:

We observe today not a victory of party but a celebration of freedom—symbolizing an end as well as a beginning—signifying renewal as well as change. For I have sworn before you and Almighty God the same solemn oath our forebears prescribed nearly a century and three quarters ago.

The world is very different now. For man holds in his mortal hands the power to abolish all form of human poverty and to abolish all form of human life. And, yet, the same revolutionary beliefs for which our forebears fought are still at issue around the globe—the belief that the rights of man come not from the generosity of the state but from the hand of God.

We dare not forget today that we are the heirs of that first revolution. Let the word go forth from this time and place, to friend and foe alike, that the torch has been passed to a new generation of Americans—born in this century, tempered by war, disciplined by a cold and bitter peace, proud of our ancient heritage—and unwilling to witness or

---

[*] John F. Kennedy, Inaugural Address, January 20, 1961.

permit the slow undoing of those human rights to which this nation has always been committed, and to which we are committed today.

Let every nation know, whether it wish us well or ill, that we shall pay any price, bear any burden, meet any hardship, support any friend or oppose any foe in order to assure the survival and success of liberty.

This much we pledge—and more.

To those old allies whose cultural and spiritual origins we share, we pledge the loyalty of faithful friends. United, there is little we cannot do in a host of new co-operative ventures. Divided, there is little we can do—for we dare not meet a powerful challenge at odds and split asunder.

To those new states whom we now welcome to the ranks of the free, we pledge our world that one form of colonial control shall not have passed merely to be replaced by a far more iron tyranny. We shall not always expect to find them supporting our every view. But we shall always hope to find them strongly supporting their own freedom—and to remember that, in the past, those who foolishly sought to find power by riding on the tiger's back inevitably ended up inside.

To those peoples in the huts and villages of half the globe struggling to break the bonds of mass misery, we pledge our best efforts to help them help themselves, for whatever period is required—not because the Communists are doing it, not because we seek their votes, but because it is right. If the free society cannot help the many who are poor, it can never save the few who are rich.

To our sister republics south of our border, we offer a special pledge—to convert our good words into good deeds—in a new alliance for progress—to assist free men and free Governments in casting off the chains of poverty. But this peaceful revolution of hope cannot become the prey of hostile powers. Let all our neighbors know that we shall join with them to oppose aggression or subversion anywhere in the Americas. And let every other power know that this Hemisphere intends to remain the master of its own house.

To that world assembly of sovereign states, the United Nations, our last best hope in an age where the instruments of war have far outpaced the instruments of peace, we renew our pledge of support—to prevent its becoming merely a forum for invective— to strengthen its shield of the new and the weak—and to enlarge the area to which its writ may run.

Finally, to those nations who would make themselves our adversary, we offer not a pledge but a request: that both sides begin anew the quest for peace, before the dark powers of destruction unleashed by science engulf all humanity in planned or accidental self-destruction.

We dare not tempt them with weakness. For only when our arms are sufficient beyond doubt can we be certain beyond doubt that they will never be employed.

But neither can two great and powerful groups of nations take comfort from their present course—both sides overburdened by the cost of modern weapons, both rightly alarmed by the steady spread of the deadly atom, yet both racing to alter that uncertain balance of terror that stays the hand of mankind's final war.

So let us begin anew—remembering on both sides that civility is not a sign of weakness and sincerity is always subject to proof. Let us never negotiate out of fear. But let us never fear to negotiate.

Let both sides explore what problems unite us instead of belaboring the problems that divide us.

Let both sides for the first time formulate serious and precise proposals for the inspection and control of arms—and bring the absolute power to destroy other nations under the absolute control of all nations.

Let both sides join to invoke the wonders of science instead of its terrors. Together let us explore the stars, conquer the deserts, eradicate disease, tap the ocean depths and encourage the arts and commerce.

Let both sides unite to heed in all corners of the earth the command of Isaiah—to "undo the heavy burdens . . . (and) let the oppressed go free."

And if a beachhead of co-operation can be made in the jungles of suspicion, let both sides join in the next task: creating, not a new balance of power, but a new world of law, where the strong are just and the weak secure and the peace preserved forever.

All this will not be finished in the first 100 days. Nor will it be finished in the first 1,000 days, nor in the life of this Administration, nor even perhaps in our lifetime on this planet. But let us begin.

In your hands, my fellow citizens, more than in mine, will rest the final success or failure of our course. Since this country was founded, each generation has been summoned to give testimony to its national loyalty. The graves of young Americans who answered that call encircle the globe.

Now the trumpet summons us again—not as a call to battle, though embattled we are—but a call to bear the burden of a long twilight struggle, year in and year out, "rejoicing in hope, patient in tribulation"—a struggle against the common enemies of man: tyranny, poverty, disease, and war itself.

Can we forge against these enemies a grand and global alliance, north and south, east and west, that can assure a more fruitful life for all mankind? Will you join in that historic effort?

In the long history of the world, only a few generations have been granted the role of defending freedom in its hour of maximum danger. I do not shrink from this responsibility—I welcome it. I do not believe that any of us would exchange places with any other people or any other generation. The energy, the faith and the devotion which we bring to this endeavor will light our country and all who serve it—and the glow from that fire can truly light the world.

And so, my fellow Americans: Ask not what your country will do for you—ask what you can do for your country.

My fellow citizens of the world: Ask not what America will do for you, but what together we can do for the freedom of man.

Finally, whether you are citizens of America or of the world, ask of us the same high standards of strength and sacrifice that we shall ask of you. With a good conscience our only sure reward, with history the final judge of our deeds, let us go forth to lead the land we love, asking His blessing and His help, but knowing that here on earth God's work must truly be our own.

Lyndon Johnson, The War on Poverty (1964)

Lyndon Johnson had served in Roosevelt's New Deal administrations and believed in the power of government to provide for the poor and to solve social problems. His Great Society package became the most massive reform movement in America's history, and its effects would touch more groups than any other reform movement. It is not an understatement to say that the Great Society changed the very face and to a certain extent structure of American society. The Economic Opportunity Act, proposed in this speech to Congress, was a $947.5 million appropriation to wage war on poverty. It included establishing the Job Corps, VISTA (Volunteers in Service to America), and new education programs including work-study for college students and grants for elementary education in poor districts.[*]

I have called for a national war on poverty. Our objective: total victory.

There are millions of Americans—one fifth of our people—who have not shared in the abundance which has been granted to most of us, and on whom the gates of opportunity have been closed.

What does this poverty mean to those who endure it?

It means a daily struggle to secure the necessities for even a meager existence. It means that the abundance, the comforts, the opportunities they see all around them are beyond their grasp.

Worst of all, it means hopelessness for the young.

The young man or woman who grows up without a decent education, in a broken home, in a hostile and squalid environment, in ill health or in the face of racial injustice—that young man or woman is often trapped in a life of poverty.

He does not have the skills demanded by a complex society. He does not know how to acquire those skills. He faces a mounting sense of despair which drains initiative and ambition and energy. . . .

The war on poverty is not a struggle simply to support people, to make them dependent on the generosity of others.

It is a struggle to give people a chance.

It is an effort to allow them to develop and use their capacities, as we have been allowed to develop and use ours, so that they can share, as others share, in the promise of this nation.

We do this, first of all, because it is right that we should.

---

[*] From *Public Papers of the Presidents of the United States, Lyndon B. Johnson, 1965* (Washington, D.C.: Government Printing Office, 1966).

For the establishment of public education and land grant colleges through agricultural extension and encouragement to industry, we have pursued the goal of a nation with full and increasing opportunities for all its citizens.

The war on poverty is a further step in that pursuit.

We do it also because helping some will increase the prosperity of all.

Our fight against poverty will be an investment in the most valuable of our resources—the skills and strength of our people.

And in the future, as in the past, this investment will return its cost many fold to our entire economy.

If we can raise the annual earnings of 10 million among the poor by only $1,000 we will have added $14 billion a year to our national output. In addition we can make important reductions in public assistance payments which now cost us $4 billion a year, and in the large costs of fighting crime and delinquency, disease and hunger.

This is only part of the story.

Our history has proved that each time we broaden the base of abundance, giving more people the chance to produce and consume, we create new industry, higher production, increased earnings and better income for all.

Giving new opportunity to those who have little will enrich the lives of all the rest.

Because it is right, because it is wise, and because, for the first time in our history, it is possible to conquer poverty, I submit, for the consideration of the Congress and the country, the Economic Opportunity Act of 1964.

The Act does not merely expand old programs or improve what is already being done.

It charts a new course.

It strikes at the causes, not just the consequences of poverty.

It can be a milestone in our one-hundred-eighty-year search for a better life for our people.

Students for a Democratic Society, The Port Huron Statement (1962)

Students for a Democratic Society (SDS) was organized in 1960 and became one of the largest and best-organized groups in the student movement of the 1960s, involved in the Berkeley Free Speech movement in 1965, the Columbia strike in 1968, and other protests designed to liberalize university policies and demonstrate opposition to the Vietnam war. The Port Huron Statement is a statement of political ideology, drafted by leaders of the SDS, written primarily by Tom Hayden (a student at the University of

Michigan who is now a state legislator in California), and adopted by SDS at its national convention in Port Huron, Michigan, in 1962.*

We are the people of this generation, bred in at least modest comfort, housed now in the universities, looking uncomfortably to the world we inherit.

When we were kids the United States was the wealthiest and strongest country in the world; the only one with the atom bomb, the least scarred by modern war, an initiator of the United Nations that we thought would distribute Western influence throughout the world. Freedom and equality for each individual, government of, by, and for the people—these American values we found good, principles by which we could live as men. Many of us began maturing in complacency.

As we grew, however, our comfort was penetrated by events too troubling to dismiss. First, the permeating and victimizing fact of human degradation, symbolized by the Southern struggle against racial bigotry, compelled most of us from silence to activism. Second, the enclosing fact of the Cold War, symbolized by the presence of the Bomb, brought awareness that we ourselves, and our friends, and millions of abstract "others" we knew more directly because of our common peril, might die at any time. We might deliberately ignore, or avoid or fail to feel all other human problems, but not these two, for these were too immediate and crushing in their impact, too challenging in the demand that we as individuals take the responsibility for encounter and resolution.

National Organization for Women, Statement of Purpose (1966)

There was no one organization that spoke for women in the 1960s and 1970s. Many were formed, but one of the first and certainly most influential was the National Organization for Women. NOW was a mainstream organization, founded by professional women including Betty Friedan (author of the ground-breaking *The Feminine Mystique)*, focused on raising consciousness and correcting the legal, economic, and political inequities facing women. Organized in 1966, NOW used the Equal Employment Act and the Civil Rights Act of 1964 to initiate social changes to benefit

---

* From the Port Huron Statement. Reprinted by permission of Tom Hayden.

women. This is the statement of purpose adopted at the NOW organizing conference in Washington D.C., in October 1966.*

We, men and women who hereby constitute ourselves as the National Organization for Women, believe that the time has come for a new movement toward true equality for all women in America, and toward a fully equal partnership of the sexes, as part of the worldwide revolution of human rights now taking place within and beyond our national borders.

The purpose of **NOW** is to take action to bring women into full participation in the mainstream of American society now, exercising all the privileges an responsibilities thereof in truly equal partnership with men.

WE BELIEVE the time has come to move beyond the abstract argument, discussion, and symposia over the status and special nature of women which have raged in America in recent years; the time has come to confront, with concrete action, the conditions that now prevent women from enjoying the equality of opportunity and freedom of choice which is their right, as individual Americans, and as human beings.

NOW is dedicated to the proposition that women, first and foremost, are human beings, who, like all other people in our society, must have the chance to develop their fullest human potential. We believe that women can achieve such equality only by accepting to the full the challenges and responsibilities they share with all other people in our society, as part of the decision-making mainstream of American political, economic, and social life.

WE ORGANIZE to initiate or support action, nationally, or in any part of this nation, by individuals or organizations, to break through the silken curtain of prejudice and discrimination against women in government, industry, the professions, the churches, the political parties, the judiciary, the labor unions, in education, science, medicine, law, religion, and every other field of importance in American society. . . .

Despite all the talk about the status of American women in recent years, the actual position of women in the United States has declined, and is declining, to an alarming degree throughout the 1950's and 1960's. . . . Working women are becoming increasingly—not less—concentrated on the bottom of the job ladder. As a consequence full-time women workers today earn on the average only 60% of what men earn, and that wage gap has been increasing over the past twenty-five years in every major industry group. . . .

Further, with higher education increasingly essential in today's society, too few women are entering and finishing college or going on to graduate or professional school. . . .

---

* Reprinted from the National Organization for Women "Statement of Purpose." It should be noted that this is a historical document and does not reflect all current NOW policies and priorities.

In all the professions considered of importance to society, and in the executive ranks of industry and government, women are losing ground. Where they are present it is only a token handful. . . .

Official pronouncement of the advance in the status of women hide not only the reality of this dangerous decline, but the fact that nothing is being done to stop it. The excellent reports of the President's Commission on the Status of Women and of the State Commissions have not been fully implemented. Such Commissions have power only to advise. They have no power to enforce their recommendations; nor have they the freedom to organize American women and men to press for action on them. The reports of these commissions have, however, created a basis upon which it is now possible to build.

Discrimination in employment on the basis of sex is now prohibited by federal law, in Title VII of the Civil Rights Act of 1964. . . . Until now, too few women's organizations and official spokesmen have been willing to speak out against these dangers facing women. Too many women have been restrained by the fear of being called "feminist."

There is no civil rights movement to speak for women, as there has been for Negroes and other victims of discrimination. The National Organization for Women must therefore begin to speak.

WE BELIEVE that the power of American law, and the protection guaranteed by the U.S. Constitution to the civil rights of all individuals, must be effectively applied and enforced to isolate and remove patterns of sex discrimination, to ensure equality of opportunity in employment and education, and equality of civil and political rights and responsibilities on behalf of women, as well as for Negroes and other deprived groups.

WE REALIZE that women's problems are linked to many broader questions of social justice; their solution will require concerted action by many groups. . . .

WE DO NOT ACCEPT the token appointment of a few women to high-level positions in government and industry as a substitute for a serious continuing effort to recruit and advance women according to their individual abilities. To this end, we urge American government and industry to mobilize the same resources of ingenuity and command with which they have solved problems of far greater difficulty than those now impeding the progress of women.

WE BELIEVE that this nation has a capacity at least as great as other nations, to innovate new social institutions which will enable women to enjoy true equality of opportunity and responsibility in society, without conflict with their responsibilities as mothers and homemakers. . . .

. . . WE REJECT the assumption that these problems are the unique responsibility of each individual woman, rather than a basic social dilemma which society must solve. . . .

WE BELIEVE that it is an essential for every girl to be educated to her full potential of human ability as it is for every boy—with the knowledge that such education is the key to effective participation in today's economy and that, for a girl as for a boy, education can only be serious where there is expectation that it will be used in society. . . .

WE REJECT the current assumptions that a man must carry the sole burden of supporting himself, his wife, and family, and that a woman is automatically entitled to lifelong support by a man upon her marriage, or that marriage, home, and family are primarily woman's world and responsibility—hers to dominate—his to support. We believe that a true partnership between the sexes demands a different concept of marriage, and equitable sharing of the responsibilities of home and children and of the economic burdens of their support. We believe that proper recognition should be given to the economic and social value of homemaking and child care. . . .

WE BELIEVE that women must now exercise their political rights and responsibilities as American citizens. They must refuse to be segregated on the basis of sex into separate-and-not-equal ladies' auxiliaries in the political parties, and they must demand representation according to their numbers in the regularly constituted party committees—at local, state, and national levels—and in the informal power structure, participating fully in the selection of candidates and political decision making, and running for office themselves. . . .

NOW WILL HOLD ITSELF INDEPENDENT OF ANY POLITICAL PARTY in order to mobilize the political power of all women and men intent on our goals. . . .

WE BELIEVE that women will do most to create a new image of women by acting now, and by speaking out in behalf of their own equality, freedom, and human dignity—not in pleas for special privilege, nor in enmity toward men, who are also victims of the current, half-equality between the sexes—but in an active, self-respecting partnership with men. By so doing, women will develop confidence in their own ability to determine actively, in partnership with men, the conditions of their life, their choices, their future, and their society.

Curtis Sitcomer, "Harvest of Discontent" (1967)

Among the new voices in American politics emerging in the 1960s were those of Mexican Americans. Concentrated primarily in the Southwest, Mexican Americans had suffered centuries of economic, social, and political discrimination. In the sixties, however, they began to fight back. Raza Unida, one of several grassroots Latino organizations in the Southwest, became a strong political force while other smaller groups formed to pressure for close-to-home bilingual education in the public schools. But perhaps no one better symbolized this new militancy than César Chávez, who took on what appeared to be an impossible task; the unionization of migrant workers. Despite the odds, Chávez was successful in leading these marginalized workers in strikes and boycotts to improve their working and living conditions. "Harvest of Discontent," a selection from an article that appeared in 1967 in *The Christian Science Monitor* describes the conditions of the workers and Chávez's fight.*

The broiling summer sun bakes this central California valley with one-hundred-ten-degree temperatures.

It's preharvest time. And out in the hot, muggy fields a lush grape crop and a labor movement are ripening together.

At stake is a half-million dollars in grapes and the fortunes of eighty thousand migrants who pick them.

What happens may force a redirection of California's $3.8-billion-a-year agricultural economy, which peaks right here in this fiery furnace in late August and September.

Cesar Chavez's farm labor union has been picking up momentum for two years—since its dramatic grape strike here in the fall of 1965. At the same time, [the] migrant workers' civil rights movement also crystallized.

CONTRACT PUSH PLANNED

Now with tens of thousands of acres of fruit ready for harvesting, the union plans its greatest push ever for collective-bargaining contracts.

Some three hundred growers in the San Joaquin Valley will be under pressure. Many may be forced to sign with the union or lose their crop for lack of labor.

Other factors make this perhaps the most meaningful harvest ever for the growers. In recent years, their profits have steadily dwindled as overhead soared. Higher labor costs, forced by unionization, could drive some growers out of business.

A successful union thrust in the next few weeks could mean [for the migrants] higher wages, . . . a better standard of living, improved housing, and a boost from society's cellar.

But if the union drive fails, the entire farm labor movement and its attendant civil rights cause may be set back for a decade. . . .

LA CAUSA HITS

Then came La Causa.

. . . The Mexican farm worker, virtually silent and anonymous for more than half a century, sprang from beneath the arbors and demanded a share of "the good life." He called his uprising La Causa.

He was prodded by the simple but pungent dialogue of one of his own kind, soft-spoken Cesar Chavez, a man whom an admirer called "a quiet explosion." . . .

INROADS MADE

Through his new union, the migrants asked for reform. From the grower, he demanded guaranteed wages, better working conditions, and collective-bargaining agreements with a union contract and closed shop. From the government, he demanded coverage under the National Labor Relations Act, unemployment and disability insurance, and Social Security. . . .

GOAL DESCRIBED

For the migrant, Cesar embodies the *Huelga*—the union's two-year-long strike for recognition by three hundred growers in California's lush San Joaquin Valley.

And he embodies La Causa—the dramatic civil rights-type movement aimed at pulling the poverty-stricken, uneducated, and up to now almost ignored, Spanish-speaking migrant into labor's mainstream.

Cesar is short and sturdy. He has wavy, black hair and a dark, youthful complexion.

His eyes are searching and penetrating. And they seem to add to the credibility of the simple but sometimes explosively eloquent phrases which verbalize La Causa.

"We are more than a union," he says. "But we are also less than a union."

In the first instance, he is talking about an extra dimension which most other unions don't possess. Some of the Chavez associates here call this "social conscience." He himself refers to it as "personalized service."

ACTIVITIES LISTED

. . . In some ways, Cesar Chavez, as a union leader, is reminiscent of the past. He is the union—much in the tradition of Samuel Gompers and, later, John L. Lewis.

BATTLE ALREADY WON

. . . The migratory worker is not covered under the National Labor Relations Act. He is usually ineligible for unemployment insurance. He is without specific health and welfare protection. And he has no guaranteed minimum wage.

RECOGNITION SOUGHT

Against this backdrop, La Causa fights the migrant's battle on three fronts. It presses the grower for union recognition and collective-bargaining contracts. It lobbies the state and federal governments for legislation to protect the agricultural worker. And it makes a broad appeal to the public to end social discrimination against the migrant.

"Our aims are still very elementary," explains Mr. Chavez. "The big goal is union recognition by the growers. And even when we get this, we have to teach the growers the very meaning of negotiations. Hopeful, they will then get together themselves and set up management-labor relations departments. Now they have no such thing."

Legislation giving benefits to migrants as a group [is] almost nonexistent.

"What we need in a state like California," says Mr. Chavez, "is a Little Wagner Act which would spell out our right to organize and engage in collective bargaining."

"On the national level—for the past thirty years—federal policy has said that workers in general have a right to join a union. We want this extended specifically to farm workers."

The soft-spoken migrant leader is optimistic that such coverage will come. "We have history on our side," he says.

CHANGE ANSWERED

. . . Cesar Chavez is a patient man. He realizes that it may take ten years or longer for his union to make real headway. In its first two years of operation, UFWOC has signed with only three of the three hundred growers in central California.

And although he doesn't particularly like to think of La Causa as a civil rights movement, Mr. Chavez knows that constant public exposure of the abject poverty and deprivation of the farm worker is essential to the momentum of his movement.

"Our situation," he says, "is really no different from that which exists in the Negro ghettos in other parts of the country." . . .

30

The End of the American Century

After the turmoil of the 1960s, the 1970s and 1980s were characterized by increasing social conservatism and skepticism about the power of national government. The end of the Cold War in the late eighties introduced the United States into a new role as the World's only superpower, and marked the beginning of new global trade relationships, alliances, and peace-keeping and military efforts.

The presidency of Richard Nixon, a Republican who came into office after the disastrous Democratic convention of 1968, saw attempts to reorganize and reform federal programs and federal spending including the introduction of (unsuccessful) programs for medical care and new welfare benefits. And although an opponent of school desegregation and busing himself, Nixon at least indirectly continued the integration of American society that had begun in the previous two decades through his appointment of moderates to the Supreme Court. In foreign affairs, American withdrawal from the war in Vietnam began under Nixon's watch, while in his most famous foreign policy move, Nixon went to China in 1972.

Richard Nixon was forced to resign in 1974, following disclosure of his role in the Watergate cover-up. His resignation haunted the administration of Gerald Ford; most certainly, Ford's decision to pardon Nixon factored heavily in Ford's defeat in 1976 by Jimmy Carter. Carter, the governor of Georgia, rode strong antigovernment sentiments to the presidency. Unfortunately, his "outsider" status hurt his ability to lead the nation through difficult economic and diplomatic times. Like his predecessor, he would be voted out of office in 1980 in a strong negative public reaction to his presidency.

The Carter administration was dogged by lingering traumas of the Vietnam war, Watergate, and a deteriorating economic climate. By many accounts, Carter was an ineffective political leader and lacked a cohesive legislative strategy to carry out his vision. Following the Iranian hostage crisis in 1980, which was seen to symbolize Carter's lack of leadership ability, Carter lost to former California governor (and old movie actor) Ronald Reagan in the 1980 election.

Reagan was elected with the support of an unlikely coalition of fiscal and social conservatives. The 1980 election showed for the first time the new power of so-called Christian conservatives, who overwhelmingly voted for Reagan (although Jimmy

Carter was himself a Christian fundamentalist). Though he had promised voters fiscal responsibility, by the end of his administration Ronald Reagan had produced the largest deficit in America's history. Reagan spent increasing amounts of money on defense, while promising to shrink the federal government (in fact government grew in the 1980s) and implemented supply-side economics. Such an economic policy basically dictated that taxes would be lowered for the wealthy on the theory that they would invest and spend, thus stimulating the economy. The result was an era in which conspicuous consumption was in vogue and American society became polarized into the rich and the poor.

Reagan possessed great personal charisma and was enormously popular. He easily won reelection against Water Mondale and Geraldine Ferraro. His vice president, George Bush, won the presidency in 1988, largely riding on Reagan's coattails. However, where Reagan was seen as a warm optimist, Bush often seemed patrician and distant. Bush used his presidency to advance an increasingly conservative social agenda, which included restrictions on abortion, support for prayer in schools, and deep cuts in social spending.

The Reagan and Bush presidencies saw the fall of the Soviet Union and the end of the Cold War. The Bush administration tried to capitalize on these events by positioning the United States as leader of a "new world order," the first test of which was Bush's successful international coalition to "liberate" Kuwait after its invasion by its neighbor Iraq. But despite his successes in the global arena, Bush lost the 1992 election to Arkansas governor Bill Clinton in a three-way race complicated by the independent candidacy of Texas billionaire Ross Perot. Fiscal conservatives abandoned Bush after he broke his pledge of "no new taxes" made in his 1988 acceptance speech, while other voters saw him as out of touch with ordinary Americans. He also suffered the brunt of an economic slowdown. Meanwhile, Clinton campaigned as a new kind of Democrat, fiscally conservative but committed to a progressive social agenda. Despite the president's personal charm, the first years of his administration were troubled by personnel problems and domestic policy failures like the health-care plan developed by his wife, Hillary Rodham Clinton. In the 1994 election, conservative Republican candidates, led by House Speaker Newt Gingrich, won majorities in both houses of Congress for the first time in forty years. The final two years of Clinton's presidency featured deep partisan conflicts between the conservative Congress and the presidency over the role of government in public life.

Study Questions

1.   Some scholars refer to the Nixon presidency as an "imperial presidency," in which the executive branch exercised more power than ever before. What in the Justice Committee's report might support or refute this characterization?

2.   What fundamental threat does Jimmy Carter see facing American society? In his speech, Carter says he "feels your pain." Discuss his attempts to portray himself as a populist president. How does his populism (which could be termed "touchy-feely") differ from that of previous presidents? How could it be perceived as weakness?

3. Compare Reagan's and Carter's visions of America and descriptions of the American spirit.

4. Contrast Carter's "malaise" with Reagan's "optimism." Could this have been a factor in the 1980 election?

5. Compare Daniel Wildom's decision to become politically active with Tom Hayden's as described in the Port Huron Statement. In what ways were Christian conservative activists indebted to Civil Rights and student protest leaders for some of their rhetoric and strategy? In what ways did they differ?

6. By setting out clearly articulated goals in the war against Iraq, some believed the United States would avoid what some called the "Vietnam syndrome." Some even hoped that a successful war in the gulf would exterminate the "ghost of Vietnam" hanging over the American military. What were the goals of the war against Hussein, as articulated by President Bush?

7. Compare Bush's speech and its rhetoric with Ronald Reagan's. Who is more successful?

House Judiciary Committee, Conclusion on Impeachment Resolution (1974)

During the 1972 presidential race, several employees of the Committee to Re-Elect the President (CREEP), a branch of Richard Nixon's reelection campaign, broke into the Democratic Party headquarters, searched through files, and installed listening devices. They were caught. Nixon initially denied that anyone in the White House was involved. But after one of the burglars admitted during his trial that Republican officials had known about their activities, several White House officials admitted their involvement and resigned. As more disclosures followed, it became clear that Nixon administration officials had wiretapped journalists and politicians as well as the Democratic headquarters, broken into the office of the psychiatrist treating Daniel Ellsberg (who had leaked the Pentagon Papers about Vietnam to the *New York Times* which helped to further erode public support for the war), and paid off the burglars to ensure their silence. Nixon's presidency was already shadowed by scandal—his vice president, Spiro Agnew, had been forced to resign after he was indicted on bribery and tax evasion charges, while Nixon himself had been investigated for tax evasion after he took huge deductions for donating his vice presidential papers to the National Archives. Newspapers, a Senate committee, and a Special Counsel investigated Nixon's involvement in the break-in, and John Dean, the former White House counsel under Nixon, testified that the president had known about the cover-up. Nixon, of course, was not forthcoming in the matter, and when it was revealed that he had tape-recorded all his meetings in the White House, the investigators sought those tapes in order to find out what Nixon knew. In the end, it took a Supreme Court ruling to force Nixon to hand over the tapes. The following is a copy of the conclusion of the House of Representatives on their consideration of the Impeachment Resolution for President Nixon, prepared and released before Nixon was ordered by the Court to release the tapes. Nixon resigned less than a month after this report was issued.*

After the Committee on the Judiciary had debated whether or not it should recommend Article I to the House of Representatives, 27 of the 38 Members of the Committee found that the evidence before it could only lead to one conclusion: that Richard M. Nixon, using the powers of his high office, engaged, personally and through his subordinates and agents, in a course of conduct or plan designed to delay, impede, and obstruct the investigation of the unlawful entry on June 17, 1972, into the headquarters of the Democratic National Committee; to cover up, conceal and protect those responsible; and to conceal the existence and scope of other unlawful activities.

This finding is the only one that can explain the President's involvement in a pattern on undisputed acts that occurred after the break-in and that cannot otherwise be rationally explained.

1. The President's decision on June 20, 1972, not to meet with his Attorney General, his chief of staff, his counsel, his campaign director, and his assistant, John Ehrlichman, whom he had put in charge of the investigation—when the subject of their meeting was the Watergate matter.

2. The erasure of that portion of the recording of the President's conversation with White House chief of staff H. R. Haldeman on June 20, 1972, which dealt with Watergate—when the President stated that the tapes had been under his "sole and personal control."

3. The President's public denial on June 22, 1972, of the involvement of members of the Committee for the Re-election of the President [CREEP] or of the White House staff in the Watergate burglary, in spite of having discussed Watergate, on or before June 22, 1972, with Haldeman, special counsel Charles Colson, and former attorney general John Mitchell [head of CREEP]—all persons aware of that involvement.

---

* House Judiciary Committee, *Conclusion on the Impeachment Resolution for President Nixon,* 1974, H. Rept. 93–1305, art. I, 133, 135–36.

4. The President's directive to Haldeman on June 23, 1972, to have the CIA request the FBI to curtail its Watergate investigation.

5. The President's refusal, on July 6, 1972, to inquire and inform himself what Patrick Gray, Acting Director of the FBI, meant by his warning that some of the President's aides were "trying to mortally wound him."

6. The President's discussion with Erlichman on July 8, 1972, of clemency for the Watergate burglars, more than two months before the return of any indictments.

7. The President's public statement on August 29, 1972, a statement later shown to be untrue, that an investigation by [White House counsel] John Dean "indicates no one in the White House staff, no one in the Administration, presently employed, was involved in this very bizarre incident."

8. The President's statement to Dean on September 14, 1972, the day that the Watergate indictments were returned without naming high CRP [CREEP] and White House officials, that Dean had handled his work skillfully, "putting your fingers in the dike every time that leaks have sprung here and sprung there," and that "you just try to button it up as well as you can and hope for the best." . . .

In addition to this evidence, there was before the Committee the following evidence:

1. Beginning immediately after June 17, 1972, the involvement of each of the President's top aides and political associates, Haldeman, Mitchell, Ehrlichman, Colson, Dena, LaRue, Mardinan, Magruder, in the Watergate coverup. . . .

Finally , there was before the Committee a record of public statement by the President between June 22, 1972 and June 9, 1974, deliberately contrived to deceive the courts, the Department of Justice, the Congress and the American people.

President Nixon's course of conduct following the Watergate break-in, as described in Article I, caused action not only by his subordinates but by the agencies of the United States, including the Department of Justice, the FBI, and the CIA. It required perjury, destruction of evidence, obstruction of justice, all crimes. But, most important, it required deliberate, contrived, and continuing deception of the American people.

President Nixon's actions resulted in manifest injury to the confidence of the nation and great prejudice to the cause of law and justice, and was subversive of constitutional government. His actions were contrary to his trust as President and unmindful of the solemn duties of his high office. It was this serious violation of Richard M. Nixon's constitutional obligations as President, and not the fact that violations of Federal criminal statutes occurred, that lies at the heart of Article I.

The Committee find, based upon clear and convincing evidence, that this conduct, detailed in the foregoing pages of this report, constitutes "high crimes and misdemeanors" as that term is used in Article II, Section 4 of the Constitution. Therefore, the Committee recommends that the House of Representatives exercise its constitutional power to impeach Richard M. Nixon.

Jimmy Carter, The "Malaise" Speech (1979)

During Carter's presidency the American economy was beset with inflation and high interest rates while foreign policy was troubled. By midpoint in his term, Carter's popularity was lower than any of the previous five presidents at a similar stage. Part of the problem was the enormous disparity between Carter's promises and his performance. Carter gave this speech after canceling an address on energy policy and retreating with his advisers at Camp David in 1979. Although Carter never used the term in this speech, it became known as his "malaise" speech because he complained publicly of a malaise of the American spirit.*

Good evening.

This is a special night for me. Exactly three years ago, on July 15, 1976, I accepted the nomination of my party to run for President of the United States. I promised you a President who is not isolated from the people, who feels your pain, and who shared your dreams and who draws his strength and his wisdom from you. . . .

Ten days ago I had planned to speak to you again about a very important subject—energy. For the fifth time I would have described the urgency of the problem and laid out a series of legislative recommendations to the Congress. But as I was preparing to speak, I began to ask myself the same question that I now know has been troubling many of you. Why have we not been able to get together as a nation to resolve our serious energy problem?

It's clear that the true problems of our Nation are much deeper—deeper than gasoline lines or energy shortages, deeper even than inflation or recession. And I realize more than ever that as President I need your help. So, I decided to reach out and listen to the voices of America.

I invited to Camp David people from almost every segment of our society—business and labor, teachers and preachers, Governors, mayors, and private citizens. And then I left Camp David to listen to other Americans, men and women like you. It has been an extraordinary ten days, and I want to share with you what I've heard. . . .

These ten days confirmed my belief in the decency and the strength and the wisdom of the American people, but it also bore out some of my long-standing concerns about our Nation's underlying problems.

I know, of course, being president, that government actions and legislation can be very important. That's why I've worked hard to put my campaign promises into law—and I have to admit, with just mixed success. But after listening to the American

* From *The Public Papers of the Presidents, Jimmy Carter, 1977* (Washington, D.C.: Government Publishing Office, 1978, 1980).

people I have been reminded again that all the legislation in the world can't fix what's wrong with America. So, I want to speak to you first tonight about a subject even more serious than energy or inflation. I want to talk to you right now about a fundamental threat to American democracy.

I do not mean our political and civil liberties. They will endure. And I do not refer to the outward strength of America, a nation that is at peace tonight everywhere in the world, with unmatched economic power and military might.

The threat is nearly invisible in ordinary ways. It is a crisis of confidence. It is a crisis that strikes at the very heart and soul and spirit of our national will. We can see this crisis in the growing doubt about the meaning of our own lives and in the loss of a unity of purpose for our Nation.

The erosion of our confidence in the future is threatening to destroy the social and the political fabric of America. . . .

The symptoms of this crisis of the American spirit are all around us. For the first time in the history of our country a majority of our people believe that the next five years will be worse than the past five years. Two-thirds of our people do not even vote. The productivity of American workers is actually dropping, and the willingness of Americans to save for the future has fallen below that of all other people in the Western world. . . .

Often you see paralysis and stagnation and drift. You don't like it, and neither do I. What can we do?

First of all, we must face the truth, and then we can change our course. We simply must have faith in each other, faith in our course. We simply must have faith in each other, faith in our ability to govern ourselves, and faith in the future of this Nation. Restoring that faith and that confidence to America is now the most important task we face. It is a true challenge of this generation of Americans. . . .

We are at a turning point in our history. There are two paths to choose. One is a path I've warned about tonight, the path that leads to fragmentation and self-interest. Down that road lies a mistaken idea of freedom, the right to grasp for ourselves some advantage over others. That path would be one of constant conflict between narrow interests ending in chaos and immobility. It is a certain route to failure.

All the traditions of our past, all the lessons of our heritage, all the promises of our future point to another path, the path of common purpose and the restoration of American values. That path leads to true freedom for our Nation and ourselves. We can take the first steps down that path as we begin to solve our energy problems. . . .

Ronald Reagan, Speech to the House of Commons (1982)

Ronald Reagan gave this speech, dubbed the "evil empire" speech for its description of the Soviet Union, to the British House of

Commons while there in 1982. As president, Reagan portrayed himself as tough on communism and increased military spending dramatically while in office. This speech showcases his fabulous speechmaking abilities—his use of humor, humanizing anecdotes, and aggressive anticommunism.*

We're approaching the end of a bloody century plagued by a terrible political invention—totalitarianism. Optimism comes less easily today, not because democracy is less vigorous, but because democracy's enemies have refined their instruments of repression. Yet optimism is in order because day by day democracy is proving itself to be a not at all fragile flower. From Stettin on the Baltic to Varna on the Black Sea, the regimes planted by totalitarianism have had more than thirty years to establish their legitimacy. But none—not one regime—has yet been able to risk free elections. Regimes planted by bayonets do not take root.

The strength of the Solidarity movement in Poland demonstrates the truth told in an underground joke in the Soviet Union. It is that the Soviet Union would remain a one-party nation even if an opposition party were permitted because everyone would join the opposition party. . . .

If history teaches us anything, it teaches self-delusion in the face of unpleasant facts is folly. We see around us the marks of our terrible dilemma—predictions of doomsday, antinuclear demonstrations, an arms race in which the West must, for its own protection, be an unwilling participant. At the same time we see totalitarian forces in the world who seek subversion and conflict around the globe to further their barbarous assault on the human spirit. What, then, is our course? Must civilization perish in a hail of fiery atoms? Must freedom wither in a quiet, deadening accommodation with totalitarian evil? . . .

It may not be easy to see; but I believe we live now at a turning point.

In an ironic sense Karl Marx was right. We are witnessing today a great revolutionary crisis, a crisis where the demands of the economic order are conflicting directly with those of the political order. But the crisis is happening not in the free, non-Marxist West, but in the home of Marxism-Leninism, the Soviet Union. It is the Soviet Union that runs against the tide of history by denying human freedom and human dignity to its citizens. It is also deep in economic difficulty. The rate of growth in the national product has been steadily declining since the fifties and is less than half of what it was then.

The dimensions of this failure are astounding: a country which employs one-fifth of its population in agriculture is unable to feed its own people. . . . The decay of the Soviet experiment should come as no surprise to us. Wherever the comparisons have been made between free and closed societies—West Germany and East Germany, Austria and Czechoslovakia, Malaysia and Vietnam—it is the democratic countries that are prosperous and responsive to the needs of their people. . . .

---

* From *The Public Papers of the Presidents, Ronald Reagan,* 1982 (Washington, D.C.: National Archives, 1982).

Our military strength is a prerequisite to peace, but let it be clear we maintain this strength in the hope it will never be used, for the ultimate determinant in the struggle that's now going on in the world will not be bombs and rockets but a test of wills and ideas, a trial of spiritual resolve, the values we hold, the beliefs we cherish, the ideals to which we are dedicated. . . .

I've often wondered about the shyness of some of us in the West about standing for these ideals that have done so much to ease the plight of man and the hardships of our imperfect world. This reluctance to use those vast resources at our command reminds me of the elderly lady whose home was bombed in the Blitz. As the rescuers moved about, they found a bottle of brandy she'd stored behind the staircase, which was all that was left standing. And since she was barely conscious, one of the workers pulled the cork to give her a taste of it. She came around immediately and said, "Here now—there now, put it back. That's for emergencies."

Well, the emergency is upon us. Let us be shy no longer. Let us go to our strength. Let us offer hope. Let us tell the world that a new age is not only possible but probable.

Donald E. Wildom, *The Conscience of a Conservative Christian* (1985)

Beginning in the 1970s, conservative Christians became actively involved in politics. One of the movement's early and most influential leaders, the Rev. Jerry Falwell, founded the Moral Majority in 1979 to oppose "abortion, pornography, the drug epidemic, the breakdown of the traditional family, the establishment of homosexuality as an accepted alternate life-style, and other moral cancers that are causing our society to rot from within." Conservative Christians were important supporters of Ronald Reagan in the 1980 election. Televangelists, including Pat Robertson, who would later be the founder of the Christian Coalition, Oral Roberts, and Jim Bakker, were popular political as well as religious figures in the mid-1980s, until they were struck by scandals. Right-wing evangelicals became increasingly important in the 1990s after their successes in grassroots organizing and the election of a number of their supporters in the Congressional elections of 1994. This selection is from Daniel Wildom's book, *The*

Conscience of a Conservative Christian, describing his decision to become involved in grassroots activism.*

One night during the Christmas holidays of 1976, I decided to watch television with my family. Gathered around the set in our den, shortly after 7 P.M., we prepared ourselves for a relaxing time of entertainment. We turned on the set and sat back to be entertained.

Not far into the program was a scene of adultery. I reacted to the situation in the manner I had been taught. I asked one of the children to change channels. Getting involved in the second program, we were shocked with some crude profanity. Once again reacting in the prescribed manner, I asked one of the children to change the channel. We got involved in a mystery when, without warning, on came a totally unexpected scene in which one man had another tied down and was working him over with a hammer. I again reacted as I had been instructed. I asked one of the children to turn off the set.

As I sat in my den that night, I became angry. I had been disturbed by the deterioration of morals I had witnessed in the media and society during the previous twenty-five years. This was accompanied by a dramatic rise in crime, a proliferation of pornography, increasingly explicit sexual lyrics in music, increasing numbers of broken homes, a rise in drug and alcohol use among the youth, and various other negative factors. I had managed to avoid those unpleasant changes to a large degree by staying away, turning my head, justifying my actions with the reasons most commonly expressed—freedom of speech, pluralism, tolerance.

Realizing that these changes were being brought into the sanctity of my home, I decided I could and would no longer remain silent. I decided to do something even though at that time I had no idea what that something would be. Little did I realize the magnitude of my decision. . . .

Out of that decisions came the National Federation for Decency (and out of the NFD came the Coalition for Better Television). For nearly three years I dealt with what I perceived to be the problems with television—sex, violence, and profanity. But the more I dealt with the problems, the more I realized that I was dealing only with symptoms—not the disease. . . .

We Americans are caught up in a great struggle unlike any with which we have faced before. Our struggle is not with an enemy from beyond our shores as it has been in the past; it is being waged inside our very borders. The outcome will determine the direction our country will take for the next several centuries.

This great struggle is one of values—particularly which ones will be the standard for our society and a base for our system of justice in the years to come. For 200 years our country has based its morals, its sense of right and wrong, on the Christian view of man. The Ten Commandments and the Sermon on the Mount have been our solid foundation. To be sure, we have never managed to get the system perfect in practice.

* From Donald E. Wildom, *The Home Invaders* (Wheaton, Ill: Victor Books, 1983), 7–8, 44–7. Copyright © 1985 by Scripture Press Publications, Wheaton, IL 60187. Reprinted by permission.

Nor will we ever be able to do so no regardless of what base we use. But it has been the most perfect system ever devised in the history of mankind.

Today there are those who would have us change; go in new directions; directions, they are convinced, that will free man from his chains of oppression. They are tired of this old system. They want a new one. And the new one will be based on what they perceive to be right and wrong. The standards for society will come from within themselves. They will decide for themselves and, consequently, for society, what kinds of conduct are acceptable and unacceptable. The old Christian morals will be cast aside in pursuit of a new society. . . .

If within the next five years we fail to turn the tide of this humanist value system which seeks to replace our Christian heritage, then we have—in my opinion—lost the struggle and it will be generations, if at all, before the Christian view of man will be the norm again. I don't like making such a statement. But I must write what I perceive to be the truth.

As a young minister I remember how cold chills ran over my body when I discovered what happened to unwanted bodies in Rome at the time of Christ. They were thrown into the sewer! And even in enlightened Athens unwanted children were discarded in the woods for the animals to eat. I thought about how much we have changed since then, how civilized we have become, how much more compassionate we are today than 2,000 years ago. Then I am told that every year there are more than one million abortions in this country. We haven't changed that much. We wouldn't dare throw a baby in the sewer. Today, we kill babies in the sterile atmosphere of a modern hospital or an abortion clinic and put the bodies in trash bags for disposal in garbage bins. It is so respectable that we even allocate tax money to help cover the expense. We aren't more civilized, only more efficient in our cruelty. Jesus' words, "Suffer the little children to come unto Me," seem out of place in this new society.

George Bush, Address to the Nation Announcing Allied Military Action in the Persian Gulf (1991)

In August 1990, Iraqi dictator Saddam Hussein sent troops into neighboring Kuwait. Both countries were oil-rich, and Saddam hoped that he would be able to take-over Kuwait's oil reserves and make back some of the funds he had lost during the disastrous war with Iran in the 1980s. A worldwide coalition, led by the United States, was formed to counter Iraq and push it out of Kuwait, which it did after a five-month standoff. The war was considered a success, although Saddam Hussein remained in power and the region remained somewhat unstable. In this address, President Bush announced that military action in the Gulf had begun. The president spoke from the Oval Office and his address was broadcast live on radio and television.*

Just 2 hours ago, allied air forces began an attack on military targets in Iraq and Kuwait. These attacks continue as I speak. Ground forces are not engaged.

This conflict started August 2d when the dictator of Iraq invaded a small and helpless neighbor. Kuwait—a member of the Arab League and a member of the United Nations—was crushed; its people, brutalized. Five months ago, Saddam Hussein [President of Iraq] Saddam Hussein started this cruel war against Kuwait. Tonight, the battle has been joined.

This military action, taken in accord with United Nations resolutions and with the consent of the Untied States Congress, follows months of constant and virtually endless diplomatic activity on the part of the United Nations, the United States, and many, many other countries. Arab leaders sought what became known as an Arab solution, only to conclude that Saddam Hussein was unwilling to leave Kuwait. Others traveled to Baghdad in a variety of efforts to restore peace and justice. Our Secretary of State, James Baker, held an historic meeting in Geneva, only to be totally rebuffed. This past weekend, in a last-ditch effort, the Secretary-General of the United Nations went to the Middle East with peace in his heart—his second such mission. And he came back from Baghdad with no progress at all in getting Saddam Hussein to withdraw from Kuwait.

Now the twenty-eight countries with forces in the Gulf area have exhausted all reasonable efforts to reach a peaceful resolution—have no choice but to drive Saddam from Kuwait by force. We will not fail.

As I report to you, air attacks are underway against military targets in Iraq. We are determined to knock out Saddam Hussein's nuclear-bomb potential. We will also destroy his chemical-weapons facilities. Much of Saddam's artillery and tanks will be destroyed. Our operations are designed to best protect the lives of all the coalition forces by targeting Saddam's vast military arsenal. Initial reports from General Schwarzkopf are that our operations are proceeding according to plan.

Our objectives are clear: Saddam Hussein's forces will leave Kuwait. The legitimate government of Kuwait will be restored to its rightful place, and Kuwait will once again be free. Iraq will eventually comply with all relevant United Nations resolutions, and then, when peace is restored, it is our hope that Iraq will live as a peaceful and cooperative member of the family of nations, thus enhancing the security and stability of the Gulf.

Some may ask: Why act now? Why not wait? The answer is clear: The world could wait no longer. Sanctions, though having some effect, showed no signs of accomplishing their objective. Sanctions were tried for well over five months, and we and our allies concluded that sanctions alone would not force Saddam from Kuwait.

---

* From *Public Papers of the Presidents of the United States, George Bush, 1991* (Washington, D.C.: Office of the Federal Register, National Archives and Records Service, 1992).

While the world waited, Saddam Hussein systematically raped, pillaged, and plundered a tiny nation, no threat to his own. He subjected the people of Kuwait to unspeakable atrocities—and among those maimed and murdered, innocent children.

While the world waited, Saddam sought to add to the chemical weapons arsenal he now possesses, and infinitely more dangerous weapon of mass destruction—a nuclear weapon. And while the world waited, while the world talked peace and withdrawal, Saddam Hussein dug in and moved massive forces into Kuwait.

While the world waited, while Saddam stalled, more damage was being done to the fragile economies of the Third World, emerging democracies of Eastern Europe, to the entire world, including to our own economy.

The United States, together with the United Nations, exhausted every means at our disposal to bring this crisis to a peaceful end. However, Saddam clearly felt that by stalling and threatening and defying the United Nations, he could weaken the forces arrayed against him.

While the world waited, Saddam Hussein met every overture of peace with open contempt. While the world prayed for peace, Saddam prepared for war.

I had hoped that when the United States Congress, in historic debate, took its resolute action, Saddam would realize the could not prevail and would move out of Kuwait in accord with the United Nation resolutions. He did not do that. Instead, he remained intransigent, certain that time was on his side.

Saddam was warned over and over again to comply with the will of the United Nations: Leave Kuwait, or be driven out. Saddam has arrogantly rejected all warnings. Instead, he tried to make this a dispute between Iraq and the United States of America.

Well, he failed. tonight, twenty-eight nations—countries from five continents, Europe and Asia, Africa, and the Arab League—have forces in the Gulf area standing shoulder to shoulder against Saddam Hussein. These countries had hoped the use of force could be avoided. Regrettably, we now believe that only force will make him leave.

Prior to ordering our forces into battle, I instructed our military commanders to take every necessary step to prevail as quickly as possible, and with the greatest degree of protection possible for American and allied service men and women. I've told the American people before that this will not be another Vietnam, and I repeat this here tonight. Our troops will have the best possible support in the entire world, and they will not be asked to fight with one hand tied behind their back. I'm hopeful that this fighting will not go on for long and that casualties will be held to an absolute minimum.

This is an historic moment. We have in this past year made great progress in ending the long era of conflict and cold war. We have before us the opportunity to forge for ourselves and for future generations a new world order—a world where the rule of law, not the law of the jungle, governs the conduct of nations. When we are successful—and we will be—we have a real chance at this new world order, an order in which a credible United Nations can use its peacekeeping role to fulfill the promise and vision of the U.N.'s founders.

We have no argument with the people of Iraq. Indeed, for the innocents caught in this conflict, I pray for their safety. Our goal is not the conquest of Iraq. It is the liberation of Kuwait. It is my hope that somehow the Iraqi people can, even now, convince their dictator that he must lay down his arms, leave Kuwait and let Iraq itself rejoin the family of peace-loving nations.

Thomas Paine wrote many years ago: "These are the times that try men's souls." Those well-known words are so very true today. But even as planes of the multinational forces attack Iraq, I prefer to think of peace, not war. I am convinced not only that we will prevail but that out of the horror of combat will come the recognition that no nation can stand against a world united. No nation will be permitted to brutally assault its neighbor.

No president can easily commit our sons and daughters to war. They are the Nation's finest. Ours is an all-volunteer force, magnificently trained, highly motivated. The troops know why they're there. And listen to what they say, for they've said it better than any President or Prime Minister ever could.

Listen to Hollywood Huddleston, marine lance corporal. He says, "Let's free these people, so we can go home and be free again." And he's right. The terrible crimes and tortures committed by Saddam's henchmen against the innocent people of Kuwait are an affront to mankind and a challenge to the freedom of all.

Listen to one of our great officers out there, Marine Lieutenant General Walter Boomer. He said: "There are things worth fighting for. A world in which brutality and lawlessness are allowed to go unchecked isn't the kind of world we're going to want to live in."

Listen to Master Sergeant J. P. Kendall of the 82d Airborne: "We're here for more than just the price of a gallon of gas. What we're doing is going to chart the future of the world for the next 100 years. It's better to deal with this guy now than five years from now."

And finally, we should all sit up and listen to Jackie Jones, an army lieutenant, when she says, "If we let him get away with this, who knows what's going to be next?"

I have called upon Hollywood and Walter and J. P. and Jackie and all their courageous comrades-in-arms to do what must be done. Tonight, America and the world are deeply grateful to them and to their families. And let me say to everyone listening or watching tonight: When the troops we've sent in finish their work, I am determined to bring them home as soon as possible.

Tonight, as our forces fight, they and their families are in our prayers. May God bless each and every one of them, and the coalition forces at our side in the Gulf, and may He continue to bless our nation, the United States of America.

Credits

Grateful acknowledgment is made for permission to reprint:

CHAPTER 6

Page 76. "Petition for Equal Education", 1787, in *A Documentary History of the negro People in the United States*, ed. Herbert Aptheker (Secaucus, NJ: Carol Publishing Group, 1951). Copyright © 1951 by Carol Publishing Group. A Citadel Press Book.

CHAPTER 7

Page 85. Excerpts from *The Journals of Lewis and Clark*, edited by Bernard DeVoto. Copyright © 1953 by Bernard DeVoto. Copyright © renewed 1981 by Avis DeVoto. Reprinted by permission of Houghton Mifflin Company. All rights reserved.

CHAPTER 8

Page 97. From José María Sánchez "A Trip to Texas (1828)" trans. Carlos E. Casteneda in *Southwestern Historical Quarterly*, Vol. 29, No. 4, April 1926, 270-273. Reprinted by permission of the Texas State Historical Association.

Page 101. From "The Letters of Mary Paul, 1845-1849" in *Vermont History.*, ed Thomas Dublin (Montpelier, Vt.: Vermont Historical Society, 1980). Reprinted with permission of the Vermont Historical Society.

CHAPTER 13

Page 158. From *Lucy Breckinridge of Grove Hill*, ed., Mary Robertson (Kent, Ohio: Kent State University Press, 1979). Reprinted by permission of the University of South Carolina Press.

CHAPTER 15

Page 173. Reprinted from *Black Elk Speaks*, by John G. Neihardt, by permission of the University of Nebraska Press. Copyright 1932, 1959, 1972 by John G. Neihardt. Copyright © 1961 by the John G. Neihardt Trust.

Page 181. Excepts from *Giants in the Earth* by O. E. Rolvaag. Copyright 1927 by Harper & Row Publishers, Inc. Copyright renewed 1955 by Jennie Marie Berdhal Rolvaag. Reprinted by permission of HarperCollins Publishers.

CHAPTER 16

Page 194. Reprinted from Mary Harris, *The Autobiography of Mother Jones,* 3d ed. (Chicago: Charles H. Kerr Publishing Company, 1977). Reprinted by permission of Charles H. Kerr Publishing Company.